William James and Carl Stumpf
Correspondence (1882–1910)

William James and Carl Stumpf
Correspondence (1882–1910)

Edited by
Riccardo Martinelli

DE GRUYTER

ISBN 978-3-11-077675-1
e-ISBN (PDF) 978-3-11-052553-3
e-ISBN (EPUB) 978-3-11-052467-3

Library of Congress Control Number: 2019956327

Bibliographic information published by the Deutsche Nationalbibliothek
The Deutsche Nationalbibliothek lists this publication in the Deutsche Nationalbibliografie;
detailed bibliographic data are available in the Internet at http://dnb.dnb.de.

© 2021 Walter de Gruyter GmbH, Berlin/Boston
This volume is text- and page-identical with the hardback published in 2020.
Cover image: Collage by De Gruyter. Images in the public domain: "William James", Notman Studios, Houghton Library, Harvard University; and "Carl Stumpf", Julius Cornelius Schaarwächter, Humboldt-Universität zu Berlin
Typesetting: Integra Software Services Pvt. Ltd.
Printing and binding: CPI books GmbH, Leck

www.degruyter.com

Contents

List of Illustrations —— VII

Acknowledgments —— IX

Introduction

1   A Lifelong Friendship —— 3
    1.1   Prague, 1882 —— 3
    1.2   The U.S. and Germany —— 8
    1.3   Public and Private Life —— 13

2   Scientific Themes —— 23
    2.1   Space and Relations —— 23
    2.2   Sensations, Feelings, Emotions —— 27
    2.3   Metaphysics and Epistemology —— 34
    2.4   Religion and Psychical Research —— 38

3   The Present Edition —— 43

Correspondence

William James, Carl Stumpf —— 51
    Letters (1882–1910) —— 51

Family Letters —— 183
    William James to Alice Howe (Gibbens) James —— 183
    William James to Hermine (Biedermann) Stumpf —— 187
    Carl Stumpf to Alice Howe (Gibbens) James —— 188
    Carl Stumpf to Henry James, 3rd —— 189
    Henry James 3rd to Carl Stumpf —— 194

Appendices
    I Overview of Correspondence —— 199
    II German letters of Carl Stumpf —— 208
        Briefe an William James (1882–1909) —— 208
        Briefe an die Familie James —— 245
    III Carl Stumpf, "William James nach seinen Briefen" (1927) —— 250

Abbreviations —— 289

References —— 291

Index of Names —— 303

Index of Subjects —— 307

List of Illustrations

Fig. 1 William James to Carl Stumpf, 15 November 1884 [5, 1884]. Autograph letter, first page —— **60**
Fig. 2 Carl Stumpf to William James, 12 February 1885 [6, 1885]. Autograph letter, first page —— **65**
Fig. 3 Carl Stumpf to William James, 8 September 1886 [8, 1886]. Autograph letter, first page —— **74**
Fig. 4 William James to Carl Stumpf, 6 February 1887 [10, 1887]. Autograph letter, first page —— **84**

Acknowledgments

I am grateful to many people and institutions that made this edition possible. Ms. Bay James generously granted the rights for the publication of the materials taken from the *William James Papers*, preserved at the Houghton Library, Harvard MA. The *Alexander von Humboldt Foundation* granted me a fellowship for a research stay in Berlin. In addition, the *Foundation* generously funded this publication. Along the years, competent librarians helpfully and kindly supported my research. I am particularly grateful to the people at Houghton Library, and *Staatsbibliothek zu Berlin*. Prof. Armin Stock, director at the Adolf-Würth-Center for the History of Psychology at Würzburg kindly helped my research. I am also grateful to the Vossius Center for the History of Sciences and the Humanities at the University of Amsterdam for supporting a part of my research activities.

The letters have been translated from German into English by R. Brian Tracz. Without his work, this edition would have not been possible. Stumpf's letters has been transcribed from the manuscripts by Lia Gioia, who published them as Appendix to her PhD thesis at the University of Trieste. I wish to thank Lia for kindly allowing me to build upon her work. Federico Skodler, also PhD at the University of Trieste, greatly helped me in checking manuscripts and drafts. Along the years, I had the privilege of entertaining conversations with many other scholars, junior and senior. All of them have variously encouraged, inspired or illuminated my work. Needless to say, I am the sole responsible for mistakes and omissions though.

Introduction

Riccardo Martinelli

1 A Lifelong Friendship

1.1 Prague, 1882

In September 1882, William James, the Assistant Professor of Philosophy at Harvard, took a sabbatical and sailed to Europe. James aimed at improving his acquaintance with the leading psychologists of his time and their ideas. He also had personal reasons to leave: his mother had died in January, and depression, restlessness and insomnia loomed as always.[1] At the end of October, on his way from Venice to Dresden, James stopped in Prague, where he met the eminent physiologist Ewald Hering and the polyhedric physicist and philosopher Ernst Mach. James also paid a visit to Carl Stumpf, a young professor of philosophy who had come from Würzburg in 1879.[2] The name of his unannounced American guest probably did not ring any bell in Stumpf's mind. But James was one of the few Americans who had attentively read – and enjoyed – Stumpf's book of 1873 on the origin of the perception of space.[3] I will leave a more detailed analysis of the issue of space to the next section of this Introduction; for now, let us say that Stumpf's nativistic and anti–idealistic views on the subject were highly congenial to James. During their days in Prague, James and Stumpf felt a reciprocal human sympathy that marked the beginning of a long and loyal friendship. Far beyond the mere obligations of academic courtesy, Stumpf was pleased to stroll around with the brilliant and somewhat unconventional American colleague. Stumpf's personality and his "more than hospitable reception" must have impressed James. Addressing his wife Alice the day after leaving Prague, he wrote:

> With Stumpf I spent 5 hours on Monday evening, (This is Thursday) 3 on Wednesday morning, and 4 more in the afternoon, so I feel rather intimate. [...] He had another philosopher named Marty to dine with me yesterday, a jolly young fellow. [...] I learned a

---

[1] See L. Simon, *Genuine Reality. A Life of William James*, New York, Harcourt Brace & Co., 1998, p. 174, 182; R. Richardson, *William James: in the Maelstrom of American Modernism. A Biography*, Boston, Houghton Mifflin, 2006, p. 224.
[2] H. Sprung, *Carl Stumpf. Eine Biographie. Von der Philosophie zur experimentellen Psychologie*, München-Wien, Profil, 2006, pp. 99–115. See also J. Hoskovec, "Carl Stumpf in Prag (1879–1884)", *Brentano-Studien 9*, 2001, pp. 51–62.
[3] C. Stumpf, *Über den psychologischen Ursprung der Raumvorstellung*, Leipzig, Hirzel, 1873. For an introduction to Stumpf's thought see D. Fisette, "Carl Stumpf", in *The Stanford Encyclopedia of Philosophy*, ed. by E.N. Zalta, 2019; D. Fisette, "The Reception and Actuality of Carl Stumpf", in *Philosophy from an Empirical Standpoint. Essays on Carl Stumpf*, ed. by D. Fisette and R. Martinelli, Amsterdam-Leiden-Boston, Brill-Rodopi, 2015, pp. 11–59.

https://doi.org/10.1515/9783110525533-001

good many things from them, both in the way of theory and fact, and shall probably keep up a correspondence with Stumpf.⁴

On 26 November 1882, from Paris, James opened his first letter to his new friend in a direct and informal style:

> My Dear Stumpf, I'm sure you will allow me to drop titles of ceremony with a colleague with whose person and whose ideas alike I feel so warm a sympathy; & I trust that when you write to me you will give the same token that you regard me in the light of an old friend.⁵

Stumpf gladly agreed:

> Dear James! I likewise return your greetings with sincere joy, for I have gained with your all-too-brief visit the firm impression that we not only harmonize in our scientific views and intentions in a rare way, but will also always be good friends.⁶

James and Stumpf kept up their correspondence for 28 years, until James's death in 1910. The year 1882, Stumpf writes in his *Autobiography* of 1924, "brought to us our great joy, a visit from William James, [...] with whom I soon found myself on terms of friendship".⁷ In 1927, 17 years after his friend's death, Stumpf wrote for *Kant-Studien* an essay on James's thought and personality, with reference to the first edition of his correspondence.⁸

Born in Wiesentheid in 1848, the young Carl Stumpf was introduced to philosophy by his acquaintance with Brentano in Würzburg. Like many others,

---

4 [58, 1882]. Together with Stumpf, Anton Marty (1847–1914) belongs to the first generation of Brentano's pupils. Leaving Prague in 1885, Stumpf wrote: "I [...] parted with my dear friend Marty with pain; I will never again find such a trusted and at the same time scientifically stimulating companion" [6, 1885]. In 1892 Marty reviewed James's *Principles of Psychology*: see [19, 1892]. On Marty's thought see *Mind and Language. On the Philosophy of Anton Marty*, ed. by G. Fréchette and H. Taieb, Berlin, de Gruyter, 2017; L. Cesalli, "Stumpf's (Early) Insights and Marty's Way to His (Later) *Sprachphilosophie*", in *Essays on Stumpf*, pp. 359–384.
5 [1, 1882].
6 [2, 1882].
7 "The year 1882 brought to us our great joy, a visit from William James, who had liked my book on space, and with whom I soon found myself on terms of friendship. Later we met again in Munich and we kept up our correspondence to the end, though I could not follow him in his conversion to pragmatism". Stumpf, *Autobiography*, p. 399.
8 C. Stumpf, "William James nach seinen Briefen. Leben. Charakter. Lehre", *Kant-Studien* 32, 1927, pp. 205–241; also Berlin, Pan Verlag, 1928. Reprinted in the Appendix III to this volume. Besides his personal memories, Stumpf quotes from *The Letters of William James*, Boston, Little & Brown, 1920. See below, in this *Introduction*.

Stumpf had been deeply impressed by Brentano's rigorous style of thinking, his sharp-mindedness and logical rigor.⁹ Following his mentor's advice, Stumpf went to Göttingen to attend Hermann Lotze's lectures.¹⁰ In the wake of Brentano, who was a Catholic priest, Stumpf entered seminary in 1869. However, the proclamation of the infallibility of the Pope in 1870 caused a deep religious crisis in Brentano and Stumpf, both of whom eventually took off the black robe. Not yet ordained, Stumpf faced less serious consequences than his mentor. In 1873, at the age of 25, Stumpf became Full Professor and succeeded to Brentano in Würzburg.¹¹ That was the beginning of a long and successful career for Stumpf, who subsequently taught in Prague, Halle, Munich and Berlin.

William James' education had been less linear. The son of Henry James Sr., a moralist and theologian who was friends with Ralph Waldo Emerson and was influenced by Swedenborg and Fourier,¹² William lived in a cultivated and cosmopolitan milieu. Born in New York in 1842, he grew up "zig–zagging" between Newport, Boston and long European sojourns, during which he learned good French and German.¹³ At the age of 22, James entered the medical school at Harvard, where he would start teaching in 1872. James's health was repeatedly challenged by high peaks of depression. In 1870 he went through a severe

---

9 "Towards the end of this semester came the great change, by the addition of Franz Brentano to the faculty. Elsewhere I have already described the complete change which this man's appearance, his personality, his manner of thinking and teaching wrought in me. Everything else vanished before the great problems of philosophical and religious regeneration". Stumpf, *Autobiography*, pp. 391–392. The reference here ("elsewhere ...") is to C. Stumpf, "Erinnerungen an Franz Brentano", in *Franz Brentano. Zur Kenntnis seines Lebens und seiner Lehre*, ed. by O. Kraus, München, Beck, 1919, pp. 87–149. On the relations between Brentano and Stumpf see K. Schuhmann, "Carl Stumpf (1848–1936)", in *The School of Franz Brentano*, ed. by L. Albertazzi et al., Dordrecht, Kluwer, 1996, pp. 109–129.
10 On the importance of Lotze for Stumpf's intellectual development, see N. Milkov, "Carl Stumpf's Debt to Hermann Lotze", in *Essays on Stumpf*, pp. 101–122.
11 Sprung, *Carl Stumpf. Eine Biographie*, cit., p. 75. On Stumpf's youth see W. Baumgartner, "The Young Carl Stumpf. His Spiritual, Intellectual, and Professional Development", in *Essays on Stumpf*, pp. 61–74.
12 See R.B. Perry, *The Thought and Character of William James, as Revealed in Unpublished Correspondence and Notes, Together with his Published Writings*, 2 vols., London, Humphrey Milford, Oxford University Press, 1935, p. 20 ff.
13 Richardson coined for William James the fortunate phrase "growing up zigzag" (Richardson, *William James: in the Maelstrom of American Modernism*, p. 17); see also J. Carrette, "Growing up Zig–Zag: reassessing the transatlantic legacy of William James", in *William James and the Transatlantic Conversation. Pragmatism, Pluralism, and Philosophy of Religion*, ed. by M. Halliwell and J.D.S. Rasmussen, Oxford, Oxford University Press, 2014, pp. 199–217. See also Simon, *Genuine Reality*, cit., pp. 44–45.

crisis, which he overcame after reading a philosophical essay by Charles Renouvier. James famously wrote in his *Diary*:

> I think that yesterday was a crisis in my life. I finished the first part of Renouvier's 2nd Essay and saw no reason why his definition of free will – the sustaining of a thought because I choose to when I might have other thoughts – need to be the definition of an illusion. At any rate, I will assume for the present – until next year – that it is no illusion. My first act of free will shall be to believe in free will.[14]

By the time of their Prague meeting, in 1882, the main achievements and works of the two friends were still inchoate: Stumpf's *Tonpsychologie* appeared in two volumes in 1883 and 1890; James released the *Principles of Psychology* in 1890. The year 1890, then, marks a turning point in the intellectual biographies of both thinkers. The general consensus is that after the publication of the *Principles of Psychology*, James progressively abandoned psychology and became more and more involved in philosophy.[15] Though he dropped all experimental activities, however, James was far from abruptly dismissing psychology as a whole. Rather, he began to focus on the metaphysical side of the same problems he had investigated psychologically: his correspondence with Stumpf stands among the clearest documents of this evolution.[16] Somewhat less spectacularly, the year 1890 also

---

[14] Quoted from Perry, *Thought and Character* 1, p. 323; see also Richardson, *William James: in the Maelstrom of American Modernism*, cit., p. 120; B. Kucklick, *The Rise of American Philosophy. Cambridge, Massachusetts, 1860–1930*, New Haven-London, Yale University Press, 1977, p. 161 ff. Dunham notes: "James's colourful announcement of his conversion to a belief in free will, which he credits to reading Renouvier's *Traité de psychologie rationnelle*, is frequently cited in histories of his thought and pragmatism more generally. Beyond this, however, little has been written in English on Renouvier's philosophy". J. Dunham, "Idealism, Pragmatism and the Will to Believe: Charles Renouvier and William James", *British Journal for the History of Philosophy* 23, 2015, p. 756.

[15] The year 1890 marks "the midpoint in James's creative life". J. Barzun, *A Stroll with William James*, Chicago and London, The University of Chicago Press, 1983, p. 7. However, any attempt to distinguish subsequent "phases" in his work is an oversimplification. "It is sometimes said that James began as a physiologist and ended as a religious mystic, having passed successively through psychology, epistemology, and metaphysics on the way. There is some justification of this view in his formal schooling and in the chronological sequence of his teaching and writing. [...] As a matter of fact James's scientific and religious interests were equally early and equally enduring" [*Thought and Character* 1, p. 449].

[16] "Letters to Stumpf afford a clear view both of James's varied activities during the decade of the '90s, and of the persistence of his psychological interests despite a growing preoccupation with philosophy" [*Thought and Character* 2, pp. 179–180]. In 1875 James had straightforwardly affirmed that psychology is "of course the antechamber to metaphysics". W. James, "Review of Wundt, Grundzüge der physiologischen Psychologie (1875)", *North American Review* 121, 1875, p. 195 [*Works* 17, p. 296].

marked a change in Stumpf's activity. Leaving *Tonpsychologie* unfinished with the second volume, Stumpf turned to a multiplicity of different projects, both in philosophy and psychology. Berlin was the ideal place for the development of his multi-faceted – albeit highly dispersive – activities.[17]

This parallel intellectual development was mirrored in the correspondence between the two thinkers. James repeatedly voiced his intention to focus on the ultimate questions of metaphysics and morals. In 1899 he went so far as to express to Stumpf his "horror" for experimentation:

> I fear I am ceasing to be a psychologist and becoming exclusively a moralist & metaphysician. I have surrendered all psychological teaching to Munsterberg [sic] and his assistant, and the thought of psychophysical experimentation, and altogether of brass–instrument and algebraic–formula psychology fills me with horror.[18]

Stumpf's reaction was quite interesting. Manifesting his agreement with James as to the importance of metaphysics, in 1886 he vowed to abandon experimentation on sounds and to "lay to rest the tone psychology project, in order to bring to fruition so much else that lies in my heart and my mind".[19] A glance at Stumpf's publications shows that he failed to achieve this goal.[20] Stumpf delayed the second volume of *Tonpsychologie* for four more years, and the planned third volume was eventually cancelled. It was only after his retirement in the early 1920s that Stumpf could concentrate upon philosophy. Yet he never saw the publication of his monumental *Erkenntnislehre*[21] in two volumes: the book was posthumously edited by his son Felix in 1939-1940 – that is, when its

---

17 On his intense Berlin years, Stumpf wrote: "I have been able to pursue every kind of work, often fully, in every direction that interested me. Berlin's genius loci, the all-pervading spirit of work, had caught me. Inspirations came a–plenty, and there was no question, however remote, on which one could not find an expert opinion. Berlin was, moreover, musically the foremost city of the world, and Joachim, that noblest of performing artists whom I had known for some time as a friend, was still in his prime. All the great men with whom, during these many years, I came into closer touch officially, personally, and often socially, I cannot even name here". *Autobiography*, p. 402.
18 [35, 1899]. Concerning Münsterberg, see below.
19 [8, 1886]. In 1924, Stumpf retrospectively avowed: "I never intended to spend so much of my lifetime on acoustics and musical psychological studies as I did later on. I had counted on a few years. But it was, after all, not musical science but philosophy that always remained mistress of the house, who, it is true, granted most generously great privileges to her helpmate". *Autobiography*, pp. 396–397.
20 See D. Fisette, "Bibliography of the Publications of Carl Stumpf. Bibliographie der Schriften von Carl Stumpf", in *Essays on Stumpf*, pp. 529–541.
21 C. Stumpf, *Erkenntnislehre*, 2 vols., ed. by F. Stumpf, Leipzig, Barth, 1939–1940.

reception in Germany was highly unfavoured.[22] Along with other writings, his correspondence with James is an important document of Stumpf's views on philosophy and of his permanent commitment to it.[23]

1.2 The U.S. and Germany

Besides its scientific value, the correspondence between Stumpf and James testifies to a human relationship and, at the same time, to an entire epoch.[24] Comments on friendship and loyalty play a certain role within the exchange. Quite early, the two correspondents agreed to "hear of each other *at least once a year*",[25] but that was not always the case. When James wrote his "annual" letter on the 1st of January 1904, he hadn't heard from Stumpf in three years.[26] Previously, it had been Stumpf's turn to complain about James's alleged coldness and distraction during the long-awaited second – and last – meeting of 1893.[27]

---

[22] Stumpf's late writings have been often neglected by scholars. Among the few studies on his *Erkenntnislehre* see R. Rollinger, "The Concept of Causality in Stumpf's Epistemology", in *Austrian Phenomenology: Brentano, Husserl, and Meinong on Mind and Object*. Frankfurt a.M., Ontos, 2008, pp. 263–300; R. Martinelli, "Stumpf on Categories", in *Essays on Stumpf*, pp. 203–227.

[23] Despite his activity as a psychologist, Stumpf never abandoned philosophy and permanently considered himself a philosopher. See G.M. Ash, *Gestalt Psychology in German Culture, 1890–1967. Holism and the Quest for Objectivity*, Cambridge, Cambridge University Press, 1995, p. 30. This book gives a resourceful picture of the development of Gestalt psychology at the Berlin Institute directed by Stumpf. Among the interpreters who wrongly assume that Stumpf abandoned philosophy in favor of experimental psychology see e.g. Sprung, *Carl Stumpf. Eine Biographie*, cit., p. 15.

[24] "The life of William James was widely spread, both in its roots and in its branches. It took its nourishment from many sources, grew in many directions, and bore a great variety of fruits. It was richly fertilized and abundantly fertile. Having a peculiar genius for friendship, James entered into relations of intimacy with a large circle of contemporaries [...]. Habits of travel and a knowledge of languages widened the scope of his sociability, and made him an important channel by which America was carried to Europe and Europe to America. In short, his life and mind were so interwoven with their context, so thoroughly socialized and humanized, that a record of them must necessarily be in some measure a history of his epoch" [*Thought and Character* 1, p. ix].

[25] [2, 1882].

[26] "I feel that, if I let the year 1904 begin without anything in the way an electric current passing, the way from your heart to mine is in danger of becoming obliterated by the growth of distance and time" [50, 1904].

[27] [23, 1893].

James and Stumpf sometimes spoke of a common spiritual root lying below the surface of character traits, unshaken by the undeniable differences of personality, and the (increasing) theoretical ones between them.[28] Despite all divergences, however, they somehow complemented each other. James considered Stumpf a model of moral righteousness, zeal in research and style as a writer. He praised Stumpf's writings for "exhaustive thoroughness, subtlety of discrimination, firmness and clearness of style, and incorruptible good sense";[29] he spoke of a "roman severity of style" which makes Stumpf's works "very impressive – monumental, as it were".[30]

As Stumpf noted in his essay of 1927, James's peculiar eagerness to give eulogies of people around him must be considered here.[31] But his appreciation of Stumpf's public and private writings goes beyond that. To some extent, it should be interpreted in terms of national characters. In his letters, indeed, James frequently touches upon Germany and the U.S., with interesting comparisons, appreciations and occasional criticism. Remarkably, and not by chance, some of James's most quoted pronouncements on America and "Americanism" are drawn from his correspondence with Stumpf.[32] In James's eyes, Stumpf championed a

---

[28] James wrote: "It is a strange fact – for your positive and constructive ideas seem to have no great similarity to mine – that I feel you, perhaps more than any other psychologist whom I read to day, to be a *gleichgesinnter Mensch* with myself. I am sure that if fate had allowed us to grow side by side we could have worked out many things together – a thing now probably impossible even if we were side by side, on account of the difficulties which increasing age brings to the irresponsible interchange of unmatured ideas" [17, 1891].
[29] [5, 1884].
[30] [40, 1900].
[31] Stumpf, *William James*, p. 221. From a methodological point of view, James's enthusiasm must be taken into account by scholars who don't want to be misled by his oratorical ability in endorsing different philosophical theses. See R. Gale, *The Divided Self of William James*, Cambridge, Cambridge University Press, 1999, p. 20. However, Gale's thesis of the "divided self" – i.e. the coexistence of a Promethean and a mystic self within James – is too rigid a hermeneutic criterion. J. Pawelsky, *The Dynamic Individualism of William James*, Albany, SUNY Press, 2007, suggests that James "made real progress toward integrating his two selves" (p. 108). His correspondence with Stumpf shows the he actually did. In turn, Pawelsky overrates the role of the "reflex arch" in James's psychology. Against Gale's thesis see also W. Cooper, *The Unity of William James's Thought*, Nashville, Vanderbilt University Press, 2002, p. 34 and *passim*. See also M. Gale, "The Still Divided Self of William James: A Response to Pawelski and Cooper", *Transactions of the Charles S. Peirce Society* 60, 2004, pp. 153–170.
[32] "It unsettles my americanism (that tender plant) to go too often abroad [...] It is no light matter to feel foreign in one's native land. I am just beginning to feel american again, when this temptation comes!" [29, 1895]. In response to Stumpf's remarks [30, 1896], James added a lesser famed statement: "My fear of losing my Americanism if I went abroad again was entirely complimentary to your side of the Atlantic. Civilization is so much more advanced in many

set of virtues which were not merely individual, but epitomized the good qualities of the German people.³³

Some excerpts from the correspondence may illustrate this point. In 1882, James wrote to Alice: "With the nourishing breath of the german air, and the sort of smoky and leathery German smell, vigor and good spirits have set in. I've walked well, & slept well & eaten well and read well, and in short begin to feel as I expected I should when I decided upon this arduous pilgrimage".³⁴ Positively commenting on the first volume of Stumpf's *Tonpsychologie*, James wrote: "[y]our German brains are built after another fashion from those of the rest of us, you can carry a heavier freight of facts, & handle them in a freer way".³⁵ To be sure, even the solid German cast of mind has some drawbacks. At times, especially in his later writings, James ironically voiced his distance from the German "professorial" style.³⁶ To the severe *Gründlichkeit* instilled into German philosophy by Christian

---

ways with you, and the American so quickly catches the European tone, that when he comes back he finds his own country in many ways foreign and displeasing, and it takes him a long time to resume his old, simple minded relations with it. I have suffered from this discord many times, particularly after my last return home; I am now on thoroughly good terms with my native land, and dread very much to throw myself out of tune again. Like all ideal things, harmony of this kind must be worked for and bought by certain renunciations. We have many ideal things here, and the best thing an American can do is to stay at home as much as possible, and try to increase them" [31, 1896].

33 The "ever-alluring theme of Germanic traits" [*Thought and Character*, 1, p. 280] recurs frequently in James's early correspondence, especially during his time abroad.

34 [58, 1882]. During his previous stay of 1867, from Berlin, James wrote to Edmund Tweedy: "if I had to be born a 'foreign' child at all, I don't know that I could do a more comfortable thing than have it done in Germany. The ways of living are (as a whole) so sensible and easy, there seems to be such a good, fat, homely atmosphere about the inner family life of the people, as well as about much of their public life, that a German child's early associations must have an uncommon richness and stoutness, so–to speak, even if they have not much artistic elevation. Then as a boy and youth you can certainly get the best education in the world. Perhaps, after all, it is a better place to grow up in than to live in after you have grown up. The people are a swarming set, and without ever seeming to be in a hurry, get through a great deal of work" [*Corr.* 4, p. 241].

35 [5, 1884].

36 "In a subject like philosophy it is really fatal to lose connexion with the open air of human nature, and to think in terms of shop-tradition only. In Germany the forms are so professionalized that anybody who has gained a teaching chair and written a book, however distorted and eccentric, has the legal right to figure forever in the history of the subject like a fly in amber. All later comers have the duty of quoting him and measuring their opinions with his opinion. Such are the rules of the professorial game – they think and write from each other and for each other and at each other exclusively [...] and if by chance any one writes popularly and about results only, with his mind directly focused on the subject, it is reckoned *oberflächliches zeug* and *ganz unwissenschaftlich*". W. James, *A Pluralistic Universe. Hibbert Lectures at Manchester*

Wolff – as already Kant put it[37] – James opposed a more direct and "popular" style, representative of a quintessentially American "entrepreneurial" spirit.[38] However, James largely identified the typical "German professor" with Wundt, rather than with Stumpf.[39]

Applauding Stumpf's "solidity of heartiness",[40] James explained: "it is partly *deutsch*, but not all the *Deutschen* have it; so I make the most of it. Besides, so far off, you are the ideal *homo* or *vir*, and when you speak kindly, as now of my book, it is as if I were being approved by 'the Absolute', an Absolute moreover who can write a Tonpsychologie!"[41] Needless to say, reference to the Absolute in this context adds a benign and intimately ironic touch. In sum, James swayed between a sincere admiration for Europe[42] on the one side, and the urge to cultivate his profound feelings towards America on the other.[43] Less interested in such themes, Stumpf contented himself with some comparisons between the educational systems of the two countries.[44] Significantly, however, he closed his 1927 essay on James[45] with the opening lines of Goethe's famous poem "*The United States*".

> America, you are better off
> Than our ancient continent.
> You have no tumbledown castles
> And no basalt deposits.

College on the Present Situation in Philosophy, New York and London, Longmans, Green & Co., 1909, pp. 17–18 [*Works* 4, p. 13].
37 Wolff is referred to as "the author of a spirit of well-groundedness in Germany that is still not extinguished": I. Kant, *Critique of Pure Reason*, ed. by P. Guyer and A. Wood, *The Cambridge Edition of the Works of Immanuel Kant*, vol. 2, Cambridge, Cambridge University Press, 1998, p. 120 (B 36).
38 For a contextual discussion, see H. Paul, "German Thoroughness in Baltimore: Epistemic Virtues and National Stereotypes", *History of Humanities* 3, 2018, pp. 327–350.
39 [10, 1887]. See below in this *Introduction*.
40 [14, 1890].
41 [14, 1890].
42 Especially German civilization and the Swiss landscape: see [22, 1893].
43 "He found work a cure for too much play, and play a cure for work; nature a cure for social fatigue, and civilization a cure for the emptiness of primitive nature; philosophy a cure for science and science for philosophy; he went to Europe when he suffered from America, and sought in America a cure for Europe" [*Thought and Character* 1, p. 234].
44 [4, 1884].
45 Stumpf, *William James*, p. 241. Besides rendering homage to James, with this quote Stumpf made fun of Ernst von Aster's Introduction to the German translation of James's *Human Immortality*: W. James, *Unsterblichkeit*, trans. by E. von Aster-Giessen, Berlin, Philo-Verlag, 1926.

Your inner lives are not disturbed by
Useless memories and vain strife.[46]

In all this, the reader of the correspondence should obviously keep in mind the peculiar state of transatlantic relations in the late nineteenth century, when Germany was leading the way in scientific research. American students with career ambitions regularly sailed for Germany to assimilate concepts and methods from state-of-the-art psychological laboratories. Occasionally, James also recommended American pupils or researchers to Stumpf's benevolence.[47] The opposite shore of the Atlantic Ocean was not as attractive at the time. Though he accepted a position at Harvard, for instance, Hugo Münsterberg strove to go back to Germany for a long time.[48] Münsterberg was in charge for experimental activities at Harvard, to James's great relief: "I may say that I myself enjoy inward peace and a good professorial conscience for the first time, now that Münsterberg has taken charge of the entire experimental field".[49]

---

[46] "Amerika, du hast es besser / Als unser Kontinent, das alte, / Hast keine verfallne Schlösser / Und keine Basalte. / Dich stört nicht im Innern / Zu lebendiger Zeit / Unnützes Erinnern / Und vergeblicher Streit". J.W. Goethe, "Den vereinigten Staaten", from *Zahme Xenien*, 1827. J.W. Goethe, *Sämtliche Werke, Briefe, Tagebücher und Gespräche*, Sect. 1, vol. 2: *Gedichte 1800–1832*, Frankfurt a.M., Suhrkamp, 1988.

[47] Arthur H. Pierce [27, 1894]; George M. Stratton [28, 1895]; Mary W. Calkins [49, 1902]. For Pierce's negative feedback concerning Stumpf's lab in Berlin, see the footnotes to [27, 1894] and [28, 1895].

[48] "Although Münsterberg first came to Harvard in 1892 as a visiting professor, it would not be until 1897 that he accepted a permanent position. During the early and middle 1890s James courted him as his replacement in the Harvard Psychological Laboratory. [...] Hugo wanted a prestigious position in a German university. In experimental psychology that meant either Leipzig or Göttingen. And unfortunately for his prospects he had criticized both Wundt and Göttingen's laboratory experimentalist, Georg Elias Müller. Moreover, there was little indication that being a Jew enhanced prospects for professional advancement". D.W. Bjork, *The Compromised Scientist: William James in the Development of American Psychology*, New York, Columbia University Press, 1983, p. 45. On 7 March 1892, accepting James's invitation, Münsterberg wrote: "Under no circumstance would I stay more than three years in America. I want to remain a German, and I consider the whole thing merely as a big beautiful instructive travel" [*Corr.* 7, p. 246].

[49] [26, 1894]. On Münsterberg's calling to Harvard see [19, 1892]. The decision eventually proved to be a bad one: "Münsterbergian anecdotes abounded. All alluded to his German background or academic elitism, which often were conflated"; later, "the anecdotes ceased to be amusing tales about a blustering foreigner and became woven into the suspicion that he was a subversive. Münsterberg's unceasing attempts to promote a German-American scholastic alliance, his intercession into delicate early twentieth century diplomacy between the United States and Germany, and finally the hysteria of World War I changed him from a caricature into an enemy. [...] Fortunately James did not live long enough to see Münsterberg's tragic failure". Bjork, *The Compromised Scientist*, cit., pp. 54–55.

This historical situation influenced German institutions and, indirectly, Stumpf's career. For the most part, American students headed to Leipzig, where Wundt had established a renowned experimental laboratory in 1879. No wonder that the Berlin *Friedrich-Wilhelm Universität* determined to challenge this primacy by establishing a prestigious Institute of Psychology in the capital. Following the influential advice of Wilhelm Dilthey, who sought a man with both experimental skills and robust philosophical training, the direction was offered to Stumpf, who was in Munich at the time.[50] After some hesitation and against Brentano's opinion,[51] in 1894 Stumpf finally accepted. His move to Berlin was frequently discussed in the correspondence: James insisted that the "helmeted" manners of the Prussian would eventually overwhelm his friend.[52] All in all, he was right. After some resistance, Stumpf eventually conceded that James had a point in disapproving of the frenetic lifestyle of the tentacular capital.[53] However, in 1924 he retrospectively noted that "after thirty years, I still believe that my decision was for the best".[54] As for James, even the relatively smaller dimension of the American college eventually proved too demanding: in 1907 he resigned from Harvard to exclusively devote himself to research.[55]

1.3 Public and Private Life

Along with letters and postcards, James and Stumpf regularly sent to each other their most representative publications. Commentaries and criticisms on these works make up the most significant part of the correspondence from a

---

50 On the circumstances around Stumpf's calling to Berlin see Ash, *Gestalt Psychology*, pp. 31–35. See also Sprung, *Carl Stumpf. Eine Biographie*, cit., p. 124 ff.; V. Gerhart, R. Mehring, J. Rindert, *Berliner Geist. Eine Geschichte der Berliner Universitätsphilosophie bis 1946*, Berlin, Akademie-Verlag, 1999, p. 168.
51 See a letter to Stumpf dated 8 September 1893, in F. Brentano, *Briefe an Carl Stumpf 1867–1917*, ed. by G. Oberkofler, Graz, Akademische Druck-und Verlagsanstalt, 1989, p. 100.
52 "I only feared that Berlin might prove a rasping, fatiguing, and *ungemüthlich* place to live in, and that you might be buying honour, if you accepted the appointment, at the price of peace of soul". [26, 1894]; "I am always overworked, and I hope that on your part Berlin is not proving too terrible a taskmistress". [28, 1895]. See also [29, 1895]; [31, 1896]; [33, 1899]; [50, 1904]; [54, 1907].
53 [51, 1904].
54 *Autobiography*, p. 402.
55 [54, 1907].

scientific point of view. Unsurprisingly, the widest epistolary discussions concern the correspondents' major works: Stumpf's *Tonpsychologie* vols. 1 and 2 (1893, 1890) and James's *Principles of Psychology* (1890) and *Varieties of Religious Experience* (1902).[56] In addition to their own, James and Stumpf also discussed the works and ideas of others: leading scientists and philosophers of the time recur in the correspondence along with names now forgotten. The footnotes added to the letters provide a reasonably detailed account concerning both categories. In this *Introduction*, attention will be paid exclusively to three outstanding authors: Wundt, Mach, and Brentano.

Wilhelm Wundt is by far the most quoted scientist in the correspondence. James had a somewhat ambivalent attitude towards him. His first meeting with Wundt in 1882 left James with a positive impression of the man.[57] At the time, James and Stumpf frequently targeted Wundt's early theories. They attacked with particular insistence the "relativity of sensations" and the hypothesis of *Innervationsgefühle*.[58] However, James later softened his tones against Wundt: he did maintain a critical attitude, yet he tried to do justice to Wundt's respectability more than Stumpf expected him to do. In James's eyes, Wundt represented the quintessential "German professor", halfway between Wolff's scholastic encyclopedism and Napoleon's bravery in tackling a multiplicity of enemies at once.[59] Indeed, in James's view, Wundt's work was fragmentary, it had no core: "[c]ut him up like a worm, and each fragment crawls; there is no noeud vital in his mental medulla oblongata, so that you can't kill him all at once".[60] Interestingly, in a letter to Alice of 18 November 1882, James directly contrasts the impressions made upon him by Wundt and Stumpf:

---

[56] C. Stumpf, *Tonpsychologie*, vol. 1, Leipzig, Hirzel, 1883; *Tonpsychologie*; vol. 2. Leipzig, Hirzel, 1890. W. James, *The Principles of Psychology*, New York, Holt, 1890; W. James, *The Varieties of Religious Experience. A study in Human Nature, being the Gifford Lectures on Natural Religion delivered at Edinburgh in 1901–1902*, New York, London and Bombay, Longmans, Green and Co., 1902.

[57] "Wundt in Leipzig impressed me very agreeably personally. He has a ready smile and is entirely unaffected and unpretending in his manner. I heard him twice, and was twice in his laboratory, he was very polite but showed no desire for a further acquaintance" [1, 1882]. Suggesting that James had no previous acquaintance with him, this formulation is consistent with Horst Gundlach's claim that James did not pay visit to Wundt in Heidelberg in 1867. H. Gundlach, "William James and the Heidelberg Fiasco", *History of Psychology* 21, 2018, pp. 47–72.

[58] [2, 1882], [5, 1884], [8, 1886]. See below, ch. 2 of this *Introduction*.

[59] [10, 1887], [24, 1893].

[60] [10, 1887]. For a commentary, see S. Araujo de Freitas, *Wundt and the Philosophical Foundations of Psychology. A Reappraisal*, Cham, Springer, 2016, p. 18.

[Wundt] made a very pleasant and personal impression on me, with his agreeable voice and ready, tooth-showing smile. His lecture also was very able, and my opinion of him is higher than before seeing him is. But he seemed very busy and showed no desire to see more of me than the present interview either time. The psychologische Gesellschaft I stayed over to see was postponed, but he did not propose to me to do anything else – to the gain of my ease, but to the loss of my vanity. Dear old Stumpf has been the friendliest of these fellows. With him I shall correspond.[61]

Stumpf's opinion on Wundt was definitely less indulgent. He considered Wundt little else than a charlatan who misled more than a generation of researchers.[62] Stumpf and Wundt stayed on indirectly hostile terms for a long time: for example, Wundt's "completely perfidious" review of Stumpf's *Tonpsychologie* appeared as anonymous.[63] Crossing swords became unavoidable when Stumpf harshly criticized the work of Carl Lorenz, a pupil of Wundt who, so to speak, invaded Stumpf's field by investigating the psychological foundations of musical consonance.[64] The polemic between Wundt and Stumpf soon reached a "dangerous stage", to use James's effective expression.[65] Diverging opinions about Wundt occasioned some misunderstandings between James and Stumpf. For example, after a long criticism of Wundt in a letter of 1886, Stumpf was afraid of having crossed the line, annoying James with his "demeanor" against the Leipzig psychologist.[66] Reassuring his friend, though, James proved the concern completely misplaced.[67]

---

61 *Corr.* 5, p. 301.
62 "He makes students and others believe that the ever repeated measurements of reaction times inaugurates a completely new 'experimental psychology', which can only look back at older psychology with derision and scorn. [...] As if something important were to follow from time measurements, as if they did not have to be interpreted themselves only through inner observation, and finally as if numbers and not, rather, clear concepts were the main point!" [8, 1886].
63 See Sprung, *Carl Stumpf. Eine Biographie*, cit., pp. 109–111, and [6, 1885].
64 Following Wundt's methodology of "intermediate graduation" (*mittlere Abstufung*) Lorenz determined that the fifth is the (psychologically) intermediate sound within an octave. Owing to this peculiar position, Lorenz concluded, the fifth is consonant. Stumpf objects that – on the contrary – the fifth tends to emerge in Lorenz's experiments of intermediate graduation *because* it is a consonant interval. For all references, see the footnotes added to [13, 1890] and [17, 1891].
65 [17, 1891].
66 [23, 1893]. In his obituary of Stumpf, Kurt Lewin recalls that Wundt's name "was nearly taboo in the Berlin Institute". K. Lewin, "Carl Stumpf", *The Psychological Review* 44, 1937, p. 194.
67 [24, 1893].

Another interesting case is that of Ernst Mach. Mach believed that the basic elements of the world – he called them "sensations" – become part either of the physical or of the mental world as soon as they aggregate with other elements.[68] Stumpf was definitely skeptical of this view, which he considered a philosophically unsophisticated and ultimately untenable pseudo-explanation.[69] As a case in point, Stumpf's opening address at the third Congress of Psychology, held in Munich in 1896 under his presidency, was devoted to a ruthless criticism of Mach's principle of psycho-physical parallelism.[70] Remarkably, at the time James

---

[68] "On a bright summer day under the open heaven, the world with my ego suddenly appeared to me as one coherent mass of sensations, only more strongly coherent in the ego. Although the actual working out of this thought did not occur until a later period, yet this moment was decisive for my whole view". E. Mach, *Beiträge zur Analyse der Empfindungen*, 1886; Eng. trans. *Contributions to the Analysis of the Sensations*, Chicago, Open Court, 1897, p. 23. In his interesting foreword to this English edition, Mach wrote: "I am of opinion [...] that the idea advanced in the present work, agreeably to which as many physico-chemical neural processes are to be assumed as there are distinguishable qualities of sensation, is [...] possessed of heuristic value, and that there is reasonable hope that at some future time it, too, will receive elucidation from the side of physiological chemistry. Admittedly, this idea [...] is but a consistent, monistic conception of Muller's principle of the specific energies [...]. (p. v).

[69] "*Mach's* text was a cause of much enjoyment for me; but if one looks more closely at it, much of it dissolves into Aperçu's writings, which are more witty than true" [8, 1886]. Stumpf reviewed Mach's book both in the 1886 edition and in the subsequent augmented one, published under the title *Die Analyse der Empfindungen*. See [8, 1886] and the relative footnotes.

[70] C. Stumpf, "Eröffnungsrede des Präsidenten, Prof. Dr. Carl Stumpf", in *Dritter International Congress für Psychologie in München vom 4–7 August 1896*, München, Lehmann, 1897, pp. 3–16. Published with some modifications as "Leib und Seele" in C. Stumpf, *Philosophische Reden und Vorträge*, Leipzig, Barth, 1910, pp. 65–93. For contingent reasons, Mach reacted late to Stumpf's speech. E. Mach, "Sinnliche Elemente und naturwissenschaftliche Begriffe", *Pflügers Archiv für die gesamte Physiologie des Menschen und der Tiere*, 136, 1910, pp. 263–274. He writes: "At the opening of the International Congress for Psychology in Munich, a meeting held on August 4, 1896, Prof. Dr. Carl Stumpf gave an address in which he also undertook to criticize my epistemological views in psychology. I was indeed inscribed as a participant of the Congress, but because of its strongly hypnotic–telepathic program did not attend. Since I was then occupied with other things and just afterwards stricken by serious illness, Stumpf's speech came to my attention late. In a series of editions of *Analyse der Empfindungen*, I have indeed answered the objections of Carl Stumpf and others, which I view neither as personal nor malicious, but *typical*, but since Stumpf's talk has recently gone into a third edition, I want to add here a comparison between my representation and the main passages of his speech in so far as they relate to me". Quoted from the English translation: E. Mach, "Sensory Elements and Scientific Concepts" in *Ernst Mach. A Deeper Look. Documents and New Perspectives*, ed. by J.T. Blackmore, Dordrecht, Kluwer, 1992, pp. 125–126.

commented positively on Stumpf's address.[71] Ten years after Mach's *Beiträge*, then, James was far from sharing Mach's positions without reservations, let alone defending them against Stumpf's uncharitable attack. Still, James had a different attitude toward the Viennese scientist. He highly esteemed Mach, whom he considered a "genius".[72] What is more, James's late "radical empiricism" is undeniably reminiscent of Mach's views.[73] For this reason, Stumpf voiced his disagreement with James's doctrine friendly, but decidedly.[74]

Franz Brentano also undoubtedly deserves a mention in this context. Both as a man and as a thinker, Brentano had a great influence over Stumpf. Besides his intellectual debt to him, Stumpf was friends with Brentano, whom he greatly admired. Of course, his friendship with James was quite different:[75] Stumpf found

---

71 "I read the address with extreme satisfaction. I think it is high time that someone in such an authoritative position should raise a voice against the excessively shallow dogmatism of the parallelists, who simply affirm the truth of a conception that they conceive as neat and pretty. You did the business in a perfectly masterly way. I especially admired the breadth of the treatment and the skill with which you avoided entering into any minute or secondary considerations. I can't help thinking that the day of the cruder parallelism, as the last word of scientific philosophy, is passed. That thistle needs only to be firmly grasped to show its feebleness! [...]" [31, 1896].

72 In 1882, James wrote to Alice: "Mach came to my Hotel and I spent 4 hours walking & supping with him at his Club – an unforgettable conversation. I don't think anyone ever gave me so strong an impression of pure intellectual genius"; furthermore: "Mach, Professor of Physics, & genius of all trades" [58, 1882]. James to Stumpf: "[...] Professor Mach, that truly "*genialer*" man" [7, 1886]. By contrast, James considered Wundt typically devoid of *genius*: Wundt "isn't a genius, he's a *professor*", he is a "Napoleon without genius" [10, 1887]; "If only he [Wundt] could show a spark of creative genius *dabei*!" [24, 1893]. In a letter to A. Thomsen of 1911, Mach recalls James's visit: "My personal memories of William James are very pleasant; he visited me while still in Prague in 80 or 81. I remember no one with whom, despite the divergence of viewpoints, I could discuss so well and fruitfully. He opposed me almost everywhere and yet I benefited almost everywhere by his objections. Already at that time he avoided any drop of wine or coffee so that I believed him more of a nervous hypochondriac than a really sick man. The center of his work certainly lies in his excellent Psychology. I cannot quite come to terms with his Pragmatism. 'We cannot give up the concept of God because it promises too much'. That is a rather dangerous argument". Quoted from E. Banks, *Ernst Mach's World Elements. A Study in Natural Philosophy*, Dordrecht, Springer, 2003, p. 143; German text in *Ernst Mach als Aussenseiter*, ed. by J.T. Blackmore and K. Hentschel, Wien, Braumüller, 1985, p. 86

73 See below in this *Introduction*.

74 "A growing divergence appears to be occurring in our views, dear and revered friend. [...] The positivistic theory of knowledge, in which you agree Mach, seems to me impossible, or barren" [53, 1907].

75 L. Sprung, "Brüder im Geiste. Franz Brentano und William James", in Sprung, *Carl Stumpf. Eine Biographie*, cit., p. 193.

in James an allied spirit who – both in personal and in scientific matters – was tremendously distant from the scholastic style prevailing within the school of Brentano. Indeed, even though Stumpf has long been considered an orthodox follower of Brentano in philosophy, recent research has highlighted the influence exerted by Lotze.[76] In fact, Stumpf eventually took his distance from both of his mentors and developed an original philosophy of his own: the correspondence testifies to the remarkable role played by William James in this evolution.

In the James-Stumpf correspondence, Brentano's name comes up twice. In 1884, Stumpf defended his teacher from a critical remark by James in *Some Omissions of Introspective Psychology*, where Brentano's view that introspection is infallible is ridiculed.[77] Stumpf objects that while Brentano did affirm the infallibility of "internal perception", he also claimed that psychology depends on short-term memory, which is far less reliable.[78] The nuanced formulation adopted for the correspondent discussion in *The Principles of Psychology* shows that James took note of this remark.[79] Fifteen years later, in 1899, Stumpf announced to his American friend that Brentano unexpectedly supported James's theory of emotions.[80] That was quite surprising to Stumpf, and is still surprising

---

[76] Stumpf's rigorous adherence to Brentanism has been stressed by K. Schuhmann, *Carl Stumpf (1848–1936)*, cit., p. 128. Concerning Lotze's influence see Milkov, *Carl Stumpf's Debt to Hermann Lotze*, cit., and B. Centi, "Stumpf and Lotze on Space, Reality, Relation", in Carl Stumpf, *From Philosophical Reflection to Interdisciplinary Scientific Investigation*, ed. by S. Bonacchi and G.-J. Boudewijnse, Wien, Krammer, 2011, pp. 69–81. A balanced evaluation was given by Denis Fisette: "Some claim that Stumpf is a truly orthodox Brentanian [...] while others [...] argue that Stumpf gradually distanced himself from Brentano's thinking and moved closer to that of Lotze. The truth must lie somewhere in the middle". D. Fisette, "Carl Stumpf", *The Stanford Encyclopedia of Philosophy*.

[77] "As is well known, contradictory opinions about the value of introspection prevail. Comte and Maudsley, for instance, call it worthless; Ueberweg and Brentano come near calling it infallible. Both opinions are extravagancies". W. James, "On Some Omissions of Introspective Psychology", *Mind* 9, 1884, p. 1 [*Works* 13, p. 142].

[78] "You do Brentano an injustice [...] if you ascribe to him such an extreme view. He emphasizes indeed that psychology is essentially dependent on observation in *memory* and that this is by no means infallible" [4, 1884].

[79] See the footnotes to [4, 1884].

[80] "I thought that I quite agreed with him [Brentano] regarding emotions, but then I received a 7-sheet long letter from him in which he declared himself decisively for *your* view and against mine" [34, 1899]. For an interpretation that links James's doctrine of emotions to intentionality (without reference to Brentano) see M. Ratcliffe, "William James on emotion and intentionality", *International Journal of Philosophical Studies* 13, 2, 2005, pp. 179–202. According to Ratcliffe, it is incorrect to argue that James denied that emotions are cognitive states: rather, James remarked that bodily feelings also belong to intentionality.

in the light of the common understanding of his doctrine.[81] However, by stating that Brentano endorsed James's view on emotions, Stumpf oversimplified a much more complicated state of affairs.[82] Stumpf had taken his distance from the James-Lange hypothesis in an essay of 1899, entitled *Über den Begriff der Gemüthsbewegung*.[83] Reacting to it, Brentano criticized Stumpf's solution and rather endorsed James.[84] However, in that circumstance Brentano avowed that he knew the James-Lange doctrine only "partially" and "indirectly" – and mainly from Stumpf's essay. In fact, Brentano never simply adhered to the James-Lange view of emotions: rather, he developed a position of his own and rejected Stumpf's "heterodox" stance.[85]

Speaking of Brentano, it might be worth making some remarks on the role of phenomenology in the correspondence. Scholars who endorse a phenomenological interpretation of James's thought[86] may reasonably expect his correspondence with Stumpf to offer some support to their reading. Yet this is not necessarily the case. Needless to say, neither James nor Stumpf are best interpreted from the point of view of Husserlian phenomenology.[87] By contrast, if

---

81 Reisenzein and Schönpflug note: "Stumpf [...] took it to be a strength of his theory that – in contrast to the theories of Wundt and James – it was in fundamental agreement with both common sense and with what he and Brentano (1874/1971) regarded as the dominant traditional line of emotion theorizing: the cognitive tradition exemplified by Aristotle, Thomas Aquinas, Descartes, and Spinoza". R. Reisenzein, W. Schönpflug, "Stumpf's Cognitive-Evaluative Theory of Emotion", *American Psychologist* 47, 1, 1992, p. 38.

82 "In short, Stumpf's position on this issue is *prima facie* a kind of compromise between James's and Brentano's views in that he argues against Brentano that sensory feeling are necessary conditions of emotional experience in general, and against James, that this phenomenal dimensional of emotional experience is not by itself a sufficient condition". D. Fisette, "Mixed Feelings. Carl Stumpf's Criticism of James and Brentano on Emotions", in *Themes from Brentano*, ed. by D. Fisette and G. Fréchette, Amsterdam and New York, Rodopi, 2013, p. 282.

83 C. Stumpf, "Über den Begriff der Gemüthsbewegung", *Zeitschrift für Psychologie und Physiologie der Sinnesorgane* 21, 1899, pp. 47–99.

84 Brentano, *Briefe an Carl Stumpf 1867–1917*, p. 115 (18 August 1889).

85 See the footnotes to [34, 1899].

86 In my view, Herzog's claim that the "place of honor as a founder of phenomenological psychology [...] belongs to James" fails to provide a correct interpretative framework. M. Herzog, "William James and the Development of Phenomenological Psychology in Europe". *Journal of the Human Sciences*, 8, 1, 1995, pp. 29–46. See also B. Wilshire, *William James and Phenomenology: A Study of "The Principles of Psychology"*, New York, AMS Press, 1979; J.M. Edie, *William James and Phenomenology*, Bloomington, Indiana University Press, 1987.

87 Husserl dedicated *Logische Untersuchungen* to Stumpf, who was his teacher in Halle. On the relationship between them, see D. Fisette, "A Phenomenology without Phenomena? Carl Stumpf's Critical Remarks on Husserl's Phenomenology", *Essays on Stumpf*, pp. 321–358; see also R. Rollinger, *Husserl's Position in the School of Brentano*, Dordrecht, Kluwer, 1999. James,

one understands "phenomenology" *lato sensu* and in close connexion with psychology, the term might capture a relevant feature of their thought, in line with what James calls their "sensationalistic" point of view".[88] In any case, the word "phenomenology" never recurs in the James–Stumpf correspondence.

The correspondence also includes a number of discussions concerning institutional matters. At the time, psychology was going through an impressive process of institutionalization: the foundation of laboratories and journals went hand in hand with the organization of grand international conferences.[89] James and Stumpf occasionally declared to be horrified by overcrowded meetings;[90] yet there are exceptions. The first Congress of Psychology in Paris (1889) admittedly exerted a positive effect upon James, encouraging him in the troubled redaction of his *Principles of Psychology*.[91] As for Stumpf, he was personally involved in the organization of the third Munich congress of 1896. Handling the congress-related correspondence exhausted him;[92] however, he defended the organization against Balwin's criticism.[93] Besides, in their letters the two friends occasionally linger on their (mostly unsuccessful) attempts at translating James's works into German, or Stumpf's into English.[94] In 1893, James asked Stumpf to join the editorial board of the Psychological Review.[95] Later, Stumpf successfully nominated James for the prestigious *Akademie der Wissenschaften* of Berlin.[96] James's curiosity as to the number and the names of

---

who had no personal acquaintance with Husserl, gave negative advice as to a translation into English of *Logische Untersuchungen*. See H. Spiegelberg, *The Phenomenological Movement. A Historical Introduction*, Den Haag, Nijhoff, 1960, pp. 112–113.

88 See below, sect. 2 of this *Introduction*. As to Stumpf's relatively narrow definition of phenomenology, see R. Rollinger, "Stumpf on Phenomena and Phenomenology", *Austrian Phenomenology: Brentano, Husserl, and Meinong on Mind and Object*. Frankfurt a. M., Ontos, 2008, pp. 139–156.

89 M. Savourin, S. Cooper, "The first International Congress of Physiological Psychology (Paris, August 1889): The birth of the International Union of Psychological Science", *International Journal of Psychology* 49, 2014, pp. 222–232. See also H. Piéron, "Histoire succincte des Congrès internationaux de Psychologie", *L'année psychologique* 54, 1954, pp. 397–405.

90 [15, 1891], [16, 1891].

91 [12, 1899]. The *Congrès international de psychologie* took place in Paris, 6–10 August 1889.

92 Stumpf complains: "I had unending correspondence with foreign scholars and with the general secretary" [30, 1896].

93 J.M. Baldwin, "The Third Congress of Psychology", *The Nation. A Weekly Journal Devoted to Politics, Literature, Science and Art* 63, No 1628, 1896, pp. 192–193. See [30, 1896] and the relative footnotes for further reference.

94 [15, 1891], [16, 1891], [18, 1891], [29, 1895], [30, 1896], [31, 1896].

95 [25, 1893].

96 [38, 1899].

the scientists appointed together with him reveal that he attached a degree of importance to this invitation.[97] He did not attend the ceremony though.[98]

Personal matters like travels, family, and health also find their way in the correspondence. As already pointed out, a second meeting took place in Munich in 1893. The outcome of this long-awaited event was disappointing for Stumpf. In a letter of 17 May 1893, he complains that in the course of a whole year spent in Europe together with his family, James devoted to him only a couple of hurried hours.[99] He also regrets to have missed the chance of meeting James's wife.[100] James's reassuring words deserve a long quotation:

> Your letter of the 17th., just received, touches me very much, and confirms me in my habitual belief that your heart is as strong and active an organ as your head. But how *could* I have conveyed to you the impression that my feeling of personal affection for you, and satisfaction in being able to count you as a friend, had grown less in the past ten years? Older I am indeed, and probably much duller, but I speak sincerely when I say that during my last visit I felt more intimately and closely the charm of your character and our intellectual kinship than when we were together ten years ago in Prag.[101]

The correspondence tells of subsequent unsuccessful attempts to arrange a meeting. James missed the 1896 Munich congress organized by Stumpf.[102] In 1899, James sailed again to Germany to recover at Nauheim's medical baths. Rather depressed, he did not feel like meeting people; when he finally wrote to Stumpf, it was too late to arrange a visit.[103]

---

97 [42, 1900].
98 [40, 1900].
99 "You are in Europe for a full year – a year that I have been looking forward to for 10 years – and of this year, few hours were allotted to seeing each other again, hours in which your thoughts and feelings were still occupied by urgent matters! I cannot reproach you for this, of course, but I am sad about it; so sad, that – to say it openly – I have the uncertain feeling that your friendship has lost some of its liveliness through the years, that you perhaps have not found in it what you promised yourself initially, or that something about me has proven alien or unpleasant to you" [23, 1893].
100 "I am infinitely sorry that we did not see your dear wife more at all, and that *I* did not get acquainted with her at all! My wife and sister-in-law were so delighted by her that I have to view it as a great loss" [23, 1893].
101 [24, 1893].
102 "I ruined myself financially by my last excursion en famille to Europe, and nothing but the need of foreign travel for my health could justify so speedy a repetition of the process. Moreover, it unsettles my americanism (that tender plant) to go too often abroad, and that must be weighed against the intellectual and social advantages of the Congress" [29, 1895].
103 [33, 1899].

The correspondents also touch upon family matters. New births and, sadly, the loss of James's child in 1885[104] are registered in the course of the years. During his sabbatical in 1882, James had left Alice with their second child of three months.[105] At the time, Stumpf introduced him to his wife Hermine – "a nice little German professor's wife, with many ach Gotts & Herrjeses'es" – and the "little Rudolf or Rudi, 14 months old, with a sharp aquiline nose like his father's and a large white forehead on which one might draw the plan of the city".[106] An irresistibly amusing touch is added by an episode occurred to the Jameses during their stay in Florence in 1893: "If you could have seen the confusion in which my last six weeks have been spent [...], you would excuse any derelictions on my part. *Incessant* sociability in florence, pushed to such an extreme that one pair of young American friends came and *had a baby* (!!!) in our appartment, there being no other convenient place for the event to take place in".[107] Finally, the letters occasionally touch upon politics, the main topic being the Dreyfus affair.[108] Both friends were shocked by the attempt to condemn an innocent; even their sympathy for France and the French yielded as a consequence. James's letters also interestingly reflect his anti-imperialism.[109]

---

104 [7, 1886].
105 Alice and William James had five children: Henry (1879–1947), William (1882–1961), Herman (1884–1885), Margaret Mary (1887–1950) and Alexander Robertson (1890–1946).
106 Quoting from James's letter to his wife Alice [58, 1882]. Hermine and Carl Stumpf had three children: Rudolf (1881–1945), Felix (1885–1970), and Elisabeth (1891–1976).
107 [22, 1893].
108 [33, 1899], [34, 1899], [35, 1899]. See D. Weinfeld, "*Les Intellectuels* in America: William James, the Dreyfus Affair, and the Development of the Pragmatist Intellectual", *The Journal of American History*, 2018, pp. 19–44.
109 [45, 1900], [47, 1901]. See A. Livingstone, *Damn Great Empires! William James and the Politics of Pragmatism*, Oxford, Oxford University Press, 2016.

2 Scientific Themes

2.1 Space and Relations

The James-Stumpf correspondence testifies to the main steps in the development of their psychological researches and philosophical ideas. When they met in Prague, James and Stumpf agreed on many significant scientific themes. Thereafter, their philosophical ideas developed differently, so that Stumpf's eventual rejection of pragmatism and radical empiricism does not come as a surprise. However, there is no point in exaggerating the distance between them. In psychology, James and Stumpf always shared a number of relevant principles and ideas. In philosophy, despite all divergences as to the theory of knowledge, they agreed on the critique of metaphysical monism[110] and embraced pluralism in cosmology, although with different nuances. Last but not least, their views on religion have much in common. Let us see the reasons for their agreement and disagreement in some detail.

James's appreciation of Stumpf's *Über den psychologischen Ursprung der Raumvorstellung* of 1873 is a good starting point.[111] In this book, Stumpf defends a nativist stance by claiming that the idea of space originates from a spatial element embedded within perception. Each visual item is endowed with "partial contents": extension, quality, and intensity. Partial contents (or "psychological parts") can *vary* independently, but cannot *exist* independently of each other.[112] This explanation, partly inspired by Lotze,[113] ruled out both

---

110 James's late philosophy can be interpreted as a form of epistemic monism: as we shall see, this will be a source of disagreement with Stumpf. At any rate, as a metaphysician James always endorsed a pluralistic view of the universe in fierce opposition to "tender-minded" views of it. For a survey of general interpretations of James's ideas, see Cooper, *The Unity of William James's Thought*, pp. 36–40.

111 "James came across Stumpf's work while writing on space perception. He had announced his theory in an article entitled 'The Spatial *Quale*' (1879), theory that later developed in the longest chapter of the *Principles of Psychology*. James was definitely in harsh disagreement with all the empiricists such as Thomas Brown or Alexander Bain or John Stuart Mill who argued in favor of a purely empirical theory of space–perception, starting from the assumption that space is not found in elementary sensations". N. Dazzi, "James and Stumpf. Similarities and Differences", *Psychologie und Geschichte* 6, 1999, p. 248.

112 Stumpf, *Raumvorstellung*, p. 121, 139. On Stumpf's mereology see M. Kaiser-el-Safti, "Carl Stumpfs Lehre vom Ganzen und den Teilen", *Axiomathes* n.s. 5, 1994, pp. 87–122.

113 Stumpf, *Raumvorstellung*, pp. 81–82. See B. Centi, *Stumpf and Lotze on Space, Reality, Relation*, cit., p. 70.

https://doi.org/10.1515/9783110525533-002

British associationism[114] and the attempts at a reinstatement of Kant's *a priori*.[115] James definitely agreed with this line of thought.[116] His copy of Stumpf's space-book bears the traces of intensive study. The final blank pages are full of handwritten notes and commentaries, among which: "Denial of association! [...] S[tumpf]'s great argument is that we cannot construct space out of mental elements which themselves have no spatial quality originally. (In other words he maintains that the antecedent of the space vorstellung [sic] must be physiological only & not logical)".[117] In 1882, James read *Aus der vierten Dimension*: another essay by Stumpf on the problem of space, where he makes fun of the hypothesis of a fourth spatial dimension.[118] The discussion on space was later revived by Stumpf's review of a book by Theodor Lipps[119] and by the publication of James's essay *The Perception of Space* in the journal *Mind*.[120]

James and Stumpf also shared the view that *all* perceptions, and not just visual ones, are endowed with some sort of spatiality. As far as sounds are concerned, James claims that e.g. a "high tone is felt as a thin, bright streak on a broader, darker background";[121] while Stumpf does not hesitate to affirm that a

---

[114] An English review of *Raumvorstellung* came out in *The Academy*. The reviewer points out Stumpf's opposition to mainstream associationism. "English writers upon this subject have not sufficiently distinguished from each other the separate interests of physiology and psychology, and our physiologists have been too much inclined to believe that their investigations have exhausted the whole of the subject and not one side of it merely; while, if we except Mr. Herbert Spencer, our psychologists are so completely carried away with the idea of the omnipotence of "Association" to explain all things and everything, that their theories are never able to satisfy the requirements of the phenomena". Th. Lindsay, "Review of Stumpf, C. Über den psychologischen Ursprung der Raumvorstellung", *The Academy* 6, 1873, p. 172.

[115] Stumpf agreed with Lotze that although space is intuitive rather than intellectual (as Kant believed), one must distinguish between formal extension and real *place*. In addition, "Stumpf further developed Lotze's objective conception of space [...] into the idea that places [...] are perceptual contents (*Sinnesinhalte*)". Milkov, *Carl Stumpf's Debt to Hermann Lotze*, p. 116.

[116] On James's theory of space see G.F. Myers, *William James. His Life and Thought*, New Haven and London, Yale University Press, 1986, pp. 114–122.

[117] Consulted at Houghton Library, Cambridge (MA). Ref. WJ 783.89.

[118] C. Stumpf, "Aus der vierten Dimension", *Philosophische Monatshefte* 14, 1878, pp. 13–30. James positively comments on it in [1, 1882].

[119] See [7, 1886] and the relative footnotes for further reference.

[120] [10, 1887]. See W. James, "The Perception of Space", *Mind*, 12, 1887, pp. 1–30, 183–211, 321–353, 516–548. Reprinted with revisions as Chapter 20 of *Principles of Psychology* [*Works* 9, pp. 776–912]; textual variants in *Works* 10, pp. 1434–1440.

[121] W. James, "The Spatial Quale", *Journal of Speculative Philosophy* 13, 1879, p. 84 [*Works* 13, p. 80].

"greater extension belongs to the low tones in consciousness".¹²² More generally, in volume 2 of *Tonpsychologie,* Stumpf echoes James's tenet that "a certain spatial quantification" is "a universal datum of sensibility".¹²³ Stumpf adds that this is no "formal" element in Kant's sense, but rather "a content of sensation: a 'Spatial Quale'".¹²⁴

The seminal importance of these early reflections on space must be adequately highlighted. It is not arbitrary to assume that the reading of *Raumvorstellung* influenced James: when he wrote *The Spatial Quale,* he was certainly familiar with Stumpf's space-book.¹²⁵ Indeed, in 1887 he praised Stumpf: "as you know, of all writers on space you seem to me the one who, on the whole, has thought out the subject most *philosophically*".¹²⁶ What is more, the explanation of space shared by James and Stumpf was no isolated solution: rather, it epitomized a conceptual model that could be successfully applied to further philosophical questions, especially that of *relations* (see below).¹²⁷

In 1884, upon reading vol. 1 of *Tonpsychologie,* James congratulated Stumpf on his adoption of a "sensationalistic"¹²⁸ point of view and on his criticism of relativity. James subscribed to the main tendency of the book.

---

122 *Tone Psychology* 1, p. 130 [*Tonpsychologie* 1, p. 207]. These pages of Stumpf's book are referred to by James at the beginning of the chapter on space in the *Principles of Psychology* (2, p. 135 [*Works* 9, p. 777]). See also [17, 1891].
123 James, *The Spatial Quale,* cit., p. 74 [*Works* 13, p. 71]; quoted by Stumpf in *Tonpsychologie* 2, p. 59.
124 *Tonpsychologie* 2, p. 59 [English in the original].
125 Stumpf is approvingly referred to when it comes to rebut an objection to James's nativism, concerning the third dimension: "If one should admit that the first two dimensions of space may [...] be called part of the simple retinal sensation, but that the intuition of depth cannot be so given, I would not only reply, with Stumpf, that we cannot feel plane space as a space without in some way cognizing the cubic spaces that the plane separates [...]" [*Works* 13, p. 68]. The reference is to *Raumvorstellung,* pp. 178–179.
126 [10, 1887]. Stumpf's influence on James is discussed by Perry in *Thought and Character* 2, pp. 59–71.
127 "With his theory of 'psychological parts' Stumpf goes above and beyond the problem of the 'origin of the idea of space'". Mereology is "the core" of *Raumvorstellung* and the "basis for phenomenology". Kaiser-el-Safti, *Carl Stumpfs Lehre vom Ganzen und den Teilen,* pp. 103–104.
128 As to the problem of space, "Sensationalist" is synonymous to "Nativist": James, *The Spatial Quale* [*Works* 13, p. 72]. Elsewhere James opposes his own "sensationalistic" point of view to the "intellectualistic" one. *Principles of Psychology* 1, pp. 244–245 [*Works* 8, pp. 237–238] (on relations). When endorsing sensationalism James avows his debt to Stumpf (*Principles of Psychology* 2, p. 282 [*Works* 9, p. 911]); by contrast, Helmholtz and Wundt are to him the most eminent "intellectualists". James, *The Perception of Space (III),* pp. 350–353 ("The Intellectualist Theory of Space"). With a new title ("Sensations which we ignore"), the chapter is partly reprinted in the chapter on space of *Principles of Psychology* 2, pp. 240–243 [*Works* 9, pp. 872–875].

> What I *care for* most in the book is of course its general theoretical tendency, away from "psychomythology" and logicalism, and towards a truly empirical and sensationalistic point of view, which I am persuaded is the only practical and solid basis for psychological science.[129]

James also praised Stumpf's rebuttal of the so-called "doctrine of relativity" of sensations, defended by several authors at the time, including Wundt. According to that doctrine, there are no absolute sensations (e.g., of a sound): rather, what we get is invariably the contrast to a previous or concomitant state (e.g., silence, or another sound of different pitch).[130] James indeed agreed with Stumpf in his severe criticism of this philosophical tenet.[131] Previously, James and Stumpf had already been involved in a criticism of the so-called *"Innervationsgefühle"*, introduced by Johannes Müller[132] and defended among others by Wundt (at the time) in the explanation of will-related acts.[133] Accordingly, the act e.g. of moving a limb results from an innervation-feeling, that is, from an efferent discharge of neural energy. James and Stumpf considered this doctrine a perfect sample of "psycho-mythology": pseudo-explanations made up of unascertainable entities.[134] Significantly, they left room for a pure act of volition – e.g., the will to move the limb – independently of any alleged efferent neural discharge.[135]

Elsewhere Stumpf is defined a "sensationalist writer" for his opinions on the problem of psychological distance. *Principles of Psychology* 2, p. 221 [*Works* 9, p. 854]. As to Stumpf's views on psychological distance, see also *Principles of Psychology* 1, p. 530 [*Works* 8, p. 501]).

129 [5, 1884]. James speaks of "mythological" psychology with reference to the Kantian assumption that space is a "super–sensational mental product". *Principles of Psychology*, 2, p. 273 [*Works* 9, p. 903].

130 Against relativity, see *Tone Psychology* 1, pp. 5–12 [*Tonpsychologie* 1, pp. 7–22].

131 "Your opening pages about the doctrine of relativity did my very heart good – I had been longing for years for something like that. It seems to me that what you have said is final" [5, 1884]. Touching upon relativity in the *Principles of Psychology*, James refers to Stumpf's *Tonpsychologie* (*Principles of Psychology* 2, p. 11 [*Works* 9, p. 660]).

132 "We have [...] a representation and a pre-determination of the amount of neural stimulation emanating from the brain, which is necessary to produce a certain degree of movement". J. Müller, *Handbuch der Physiologie für Vorlesungen*, Coblenz, Hölscher, vol. 2, 1835, p. 500.

133 [2, 1882], [4, 1884], [8, 1886]. Wundt later changed his mind: see [23, 1893] and the relative footnotes for further reference. In addition, James and Stumpf criticized the so-called "articulation-feelings", supposedly apt to explain human language: see [7, 1886].

134 Herbert S. Langfeld attended Stumpf's lectures on psychology in 1906–1907. He reports: "Stumpf felt that the innervation feelings played a rather unfortunate role in preceding decades and that James [...]" deserved much credit for his arguments against the theory. H.S. Langfeld, "Stumpf's 'Introduction to Psychology'", *The American Journal of Psychology* 50, 1937, p. 41.

135 See [4, 1884], [8, 1886] and the relative footnotes.

In line with the above mentioned "sensationalistic" point of view, James and Stumpf believed that perceptual experience comprises both simple elements and the *relations* that exist between them.¹³⁶ Commenting on volume 1 of *Tonpsychologie*, where Stumpf systematically deals with this problem, James avows that he enjoyed "immensely" Stumpf's treatment of relations as "immediate perceptions of sense, and not logical inferences from other related facts". Many – James goes on – wrongly believe that "if you can *develop* a thing's relations, and *define* it in terms of those relations, then it can never have had any other *status* in the mind than as a perception of those relations".¹³⁷ Undeniably, space and motion *can* be described in that way, but James insists that the "feeling" of space (or of motion) does not entail any hint at those definitions. Stumpf's "noble book" has dealt "one of the very heaviest of blows" to the adverse theory. Remarkably, however, James and Stumpf adopt a different terminology: whereas Stumpf claims that some classes of relations "are immanent to sensations, not actualized only by judgments",¹³⁸ James insists that no argument can ever substitute the *feeling* of a certain sensory situation.¹³⁹ This apparently slight difference actually marks a divergency that will become manifest later.

2.2 Sensations, Feelings, Emotions

Despite agreeing with his general stance, James criticizes some of Stumpf's choices. Stumpf distinguishes between sensation and judgment: "When we

---

136 This stance reveals the influence that Hermann Lotze had on the American thinker. James's intellectual debt to Lotze had been already highlighted by Perry, *Thought and Character* 1, pp. 586–587. James's acquaintance with Lotze's thought dates back to 1865. O. Kraushaar notes that "Lotze's great vogue in the last quarter of the 19th century may be credited to [t]his ability to draw the attention of both the 'tender minded' and the 'tough minded'. James was especially attracted to Lotze's doctrine because he too sought to justify and defend the validity of spiritual experience in the face of a growing acceptance of mechanistic principles". O. Kraushaar, "What James's Philosophical Orientation Owed to Lotze", *The Psychological Review* 47, 1938, p. 519. See also O. Kraushaar, "Lotze's Influence on the Psychology of William James", *The Psychological Review* 43, 1936, pp. 235–257; "Lotze as a Factor in the Development of James's Radical Empiricism and Pluralism", *The Psychological Review* 48, 1939, pp. 455–471; "Lotze's Influence on the Pragmatism and Practical Philosophy of William James", *Journal of the History of Ideas* 1, 1940, pp. 439–458.
137 [5, 1884].
138 *Tone Psychology* 1, p. 54 [*Tonpsychologie* 1, p. 97].
139 With reference to the criticized theories, James writes: "Thus motion is a synthesis of *terminus a quo* and *terminus ad quem*, with earlier & later moments of time, and cannot be a simple feeling; Space is a synthesis of *positions*, and no feeling" [5, 1884].

designate a sensation as the tone a or as the third of f, what we express by saying this is a sensory judgment, i.e. a judgment that concerns sensory phenomena and that is evoked by them".[140] More specifically, he speaks of a threshold between sensation and judgment.[141] When we fail to notice a part of the sensory content, the correspondent sensation remains unnoticed, that is, below the threshold. Unnoticed sensations can nevertheless exert a remarkable effect upon the overall content and, consequently, upon the judgment. For instance, overtones influence tonal impressions, yet they remain unnoticed, at least until we concentrate upon hearing them intentionally. Thus, Stumpf moved away from Fechner's psychophysics[142] and the related hypothesis of *unconscious* – rather than *unnoticed* – sensations.

James complains: "you speak as if the sensation to be judged were an unvarying and permanent bit of content, no matter what its concomitants".[143] In *Some Omissions of Introspective Psychology*,[144] James had opposed this view. He made it clear that we "never have the same subjective modification twice".[145] What we get twice – James argues – is the same *object*:

> For the judgement to be identical, it seems to me that there is no need of supposing that the sensation that underlies it maintains an absolutely unchanged individuality. When the attention discriminates an overtone that a moment before it did not notice, I don't think we ought to say that the overtone was already there *as a sensation*. It surely was *not* there as the sensation *we now get of it*; and I think the more rational way of considering the matter is to say that the *sound* was there as an object that with our brain in one state and our consciousness in the corresponding state we defined that object in one way, but that with our brain and consciousness in a better more active state, we now define the *same* sound in *another* way, namely as having an overtone.[146]

Stumpf rejoices for James's overall positive reception of his book: "your recognition is, for me, more valuable than that of the majority of my German colleagues".[147] As for James's criticism, Stumpf replies somewhat elusively:

---

140 *Tone Psychology* 1, p. 3 [*Tonpsychologie* 1, p. 3].
141 *Tone Psychology* 1, p. 19 [*Tonpsychologie* 1, pp. 33–34]. See below, [5, 1884] and the explanatory footnotes.
142 *Tone Psychology* 1, p. 30 [*Tonpsychologie* 1, p. 54].
143 [5, 1884].
144 "However it may be of the stream of real life, of the mental river the saying of Herakleitos is probably literally true: we never bathe twice in the same water there". James, *On Some Omissions of Introspective Psychology*, cit., p. 11 [*Works* 13, p. 152].
145 [5, 1884].
146 [5, 1884].
147 [6, 1885].

> I need to reflect on the remarks you made in your letter, [...] for which I am very thankful; perhaps volume II will provide the opportunity to come back to it. I remember earlier having a similar view on the matter myself; but the theory would not let itself be carried out. Perhaps there is some middle way to be found. I hope to be done with volume II by the end of this year.

Indeed, one can see a development of this topic in the second volume of *Tonpsychologie*. James finished reading it during his voyage to Europe in autumn 1891. Writing from London, he expressed a positive comment: "You have done a monumental piece of work, which will be a model to all time of the way in which general views and the minute study of details can be combined".[148] James admired Stumpf's ability in squeezing "the last drops of formulable truth out of the facts"; his "strong point" consisted in his "incorruptible critical clear headedness".[149] James also praised the style of Stumpf's book: "What a strange thing an intellectual *atmosphere* is! To many of your 'popular scientists' readers you must seem displeasingly cool-blooded, but it was a constant delight to me to feel the firm and close knit *texture* of your thought".[150]

Nevertheless, James had two reservations. In the first place, he was unsatisfied with Stumpf's treatment of "the sense of similarity and the metaphysics thereto appertaining". What disturbed James was Stumpf's dismissal of the definition of similarity in terms of partial identity: "It seems to me an almost irresistible *postulate* that resemblance should be analyzable into partial identity".[151] This criticism is somehow puzzling, and calls for explanation. In the first volume of *Tonpsychologie*, Stumpf had claimed that "*[t]he equality of sensory phenomena is nothing but extreme similarity. The lack of this extreme is difference*".[152] This view is also defended in James's *Principles of Psychology*, where Stumpf is quoted

---

148 [17, 1891]. As Dazzi puts it, even though James criticizes Stumpf's allowance for unnoticed sensations, "there is however a Stumpf he continues to like, the antiatomist Stumpf, the Stumpf who criticizes artificial and complicated explanations, who supports direct experience". Dazzi, *James and Stumpf. Similarities and Differences*, cit., p. 251.
149 "It is not certainly the clear headedness of a purely and dryly logical mind which always seems negative and shallow, but that of a mind whose dissatisfaction with vague and facile formulas proceeds from his own sense of the presence of profounder sources of truth" [17, 1891].
150 [17, 1891]. As to positive aspects of the book, James contents himself with some general remarks concerning the treatment of timbre (*Klangfarbe*) and that of tonal fusion: "Let me say that § 28 particularly interested me, especially the part about klangfarbe. After that, § 22 In the 'Verschmelzung' business you have no doubt struck a fertile new conception, and I am curious to see what its farther developments will be".
151 See [17, 1891] and the explanatory footnotes.
152 *Tone Psychology* 1, p. 62 [*Tonpsychologie* 1, p. 111].

in support of said thesis.[153] Furthermore, in a discussion of this topic in 1893 – that is, after the letter of 1891 where James criticized Stumpf – James went so far as to defend, against Bradley, his solution concerning resemblance, "or rather Stumpf's (for in my book I am but the humble follower of the eminent Munich psychologist) [...]".[154] So why did James object to Stumpf's definition of resemblance?

This is one of the most intricate subjects dealt with in the correspondence. For the benefit of a reconstruction, the footnotes present the reader with additional materials drawn from James's and Stumpf's works, along with some remarks on Mach and Bradley.[155] For now I will only say that in 1890 (*Tonpsychologie* 2) Stumpf explicitly reaffirmed his view on similarity as expressed in 1883 (*Tonpsychologie* 1), defending it against an argument autonomously developed by Ernst Mach in *Beiträge zur Analyse der Empfindungen* (1886). Now, though he approved of Stumpf's original definition of similarity (1883), which he reaffirmed against Bradley (1893), in his letter of 1891 James also leaned for Mach's arguments of 1886. Confronted with Bradley, James stuck to Stumpf's original doctrine and denied that similarity necessarily follows on partial identity; confronted with the Stumpf of 1890, he shifted toward Mach's view – which is astoundingly akin to Bradley's: resemblance always depends on the identity of parts.[156]

On closer inspection, however, James's position appears more consistent than what it may seem at first. He does share with Stumpf the view that identity is the extreme degree of similarity (and not *vice versa*); yet he refuses to conclude from that, as Stumpf does,[157] that similarity doesn't imply partial identity. In fact, James draws a preliminary distinction: "It is supposed perhaps, by most people, that two resembling things owe their resemblance to their absolute identity in respect of some attribute or attributes, combined with the absolute non-identity of the rest of their being. *This, which may be true of compound things, breaks down when we come to simple impressions*".[158] With this subtle distinction, James makes room for two apparently opposite doctrines: the commonsense doctrine advocated by Mach, valid for the case of compound things; and Stumpf's view,

---

153 *Principles of Psychology* 1, p. 532 [*Works* 9, p. 502].
154 W. James, "Mr Bradley on Immediate Resemblance", *Mind* n.s. 2, pp. 208–210, and "Immediate Resemblance", *Mind* n.s. 2, 1893, pp. 509–510.
155 See the footnotes to [17, 1891], [18, 189s1], [23, 1893] [24, 1893].
156 On the polemic between James and Bradley see T.L.S. Sprigge, *James and Bradley. American Truth and British Reality*, Chicago and La Salle, Open Court, 1993, pp. 385–393; Myers, *William James. His Life and Thought*, pp. 111–112.
157 *Tone Psychology* 1, p. 62 [*Tonpsychologie* 1, p. 111]; see also *Tonpsychologie* 2, p. 272.
158 *Principles of Psychology* 1, p. 532 [*Works* 9, p. 502], emphasis added.

which holds for simple impressions.[159] At any rate, James omits any reference to this specification when he criticizes Stumpf in the letter of 1891.

Secondly, James questions the masterpiece of his German friend from another, more radical point of view. He notes that Stumpf's entire "doctrine of multiplicity" (*Mehrheitslehre*) "and of existent sensations not discriminated is at variance with the formulas I have used in my book [scil. *Principles of Psychology*], and seems to me hard to keep clear of entanglement with psychic chemistry etc".[160] In the first chapter of *Tonpsychologie* vol. 2, Stumpf discusses the problem of mental multiplicity. Consider the case of hearing a chord: should we say that we perceive *many* sounds at once, or *one* chord? In this formulation, the question may seem trivial, yet it becomes more intriguing when we think that a sound (e.g. of a violin, a guitar, etc.), is in turn made up of a multiplicity of simple tones, the so-called upper partials.[161] As a consequence, hearing a *single* sound amounts to perceiving a *multiplicity* (of upper partials). Tackling this theoretical difficulty, Stumpf distinguishes three main options: the doctrines of multiplicity, of unity, and of contrast.[162] These three hypotheses respectively imply that we perceive either a real multiplicity of sensory appearances, or a unitary impression, or else two swiftly alternating impressions (like a musical *trillo*). After a detailed evaluation of the pros and cons, Stumpf embraces the doctrine of multiplicity (*Mehrheitslehre*).[163] In other words, he advocates the opinion that perceiving multiple sensory instances (e.g. chords if compared with sounds, or sounds with upper partials, etc.) implies the apprehension of a *real* multiplicity.

While he agrees that the matter has great philosophical importance, and although he does share[164] some presuppositions with Stumpf, James cannot subscribe to his friend's *Mehrheitslehre*. Given his claim that each state of mind is

---

159 See also [23, 1893] and Myers, *William James. His Life and Thought*, cit., pp. 110–111.
160 [17, 1891].
161 The theory had been worked out by H. Helmholtz in *Die Lehre von den Tonempfindungen, als physiologische Grundlage für die Theorie der Musik*, Braunschweig, Vieweg, 1863.
162 *Tonpsychologie* 2, p. 12 (Mehrheitslehre, Einheitslehre, Wettstreitslehre). See [17, 1891] and the footnotes.
163 *Tonpsychologie* 2, p. 40 ff.
164 Reed affirms that James "probably" follows Stumpf when he "argues against the idea that, although single waves of air pressure give no sensation of pitch (one hears a thump or click), a series of such waves do produce a pitch sensation". Reed concludes that "James did not criticize physical or stimulus atomism in anything like the way he criticized sensory atomism. In this regard he is much closer to Stumpf than to Stumpf's student Köhler, with his concept of 'physical Gestalten' [...]". E. Reed, "The psychologist's fallacy as a persistent framework in William James's psychological theorizing", *History of the Human Sciences* 8, 1995, p. 66.

the product of that unique momentary situation, one could suspect that James rather leans for what Stumpf calls the "unity-hypothesis". Indeed, James often comes close to that option: "When I think the seven colours of the rainbow, I do not have seven thoughts of a colour, and then a thought of a bow; that would be eight thoughts. What I have is just one thought of the whole object".[165] More generally, "Whatever is known *together* is and must be known through a single modification of thought's stream".

By 1891, however, James already explored new explanatory strategies on this point:

> I believe that there will be no satisfactory solution of that whole matter except on some *erkenntnistheoretische* Basis, which will succeed in clearing up the relations between the "state of mind" and its "object". This is an obscure matter about which I have aspirations to write something which shall do away with the contradictions which occur so much on the psychological plane. I mean no ontological theory of knowledge, but an analysis of the way in which we come to treat the phenomenon or datum of experience sometimes as a thing sometimes as a mental representation of a thing etc etc. But this is unintelligible![166]

This is an early, sketchy and still admittedly "unintelligible" announcement of James's doctrine of "radical empiricism", which he would later develop. Rather than endorsing the most credible solution discarded by Stumpf (the *Einheitslehre*), James aims at a sea change that allows him to elude all of Stumpf's alternatives altogether.[167]

Considering all his criticism of both volumes of *Tonpsychologie*, James refuses to admit: 1) that there are unnoticed sensations (because each mental state is unitary); 2) that resemblance can be independent of partial identity; and 3) that there is a real multiplicity of simultaneous impressions in the mind instead of a unitary, unanalyzable complex mental state.

This time, Stumpf's answer was detailed and articulated. He replied to James's letter less than a month later:

> I also understand completely the objections you had to make against many specific points, and I can sufficiently sense their weight to empathize with you also on these points that divide us. This holds in particular for your opposition to unperceived sensations. I myself would have rejected them 12 years ago; however, the consequence of

---

165 James, *On some Omissions of Introspective Psychology*, cit., p. 10 [*Works* 13, p. 151].
166 [17, 1891].
167 As Lamberth notes, this letter provides evidence for "the early date of James's turn to metaphysics": D. Lamberth, *William James and the Metaphysics of Experience*, Cambridge, Cambridge University Press, 1999, p. 72. In support of his interpretation Lamberth (pp. 72–73) also refers to [29, 1895], and [31, 1896].

numerous individual observations appears to me to lead to the fact that we must distinguish between actual "unconscious" representations and unnoticed parts of a whole; I consider the first inadmissible, the latter necessary. I do not believe that it is the "psychologist's fallacy" which carries the blame here, but rather only certain specific arguments in detail. However, this matter requires a thorough investigation of principle, which will *necessarily* lead to an understanding.

Stumpf's reference to "psychologist's fallacy" hints at a concept formulated in the *Principles of Psychology* where James notes that the "great snare of the psychologist is the *confusion of his own standpoint with that of the mental fact* about which he is making his report". This he calls "the 'psychologist's fallacy' *par excellence*".[168] Stumpf was one of the psychologists accused of this fallacy, because he argued for the fusion of many sensations into one.[169] The quotation above, then, can be read as Stumpf's answer to this criticism from James. Be that as it may, Stumpf goes on to unfold the consequences of James's overall position:

> If I understand you correctly, according to you, there are in general no *parts* in the content of representation; each is an absolutely simple quality. All "analysis", instead of an actual analysis, is a discovery or production of entirely *new* simple qualities. The consequence of this, I think, is that there is also no classification. *Nothing* then is common to individual appearances; every general concept is itself in turn a new simple quality sui generis. Is that your opinion? I can also appreciate your opposition to "simple similarities", since this claim did not impose itself on me until lately, and since I still find certain difficulties in it. However, precisely from *your* standpoint, this assumption seems the least avoidable. For if in general there are no parts in sensations, how ought we then define "similarity" by "partial sameness or identity"?[170]

Unfortunately, James never replied. His subsequent letter to Stumpf was sent from Lucerne:[171] at the beginning of a long stay in Europe, James was preoccupied with other things and made no mention of the criticism.

To sum up, James highly esteemed Stumpf's early views on space, together with the general stance of both volumes of *Tonpsychologie*, which he considered representative of a general tendency which he himself shared. Besides Stumpf's thoroughness and precision, James appreciated his opposition to idealism and relativism, and his acknowledgment of the fact that some relations are intrinsically given within the appearances, and not superimposed by a logical act of the mind. He mainly disagreed as to the possibility of unnoticed parts of the same content, and to the idea of simple similarity. Stumpf generally conceded that the

---

168 *Principles of Psychology* 1, p. 196 [*Works* 8, p. 195].
169 *Principles of Psychology* 1, pp. 493–494 [*Works* 8, p. 493].
170 [18, 1891].
171 [19, 1892].

two issues are controversial, but keenly noted that the two arguments contradict each other.

Did James take note of Stumpf's objection? Notwithstanding his silence in the correspondence, I think he did. Abandoning a crucial tenet of his *Principles of Psychology*, in his Presidential Address before the American Psychological Association at Princeton in December 1894, James dropped the view that each mental state is an indecomposable unity.[172] Confronted with the neatly defined alternative – either the unity of the mental state (and simple similarity), or decomposable mental states (and similarity as partial identity) – James eventually opted for the latter. Of course, he did so in his own characteristic way.[173] The described exchange of views with his German friend can be counted among the reasons that induced James to embrace his mature view. To be sure, Stumpf's criticism interacted with many other factors in James's highly receptive mind. Considering all of these factors systematically exceeds the aims and limits of this introductory essay. At any rate, it is surely no exaggeration to say that the correspondence with Stumpf deserves serious attention by those interpreters who are interested in James's intellectual development.

2.3 Metaphysics and Epistemology

James and Stumpf always shared a fierce opposition to the speculations of idealism, and especially to its monistic metaphysics. James was undoubtedly the one who voiced his opposition to the "Absolute" in the most radical terms.[174] In a less vehement language, Stumpf devoted the first part of his official prolusion as Rector of the Berlin University (that is, where Fichte, Hegel and the later Schelling had taught ...) to a radical criticism of idealism. As a consequence of its pseudo-scientific speculations, Stumpf claimed, philosophy had gone rack

---

[172] W. James, "The Knowing of Things Together", *Psychological Review*, 1895, 2, pp. 105–124. See Lamberth, *William James and the Metaphysics of Experience*, p. 73.

[173] Actually, James was tempted to accept both horns of Stumpf's dilemma. "James's [...]radical empiricism revised, but did not abandon the traditional version": his pluralistic universe "remained, in essence, a universe of pluralities". Ash, *Gestalt Psychology*, cit., p. 71.

[174] "Damn the Absolute!" is the commentary added to the photographs portraying James and Royce in *The Letters of William James*, ed. by Henry James 3rd, Boston, Little & Brown, 1920, p. 134. The text reads: "Chocorua, September, 1903. One morning James and Royce strolled into the road and sat down on a wall in earnest discussion. When James heard the camera click, as his daughter took the upper snap-shot, he cried, 'Royce, you're being photographed! Look out! I say *Damn the Absolute!*'".

and ruin. The regeneration and "rebirth" of the discipline would go hand in hand with a new, informed and respectful alliance with natural science.[175]

According to Stumpf, monistic world-views are indefensible: despite all other differences, both Hegel's idealism and Mach's positivism fall into this class. Going off from the circumstance that the primary data of experience, namely "appearances" and "mental functions", irremediably differ, Stumpf rather endorses dualism.[176] The entire system of human knowledge cannot escape this duality: whereas the hard sciences build on the appearances, psychology and the human sciences start from mental functions.[177] Along with this dualistic epistemology, Stumpf allows for a pluralistic metaphysics. A full development of his thoughts on this subject came with *Spinozastudien*, where Stumpf interprets Spinoza's parallelism and his doctrine of infinite attributes.[178] On Stumpf's reading, Spinoza's parallelism has nothing to do with the abhorred "psychophysical parallelism" of Fechner, Wundt and Mach; rather, *Ethica more geometrico demonstrata* re-echoes the traditional tenet that the worldly things (*res*) are the *intentional objects* of God's thoughts (*ideae*).[179] From this perspective angle, Stumpf proceeds to untangle another obscure aspect of Spinoza's philosophy. As a consequence of God's infinity, the two known "attributes" of extension and thought partake in a list of infinite other attributes, wholly unknown to us; now, Stumpf explains, all of these innumerable attributes are "intentionally" paired with each other, just like extension and thought.[180]

Stumpf published *Spinozastudien* in 1919, long after James's death. However, he had already touched upon cosmological problems in a speech on evolutionism

---

175 C. Stumpf, *Die Wiedergeburt der Philosophie. Rede zum Eintritt des Rektorates der königlichen Friedrich-Wilhelms-Universität Berlin, 15 Oktober 1907*, Berlin, Francke, 1907; also in *Reden und Vorträge*, pp. 161–196. See R. Martinelli, "A Philosopher in the Lab. Carl Stumpf on Philosophy and Experimental Sciences", *Philosophia Scientiae* 19, 2015, pp. 23–43.
176 C. Stumpf, "Erscheinungen und psychische Funktionen", *Abhandlungen der Königlich-Preußischen Akademie der Wissenschaften, Philosophisch-historische Classe* 4, 1906, pp. 3–40.
177 C. Stumpf, "Zur Einteilung der Wissenschaften", *Abhandlungen der Königlich-Preußischen Akademie der Wissenschaften, Philosophisch-historische Classe* 5, 1906, pp. 1–94.
178 C. Stumpf, "Spinozastudien", *Abhandlungen der Königlich-Preußischen Akademie der Wissenschaften*, Berlin: Verlag der Königlich Akademie der Wissenschaften, 1919, pp. 1–57.
179 "The proposition *ordo et connexio idearum idem est ac ordo et connexio rerum* means that the order and connection of the divine acts of presentation is the same as that of the divine content of presentation. It is the parallelism of Aristotelian psychology, transposed to the deity, whose modes are our individual minds and bodies, and their states". Stumpf, *Spinozastudien*, cit., p. 24.
180 See R. Martinelli, "Intentionality and God's Mind. Stumpf on Spinoza", in *Carl Stumpf: From Philosophical Reflection to Interdisciplinary Scientific Investigation*, ed. by S. Bonacchi and G.-J. Boudewijnse, Vienna, Krammer, 2011, pp. 51–67.

published in 1899: *Der Entwicklungsgedanke in der gegenwärtigen Philosophie*.[181] Tackling the riddle of the emergence of the mind within the natural world, Stumpf seeks a metaphysical explanation compatible with the scientific worldview. The origin of consciousness is explained by the analogy with a sluice gate, opened by an inner force whose "floodwaters ripple over the land to spawn a peculiar vegetation".[182] Accordingly, metaphysicians are allowed to rebut materialism by assuming that "the multiplicity of substances rests on a transcendent unity". This thought is in line with his reading of Spinoza: no one can exclude that the above mentioned "sluice gate" mechanism, in addition to the mind, may spawn totally new forms of being, largely (or only momentarily) unknown to us. In *this* sense, mindful of Spinoza, Stumpf comes close to James's tenet that the universe is plural.

Responding to Stumpf's essay of 1899, James calls his friend's attention

> to the logical possibility that out of a world of complete chance at the origin, during infinite time, systems of coherent order were sure to have developed, of which our world may be one, all the chance facts disconnected and ununified with that world, having long since disappeared, either from existence, or from observation from that world's point of view. In my second Course of Gifford lectures, I am going to defend *radical* pluralism and tych-ism, and I hope to make a convert of you.[183]

Apparently, this point of view is similar to Stumpf's. Both thinkers assume that the universe is open to unknown and unexpected developments. Once again, however, a slight difference of accent conveys a broader divergence. Whereas Stumpf's pluralistic universe admits a common metaphysical ground – an equivalent of Spinoza's unique substance – James defends a far more radical point of view. Stumpf is adamant in making this point clear:

> [...] our views are close in many respects. Even your pluralism is not so alien to me as it probably is to most of our colleagues (although I believe that you underestimate the value of the feeling of unity of what is highest).[184]

As Stumpf noted in his posthumous portrait *William James nach seinen Briefen*, "pluralism" was quintessentially synonymous to indeterminism in James's eyes. Far from any form of materialistic pluralism, he rather revived the doctrine of those Ancients who juxtaposed a material, negative counterpart to the godly

---

181 C. Stumpf, *Der Entwicklungsgedanke in der gegenwärtigen Philosophie*, Berlin, Lange, 1899; quoted from *Reden und Vorträge*, pp. 94–124.
182 Stumpf, *Der Entwicklungsgedanke in der gegenwärtigen Philosophie*, cit., p. 112.
183 [40, 1900].
184 [51, 1904].

intellect. Along with the "*noûs*", they admitted a "*hylē*" that can be held responsible for evil.[185] This "hyletic" principle implies a plurality, which adequately accounts for the infinity of the world, open to more possibilities than we can envision from our specific perspective angle.

James repeatedly struggled to give a more systematic form to these thoughts. In 1901 he wrote: "After my lectures on religious experience are published, I hope to write a more systematic attempt at a Weltanschauung on a radical empiricist and pluralist basis, seeking to destroy the notion of a monistic Absolute of any sort".[186] Unfortunately, he never did.[187] James remained permanently committed to his popular style, successful (and remunerative) but regrettably open to misunderstandings. In sum, James's and Stumpf's metaphysical thoughts were singularly akin, though they put a different accent on the metaphysical unity of the whole.

By contrast, James and Stumpf deeply diverged as to the theory of knowledge. Stumpf's interpretation of this gap is interesting. In a letter of 1907, he notes that a "growing divergence" could be seen in their views:

> I cannot befriend pragmatism [...]. The positivistic theory of knowledge, in which you agree with Mach, seems to me impossible, or barren. [...] You will label this a standpoint that you have *abandoned*; I agree with the earlier James more than with the present one.[188]

Stumpf thus distanced himself from two different aspects of James's philosophy: pragmatism and radical empiricism (the "positivistic theory of knowledge"). To be sure, pragmatism was not the main target of Stumpf's polemic: occasionally, he conceded that there was a grain of wisdom in it.[189] By contrast, radical empiricism was absolutely unacceptable to him. Rather than a development, he saw it as a regrettable u-turn in his friend's views: all the more so, because James's new position implied adherence to Mach's execrated metaphysical monism.[190]

---

185 Stumpf, *William James*, p. 235.
186 [48, 1901].
187 Some reasons for James's failure to write a systematic metaphysics are illustrated by C.H. Siegfried, *William James's Radical Reconstruction of Philosophy*, Albany, SUNY Press, 1990, pp. 333–341.
188 [53, 1907].
189 Stumpf, *Erkenntnislehre* 1, p. 71 ff.
190 According to E. Banks, most of James's radical empiricism is "actually found in Mach's 1886 *Analysis of Sensations*, not surprisingly given the close relationship between Mach and James [...]. However, James finally goes *beyond* Mach in developing a direct realist theory of perception". E. Banks, *The Realistic Empiricism of Mach, James, and Russell. Neutral Monism Reconceived*, Cambridge, Cambridge University Press, 2014, p. 91. More convincingly, Ash notes that James's "empirical parallelism" was "similar in logical structure to the doctrines of Mach

2.4 Religion and Psychical Research

When Stumpf read *The Sentiment of Rationality* in 1884, his attention was drawn by a remark concerning faith.[191] In that essay, James had pointed out that empiricism and "imaginative faith" join hands in confessing that there must be a logically opaque "bottom of Being", that is, something more than mere empirical facts. Empiricism – James went on – warns against any anthropomorphic identification of this entity. By contrast,

> Faith says: "you have no right to extend to it your denials". The mere ontologic emotion of wonder, of mystery, has in some minds such a tinge of the rapture of sublimity, that for this aesthetic reason alone, it will be difficult for any philosophical system completely to exorcise it.[192]

Commenting on these lines, Stumpf suggested leaving aside any direct reference to faith in philosophy. He briefly recalled his juvenile "painful experience" as a would-be priest that I have illustrated above. However, James was right in claiming that the issue must be placed within the public debate. If compared to the perennial problem of the destiny of the human being, Stumpf's experimental work became irrelevant in his own eyes.[193] In 1885, upon receiving *The Literary Remains of the Late Henry James* – a collection of writings by his father Henry James Sr., posthumously edited by William – Stumpf reiterated that "the relation of religion to morality is [...] one of the most important questions for me".[194]

---

and Avenarius, but not in its content. Mach demanded for two similar figures corresponding nerve-processes with 'identical components,' a point-to-point isomorphism. For James, perception and thinking are integral processes". Ash, *Gestalt Psychology*, cit., p. 71.

191 "Your remarks regarding philosophical faith interested me quite above all" [4, 1884]. Reference is to W. James, "The Sentiment of Rationality", *Mind* 4, 1879, pp. 317–346. See M. Slater, *William James on Ethics and Faith*, Cambridge, Cambridge University Press, 2009.

192 James, *The Sentiment of Rationality*, cit., p. 59.

193 "[...] I regard all of the detailed work that I pursue to be very minor compared to that great question, which will compose the core and the soul of philosophy forever" [4, 1884].

194 [6, 1885]. The reference is to *The Literary Remains of the Late Henry James*, edited with an Introduction by William James, Boston and New York, Houghton Mifflin, 1884. After a long description of his father's theological thoughts, in the last part of his *Introduction*, pp. 113–119 [*Works* 11, pp. 60–63], William adds a commentary of his own. He contrasts two states, labelled as *morality* and *religion*. The healthy subject embraces *morality*, i.e. opts for activity and pluralism – though not in the *philosophical* sense: James means here something close to polytheism (which "[...] has always been the real religion of common people, and is so still to-day": *Varieties*, p. 526 [*Works* 15, p. 413]). However, "healthy-mindedness is not the whole of life; and the *morbid* view, as one by contrast may call it, asks for a philosophy very different from that of absolute moralism" (W. James, "Introduction", in The *Literary Remains*, cit., p. 117 [*Works* 11, p. 62]). The latter view is that of *religion*. In short, "that of religion and moralism, the morbid and

Again, in 1898 Stumpf thanked James for sending him the essay *On Human Immortality*. He wrote:

> It is good that representatives of scientific psychology are taking this issue of the human heart into hand once again, instead of always investigating mere reaction times. I can say that this has occupied me all my life more than anything else, and lately I have also learned to consider the influence of the belief in immortality on ethical intuitions ever more highly.[195]

By contrast, Stumpf was wholly unsympathetic to the so-called "psychical research". James introduced the subject in 1886: "I don't know whether you have heard of the London 'Society for Psychical Research', which is seriously and laboriously investigating all sort of 'supernatural' matters, clairvoyance, apparitions etc".[196] According to James, "the present condition of opinion regarding it is scandalous": people capable of "a critical judgement" would not even consider the increasing mass of testimony or "apparent testimony". James was among the founders of an analogous society in America.[197] Stumpf's response to this solicitation was respectful, but lapidary:

> Since you asked me about my take on this research, I acknowledge my agreement with the general principles that you speak of in the letter, and believe myself to be free of the prejudice which holds the unusual to be impossible. But I believe these things assume actual meaning only if they serve at the same time to bring the unusual into connection with what is already explained. Now everyday phenomena already offer us so many riddles in psychical life, that it would not seem right to me if we were to turn our best powers to those extraordinary phenomena. I also do not believe that *you* do this or intend to do this.[198]

James actually wasted a lot of time in the investigation of psychical phenomena. His cooperation with people like Myers or Gurney, grossly cheated by

---

the healthy view, it may be said that what is meat to the one is the other's poison. Any absolute moralism is a pluralism; any absolute religion is a monism" (p. 118 [*Works* 11, p. 62]). How to solve this contradiction? James concludes: "By their fruits ye shall know them. *Solvitur ambulando*; for the decision we must perhaps await the day of judgment. Meanwhile, the battle is about us, and we are its combatants, steadfast or vacillating, as the case may be. It will be a hot fight indeed if the friends of philosophic moralism should bring to the service of their ideal, so different from that of my father, a spirit even remotely resembling the life–long devotion of his faithful heart" (p. 119 [*Works* 11, p. 63]).
195 [32, 1898].
196 [7, 1886]. See J. Oppenheim, *The Other World: Spiritualism and Psychical Research in England, 1850–1914*, Cambridge, Cambridge University Press, 1985.
197 See Richardson, *William James: in the Maelstrom of American Modernism*, cit., p. 257 ff.; T. Ruetenik, *The Demons of William James. Religious Pragmatism Explores Unusual Mental States*, London, Palgrave Macmillan, 2018, p. 54 ff.
198 [8, 1886].

alleged spirit-seers, is somewhat embarrassing.[199] For instance, James comments on Gurney's *Phantasms of the Living*[200] in the following terms: "I should not at all wonder if it were the beginning of a new department of natural history. But even if not, it is an important chapter in the statistics of *Völkersychologie*, and I think Gurney worthy of the highest praise for his devotion to this unfashionable work".[201] As it turned out, neither was the case. Nevertheless, James's somewhat imprudent adherence to this line of research is instructive. In a provocative vein, he went so far as to affirm that the quest concerning human immortality had to be dealt with scientifically.[202] Investigating the forms of religious experience was in line with this unconventional stance.

The publication of *The Varieties of Religious Experience* in 1902 marks a turning point in the correspondence. The result of an attentive reflection upon James's book, Stumpf's long letter of 26 March 1904 unveils his deepest thoughts on religion. Once again, Stumpf recalls his infelicitous juvenile experience:

> [...] in my youth, for years I harbored the plan of becoming a Catholic priest and of burying myself in theology, until the inner contradictions of the dogmas drove me away under the heavy agony of my heart.[203]

In the light of that experience, Stumpf had a deep understanding for the pathological aspects of the religious experiences investigated by James. He believed that the most sentimental aspects of religion were at odds with human dignity.[204]

---

199 M. Ford, "William James's Psychical Research and Its Philosophical Implications", *Transactions of the Charles S. Peirce Society* 34, 1998, pp. 605–626. Some of James's contemporaries were "embarrassed" by his interest in psychical research, and "thought it best to distance themselves and their emerging disciplines from such research" (p. 614). Notwithstanding the respectful tone of his letters, this undoubtedly holds for Stumpf as well.
200 The reference is to E. Gurney, F.W.H. Myers, F. Podmore, *Phantasms of the Living*, 2 vols., London, Trübner, 1886. See Oppenheim, *The Other World*, cit., pp. 144–145.
201 [10, 1887].
202 "I have said nothing in my lectures about immortality [...] It seems to me that it is eminently a case for facts to testify. Facts, I think, are yet lacking to prove spirit–return, 'though I have the highest respect for the patient labors of Messrs. Myers, Hodgson, and Hyslop, and am somewhat impressed by their favorable conclusions. I consequently leave the matter open, with this brief word to save the reader from a possible perplexity as to why immortality got no mention in the body of this book": *Varieties*, p. 524 [*Works* 15, p. 412]. On this theme, see S. Madelrieux, "De l'âme à l'inconscient. Métaphysique et psychologie chez James et Bergson", in *Bergson et James, cent ans après*, Paris, Presses Universitaires de France, 2011, pp. 99–121.
203 [51, 1904].
204 "I find anything sentimental, enrapturing, cutesy, and unctuous about these things extremely repugnant in grown people" [51, 1904].

Contrition and consciousness of sins were misplaced: evil, he thought, does not only dwell within human beings, but characterizes the external world as well, as created by God. The "religion of the religious" was "preposterous and unnatural";[205] by contrast, Stumpf agreed with James's broad view of religion, subscribing to his emphasis on our connection with a spiritual world and its irradiating energy. In the end, for Stumpf, allegiance to "active altruism" was the only meaningful value.

Stumpf's commentary on what James calls "over-belief" belongs to the most intense pages of the correspondence. In the *Varieties*, James had noted that "high–flying speculations like those of either dogmatic or idealistic theology" must be classed "as over–beliefs, buildings–out performed by the intellect into directions of which feeling originally supplied the hint".[206] Over-beliefs are conceptual constructs built over, and in support of, one's feelings concerning God and immortality. Reacting to James's pages, Stumpf wrote:

> Should I now tell you something about my "over-belief"? I do not know whether I will decide to publish such thoughts, which occupy me every day of my life. However, I will gladly share them with you confidentially. Personal immortality stands in the foreground for me. [...] Indeed, the actualization of ideals is only possible under the presupposition of individual immortality. [...] If the congealment of the earth occurs, and therefore no more new individuals arise, where does the actualization of ideals reside, if what is spiritual does not endure? For me, this is the first condition, if life is not to be absolutely bleak and meaningless.[207]

For Stumpf, mental individuality disappears in the afterlife: what survives after death is the moral principle within the individual. One's afterlife state, he fancies, is akin to the enjoyment of an artistic masterpiece. Freed from all casual trivialities, in those sublime moments the self is there, yet it is "elevated into a higher sphere, and accompanied by the blissful feelings of being-one with all the good and high spirits of all times".[208] These thoughts, Stumpf claims, agree with the core statements of his psychological and epistemological writings.[209]

---

205 [51, 1904].
206 *Varieties*, p. 431 [*Works* 15, p. 341].
207 [51, 1904].
208 [51, 1904].
209 "I do not want to explain in further detail how I make these thoughts work with my psychological and natural philosophical views. Anyway, you will easily detect some lines of connection with my short essays on the body and the soul and with my thoughts on evolution" [51, 1904]. The reference is to two essays reprinted together in 1903: C. Stumpf, *Leib und Seele. Der Entwicklungsgedanke in der gegenwärtigen Philosophie. Zwei Reden*, Leipzig, Barth, 1903. As previously shown, Stumpf would further develop these views in the subsequent *Spinozastudien* of 1919.

Indeed, his view on the origin of consciousness within cosmological evolution is in line with these metaphysical speculations.

James had a different approach to immortality. In the final chapter of the *Varieties*, he states:

> I have said nothing in my lectures about immortality or the belief therein, for to me it seems a secondary point. If only our ideals are cared for in 'eternity', I do not see why we might not be willing to resign their care to other hands than ours.[210]

James softened this view by affirming his sympathy "with the urgent impulse to be present ourselves, and in the conflict of impulses, both so vague and yet both noble, I know not how to decide". He ultimately submitted the issue to the court of experience: "It seems to me that it is eminently a case for facts to testify. Facts, I think, are yet lacking to prove 'spirit-return'" notwithstanding some evidence provided by the "psychical researchers".[211] Sporting enough "tough-mindedness" to deal with human immortality as an empirical question was probably meant to impress the mostly clerical audience of the Edinburgh Gifford Lectures. But James was not being completely genuine – which is fortunate. Some of the darkest hours of his life are due to that attitude: I am thinking of him sitting in a hospital aisle soon after Myers' death, ready to report the promised signals from the afterworld.[212] What James wrote in response to Stumpf's highly confidential letter of 1904 points to a different view.

> Your own confidences as to your religions state of mind interest me deeply. I agree that a *God of the totality* must be an unacceptable religious object. But I do not see why there may not be superhuman consciousness of *ideals* of ours, and that would be *our* God. It is all very dark. I never felt the *rational* need for immortality as you seem to feel it; but as I grow older I confess that I feel the practical need of it much more than I ever did before; and that combine with reasons, not exactly the same as your own, to give me a growing faith in its reality.[213]

---

210 *Varieties*, p. 526 [*Works* 15, p. 412]. See also W. James, *Human Immortality: Two Supposed Objections to the Doctrine*, Boston and New York, Houghton Mifflin, 1898.
211 *Varieties*, p. 524 [*Works* 15, p. 412].
212 The story was told by a testimony, the Swedish doctor A. Munthe: "James sat just outside the door, overwhelmed with grief, but waiting with notebook and pencil to receive the message that Myers had promised to send after his death [...]" [*Thought and Character* 2, p. 167]. See also Richardson, *William James: in the Maelstrom of American Modernism*, cit., pp. 401–402.
213 [52, 1904]. See also T. Carlson, "James and the Kantian Tradition", in *The Cambridge Companion to William James*, ed. by R.A. Putnam, Cambridge, Cambridge University Press, 1997, p. 381.

3 The Present Edition

After James's death in 1910, his son Henry (3rd) planned an edition of his father's letters. In 1912, upon request,[214] Stumpf sent to "Harry" all of the letters he had received from William.[215] Henry's edition eventually came out in 1920, under the title *The Letters of William James*.[216] Thereafter, in accordance with an existing agreement,[217] Henry took contact with Stumpf,[218] ready to send back the letters, but tactfully suggesting an alternative:

> If you do not care to have the manuscript of your letters returned to you, or if at any later time you have no other disposition that you care to make of them, I shall always be glad to place them with the collection that is being preserved in Cambridge, but hope you will understand that in informing you of this possibility, I am not pressing you to do anything with the manuscripts that really belong to you, except what you may prefer to do with them.[219]

Fortunately enough, Stumpf agreed to leave most of William's letters in Cambridge. As a token of affection, he just asked for a couple of letters back, which Henry sent in 1922.[220] As a consequence, both Stumpf's and James's letters are now almost entirely preserved at the Houghton Library in Cambridge (MA).[221] Before Henry's request, two manuscript letters by William James had been already given by Stumpf to the collection of autographs at the Berlin *Königliche Bibliothek*.[222] Stumpf sent Henry two accurate handwritten

---

214 [61, 1911]. Henry must have formulated his request together with the shipment of William James's *Memories and Studies*.
215 [63, 1912], [64, 1912].
216 *The Letters of William James*, ed. by H. James 3rd, Boston, Little & Brown, 1920.
217 "If you do not require them any longer, I would like to ask for them back, since they are a cherished keepsake of a friend and colleague, with whom I was joined for so long in the warmest sympathy" [63, 1912].
218 [65, 1921].
219 [65, 1921].
220 [66, 1922]. The letters referred to are [29, 1895] and [57, 1910]. The copies of these letters preserved at the Houghton Library are typed. The German word 'Abschrift' ("copy") has been added at the top. I have no clue as to the whereabouts of the manuscripts sent over to Stumpf.
221 *William James Papers*, Houghton Library, Harvard University, Series I.: bMS Am 1092.9: *Correspondence*. From Carl Stumpf: bMS Am 1092.9, 620–642; to Carl Stumpf: bMS Am 1092.9, 3778–3811; family letters: bMS Am 1092.9, 4336, 172, 265. See the Overview of correspondence in the Appendix I for further details.
222 [47, 1901] and [49, 1902]. The copies preserved at the Houghton Library have been drafted on the letterhead paper of the Royal Library (*Königliche Bibliothek – Autographen Sammlung Darmstaedter*).

copies of these letters: the original manuscripts are still preserved at the *Staatsbibliothek zu Berlin*.[223]

The correspondence is bilingual: James wrote in English, Stumpf in German. His familiarity with the British literature on music psychology vouches for Stumpf's good understanding of the English language.[224] James occasionally reports that the prolonged lack of practice undermined his German, but he clearly thinks of speaking fluency, not of reading, when saying so.[225] In the present edition, all the letters are published in English, in chronological order. Stumpf's letters have been translated from German into English by R. Brian Tracz. The German originals are included in the Appendix II. Stumpf's essay *William James nach seinen Briefen* is reproduced in the Appendix III.[226] The edition is supplemented by a number of further documents: a letter written by James to his wife Alice, with regard to the Prague stay of 1882,[227] a charming letter written by James to Stumpf's wife Hermine, preserved at the *Adolf Würth Zentrum für Geschichte der Psychologie* at Würzburg,[228] and the correspondence between Stumpf and the James family after William's death.[229] The Overview of correspondence in the Appendix I provides information concerning the source of each letter with its archival number and previous publication.

Twenty-one letters by Stumpf, and seven by James are being published in this edition for the first time, at least in a complete form.[230] With one exception, the family letters appear here for the first time.[231] James's remaining letters to Stumpf

---

[223] Staatsbibliothek zu Berlin – Preußischer Kulturbesitz. Ref.: Sammlung Darmstaedter 2a 1890: James, William Bl. 5 r/v (D3589.10)
[224] C. Stumpf, "Musikpsychologie in England", *Vierteljahrsschrift für Musikwissenschaft* 1, 1885, pp. 261–349.
[225] [36, 1899].
[226] C. Stumpf, "William James nach seinen Briefen. Leben. Charakter. Lehre", *Kant-Studien* 32, 2–3, 1927, pp. 205–241; also Berlin, Pan Verlag, 1928.
[227] [58, 1882].
[228] [59, 1893]. William James an Hermine Stumpf, 14.03.1893. Adolf-Würth-Zentrum für Geschichte der Psychologie, Würzburg. Archiv: Carl Stumpf (1848–1936) *expansion 2014* (K2).
[229] From [60, 1911] to [66, 1922].
[230] Prior to this edition, all of Stumpf's letters to William James have been transcribed from the manuscripts and published by Lia Gioia in her PhD thesis at the University of Trieste: L. Gioia, *William James e Carl Stumpf. Un rapporto scientifico e personale attraverso le lettere*, PhD Thesis, University of Trieste, 2013. For the present edition, the text of Stumpf's letters has been revised.
[231] See the letters nn. 59 to 66.

have been already published in *The Correspondence of William James*;[232] non-published letters (including, oddly enough, James's first letter to Stumpf) are calendared and briefly summarized at the end of each volume. In addition, the *Correspondence of William James* includes two letters from Stumpf to James, in the original German,[233] whereas the remaining ones are calendared. Previously, some of Stumpf's letters had been published by Ralph Barton Perry in the second volume of *The Thought and Character of William James*.[234] The seven letters chosen by Perry, however, are incomplete. In some cases, the omissions clearly ensue from the difficulty of deciphering Stumpf's handwriting.[235]

The body of correspondence is incomplete. The existence of at least five missing letters or postcards can be inferred from the existing documents. In a letter of 1887, Stumpf mentions two unpreserved postcards by James.[236] In a note published in *Mind* in April 1887, James refers to a lost letter by Stumpf.[237] In 1887, James thanked Stumpf for an unidentified "charming letter" and expresses his sorrow for Stumpf's "aural troubles", unmentioned in the preserved correspondence.[238] Stumpf's letter of invitation to the Munich congress of 1896 is only known of from James's answer.[239] None of these losses, however, are irremediable, there being enough indirect evidence as to the missing contents.

All of the items included in Stumpf's personal library, now in Japan,[240] have been catalogued by Miko Takasuna, whose work is a valuable tool

---

[232] *The Correspondence of William James*, ed. by I. Skrupskelis and E.M. Berkeley, Charlottesville-London, University Press of Virginia, 12 vols., 1992–2004. James's letters to Stumpf are scattered over several volumes.
[233] [18, 1891], [23, 1893].
[234] *Thought and Character*, pp. 738–744.
[235] The same hand put into square brackets the parts of the letters selected for publication, and drafted a question mark upon the manuscripts nearby omitted words or sentences. This happens, for instance, with the word "*Grossmannssucht*" ("quest for greatness") [8, 1886]. Cf. *Thought and Character* 2, p. 738.
[236] [9, 1887].
[237] W. James, "Correction to 'The Perception of Space' (1887)", *Mind* 12, 1887, p. 318. The table of contents of the journal registers these few lines by James under "Miscellaneous". See [11, 1887], footnotes.
[238] [12, 1889]. See *Autobiography*, p. 409.
[239] "It did my eyes good to see our handwriting once more and I was gladder still to hear the pleasant words in which you urge me not to be absent from Munich next summer" [29, 1895].
[240] On the circumstances behind the relocation of Stumpf's library at the Kyushu University see M. Takasuna, "Die Stumpf-Sammlung in Japan", in Sprung, *Carl Stumpf. Eine Biographie*, pp. 450–454.

in the reconstruction of the essays referred to in the correspondence: incidentally, James is the best-represented author in Stumpf's library.[241] As to the different editions of James's writings, Ralph Barton Perry's *Annotated Bibliography of the Writings of William James* of 1920 still offers a quick and reliable orientation.[242]

As usual, words underlined in the original manuscripts are printed in italics; words underlined twice are printed both in italics and underlined.[243] Stumpf's essay *William James nach seinen Briefen* comprises both italicized words and words highlighted by separating the letters: the former are printed in italics, the latter underlined. Small capital letters in the address of a letter refer to a preprinted letterhead or a stamp. New lines in the address or in the signature of a letter are indicated by a vertical line (|).

In some cases, additions have been necessary in order to make sense of what was being said: added words or signs are marked in square brackets. For instance, "I had take" becomes "I had [to] take", etc. By contrast, omissions of capital letters and minor exceptions have been ignored: e.g. "I can hardly speak german", etc. Typically, James frequently inserts German words in his phrasing: the translation is given in the corresponding footnote.

Throughout this book, the letters are referred to by a number in square brackets, followed by the year. For instance, [5, 1884] designates William James's letter to Carl Stumpf of 15 November 1884, which is the fifth letter in this edition. All abbreviations are listed at the end of the volume. After the first occurrence, books and essays are referred to in an abridged but intuitively understandable form (e.g. *Autobiography*); the complete bibliographic data can be found in the list of References, where items by the same author are ordered chronologically. Stumpf's essay *William James nach seinen Briefen*, reprinted in Appendix III, is quoted according to the pagination of *Kant-Studien*, vol. 32, 1927, which is given in the present edition in square brackets. For the most part, references in the footnotes are to the original

---

241 M. Takasuna, "Reconstruction of Stumpf Collection and Barth Collection: Using Bibliographical Cards as Resource in the Main Library at Kyushu University", *History of Psychology and Psychological Studies* 5, 2003, pp. 37–68.
242 R.B. Perry, *Annotated Bibliography of the Writings of William James*, New York, Longmans, Green & Co., 1920.
243 Small capital letters have been used for the word 'lazy', underlined four times by James in [19 1892].

edition of James's and Stumpf's works: this choice allows me to preserve the pagination of those original editions, when they are referred to in the letters. However, the reference to the standard edition *The Works of William James*[244] is always added in square brackets, with the indication of the corresponding volume and page.

---

[244] *The Works of William James*, ed. by F.H. Burkhardt, F. Bowers and I.K. Skrupskelis, Cambridge-London, Harvard University Press, 17 vols., 1975–1988.

Correspondence

English translation of Stumpf's letters by R. Brian Tracz

William James, Carl Stumpf
Letters (1882–1910)

[1, 1882]

Paris, 26.11.1882

My Dear Stumpf,
I'm sure you will allow me to drop titles of ceremony with a colleague with whose person and whose ideas alike I feel so warm a sympathy; & I trust that when you write to me you will give the same token that you regard me in the light of an old friend.

I mailed you the papers you were kind enough to lend me the day before yesterday.[1] I hope they will reach you safely. When I say that I actually had no time to finish reading them before I got to Paris, which was three days ago, it will give you an idea of the busy character of my life since leaving Prague. Both in Leipzig and in Berlin I found a host of old american friends, many of them former students. I stayed in Berlin a week, in Leipzig 5 days, in Liege 2 1/2 days with Delboeuf. In each place I heard all the university lectures I could, and spoke with several of the professors. From some I got very good hints as to how *not* to lecture. Helmholtz for example gave the very worst lecture I ever heard in my life except one – (that one was by our most distinguished american mathematician). The lecture I heard in Prag from Mach was on the same elementary subject as Helmholtz's and one of the most artistic lectures I ever heard. Wundt in Leipzig impressed me very agreeably personally.[2] He has a ready smile and is entirely unaffected and unpretending in his manner. I heard him twice, and was twice in his laboratory, he was very polite but showed no desire for a further acquaintance. *Überhaupt* I must say that the hospitality of Prag towards wandering philosophers much surpasses that of Berlin and Leipzig. In greater capitals it is more difficult to give one's time to strangers. I found M. Delboeuf a most delightful man, full of spirit and originality, and altogether I enjoyed extremely my sojourn in Liège.[3] I'm not yet settled in Paris. I find my chronic insomnia rather worse in Europe than it was at home, so I

---

[1] Most probably C. Stumpf, "Aus der vierten Dimension", *Philosophische Monatshefte* 14, 1878, pp. 13–30, and "Die empirische Psychologie der Gegenwart", *Im neuen Reich* 4, No 2, 1874, pp. 201–226. Besides a self-announcement of his book on space, Stumpf had no other short essay at the time.
[2] On Mach and Wundt see the *Introduction*.
[3] Concerning his visit to Joseph R.L. Delboeuf (1831–1896) in Liège, James wrote to his wife Alice: "I must confess I haven't gained enormously from talking philosophy with him, or with

may possibly return before many weeks. I read your "Aus der *4ten* Dimension" with lively interest and admiration.[4] Where did it appear? I should like the reference for the use of my students. I make a couple of them work up that subject in an essay every year. I hope that this will find you, the Frau Professorin and the youthful Rudi all well. It will be long ere I forget those pleasant days in old Prague – pleasant chiefly on account of you. With best regards to Professor Marty when you meet him, and extra best to Mrs Stumpf, believe me always faithfully yours

Address: Cave of Baring Bros. & Co   Wm James
London England

---

any other except a little with Stumpf. Probably we can never do so but with exceptional individuals [...]" [*Corr.* 5, p. 302].
4 After fiercely criticizing Johann K.F. Zöllner's arguments in support of the 4th dimension of space, Stumpf concludes in the tone of a scientific satire, inviting the reader to step through the back door of fantasy, hand-in-hand with Zöllner, and have a stroll in the 4th dimension. C. Stumpf, "Aus der vierten Dimension", *Philosophische Monatshefte* 14, 1878, p. 24. There he will meet Kant's Thing-in-itself, Plato's Ideas, the Site of the Soul, the Unconscious etc., together with a ready-made solution for all philosophical and scientific problems. Stumpf concludes: "there is no third way between science and fairytales. Philosophy occasionally sought for a middle way between them, but the attempt never gave good results" (p. 29). Here he probably refers to German Idealism: see also C. Stumpf, "Die Wiedergeburt der Philosophie", in *Reden und Vorträge*, pp. 161–196.

[2, 1882]

Smichov-Prague 8 Dec 82

Dear James!
I likewise return your greetings with sincere joy, for I have gained with your all-too-brief visit the firm impression that we not only harmonize in our scientific views and intentions in a rare way, but will also always be good friends.

I am much obliged for the restitution of my short essays, but far more for the delivery of both of your essays.[5] Regarding the latter – since my hands are currently full with the printing of my Tonpsychologie –, I have only read one, "The Feeling of Effort",[6] and am in almost complete agreement with your basic remarks; I am also glad that I was able to refer to it once for support[7] in the Tonpsychologie (in particular, the "innervation feelings [*Innervationsgefühle*]"[8] play their questionable role there, too).[9]

My essay about the fourth dimension appeared in the Philosoph. Monatsheften edited by Schaarschmidt (1878).[10]

---

5 The essays referred to by Stumpf are: "The Feeling of Effort" (see below, in this letter), and "The Sentiment of Rationality", discussed in a subsequent letter [6, 1885]. From Germany, James wrote to Alice: "I wish you could send me all the copies of the Feeling of Effort, of the Sentiment of Rationality [...]" [58, 1882].
6 W. James, *The Feeling of Effort*, Anniversary Memoirs of the Boston Society of Natural History. Boston, 1880 [*Works* 13, pp. 83–124].
7 Among the opponents of the innervation-feelings, Stumpf mentions Lotze, Georg Elias Müller and David Ferrier, adding: "For a most thorough-going job, see W. James, an excellent psychologist of the new world, professor in New Cambridge, near Boston, in his article 'The Feeling of Effort' [...]". *Tone Psychology* 1, p. 271 [*Tonpsychologie* 1, p. 167 fn.].
8 "Innervation feelings" were supposed to accompany the will to make a bodily movement. Whereas muscular sensations are centripetal (*afferent*), innervation feelings go the other way around (*efferent*). In *The Feeling of Effort* James writes: "In opposition to this popular view, I maintain that the feeling of muscular energy put forth is a complex affert sensation coming from the tense muscles, the strained ligaments, squeezed joints, fixed chest, closed glottis, contracted brow, clenched jaws, etc. etc. That there is over and above this another feeling of effort involved, I do not deny; but this latter is purely moral and has nothing to do with the motor discharge". [*Works* 13, p. 85]. James touches on the question again in chapter 26 ("Will") of the *Principles of Psychology* [*Works* 9, pp. 1104–1130]. For further reference see below, [23, 1893] and the explanatory footnotes.
9 "In consciousness I find the will to a particular movement in connection with a muscular presentation that has stayed in my memory from earlier executed (at first involuntary) movements"; by contrast, Stumpf attacks, "I notice no *sensation* (*Empfindung*) at all [...]". *Tone Psychology* 1, p. 109 [*Tonpsychologie* 1, p. 167].
10 C. Stumpf, "Aus der vierten Dimension", *Philosophische Monatshefte* 14, 1878, pp. 13–30. See above, [1, 1882].

I hope that this letter will still find you in London, and indeed in better health. Perhaps the erratic lifestyle that you revere in Europe had an unfavorable influence on your nerves? I, at least, would long since have been ruined by it. But you must know yourself better than I.

Your notes on Helmholtz and Delboeuf, among others, were interesting to me. I hope very much that in the future we will hear of each other *at least once a year*. The next sign of me will certainly be delayed somewhat longer, since for now and foreseeably throughout the whole of 1883, I will find myself "under the press" and unable to catch my breath.

Heartfelt greetings from me as well as from my wife and Marty, who have received your greetings thankfully and with joy.

All the best!

Your dear | C. Stumpf

[3, 1884]

Cambridge (Mass) U.S.A. | Jan 9. 1884

My dear Stumpf,

I had only been awaiting the sight of your book, which I saw announced six weeks ago, to write you the annual letter we agreed upon last winter. Today I was most agreeably surprised at the reception of the copy you have so kindly sent me.[11] I had already ordered one which has not arrived, but which I can easily transfer to a friend. I shall devour it most eagerly, and expect to be greatly nourished in consequence, though unhappily my eyes are no better and the rate of my reading is excessively slow. I feel sometimes quite desperate about it, but the insensibility of habit comes to my aid, and lets me often not think of it. But for the man, who, with as much university teaching as yours, and complaining as you do of imperfect health, can not only write, but actually publish, a volume of 400 pages, – for such a man I have a feeling of admiration and envy such as few other phenomena are capable of exciting in me. My own work has hardly been advanced at all in the past 6 months, – a most humiliating confession.[12]

I am much the better physically however, for my trip to Europe, and find myself already making plans whereby my next sabbatical year, 7 years hence, shall be more successful than this last one was in certain respects. There was no episode of the last of which I think with more pleasure than of my visit to Prag, and of the more than hospitable reception you gave me. I am working away at the old routine of teaching, and will send you the list of our courses which may interest you. The method of teaching throughout is with us more laborious for the professor, though I think better for the student, than it is with you.[13] In all of our courses the students are interrogated, and stirred up, and frequently made to give an account of themselves in writing in a way that I fancy only happens with you in the courses marked "Privatissime". But I fear, for all that, that our students remain behind yours in the spirit of work and the degree of real respect paid to intellectual things.

We have no schools comparable to your Gymnasia, and the results make themselves felt all through the college course. It is true that our so-called "college" 4 years, followed by about 1000 students whose ages average from 18 1/2 to 22 1/2, is preliminary to business and law, medicine, and theology, and not,

---

11 Stumpf, *Tonpsychologie* 1.
12 The reference is to the *Principles of Psychology*. On the gestation of the book, see *Works* 10, pp. 1532–1578 and Perry, *Thought and Character* 2, pp. 34–50.
13 James had worried about pedagogics since 1876: W. James, "The Teaching of Philosophy in our Colleges", *Nation* 23, 1876, pp. 178–179.

like your philosophical faculty, coordinate with the latter three. We are seeking, if possible, to heighten the standard of admission without raising the age, and to make the course 3 years instead of 4, but it is hard to improve the schools.[14]

I have made no discoveries during the past year. I have two or three little mustard seeds of experimental investigations on hand, but I very much doubt if they grow into anything important. I have sent a couple of articles to *Mind* of which you shall receive reprints in due time.[15] But this seems on the whole, a sterile year with me. Family misfortunes both of my own and my wife's have followed thick and fast and taken much of my time and thought.[16]

I am sorry I have no more jovial account to give you of myself. In spite of it all I am cheerful and sanguine of the future.

The appearance of your book makes me believe that everything must have been going well with you. I will write you my opinion of it as soon as I have succeeded in getting through it, which may possibly not be for some months.[17] Mach's book which he sent me last summer and which I hoped to have read ere now, I have, Alas! hardly been able to look at.[18] Pray give him my best regards if you see him and do the same to Professor Marty, who I hope will not forget me. My wife, who holds the pen, sends friendliest greetings to your Frau Gemahlin, in which I cordially join.

Believe me, with many thanks, and the warmest good wishes,

Yours always | Wm. James

---

14 See also a later writing of 1891: W. James, "The Proposed Shortening of the College Course", *Harvard Monthly* 11, 1891, pp. 127–137.
15 W. James, "On Some Omissions of Introspective Psychology", *Mind* 9, 1884, pp. 1–26: see below, [4, 1884]; W. James, "What is an Emotion?", *Mind* 9, 1884, pp. 188–205: see below, [34, 1899]. In this "sterile" year James published his epochal theory of emotions.
16 His father Henry James Sr. died in December 1882, when William was still in Europe. In 1883, William's sister Alice entered an asylum for mental health problems; his brother Garth Wilkinson died in November. As to the "misfortunes" of William's wife Alice see Simon, *Genuine Reality*, cit., pp. 182.
17 See below, [5, 1884].
18 E. Mach, *Die Mechanik in ihrer Entwickelung historisch-kritisch dargestellt*, Leipzig, Brockhaus, 1883.

[4, 1884]

Prague, Smichov 4 Feb 84

My dear James!
You have my strongest gratitude for your dear letter, and the same goes for your revered wife for her writing! It is curious that you received my book so late, since I gave Hirzel the order to send it to you already in the second half of October, and the other parcels were all delivered at that time. It must have lain for a while on the way. For the friendly words that you said to me about it, I am thankful with all my heart; up to now, the recognition that I have found has been extremely slight and restricted to 2–3 letters. I also cannot hope that the book will find many readers; it goes too much into detail. "Mind" published a note expressing the suspicion that I was still unfamiliar with Gurney.[19] This, thanks to your recommendation,[20] is not the case – I have been familiar with his work for over a year (my book was printed up to, say, § 11 when I read it), but unfortunately I haven't found as much in it as I had hoped. It has nothing to do with volumes 1 and 2 of my book; I will only be able to use it for volume 3.[21] I am now working on volume 2, which, however, will not appear before Easter 1885,[22] since my nerves cannot stand greater strain; in it, I will provide a new theory of consonance.[23]

---

[19] "This is a complete psychology of Tone as a basis for musical theory. This task on the scale conceived by our author can hardly be said to have been attempted before. Helmholtz's classical work, though it certainly penetrates into the psychological territory, is in the first instance a physico-physiological treatise. The most complete treatment of the psychological base of music is the work of Mr. E. Gurney, which seems oddly enough to be unknown to Dr. Stumpf". Stumpf's "full and penetrating" treatment "is pretty certain to count as a solid contribution to the pure science of psychology" rather than to psychology of music. J. Sully, "Review of Tonpsychologie, vol. 1", Mind 9, 36, 1884, p. 593. The reference is to E. Gurney, *The Power of Sound*, London, Smith, Elder & Co. 1889. Thereafter Gurney turned to "psychical research": see below, [10, 1887].
[20] In Prague, James had recommended Gurney's book to Stumpf. See below, [6, 1885].
[21] Though he will never publish vol. 3, Stumpf expounds and criticizes Gurney's ideas on music in C. Stumpf, "Musikpsychologie in England", *Vierteljahrsschrift für Musikwissenschaft* 1, pp. 261–349. See below, [6, 1885].
[22] Vol. 2 of *Tonpsychologie* was published in 1890.
[23] Properly speaking, the theory of "tonal fusion" in *Tonpsychologie* 2 provides the preliminary psychological basis for a theory of consonance. The latter was developed in C. Stumpf, "Konsonanz und Dissonanz", *Beiträge zur Akustik und Musikwissenschaft* 1, 1898, pp. 1–108; C. Stumpf, "Konsonanz und Konkordanz. Nebst Bemerkungen über Wohlklang und Wohlgefälligkeit musikalischer Zusammenklänge", *Zeitschrift für Psychologie und Physiologie der Sinnesorgane* 58, 1910, pp. 321–355; also in *Beiträge zur Akustik und Musikwissenschaft* 6, 1910, pp. 151–165.

I have already received your "Courses of Study" and have taken notice of it with interest.[24] The facilities appear certainly very different from ours, more scholastic, but certainly more practical. By the way, we now also have a philosophical seminar in Prague, two hours a week, led by me and Marty – it is the first in Austria.

I saw your first essay in Mind at the university library and I read the first pages, which made me eager for the rest. You do Brentano an injustice, though, if you ascribe to him such an extreme view;[25] he emphasizes indeed that psychology is essentially dependent on observation in *memory* and that this is by no means infallible.[26] Marty will send you an essay on "Subjectless propositions".[27]

Did you receive our photographs last year? My wife sent them to you together with the warmest thanks for the beautiful books by your brother, which she read with much enjoyment.[28]

I have not yet studied your essays completely, but for the most part I have, and I am glad that I agree with you on the essential points of psychology. You will find your excellent work on innervation feelings already cited in the Tonpsychologie (167). Meanwhile, I have learned from the large Handbuch der Psychologie by Hermann that Hering (Raumsinn, p. 547) and Funke (Tastsinn: 363 ff.) have expressed themselves in our terms.[29] Your remarks regarding

---

24 See above, [3, 1884].
25 "As is well known, contradictory opinions about the value of introspection prevail. Comte and Maudsley, for instance, call it worthless; Ueberweg and Brentano come near calling it infallible. Both opinions are extravagancies; the first for reasons too obvious to be given, the second because it fails to discriminate between the immediate *feltness* of a mental state and its perception by a subsequent act of reflexion". W. James, "On Some Omissions of Introspective Psychology", *Mind* 9, 1884, p. 1 [*Works* 13, p. 142].
26 F. Brentano, *Psychology from an Empirical Standpoint*, ed. by L. McAlister, London-New York, Routledge, 2009, pp. 22–26. In the *Principles of Psychology*, James mentions Brentano among the psychologists who "take high ground here and claim [...] a sort of infallibility" for inner perception; however, no one "has emphasized more sharply than Brentano himself the difference between the immediate *feltness* of a feeling, and its perception by a subsequent reflective act" (*Principles of Psychology* 1, p. 187, 189 [*Works* 8, p. 187, 189]).
27 A. Marty, "Über subjectlose Sätze und das Verhältniss der Grammatik zur Logik und Psychologie", *Vierteljahrsschrift für wissenschaftliche Philosophie*, 1884–1896. Marty criticizes the linguist F. Miklosich, who claimed that the *impersonalia* (e.g. "it rains") have *literally* no subject.
28 James sent to Hermine Stumpf two novels by his brother Henry: *Portrait of a Lady* and *The American*. See below, [58, 1882].
29 L. Hermann, *Handbuch der Physiologie*, Hrsg. von L. Hermann, 6 vols., Leipzig, Vogel, 1879–1883. Ewald Hering ("Raumsinn des Auges. Augenbewegung", vol. 3, t. 1, 1879, p. 547), notes that the hypothesis of *Innervationsgefühle* is not supported by facts. Otto Funke ("Der

philosophical faith interested me above all; yet I must confess that I withhold my agreement regarding the phenomenon itself, as well as regarding the theory of the phenomenon.[30] Too much has already been tainted by faith in philosophy, too many sins committed, that we should not strictly avoid it with this inclination. I myself have already undergone painful experiences with it, which costed me years of development.[31] But you are right that the question must be brought forward, since until now it has been nearly completely silent; and I regard all of the detailed work that I pursue to be very minor compared to that great question, which will compose the core and the soul of philosophy forever. Hopefully one day we will talk about that in conversation! But then you must stay not for days, but rather for weeks, and also bring along your revered wife. Heartfelt greetings!

Your | C. Stumpf

Tastsinn und die Gemeingefühle", vol. 3, t. 2, 1880, p. 364, 373) considers Wundt the "main representative of innervation feelings" and criticizes him.
30 W. James, "The Sentiment of Rationality", *Mind* 4, 1879, pp. 317–346 [*Works* 5, pp. 32–64]. James allows for a specific sentiment of intellectual persuasion, which is negatively conceived as absence of hurdles or interruptions in the stream of thought. This sentiment of persuasion never reaches complete fulfillment, unless one solves the ultimate ethical and religious problems. An essay with the same title, resulting from part of the 1879 article and "Rationality, Activity and Faith" (*Princeton Review*, 1882, 2, pp. 58–86), is included in W. James, *The Will to Believe and Other Essays in Popular Philosophy*, New York and London, Longmans, Green & Co., 1897.
31 See the *Introduction*, and below, [51, 1904].

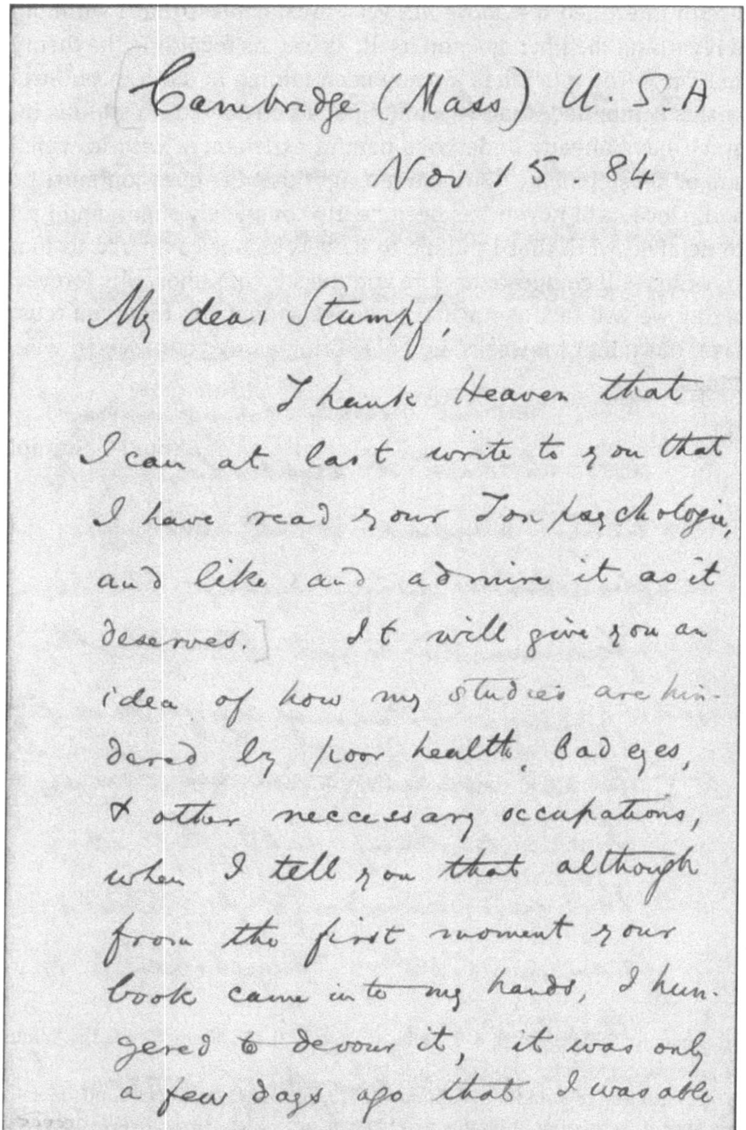

Fig. 1: William James to Carl Stumpf, 15 November 1884 [5, 1884]. Autograph letter, first page.
Source: Harvard University · Houghton Library / Stumpf, Karl, 1848–1936, recipient. 34 letters; 1882–1910. James, William, 1842–1910. William James papers, 1803–1941 (inclusive) 1862–1910 (bulk). MS Am 1092.9 (3778–3811). Houghton Library, Harvard University, Cambridge, Mass.

[5, 1884]

Cambridge (Mass) U.S.A. | Nov 15. 84

My dear Stumpf,
Thank Heaven that I can at last write to you that I have read your Tonpsychologie, and like and admire it as it deserves. It will give you an idea of how my studies are hindered by poor health, bad eyes, & other necessary occupations, when I tell you that although from the first moment your book came into my hands, I hungered to devour it, it was only a few days ago that I was able to close it, read. I had an attack of fever during the summer vacation that spoilt a good two months for me; and as my eyes are never good for more than about four hours a day, and I have eight hours of lecturing a week to get ready for, besides having during the past few months to get through the press a volume of my father's literary remains;[32] you see how near I am to being left high and dry and abandoned by the advancing tide of psychological literature.

But enough of groaning! Your book is masterly through and through; and I feel quite proud, now that everyone must rank you among the first psychologists, that I long ago discovered in your Space-book[33] the same merits that are here so conspicuous, – exhaustive thoroughness, subtlety of discrimination, firmness and clearness of style, and incorruptible good sense, – not to speak of great learning. Your German brains are built after another fashion from those of the rest of us, you can carry a heavier freight of facts, & handle them in a freer way. What I *care for* most in the book is of course its general theoretic tendency, away from "psychomythology" and logicalism, and towards a truly empirical and sensationalistic point of view, which I am persuaded is the only practical & solid basis for psychological science. Your opening pages about the doctrine of relativity[34] did my very heart good – I had been longing for years for something like that. It seems to me that what you have said is final. *We are*

---

32 *The Literary Remains of the Late Henry James*, edited with an Introduction by William James, Boston and New York, Houghton Mifflin, 1884.
33 Stumpf, *Raumvorstellung*. On James's acquaintance with the book, see the *Introduction*.
34 *Tone Psychology* 1, pp. 5–12 [*Tonpsychologie* 1, pp. 7–22]. Among the supporters of the "law of relativity", Stumpf mentions Wundt, Alexander Bain and Alois Riehl. Stumpf distinguishes between five different formulations of this law: (1) there are no pure sensations, every sensation is related to others; (2) there are pure sensations, but we become aware of them only by distinguishing them and relating them to each other; (3) sensations are as such something relative: we don't feel any absolute content, but rather relations, distinctions and changes; (4) sensations are a function of the change of the stimulus; (5) sensations depend on the previous (or simultaneous) state of the sense organ. Stumpf rules out all of these formulations: in his view, "the existence of a sensation in consciousness is, without exception, connected

especially pestered just now by the relativity doctrine in its most extreme form, from the side of the anglo- & americano-hegelians, who are getting very active. The best proof that there is something absolute & positive in our "simple ideas" (as Locke calls them) has always seemed to me to be the existence of *problems*. A problem is a *quaesitum* of which one knows the *relations*, but which one ignores as a *term*, with an intrinsic quality of content. Who, if asked to furnish a sound which should be both higher and yet the same in quality with a given sound, would think of the *octave*, unless he had already *felt* it? etc, etc.

For similar reasons I enjoyed immensely your treatment of *Aehnlichkeit*,[35] of *Distanz*,[36] and of *Tonhöhe*,[37] as immediate perceptions of sense, and not logical inferences from other related facts. Most psychologists, and what is worse, ordinary people, seem to think that if you can *develop* a *thing's* relations, and *define* it in terms of those relations, then it can never have had any other *status* in the mind than as a perception of those relations. Thus motion is a synthesis of *terminus a quo* and *terminus ad quem*, with earlier & later moments of time, and cannot be a simple feeling; Space is a synthesis of *positions*, and no feeling; Action, because happiness is an incident of its successful performance, must have been *motivated* by that happiness – everywhere confusion of the worst sort, to which you, in this noble book, have dealt one of the very heaviest of blows. I wish very much you might continue in this same line for a good while to come.

There is but one matter in relation to which it seems to me that the psychology of the future may find something to correct in your pages. In your treatment of *subjective Zuverlässigkeit*,[38] you speak as if the sensation to be judged were

---

with certain judgements about their relation to other presentations". Tone Psychology 1, p. 12 [*Tonpsychologie* 1, p. 22].

35 "Similarity". Stumpf claims that *"[t]he equality of sensory phenomena is nothing but extreme similarity"*. Tone Psychology 1, p. 62 [*Tonpsychologie* 1, p. 111]. Most scholars, on the contrary, claim that resemblance is tantamount to partial identity. For Stumpf, resemblance *can* follow from partial identity, but *needs not* to: "the similarity between two objects can in certain cases be measured by dividing them into equal and unequal elements. But not in all cases". Tone Psychology 1, p. 62 [*Tonpsychologie* 1, p. 112]. On James's stance, see the *Introduction* and below, [17, 1891].
36 "Distance". Tone Psychology 1, p. 69 [*Tonpsychologie* 1, p. 122].
37 "Pitch". Tone Psychology 1, p. 90 ff. [*Tonpsychologie* 1, p. 134 ff.].
38 "Subjective reliability". Tone Psychology 1, pp. 17–24 [*Tonpsychologie* 1, pp. 31–43]. This concept plays an important role in Stumpf's doctrine. It is often believed that our judgments are always completely trustworthy from the point of view of *subjective* reliability. If I have e.g. tinnitus, there is no physical sound (in Stumpf's terminology: lowest *objective* reliability), but I nevertheless do perceive a sound (highest *subjective* reliability). Yet Stumpf insists that errors may occur in the latter case too, because of the the so-called "unnoticed sensations"

an unvarying and permanent bit of content, no matter what its concomitants. In "Mind" for January last, I gave some reasons for thinking that we never have the same subjective modification twice.³⁹ When we judge, name or estimate a sensation, just as when we judge an outward thing, we are dealing with an *object*. What we mean by C^3 for example is an *ideal* note abstracted from several sensible experiences, never *felt* except as entering into some total consciousness of the moment, tinging to be sure that consciousness, but also tinged by it, and *judged* by us in a unitary mental state that probably never recurs in just the same way.⁴⁰ For the judgment to be identical, it seems to me there is no need of supposing that the sensation that underlies it maintains an absolutely unchanged individuality. When the attention discriminates an overtone which a moment before it did not notice, I don't think we ought to say the overtone was already there *as a sensation*.⁴¹ It surely was *not* there as the sensation *we now get of it*; and I think the more rational way of considering the matter is to say that the *sound* was there as an object, that with our brain in one state and our consciousness in the corresponding state we defined that object in one way, but that with our brain and consciousness in a better more active state, we now define the *same* sound in *another* way, namely as having an overtone.

(*unbemerkte Empfindungen*). "There is thus not merely a threshold that the difference in the stimulus must overcome in order to produce differences in sensations, but also a threshold that the difference in sensations must overcome to be noticeable. The latter, in contrast with the sensation-threshold, can be designated as a *judgement-threshold* [...]". *Tone Psychology* 1, p. 19 [*Tonpsychologie* 1, pp. 33–34].

39 "The demand for atoms of feeling, which shall be real units, seems a sheer vagary, an illegitimate metaphor. Rationally, we see what perplexity it brings in its train; end empirically, no facts suggest it, for the actual contents of our minds are always representations of some kind of an *ensemble*". James, *On Some Omissions of Introspective Psychology*, cit., p. 11 [*Works* 13, p. 152].

40 "In my earlier studies on poetics – writes Wilhelm Dilthey – I have shown the indefensibility of the theory of the lifeless reproduction of images. The same memory image will not recover given new circumstances, just as the same leaf will not reappear on a tree the following year. This very thesis was recently confirmed by James due to his astonishing realistic power of inner perception". W. Dilthey, "Ideas for a Descriptive and Analytic Psychology" (1894), Eng. trans. in *Selected Works*, vol. 2, ed. by R.A. Makkreel and F. Rodi, Princeton and Oxford, Princeton University Press, 2010, p. 151.

41 A similar criticism will be independently formulated by a pupil of Stumpf's, the Gestalt psychologist Wolfgang Köhler, in "Über unbemerkte Empfindungen und Urteilstäuschungen", *Zeitschrift für Psychologie* 66, 1913, pp. 51–80. James is not mentioned in this essay; at any rate, in Stumpf's lectures "Köhler and Koffka learned of William James's Principles of Psychology (1890)". G.M. Ash, *Gestalt Psychology in German Culture, 1890–1967. Holism and the Quest for Objectivity*, Cambridge, Cambridge University Press, 1995, p. 70.

Sully has something to the same effect in his review of you in Mind, but I'm not sure it is from the same point of view.[42] Still less am I sure I have made my own point of view clear to you. But enough. Your book is solid, & will be a model for the future. I expect with great interest the aesthetic part, and only wish my own organization were not so unmusical. Pray tell Herr Marty that (for reasons already stated), I have only read the first chapter of his Subjectlose Sätze but hope now soon to do the rest.[43] The Prager University seems to me to flourish well, with such men as you twain, Mach, Hering etc.

As for me, we are all getting on fairly well in the family, and I am thinking of building a house of my own ere long, to lodge my 3 boys in. My "psychology" makes *no* progress, literally. But whilst there's life there's hope. I always think with the keenest sympathy of you, and with the keenest pleasure of the days I spent in Prag. Please give my very best regards to Mrs Stumpf, and tell her my wife sends the same. My little Harry, 5 years old, who has been threatened with diphtheria but is now playing about in his dressing gown, sends the same to *Rudi*! Let me hear from you soon and believe me faithfully yours

Wm. James

---

[42] "Dr. Stumpf, in his opposition to the relativism of Bain, Wundt and others, seems to fall into the other extreme of absolutism. To him the particular content of a sensation is something wholly independent of any reference to other sensations". This "may perhaps be justified as a kind of mathematical fiction, of great service for his special purposes, namely, measurement of sense-judgment and its factors", but hardly corresponds to the real life of the mind. J. Sully, "Review of Stumpf, *Tonpsychologie* (1)", *Mind* 9, 1884, p. 600.

[43] See above, [4, 1884]. In the first article read by James, Marty argues that purely logical judgements need no empirical linguistic counterpart.

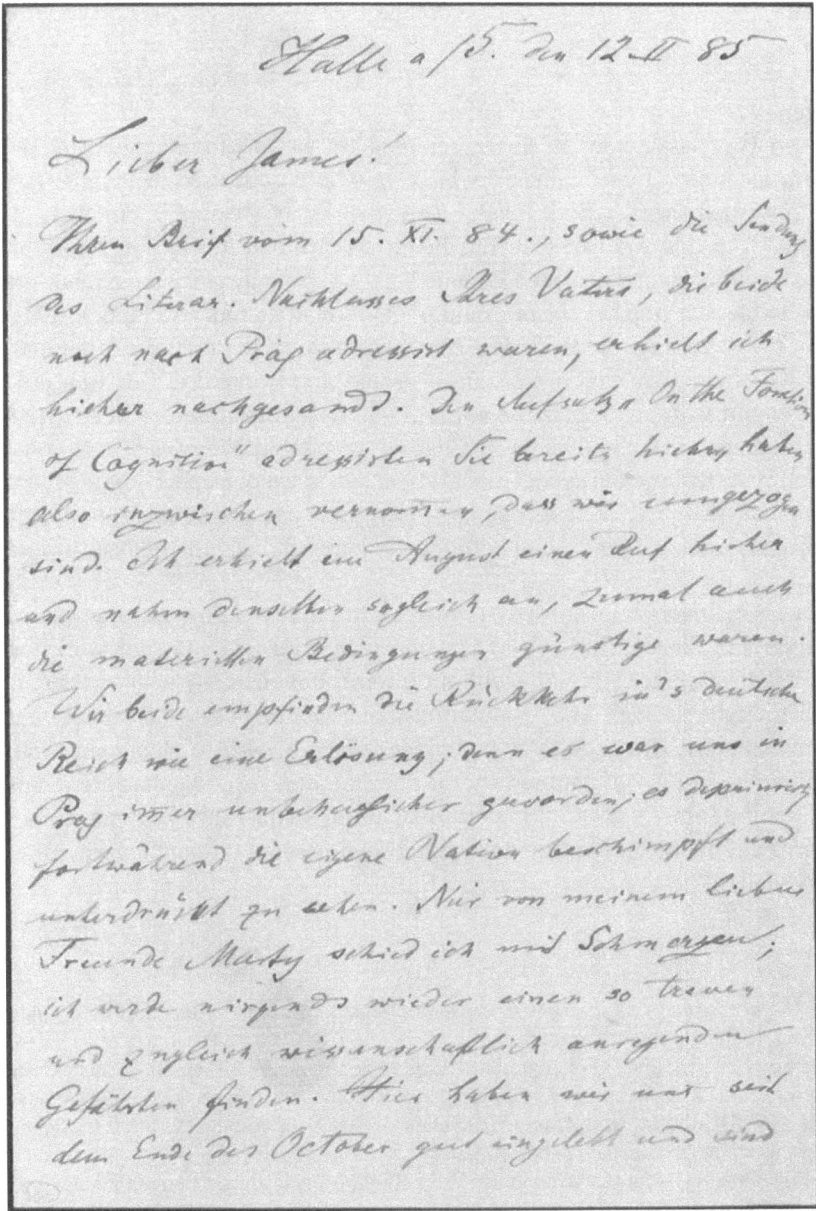

Fig. 2: Carl Stumpf to William James, 12 February 1885 [6, 1885]. Autograph letter, first page.
Source: Harvard University – Houghton Library / James, William, 1842–1910. William James papers, 1803–1941 (inclusive) 1862–1910 (bulk). MS Am 1092.9 (620–642). Houghton Library, Harvard University, Cambridge, Mass.

[6, 1885]

Halle a/S, 12 Feb. 1885

Dear James!

I received your letter from 15 November 1884, as well as the shipment of the "Literary remains" of your father,[44] which were both addressed to Prague, and were forwarded here. You already sent the essay "On the Function of Cognition"[45] to this address, and thus heard that we had moved. I received an offer here in August and accepted it immediately, especially since the terms were also favorable. We both see the return into the German Empire as a kind of salvation; for it was getting constantly less comfortable for us in Prague; it is depressing to see one's own nation constantly reviled and oppressed.[46] It was only painful to part with my dear friend Marty; I will never again find such a trusted and at the same time scientifically stimulating companion. We have settled down here well since the end of October and are satisfied in every respect – particularly with the collegial circles. Eight days ago, our luck was yet doubled, since my wife gave me a second boy,[47] and both the mother and the child are healthy and cheerful.

However, I heard with sorrow from your letter that you have not had such a good time and constantly have to struggle with your eyes. Do not work too much, my dear friend! You write without interruption. Of course, everything is so well thought through and stimulating that I would like to take back that wish immediately. Our science so badly needs new powers to tackle old problems in a more *impartial* manner, that it does me unending displeasure to see one of the best among them hindered in action by bad health. But one cannot go on without fresh nerves in the long run. I say the same thing to myself, and I am very vigilant now against overwork.

---

44 *The Literary Remains of the Late Henry James*, edited with an Introduction by William James, Boston, Houghton Mifflin, 1884.
45 W. James, "On the Function of Cognition", *Mind* 1885, 10, pp. 27–44; repr. in W. James, *The Meaning of Truth. A Sequel to 'Pragmatism'*, London, Longmans, Green & Co., 1909. James probably sent the text he read at the Aristotelian Society on December 1, 1884. In *Stumpf Collection*, p. 52, the text appears to be nondated.
46 "During the struggle for our nationality, [...] I myself became a good German and learned to hold the Bohemian Germans in high esteem as a serious industrious branch of our people steeled by centuries of fighting for their national existence". He goes on: "In the summer of 1884 I received a call to Halle [...]. My longing for the German Fatherland had become so intense that I accepted the call with great rejoicing". Stumpf, *Autobiography*, pp. 399–400.
47 Felix Stumpf (1885–1970), who will edit his father's *Erkenntnislehre*.

I have been unable, as yet, to become more closely acquainted with your father's book, with your extensive introduction,[48] or with your last essay; what is lacking is the time, not the interest. Like the philosophy of religion, the relation of religion to morality is also one of the most important questions for me, and I am eager to become acquainted with both of your views more exactly; hopefully, the vacation will bring me the required leisure to devote evenings to them, since the days must be dedicated to my book. Now, in the evening, I am either too tired or must take part in social events that also unfortunately take away a great deal of time and energy here, but such things are not to be avoided when starting a life in a new city.

I wish to give you my most heartfelt thanks for your good opinion of my Tonpsychologie; your recognition is, for me, more valuable than that of the majority of my German colleagues. Wundt has written a completely perfidious *anonymous* review in the Literar. Centralblatt,[49] which must give the impression that a *third person* placed himself on Wundt's side precisely on the points on which I had attacked Wundt. Otherwise, I have been certainly surprised by the fair number of friendly reviews; Sully's was quite expert, only he has totally misunderstood my argument given on p. 33[50] – his objection against it is

---

48 W. James, "Introduction", in *The Literary Remains of the Late Henry James*. See my Introduction in this volume.

49 "Stumpf, Dr. Carl, Prof., *Tonpsychologie*, 1. Bd. Leipzig, 1883. Hirzel", *Literarisches Centralblatt* 16, 1884. The reviewer notes that Stumpf's opposition against widespread doctrines such as those of "local signs" and of "innervation feelings" is the "expression of a subjective opinion" rather than the result of systematic experimentation; furthermore, in his discussion of the "doctrine of relativity", Stumpf merely attacks a straw-man (col. 547).

50 Stumpf's argument was: given e.g. three sounds a, b, c, and assumed that we can notice neither the difference between a and b, not that between b and c, we could nevertheless perceive the difference between a and c: "Suppose that a, b, c, ... z are all the sensations of tones. When gradually increasing the number of vibrations of the tonal stimulus from the lower to the higher auditory limit, these sensations are simply no longer discerned as different (a not [as different] from b, b not from c, c not from d, etc.) by the most experienced and attentive observers. Under the above presupposition, there would be no distinction between all these sensations of tone. All the tones from the lowest to the highest would be equal to each other. There would be only one. And further, where those observers distinguish a from c, then $a = b$, $b = c$, and in fact not $a = c$". *Tone Psychology* 1, p 19 [*Tonpsychologie* 1, p. 33]. Sully's reconstruction goes: "Thus, in the case of sensations of pitch, by making the differences in the number of vibrations small enough, we obtain a series of sensations which can no longer be discriminated by the most observant and practised observer. And if the limits of observation were also those of sensibility, it would follow that all members of the series were alike, that is to say, there would be only one sensation of tone. It follows that there are differences among sensations smaller than the least perceptible". Sully, *Review of Tonpsychologie* (1), cit., p. 595.

obviously invalid.[51] I need to reflect on the remarks you made in your letter, which nearly coincide with one of Sully's main points, as you said yourself, and for which I am very thankful; perhaps volume II will provide the opportunity to come back to it. I remember earlier having a similar view on the matter myself; but the theory would not let itself be carried out. Perhaps there is some middle way to be found. I hope to be done with volume II by the end of this year. The move and the new position have left me behind in my work. Since November, I have nearly completed only one essay, "Über englische Musikpsychologie oder über Sprachmusik und Thiermusik", which should come out in the new *Vierteljahrsschrift für Musikwissenschaft*, but only in July.[52] It also contains studies for volumes II and III and provides extensively much of what will then be treated more briefly in the book. Spencer, Sully, Darwin, Gurney, and Pole are critiqued in it.[53] Are you familiar yet with recent work on the psychology of music in England? I have already considered Gurney based on your suggestion in December 1881,[54] but could begin nothing with it for volume I; for this reason, Sully notes unjustly that this work "oddly enough"[55] appeared to be unknown to me.[56] I will unfortunately also be able to use little

---

[51] Sully's criticism runs as follows: "A sensation is a product of external and internal conditions combined. Its particular content is of course determined, largely at least, by the former, but this content is only realised when the internal conditions are added. Much the same line of remark might be followed with respect to the author's conception of relations of difference &c. among sensations. In a manner, of course, the difference is independent of our observation. That is to say, there are the conditions present for the perception of difference, supposing the supplementary internal conditions are added. These conditions involve a certain amount of difference in the stimuli concerned; and the simple recognition of this fact [...] at once gives us a solution to the puzzle about all sensations of pitch becoming one sensation with which the author, showing an excess of ingenuity not unprecedented in his writings, perplexes his unwary reader". Sully, *Review of Tonpsychologie* (1), cit., p. 599–600.
[52] C. Stumpf, "Musikpsychologie in England", *Vierteljahrsschrift für Musikwissenschaft* 1, 1885, pp. 261–349.
[53] See E. Valentine, "Carl Stumpf and English Music Psychology", *Brentano-Studien* 9, 2001, pp. 251–266.
[54] Should be November 1882.
[55] English in the original.
[56] Sully, *Review of Tonpsychologie* (1), cit., p. 595. See above, [4, 1884]. In turn, Gurney admits: "I have not read any of the German systems of aesthetics, general or musical". Gurney, *The Power of Sound*, cit., p. vi.

positive material from it in the following volume; the appeal to a "musical sense"[57] is no explanation.[58]

Last year, my wife sent you our photographs, and I later wrote a letter to you, in which, among other things, I discussed briefly your work on the philosophy of religion (I do not remember the other contents). Have you received both of them?[59] Please respond in the next letter about them. It would be generally good if we regularly mentioned receiving the other's latest letter and any parcels, no? Now take care, dear friend, and give your revered wife and family the most heartfelt and best wishes from us both, who think back with true joy on your presence. May things go well for you in the new year!

Your C. Stumpf

---

57 English in the original. For instance: "[...] the consideration of the special process, of the exercise of the special *musical faculty*, will necessitate for its comprehension a careful scrutiny of the structure of melodic forms; and even after that, such is the uniqueness of this peculiar faculty, that our comprehension of it will greatly consist in carefully making out what it is not, and so removing some very general misconceptions with regard to it". Gurney, *The Power of Sound*, cit., p. 112. Furthermore: "the unifying bonds of large musical structure [...] though instinctively recognised by the musical sense, are so unlike anything else as to be specially hard to analyse from outside and describe in general and untechnical language" (p. 217). See also Gurney, *The Power of Sound*, cit., pp. 230, 232, 250, 308, 317, 331 and *passim*.

58 For Gurney, Stumpf notes, "the phrase 'sense of ... ' is a favorite one, representing invariably [...] a non-analyzable faculty". Gurney speaks e.g. of "musical sense", of a "sense of the characteristic of the melodic form", etc. Gurney's explanations then amount to the notorious answer given in Molière's *Imaginary Invalid* by the candidate, who explains the effect of opium by means of a supposed *"virtus dormitiva"*. The same – Stumpf remarks – holds for any pseudo-explanation appealing to the "vital force", the "spirit of the people", the "sense for language", the "moral sense" – and Gurney's "musical sense". Stumpf, *Musikpsychologie in England*, cit., p. 332.

59 Stumpf refers to [4, 1884], where he already asked about the photograph.

[7, 1886]

Cambridge (Mass) | Jany 1. 1886

My dear Stumpf

The first of January is a good day for sending you my annual letter, with a hearty New Year's Greeting to yourself and all your family, especially the amiable Frau Professorin. I was reminded of you only a week or so since, as I accidentally fell upon a number of the Deutsche Literaturzeitung which contained a review[60] of Lipps's Psychologische Studien[61] (if that is the title) which I had just read and admired for their originality and acuteness, – although his argument against the *Tiefendimension* had failed to convince me as much as it failed to convince you.[62] Your rallying to the fight strengthened my own steadfastness in the faith.[63] The feeling of distance *is* a feeling, or nothing is a feeling. That immediate simple fact of introspection cannot be overthrown by any amount of argument. The only thing to argue about is the explanation of its variations. All that Lipps proves, if I remember rightly, (– I no longer have the book by me –)

---

60 C. Stumpf, "Review of Lipps, Psychologische Studien I", *Deutsche Litteraturzeitung* 45, 1885, cols. 1580–1581.

61 Th. Lipps, *Psychologische Studien*, Leipzig, Dürr, 1885.

62 In 1873, Stumpf had argued that the third dimension of space originates within ordinary visual perception: when we see a surface, the representation of the third dimension is already there "together with it" (*Raumvorstellung*, p. 176). Tackling this argument, Lipps contends that the third dimension is neither *seen* nor *represented*: rather, it is "a thought or a belief: knowledge, not perception" (Lipps, *Psychologische Studien* 1, cit., p. 84). In his review, Stumpf replies that he conceives of the third dimension in a different manner from – say – the fourth of the fifth. A four-dimensional world is indeed mathematicaly conceivable: we do have a "thought" of the fourth dimension in Lipps's sense. In addition, the third dimension (and *only* the third dimension) "can be represented". Stumpf, *Review of Lipps, Psychologische Studien*, col. 1580. See also Stumpf, *Aus der vierten Dimension*, quoted above in [1, 1882] and [2, 1882]; *Raumvorstellung*, p. 170.

63 James writes: "Professor Lipps, in his singularly acute Psychologische Studien (p. 69 ff.), argues [...] that it is logically impossible we should perceive the distance of anything from the eye by sight; for a seen distance can only be between seen termini; and one of the termini, in the case of distance from the eye, is the eye itself, which is not seen. [...] But no arguments in the world can prove a feeling which actually exists to be impossible. The feeling of depth or distance, of farness or awayness, does actually exist as a fact of our visual sensibility. All that Professor Lipps's reasonings prove concerning it is that it is not linear in its character, or in its immediacy fully homogeneous and consubstantial with the feeling of lateral distance between two seen termini; in short, that there are two sorts of optical sensation, each inexplicably due to a peculiar neural process". W. James, "The Perception of Space (III)", *Mind* 12, 1887, p. 330 [*Works* 9, p. 855]. See also W. James, "Review of Th. Lipps's Psychologische Studien", *Science* 6, 1885, pp. 308–310.

is that it cannot be a feeling of exactly the same *sort* as the feeling of lateral extension seen – which may very well be true, and yet leave it susceptible of being quantitatively interpreted, and compared and equated with feelings of lateral extension. I have got Lipps's larger book,[64] but not yet had a chance to read a page of it. He is evidently a very able writer, with whom one must reckon in Psychology.

But a truce to Lipps. Let me tell you of my own fate since I wrote you last. It has been an eventful and in some respects a sad year. We lost our youngest child in the summer – the flower of the flock 18 months old, – with a painful and lingering whooping cough complicated with pneumonia.[65] My wife has borne it like an angel, however, which is something to be thankful for. Her mother, close to whom we have always lived, has had a severe pulmonary illness, which has obliged her to repair to Italy for health – she is now on the Ocean, with her youngest & only unmarried daughter, the second one having only a month ago become the wife of that *Salter* whose essays on Ethics have lately been translated by v. Gizycki in Berlin.[66] So I have gained him as a brother-in law, and regard it as a real gain. I have also gained a full Professorship with an increase of pay, and have moved into a larger and more commodious house. My eyes, too, are much better than they were a year ago, and I am able to do more work, so there is plenty of sweet as well as of bitter in the Cup. I don't know whether you have heard of the London "Society for Psychical Research," which is seriously and laboriously investigating all sorts of "supernatural" matters, clairvoyance, apparitions etc.[67] I don't know what you think of such work: but I think that the present condition of opinion regarding it is scandalous, there being a mass of testimony or apparent testimony about such things, at which the only men capable of a critical judgment, – men of scientific education – will not even look. We have founded a similar society[68] here within the year – some of us thought that the publications of the London society deserved at least to be treated as if worthy of experimental disproof – and although work advances very slowly owing to the amount of disposable time on the part of the members who are all very busy

---

64 Th. Lipps, *Grundtatsachen des Seelenlebens*, Bonn, Cohen, 1883.
65 The reference is to Herman James.
66 William M. Salter, *Die Religion der Moral*, Leipzig, Friedrich, 1885. The book results from Salter's speeches in Chicago, translated by Georg von Giżycki. The English edition came out four years later: W.M. Salter, *Ethical Religion*, Boston, Roberts, 1889.
67 Founded in 1882 by a group of scholars around Henry Sidgwick, who became its first president. The scholars included Frederic W.H. Myers, Edmund Gurney and Arthur Balfour, who would later serve as Prime Minister.
68 In 1884, its founders included William James, G. Stanley Hall (who later polemically resigned), and George Stuart Fullerton. The first President was the astronomist Simon Newcomb.

men, we have already stumbled on some rather inexplicable facts out of which something may come. It is a field in which the sources of deception are extremely numerous. But I believe there is no source of deception in the investigation[69] of nature which can compare with a fixed belief that certain kinds of phenomenon are *impossible*. My teaching is much the same as it was – a little better in quality I hope. I enjoy very much a new philosophic Colleague, Josiah Royce from California, who is just 30 years old and a perfect little Socrates for wisdom & humour. I still try to write a little psychology, but it is exceedingly slow work. No sooner do I get interested than bang! goes my sleep, and I have to stop a week or ten days, during which my ideas get all cold again. Nothing so fatiguing as the eternal hanging on of an uncompleted task. A propos to which let me hope that your second volume is soon to see the light and leave you with *that* fatigue relieved. If it is as good as vol 1, the whole will form a great book, whose fame will always endure. I have just received from Professor Mach, that truly *"genialer"* man, the bare announcement of a new theory of sensations of sound, which reads as if it might be very important.[70] His book, too, he writes me is about to appear.[71] I am thirsty to read it, altho my reading goes on very slowly. I try to spend two hours a day in a laboratory for psychophysics which I started last year, but of which I fear the *fruits* will be slow in ripening, as my experimental aptitude is but small. But I am convinced that one must guard in some such way as that against the growing tendency to *subjectivism* in one's thinking, as life goes on. I am *hypnotizing* on a large scale the students, and have hit upon one or two pretty unpublished things of which some day I hope I may send you an account. Spending a number of hours a week in a laboratory is not however a sure remedy for subjectivism, as the case of Stricker proves.[72] I have just read your note about him in the Revue Philosophique.[73] Was there ever such an ass,

---

69 The manuscript reads 'investigestion'.
70 E. Mach, "Zur Analyse der Tonempfindungen", *Sitzungsberichte der Kaiserlichen Akademie der Wissenschaften. Mathematisch-naturwissenschaftliche Klasse* 92, 1885. Rejecting Helmholtz's view that there are as many "specific sensory energies" as there are audible pitches, Mach proposes to reduce them to two, called *"dumpf"* (dull) and *"hell"* (bright). Different pitches originate from the different proportion of these two "sensory energies" in each tonal sensation.
71 E. Mach, *Beiträge zur Analyse der Empfindungen*, Jena, Fischer, 1886.
72 The Viennese physiologist Salomon Stricker (1834–1898). When criticizing him, James refers to Stumpf. *Principles of Psychology* 2, pp. 62–64 [*Works* 9, pp. 709–711].
73 The reference is to C. Stumpf, "Sur la représentation des mélodies", *Revue philosophique de la France et de l'étranger* 20, 1885, pp. 617–618. According to Stricker (*Studien über die Sprachvorstellungen*, Wien, Braumüller, 1880, pp. 69), when we silently imagine a piece of music, we always perform a subtle larynx movement. In 1883 Stumpf proceeded (*Tone Psychology* 1, pp. 102–109 [*Tonpsychologie* 1, pp. 155–167]) to a punctual confutation of this

such an intellectual barbarian as that man! with his Procrustes-bed of articulations empfindungen into which he insists that the Psyche of everyone must be jammed! Bah! – Well, this is all the news. –

I hope you still like Halle, and are well, and in good working condition. I don't yet see my way clearly to another trip abroad within five years. Many changes may occur in both of us before then. Let me hear how things go with you erelong. Meanwhile, once more the heartiest of Gluckwünsche zum Neuen Jahre to both yourself and Frau Stumpf from both of us!

Ever faithfully yours | Wm James

---

claim, which he considered a variation of the doctrine of the innervation feelings. Stricker replied to Stumpf in the French translation of *Studien über die Sprachvorstellungen*, published under the title *Du langage et de la musique*, Paris, Alcan, 1885, pp. 169–172. In it, he confirmed that recalling a melody involves the muscular feelings of the larynx. As Stricker put it: "I say that the inner melody, deprived of auditory image, has its origin in movements", while Stumpf believed that "it is abstract". Stricker, *Du langage et de la musique*, cit., pp. 166–167. Stumpf counterattacked: "pure muscular representations of that kind cannot be considered melodic souvenirs any more than the recollection of a gym exercise". Stumpf, *Sur la représentation des mélodies*, cit., p. 618.

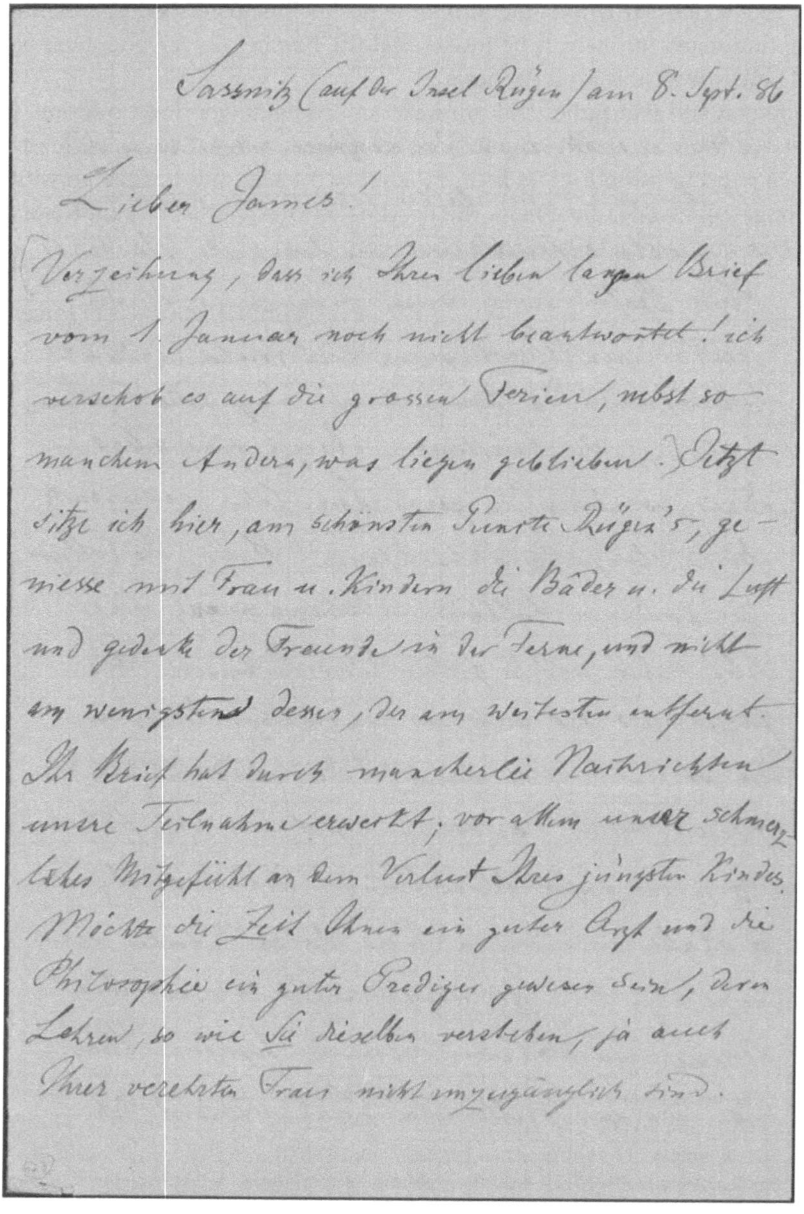

Sassnitz (auf der Insel Rügen) am 8. Sept. 86

Lieber James!

Verzeihung, dass ich Ihren lieben langen Brief vom 1. Januar noch nicht beantwortet! ich verschob es auf die grossen Ferien, nebst so manchem Andern, was liegen geblieben. Jetzt sitze ich hier, am schönsten Punkte Rügen's, geniesse mit Frau u. Kindern die Bäder u. die Luft und gedenke der Freunde in der Ferne, und nicht am wenigsten dessen, der am weitesten entfernt. Ihr Brief hat durch mancherlei Nachrichten unsere Teilnahme erweckt, vor allem unser schmerzliches Mitgefühl an dem Verlust Ihres jüngsten Kindes. Möchte die Zeit Ihnen ein guter Arzt und die Philosophie ein guter Prediger gewesen sein, deren Lehren, so wie Sie dieselben verstehen, ja auch Ihrer verehrten Frau nicht unzugänglich sind.

Fig. 3: Carl Stumpf to William James, 8 September 1886 [8, 1886]. Autograph letter, first page. **Source:** Harvard University - Houghton Library / James, William, 1842–1910. William James papers, 1803–1941 (inclusive) 1862–1910 (bulk). MS Am 1092.9 (620–642). Houghton Library, Harvard University, Cambridge, Mass.

[8, 1886]

Sassnitz (on the island Rügen) on 8 Sept. 1886

Dear James!
Pardon me for not answering your long and lovely letter of 1 January![74] I postponed doing so until my long vacation, along with so many other things that have been left behind. Now I'm sitting here, in the most beautiful point of Rügen, enjoying the baths and the air with my wife and children and thinking of distant friends, and more than a little of the one who is most remote. Your letter has aroused our commiseration for a variety of news, and above all our painful sympathy for the loss of your youngest child. I hope that time has been a good doctor to you and philosophy a good preacher whose teachings, as soon as *you* understand them, are indeed not inaccessible to your adored wife. And regarding the concern for your mother-in-law, I hope that it is alleviated by the trip to Italy.

We were very delighted by the news of your promotion to ordinary professor, which I am convinced you had earned much earlier; also the better external location, the more comfortable apartment, and your healthier eyes are all things of which I am glad to hear. For our part, we also ought not complain. Halle, my colleagues, and my relationships with students suit me; I live quietly and in good arrangements. We feel like we have been removed from an unsettled sea and placed into a silent harbor. The students are industrious, my lectures well attended (about 70 at the logic seminar this summer). Just as in Prague, there is pollution from factories in Halle, but not in the same degree by far. Extremely comfortable apartment. This is a *cultivated* country, while I would count Bohemia and especially Prague among the half-cultivated areas. Our children (Rudolf now 5 1/4, Felix 1 2/3 years old) are thriving on the whole, so that we only have temporary and small concerns and rather many joys with them. I myself still fail to get lasting and constantly good sleep; for every seven deficient nights, there is only one really good night. This inhibits my activity and often impairs my cheerfulness; but one must come to terms with it and not let one's hopes sink. So, I hope to have another good winter, particularly because of this sea spa resort, and hopefully my hopes will not betray me. Under this assumption, I also hope to finally finish volume 2 of the Tonpsychologie, on which I could only work extremely slowly and with continual interruptions this year; partially because of my sick nerves, partially because of academic duties. A third volume, whose basic outline has also long been certain, will follow

---

[74] [7, 1886].

the second volume, God willing.[75] Then I want to celebrate and lay to rest the tone psychology project, in order to bring to fruition so much else that lies in my heart and my mind. But how short life is! One sees this clearly if one is already done with the first half; before it lay like an ocean, with unforeseeable borders, and now – one must be thankful for every new day, every hour of fresh work, every moment of sunshine, as if it were an unexpected gift.

I do not think quite so favorably about *Lipps* as you do; he seems to me indeed full of talent, but not very mature. It would be useful for him if he paused his publishing activity for some years and did not conduct his academic studies before the public. But our young generation is quite ambitious. *Mach's* text was a cause of much enjoyment for me;[76] but if one looks at it more closely, much of it dissolves into Aperçu's writings, which are more witty than true. I took it upon myself to indicate this as politely as possible in my review in the "Deutschen Litt. Ztg.",[77] and learned to my joy that Mach did not take offence at my dissent. Rather, he expressed his thanks. I also recently reviewed Spencer's Psychology in the same journal[78] and have become very clear there about Spencer's actual essence; he is basically a modernized Hegel, doesn't it seem that way to you? If you would like to have prints of the reviews, I will send them. Two other pieces of work have also cost me much time: a talk on Ellis' investigations on exotic musical scales,[79] which was very difficult to study, and

---

[75] The planned third volume was never published.

[76] Mach, *Beiträge zur Analyse der Empfindungen*, cit.

[77] C. Stumpf, "Review of E. Mach, Beiträge zur Analyse der Empfindungen", *Deutsche Litteraturzeitung* 27, July 3, 1886, cols. 947–948. Stumpf rejects Mach's hypothesis concerning tone sensations (see above, [7, 1886]): being themselves part of the musical scale, Mach's two alleged basic tonal elements ("dull" and "bright") cannot account for the remaining notes; furthermore, two tones do not mix up to form a middle-pitched one. Stumpf, *Review of Mach, Beiträge*, col. 948. Four years later, Stumpf critically reviewed Mach's second augmented edition, published under a different title: E. Mach, *Die Analyse der Empfindungen und das Verhältnis des Physischen zum Psychischen*, Jena, Fischer, 1900. Stumpf notes Mach's proximity to William James: however, it is "a proximity also in drawbacks". C. Stumpf, "Review of E. Mach, Die Analyse der Empfindungen und das Verhältnis des Physischen zum Psychischen", *Deutsche Litteraturzeitung* 51/52, 1900, col. 3292.

[78] C. Stumpf, "Review of H. Spencer, System der synthetischen Philosophie, 5er Bd.: Die Principien der Psychologie", *Deutsche Litteraturzeitung* 7, 34, August 21, cols. 1194–1196. For Stumpf, Spencer is a "mainly dogmatic and deductive thinker": in his system, every mental fact is defined by the processes of differentiation and integration, so that "doubts or unsolved problems" are largely ruled out (col. 1196).

[79] C. Stumpf, "Rev. of Alexander J. Ellis, "On the Musical Scale of Various Nations", *Vierteljahrsschrift für Musikwissenschaft* 2, 1886, pp. 511–524. As late as 1922, this seminal essay was translated into German and published in the first issue of the journal of comparative

a report about my research on the songs of the Bella Coola Indians, who we were able to see and hear last winter in Halle;[80] you should receive both in the coming months. I did send you the essay on "Englische Musikpsychologie", didn't I?[81] Do you know a Prof. *Grafe* in Leyden?[82] He visited me last summer and said that he worked on innervation sensations. He was familiar with your text on it. Yet he seems to be an *adherent* of inn[ervation]-sensations. I was particularly reminded of you by the visit of your American colleague, *Fullerton* from Philadelphia.[83] He spent a few weeks in Halle. We philosophized several times, and particularly regarding idealism (phenomenalism), which he professes, while I hold it to be unfeasible. Natural science is not possible as a science of the phenomena, since these phenomena manifest no lawfulness as such, but rather only when we add realities independent of consciousness to it that stand in lawful reciprocal action among themselves and with objects of sensation. The external world is the most general hypothesis, of which all other hypotheses and laws of natural science are only specializations. We certainly do not cognize more than the lawful *relations* among realities, therefore *not* their absolute qualities. Naturally we did not come to an agreement on this. Fullerton seems to me

---

musicology edited by Stumpf and E.M. von Hornbostel: A.J. Ellis, "Über die Tonleitern verschiedener Völker", *Sammelbände für vergleichende Musikwissenschaft* 1, 1922, pp. 1–76.

80 C. Stumpf, "Lieder der Bellakula-Indianer", *Vierteljahrsschrift für Musikwissenschaft* 2, 1886: 405–426. In 1885, in Halle, Stumpf attended the performance of a group of native Americans, brought to Europe by a German impresario. Subsequently, Stumpf had the singer repeat their chants in private auditions, and patiently noted them down. At the time, Stumpf had no phonograph yet; later on, he started making systematic recordings and grounded the *Berliner Phonogrammarchiv*. For this reason, Stumpf counts among the founders of ethnomusicology. For further reference see D. Christensen, "Erich M. von Hornbostel, Carl Stumpf, and the Institutionalization of Comparative Musicology", in *Das Berliner Phonogramm-Archiv 1900–2000. Sammlungen der traditionellen Musik der Welt*, ed. by A. Simon, Berlin, Verlag für Wissenschaft und Bildung, 2000, pp. 141–150 (German/English text); R. Martinelli, "Melting musics, fusing sounds. Stumpf, Hornbostel, and Comparative Musicology in Berlin", in *The Making of the Humanities*, vol. 3: *The Modern Humanities*, ed. by R. Bod, J. Maat and T. Weststeijn, Amsterdam, Amsterdam University Press, 2014, pp. 391–401. On a related subject see C. Stumpf, *The Origins of Music*, ed. by D Trippett, Oxford, Oxford University Press, 2012.

81 See above, [6, 1885].

82 Probably Karl Alfred Graefe (1830–1899), who is referred to in James's *Principles of Psychology* 2, pp. 507–508, 510 [*Works* 10, pp. 1117, 1120]. Graefe co-edited a handbook of ophthalmology: *Handbuch der gesamten Augenheilkunde*, ed. by K.A. Graefe and Th. Saemisch, Leipzig, Engelmann, 1874 ff. The online archive 'Leidse hoogleraren vanaf 1575' (*Lecturers at Leiden since 1575*) has no record under the name "Grafe" (https://hoogleraren.leidenuniv.nl, consulted September 218).

83 George Stuart Fullerton (1859–1925) taught philosophy at the University of Pennsylvania. He was one of the founders of the American Society for Psychical Research.

a sharp mind, though (between you and me) he seems somewhat too confident and too little informed about the philosophical literature. He is still very young, and so he might yet overcome these deficiencies. With you, dear James, I obtained a much closer feeling in a shorter time, both scientifically and personally; we are obviously quite close already in terms of our mental organization and our disposition, without knowing it.

I also received from Fullerton an extensive report about the activity of your "psychical society" described in your letter from January 1. Fullerton was indeed completely wrapped up in it and appeared to view it as the main work of his entire trip. Since you asked me about my take on this research, I acknowledge my agreement with the general principles that you speak of in the letter, and believe myself to be free of the prejudice which holds the unusual to be impossible. But I believe these things assume actual meaning only if they serve at the same time to bring the unusual into connection with what is already explained. Now everyday phenomena already offer us so many riddles in psychical life, that it would not seem right to me if we were to turn our best powers to those extraordinary phenomena. I also do not believe that *you* do this or intend to do this. Fullerton, on the other hand, seems to me more than duly taken in by these matters.

One certainly must also leave some room for individual inclination, and I do not want to come to an agreement about him in this respect, though it surprises me how he could still sense interest in further inquiry despite the unsoundness of observation that was always and everywhere confirmed by his own investigation. Now he will tell you himself about what Fechner and others confessed to him. *Hypnotic* manifestations stand up better than *spiritistic* manifestations, and no doubt they have a scientific value by analogy with many recognized phenomena. The connection to these phenomena will certainly be found sooner or later; and everyone who brings out something new about them increases the chances of this. For that reason, I wish you luck with what you found in this regard through your own experiments, as per your previous letter. If I can speak *quite* frankly, as a friend does, and as you deserve, and if for this reason you do not wish to take offence at it, I must only express my doubt as to whether it would be advisable to groom *students* in large numbers for such experiments. Through them, students may easily come to the opinion that oddities are the main point in science. Fullerton also appears to go exceptionally far in this respect; he has indeed, according to his report, conducted about 10,000 experiments on mind reading with students! But once again: we certainly largely agree on these things, and you do not think me presumptuous in saying it.

This consensus on the principles and the goals of research becomes the more valuable to me, the more I see that men, who one thought to be of the same disposition and attitude, distance themselves from that disposition and attitude. It seems to me, for example, that Sully no longer entirely makes the correct use of his great talents; he seems to me to be aiming at writing mania and popularization. His "Sensation and Intuition"[84] contains, in my opinion, more stimulating elements than his later writings; every new text goes more into breadth than into depth. Perhaps his position as an examiner prompted him to this. However, if the students laugh, science must mourn.

What I just said most certainly holds for *Wundt*. His quest for greatness and his confusion are increasing in the same degree. He makes students and others believe that the ever repeated measurements of reaction times inaugurates a completely new "experimental psychology", which can only look back at older psychology with derision and scorn. See his Essays about that;[85] see the statements of his students in the Literar. Centralblatt.[86] As if something important were to follow from time measurements, as if they did not have to be interpreted themselves only through inner observation, and finally as if numbers and not, rather, clear concepts were the main point! And what a bad example the teacher gives to students regarding clear and sharp thinking! Like his doctrine of relativity, his doctrine of apperception and almost all of his more general views are chock full of ambiguities and contradictions. No one today better understands the art of throwing sand in people's eyes with sonorous words and under the illusion of exactitude. My dear Marty has submitted Wundt's doctrine of apperception to a rousing critique in Wundt's own Vierteljahrsschrift, and appeared to upset Wundt so much, that the publisher Avenarius has in the meantime suspended the sequel.[87] But Wundt cannot respond with anything compelling against it; he will attempt to patronizingly invoke, in turn, some general phrase against it in order to rehabilitate himself, at least with his blind worshippers.

---

[84] J. Sully, *Sensation and Intuition. Studies in Psychology and Aesthetics,* London, Kegan Paul, 1880. Sully criticizes Stumpf's doctrine of space (p. 67). In his systematic essay on musical sensations (pp. 163–185) he makes no mention of Stumpf.

[85] W. Wundt, *Essays*, Leipzig, Engelmann, 1885, p. 143.

[86] The *Literarisches Centralblatt für Deutschland* (1850–1944) was a weekly collection of book reviews. In the words of its editor Friedrich Zarncke, it aimed at a "complete and quick overview over the whole literature in Germany" (Oct. 1st, 1850, col. 1). The unsigned review of Wundt's *Essays* was published in the issue of January 2nd, 1886, cols. 43–44.

[87] A. Marty, "Über Sprachreflex, Nativismus und absichtliche Sprachbildung", *Vierteljahrsschrift für wissenschaftliche Philosophie*, 1884–1892. Marty tackles Wundt in the 2nd and in the 3rd article (1886, pp. 77–105, 354–364). The journal was edited by Avenarius "in cooperation" with Max Heinze and Wundt.

My inclination goes too little towards mere polemic, so I would rather describe at once the entire register of Wundt's sins, and attempt to steer all eyes to what is true and valuable in all research, something about which the younger generation is deceived by Wundt in many ways. One will have to come back to it again by himself. How often has psychology already been made "exact"[88] in such a way, only to be then steered yet again back to its old paths, to the *psychological psychology!*[89]

Enough with complaints, my dear James, indeed far too many of them! Let us rather look out happily to what is gratifying in the world and among men, and above all to realize it in ourselves.

And so best wishes from your Carl Stumpf, who along with his wife sincerely greets you and your wife.

---

88 English in the original.
89 Stumpf mocks Wundt's allegedly *physiological* psychology: W. Wundt, *Grundzüge der physiologischen Psychologie*, Leipzig, Engelmann, 1874 (many subsequent modified editions).

[9, 1887]

Halle a/S. 2 Jan. 1887

Dear James!
This time it is my turn to congratulate you on the new year (last time it was yours)[90]; and so I am sending you across the ocean the most heartfelt wishes for your well-being and that of your family. From week to week, and often from day to day, I have postponed thanking you for your last cards[91] and for the delivery of the "Proceedings",[92] since I still wanted to write something more and could not find the time for it. Now I must catch up with everything, before the lectures begin again! I am also too late now in sending you my wishes for the jubilee of your university, which many have spoken of in our newspapers. I am pleased to read so much praise and hope for the university to which you belong, and to which you are an adornment.

After my last letter, I had a feeling which we often call a "Kater-Gefühl"[93] (you surely recognize this phrase from your students); the feeling that I had almost exclusively blamed others for and that had given free reign to my exasperation over so much unsoundness with famous authors or various colleagues; through which the appearance of hubris could arise, which for me lies far away from the bottom of my heart and is despised as the worst quality. For this reason, I was truly reassured by your card, since it showed that you had not interpreted the letter in this dreadful sense. Your judgement regarding Spencer[94] interests me; since one seldom hears such sharp words about this thinker, particularly from English or American philosophers. Each of us see more clearly deficiency and unsoundness in those who are closer to us: you in Spencer, I in Wundt.[95] In fact, the drive of the latter causes annoyance in those who see through it more closely. From all the specialists whose original thoughts he uses – mathematicians, physiologists, philosophers of language, etc. – one hears complaints that he treats their thoughts as his own, without sufficiently orienting the reader about their origin. Certainly, he always gives these ideas a somewhat different style. But not only is his choice of

---

90 See above, [7, 1886].
91 These postcards are not preserved. See the *Introduction*.
92 *Proceedings of the American Society for Psychical Research* 1, July 1886, n. 2.
93 I.e., the feeling of a hangover.
94 Perhaps with reference to a judgment expressed in the lost cards (see above), in response to Stumpf's remarks on Spencer [8, 1886]. James had criticized Spencer in his essay "Remarks on Spencer's Definition of Mind as Correspondence", *Journal of Speculative Philosophy* 12, 1878, pp. 1–18. See *Thought and Character* 1, p. 478, and the whole chapter on Spencer, pp. 474–493.
95 "James and Stumpf were united by their antipathies as well as by their sympathies, Spencer and Wundt being the most notable cases in point" [*Thought and Character* 2, p. 66].

ideas (demonstrating a particular instinct for the false and confused, e.g., the law of relativity!)[96] – rather, he regularly makes them worse still through his editing. Not to mention his unbearable writing mania[97] – yet again a thick-bodied product, the "Ethics"![98] Nothing but folk psychology and obscure talk about generalities. This "total will", towards which ethics flows for him, is indeed pure mysticism, reheated Schopenhauer! But enough with this, I am resuming the same tone. One must always be aware in such jeremiads that we have improved compared to the days of Hegel, and that on the whole issues are increasingly dealt with separately and with attentive analysis; otherwise one could despair.

In the "Proceedings", your contribution is decisively the best indeed, it seems to me, the only good one;[99] it really interested me. In particular, the note on p. 99 on the united effect of an unanalyzed sum of marks and the application to animals seemed both instructive and true.[100] On the contrary, the other contents of this volume are unable to convince me of the usefulness of this rather large apparatus for "psychical investigation" (meaning: for the investigation of *extraordinary* psychical facts). The only two facts which the president alleges in his long address[101] (75–76) are extremely weakly authenticated in relation to the sureness that one is supposed to have for such things.[102] And this pseudo-"law", garnished

---

[96] Wundt, *Essays*, pp. 162–163. On Stumpf's and James's opposition to the relativity of sensations, see above [5, 1884].

[97] "Stumpf, in contrast to Wundt, did not write easily. He published a large number of pamphlets but few books. He never compiled a systematic psychology; his doctrines must be gathered from his various publications. He gave intensive thought to his theories and every sentence he wrote had definite significance. It was difficult writing and perhaps that was why he did not produce more. When once he had put down an idea he rarely changed it in future treatises, so that the contents of his various publications are surprisingly consistent". H.S. Langfeld, "Carl Stumpf: 1848–1936", *The American Journal of Psychology* 50, 1937, p. 319.

[98] W. Wundt, *Ethik. Eine Untersuchung der Tatsachen und Gesetze des sittlichen Lebens*, Stuttgart, Enke, 1886.

[99] W. James, "Report on the Committee on Hypnotism", *Proceedings of the American Society for Psychical Research* 1, No 2, 1886, pp. 95–102.

[100] James contrasts the analytical attitude of the human mind with that of the trance-subject, who "surrenders himself to the general look" at things, a look which is lost "upon the normal looker-on, bent as he is on concentration, analysis, and emphasis". He goes on: "Is it too much to say that we have in this dispersion of the attention and subjection to the 'general effect' something like a relapse into the state of mind of brutes?" James, *Report on the Committee on Hypnotism*, cit., p. 100 [*Works* 13, pp. 194–195].

[101] S. Newcomb, "Address of the President", *Proceedings of the American Society for Psychical Research* 1, July 1886, n. 2, pp. 63–86.

[102] The two alleged "facts" (Newcomb, *Address of the President*, pp. 75–76) amount to the dubious performances of a "mesmerist" from Brighton called Smith, and of the four daughters ("as well as a waiting-maid") of Reverend A.M. Creery. The Creery sisters, supposedly able to

with physical expressions, is in itself of miserable indeterminacy and still more miserable justification, p. 82![103] Now, you indeed expressed yourself with understandable restraint in the second essay "Report"[104] and still more openly in your card. But I thank you for having better oriented me regarding this movement in your delivery of the entire journal, better than was the case until now.

Fullerton also sent me his essay on the infinite.[105] He speaks well about abstract concepts, but very insufficiently about the infinite itself. Both of my children have scarlet fever, but it is getting better again. We adults are healthy. I divide my time between my book and college. Best of luck again for 1887!

Your | C Stumpf

I am sending you a study on *Indian Songs*.[106] If you can provide me similar material or literature, or if you could prompt musically talented people to undertake similar investigations, it would be appreciated in the "Tonpsychologie". Sully delighted me with his review of "Musikpsych. in England".[107] Very few German reviewers would refer so objectively to an essay in which *they* are criticized.

---

guess objects thought of by other people, later confessed the humbug, revealing the system of signs they adopted. The disillusioning discovery of Smith's (and others') fraud was one of the reasons that might have led Gurney to commit suicide in 1888. Oppenheim, *The Other World: Spiritualism and Psychical Research in England*, cit., pp. 144–145.
103 When one individual – Newcomb argues – possesses the power of thought-transference, "there is a certain chance of its passing to another individual who chances to be an inmate of the same family". But then, "what prevents any one person from being influenced by the thoughts and feelings of the whole thousand million of other people who live in the world? In the absence of any answer by the Psychical Society, I shall suggest one: the intensity of the effect diminishes very rapidly with the distance". Newcomb, *Address of the President*, cit., p. 82.
104 W. James, "Report on the Committee on Mediumistic Phenomena", *Proceedings of the American Society for Psychical Research* 1, July 1886, pp. 102–106.
105 G.S. Fullerton, *The Conception of the Infinite, and the Solution of the Mathematical Axioms: A Study in Psychological Analysis*, Philadelphia, Lippincott, 1887.
106 C. Stumpf, *Lieder der Bellakula-Indianer*. Announced in [9, 1887].
107 With considerable understatement, Sully writes: "Prof. Stumpf next examines my own contribution to the psychology of music. The attempt to combine Mr. Spencer's theory of musical expression with Helmholtz's doctrine of musical sensations seems to our author a singularly unhappy one". J. Sully, "Rev. of Stumpf, Musikpsychologie in England", *Mind* 11, 1886, p. 582.

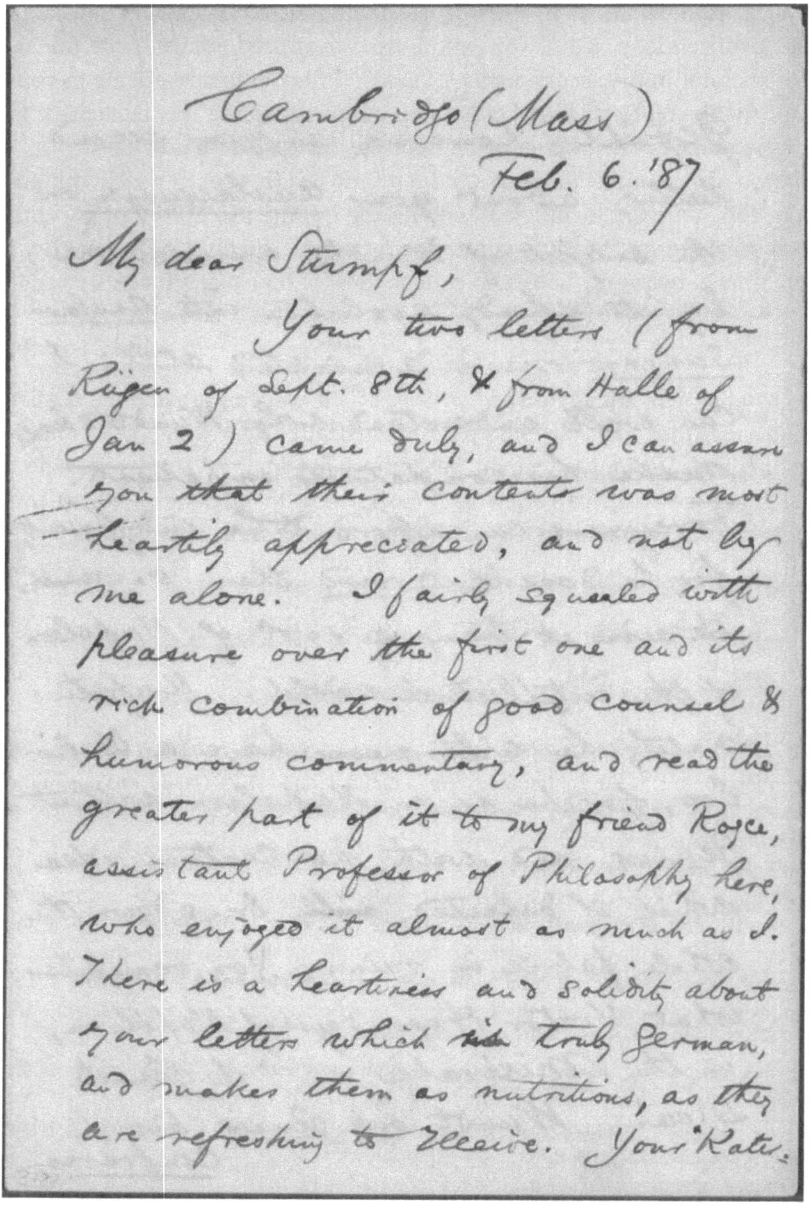

Fig. 4: William James to Carl Stumpf, 6 February 1887 [10, 1887]. Autograph letter, first page.
Source: Harvard University – Houghton Library / Stumpf, Karl, 1848–1936, recipient. 34 letters; 1882–1910. James, William, 1842–1910. William James papers, 1803–1941 (inclusive) 1862–1910 (bulk). MS Am 1092.9 (3778–3811). Houghton Library, Harvard University, Cambridge, Mass.

[10, 1887]

Cambridge (Mass) | Feb. 6. '87

My dear Stumpf,
your two letters (from Rügen of Sept. 8th, & from Halle of Jan 2) came duly, and I can assure you that their content was most heartily appreciated, and not by me alone. I fairly squealed with pleasure over the first one and its rich combination of good counsel & humorous commentary, and read the greater part of it to my friend Royce, assistant Professor of Philosophy here, who enjoyed it almost as much as I.[108] There is a heartiness and solidity about your letters which is truly German, and makes them as nutritious, as they are refreshing to receive. Your "Katergefühl," however, in your second letter, about your *Auslassungen*[109] on the subject of Wundt amused me by its speedy evolution into *Auslassungen* more animated still. I can well understand why Wundt should make his compatriots impatient. Foreigners can afford to be indifferent, for he doesn't *crowd* them so much. He aims at being a sort of Napoleon of the intellectual world. Unfortunately he will never have a Waterloo, for he is a Napoleon without genius and with no central idea which, if defeated, brings down whole fabric in ruin. You remember what Victor Hugo says of Napoleon, in the *Misérables* – "il gênait Dieu!"[110] Wundt only *gêne[r's]* his *confrères*,[111] and whilst they make mincemeat of some one of his views by their criticisms, he is meanwhile writing a book on an entirely different subject. Cut him up like a worm, and each fragment crawls; there is no *noeud vital* in his mental medulla oblongata, so that you can't kill him all at once.[112] – But surely you must admit that, since there must be professors in the world, Wundt is the most praiseworthy and never too much to be respected type of the species. He isn't a genius, he is a *professor*, – a being whose duty is to know everything, and have his own opinion about

---

108 Josiah Royce (1855–1916) came to Harvard from California in 1882 to replace William James, who was spending his sabbatical in Europe. Three years later Royce was appointed assistant professor. Like Stumpf, Royce had been a pupil of Hermann Lotze in Göttingen. J. Clendenning, *The Life and Thought of Josiah Royce*, Nashville, Vanderbilt University Press, 1999, p. 64.
109 "Outbursts".
110 "He was embarrassing God". V. Hugo, *Les Misérables*, II, 1.9.
111 "Wundt only bothers his colleagues".
112 Allusion to the theories of Pierre Flourens (1794–1857). According to Flourens, an organism ceases to breath instantly when its "vital spot" is touched: "Le mécanisme respiratoire [...] ne dépend que du point de la moelle allongée, que j'appelle, à cause de cela, *point* ou *nœud vital*". P. Flourens, *De la vie et de l'intelligence*, Paris, Garnier, 1858, p. 37.

everything, connected with his *Fach*.[113] Wundt has the most prodigious faculty of appropriating and preserving knowledge, and as for opinions, he takes *au grand sérieux* his duties there. He says of each possible subject "here I must have an opinion. Let's see! what shall it be? How many possible opinions are there? 3? 4? Yes! just 4! Shall I take one of these? I will seem more original to take a higher position, a sort of *Vermittelungsansicht*,[114] between them all. *That I will do*," etc etc So he acquires a complete assortment of opinions of his own; and, as his memory is so good, he seldom forgets which they are. But this is not reprehensible; it is admirable, from the Professorial point of view. To be sure, one gets tired of that point of view after a while. But was there ever, since Christian Wolff's time, such a model of the German Professor? He has utilized to the uttermost fibre, every gift that heaven endowed him with at his birth, and made of it all that mortal pertinacity could make. He is the finished example of how much mere *education* can do for a man. Beside him, Spencer is an ignoramus as well as a charlatan. I admit that Spencer is occasionally more *amusing* than Wundt. His "Data of Ethics"[115] seems to me incomparably his best book, because it is a more or less frank expression of the man's personal *ideal of living* – which has of course little to do with science, and which, in Spencer's case, is full of definiteness & vigor. Wundt's Ethics I have not yet seen, & probably shall not "tackle" it for a good while to come.

I was much entertained by your account of Fullerton, of whom you have seen much more than I have. I am eager to see him, to hear about his visit to Halle, and to get his account of you. But Philadelphia and Boston are 10 hours asunder by rail and I never go there and he never comes here. He seems a very promising fellow with a good deal independence of character; and if you knew the conditions of education in this country, and of preparation to fill chairs of Philosophy in Colleges, you would not express any surprise at his, or mine, or any other American's, small amount of "Information über die philosophische Literatur."[116] Times are mending, however, and within the past 6 or 8 years it has been possible, in 3 or 4 of our Colleges, to get really educated for philosophy as a profession. The most promising man we have in this country is, in my opinion, the above-mentioned Royce, a young Californian of 30, who is really built for a metaphysician, and who is besides that a very complete human being, alive at every point. He wrote a novel last summer, which is now going

---

113 "Subject".
114 "Mediating opinion".
115 H. Spencer, *The Data of Ethics*, London, Williams & Norgate, 1879. See James's review: "Review of Herbert Spencer's Data of Ethics", *Nation* 29, 1879, pp. 178–179.
116 See [8, 1886].

through the press, and which I am very curious to see. He has just been in here, interrupting this letter, & I have told him he must send a copy of his book, the Religious Aspect of Philosophy,[117] to you, promising to urge you to read it when you had time. The first half is ethical, and very readable and full of profound and witty details, but to my mind not of vast importance philosophically. The second half is a new argument for monistic idealism, an argument based on the possibility of truth and error in knowledge, subtle in itself, and rather lengthily expounded, but seeming to me to be one of the few big original suggestions of recent philosophical writing.[118] I have vainly tried to escape from it, I still suspect it of inconclusiveness, but I frankly confess that I am *unable* to overthrow it.[119] Since you too are an anti-idealist, I wish very much you would try your critical teeth upon it. I can assure you that, if you come to close quarters with it, you will say its author belongs to the genuine philosophic breed.

I am myself doing very well this year, rather light work, etc, but still troubled with bad sleep so as to advance very slowly with private study & writing. However, few days without a line at least. I found to my surprise & pleasure

---

117 J. Royce, *The Religious Aspect of Philosophy. A Critique of the Bases of Conduct and of Faith*, Boston and New York, Houghton Mifflin, 1885.

118 "Everything in Dr. Royce is radical. There is nothing to remind one of that dreary fighting of each step of a slow retreat to which the theistic philosophers of the ordinary commonsense school have accustomed us [...]. The Thought of which our thought is part is lord of all, and, to use the author's own phrase, he does not see why we should clip our own wings to keep ourselves from flying out of our own coop over our own fence into our own garden. California may feel proud that a son of hers should at a stroke have scored so many points in a game not yet exceedingly familiar on the Pacific slope". W. James, "Review of J. Royce's *The Religious Aspect of Philosophy*", Atlantic Monthly 55, 1885, pp. 840–843 [*Works* 17, pp. 387–388].

119 Royce analyzes the relativity and the "inherent absurdities" of human thought: "Every judgment, A is B, in fact does agree and can agree only with its own object, which is present in mind when it is made. With no external object can it agree or fail to agree. It stands alone, with its own object. It has neither truth nor error beyond itself. It fulfills all its intentions, and is true, if it agrees with what was present to it when it was thought. Only in this sense is there any truth or falsity possible for our thought". Royce, *The Religious Aspect of Philosophy*, cit., p. 420. How to escape this difficulty? Royce triumphantly concludes: "let us overcome all our difficulties by declaring that all the many Beyonds, which single significant judgments seem vaguely and separately to postulate, are present as fully realized intended objects to the unity of all-inclusive, absolutely clear, universal, and conscious thought, of which all judgments, true or false, are but fragments, the whole being at once Absolute Truth and Absolute Knowledge. Then all our puzzles will disappear at a stroke, and error will be possible, because any one finite thought, viewed in relation to its own intent, may or may not be seen by this higher thought as successful and adequate in this intent". Royce, *The Religious Aspect of Philosophy*, cit., p. 423. On Royce's argument in context, see B. Kucklick, *The Rise of American Philosophy. Cambridge, Massachusetts, 1860–1930*, New Haven and London, Yale University Press, 1977, pp. 140–158 and 259 ff.

that Robertson[120] was willing to print my chapter on Space in Mind even tho' it should run through all 4 numbers of the year.[121] So I sent it to him. Most of it was written 6 or even 7 years ago. To tell the truth, I am *off* of Space now, and can probably carry my little private ingenuity concerning it no farther than I have already done in this essay; and fearing that some evil fiend may put it into Helmholtz's mind to correct all his errors & tell the full truth in the new edition of his Optics,[122] I felt it was high time that what I had written should see the light and not be lost. It is dry stuff to read, and I hardly dare to recommend it to you; but if you do read it, there is no one whose favorable opinion I should more rejoice to hear; for, as you know, you seem to me of all writers on space the one who, on the whole, has thought out the subject most *philosophically*.[123] Of course the experimental patience, and skill and freshness of observation of the Helmholtz's & Hering's are altogether admirable, and perhaps at bottom *worth* more than philosophic ability. Space is really a direfully difficult subject! The third dimension bothers me very much still. – I have this very day corrected the proofs of an essay on the Perception of Time, which I will send you when it shall appear, in the Journal of Speculative Philosophy for October last.[124] (The number for "July 1886" is not yet out!) I rather enjoyed the writing of it. I have just begun a Chapter on "Discrimination & Comparison," subjects which have long been stumbling blocks in my path.[125] Yesterday it seemed to me that I could perhaps do nothing better than just translate §§ 6 & 7 of the first *Abschnitt* of your Tonpsychologie,[126] which is worth more than everything else

---

120 George Croom Robertson (1842–1892) was the first editor of *Mind* from 1876 to 1891.
121 W. James, "The Perception of Space", *Mind* 12, 1887, pp. 1–30, 183–211, 321–353, 516–548.
122 H. Helmholtz, *Handbuch der physiologischen Optik*, 3 vols., Leipzig, Voss, 1856, 1860, 1867.
123 Elsewhere James affirms: "[...] Stumpf's *Psychologischer Ursprung der Raumvorstellung* [...], a work which seems to me to give on the whole the most philosophical account of the subject yet published". James, *The Perception of Space (I)*, p. 27. Furthermore: "My own sensationalistic account has derived most aid and comfort from the writings of Hering, A.W. Volkmann, Stumpf, LeConte, and Schoen [...] Stumpf seems to me the most philosophical and profound of all these writers; and I owe him much". *Principles of Psychology* 2, p. 282 [*Works* 9, p. 911].
124 W. James, "The Perception of Time", *Journal of Speculative Philosophy*, 1886, 20, pp. 374–407; reprinted in *Principles of Psychology*, chapter 15 ("Perception of time"). See G.E. Myers, *William James. His Life and Thought*, New Haven and London, Yale University Press, 1986, pp. 144–160.
125 The reference is to chapter 13 ("Discrimination and Comparison") of the *Principles of Psychology*, pp. 483–549 [*Works* 8, pp. 457–518].
126 *Tone Psychology* 1, pp. 53–59 (§ 6: "Analysis and Comparison") and 69–76 (§ 7: "Comparisons of distances. Judgements that presuppose a standpoint"). [*Tonpsychologie* 1, pp. 96–122 and 122–132].

put together, which has been written on the subject. But I will stumble on it and try to give to it a more personal form. I shall, however, largely borrow from you. – What you say of Sully is true. But poor man! The anxieties of his life are enough to take the quality out of any man's work. His outlines of Psychology were written *merely* to sell. He is very poor, without a professorship, and in poor health, bad sleep, morbid sensitiveness to sounds etc. He is a beautiful, reasonable, unselfish character, and the "Objectivität" of which you speak, in his notice of your Musikpsych. in England is the natural result of this. I wish he could have had more money many years ago. But after all, there is no *nerve* in his mind – it vacillates. Have you seen Gurney's two bulky tomes "Phantasms of the Living," an amazingly patient and thorough piece of work?[127] I should not at all wonder if it were the beginning of a new department of natural history. But even if not, it is an important chapter in the statistics of *Völkersychologie*, and I think Gurney worthy of the highest praise for his devotion to this unfashionable work.[128] He is not the kind of stuff which the ordinary pachydermatous fanatic & mystic is made of.

My wife is well, and expects a fourth little one in 6 weeks. I bought last summer a bit of land on a lovely lake in New Hampshire with mountain 3500 feet high just behind it, and 90 acres of land, oaks, pines etc, brook, splendid spring of water, house etc, for $750,00 (!) [129] I wish you could come and spend a summer there with us! We would conspire against the whole philosophic world. Why, ah why is it that "freiheit liegt nur in dem Reich' der Träume"?[130]

Well, since 'tis so, good night! Thank you again for your splendid letters. Pray give my warmest greetings, and my wife's too to the Frau Professorin, and believe me

faithfully yours | Wm James

---

127 E. Gurney, F.W.H. Myers, F. Podmore, *Phantasms of the Living*, 2 vols., London, Trübner, 1886. Admittedly, Gurney is "solely responsible" for the book (p. iii). Myers wrote the Introduction and a "Note on a suggested mode of psychical interaction" (vol. 2, pp. 277–320); Podmore helped in the "collection, examination and appraisal of evidence" (p. iii).
128 W. James, "Review of E. Gurney's, F.W.H. Myers's, and F. Podmore's Phantasms of the Living", *Science* 9, 1887, pp. 18–20.
129 James is referring to his house at Chocorua. See Simon, *Genuine Reality*, cit., p. 208.
130 "Freedom but in the realm of vision dwells". From the final strophe of Friedrich Schiller's poem "Der Antritt des neuen Jahrhunderts". F. Schiller, *Sämtliche Werke*, ed. by J. Golz, vol. 1: *Gedichte*. Aufbau-Verlag, Berlin, 1980, p. 497 f. "Into thy bosom's holy, silent cells, Thou needs must fly from life's tumultuous throng! Freedom but in the realm of vision dwells, And beauty bears no blossoms but in song" (*In des Herzens heilig stille Räume / Mußt du fliehen aus des Lebens Drang, / Freiheit ist nur in dem Reich der Träume, / Und das Schöne blüht nur im Gesang*).

[11, 1887]

D[ear] J[ames]
So that you do not take issue again with my letter,[131] I wish to add that I do not consider, say, points (or even *mathematical* points) to be perceivable in *isolation*, but rather (as also in my book) only as parts of the entire visual field.[132] Indeed,

---

131 Stumpf probably refers to a lost letter, whose content can be deduced from a short note published by James in *Mind* in April 1887: "Professor Stumpf writes to me that in the quotation I made from him in the last No. of Mind: 27, n., I mistranslated his words *Stelle* and *Ort* by *position*, which is properly the equivalent of *Lage* or of *Stellung*, and connotes relation to some other position, as *Ort* and *Stelle* do not. I am sorry that I failed to catch a shading of his meaning which was manifestly essential. I confess, however, that I find a difficulty in thinking of *Ort* as disconnected with *Lage*, of place as not implying position, of *locus* as independent of *situs*. Prof. Stumpf develops his view in a passage which I would gladly place before the readers of *Mind* if room could be found for it in the April No.; but it does not induce me to modify my own text". W. James "Correction to 'The Perception of Space' (1887)", *Mind* 12, 1887, p. 318 [*Works* 17, pp. 126–127]. The reference is to the following passage from Stumpf's *Raumvorstellung*, translated into English and quoted by James in *The Perception of Space*: "We hold a sheet of paper before us and ask: Can different positions be distinguished, in and of themselves, when of precisely the same colour? They can, without doubt, and indeed in the same way and in the same sense in which two colours can be distinguished one from the other. It makes a difference in our experience, we notice, whether red is presented in this place or the other, just as it makes a difference whether green or red is offered. We recognise in both cases by simply looking at them that we have before us different species of the same genus. Red and green are both colours, but *different* colours as our sight assures us. Here and There in the field of vision are both positions [*Orte*], but *different* positions [verschiedene *Orte*], as again our sight proves to us. Here, There, In that place, are specified differences of place [*des Ortes*], as green, red, blue, are of colour. So then separate positions [*Orte*] are plainly distinguished as such in representation. Indeed they are so very distinct that identity never occurs between them (we cannot imagine two positions [*Orte*] the same), and the same colours can be recognised as two only through the difference of their positions. To depict this difference I am naturally unable, for it is no qualitative difference; but notwithstanding that it is a real difference and can be *felt*. I can moreover as little *define* it as I can that of the two colours (as sensations namely, not ethereal vibrations). But I can *point it out*, and upon him who does not know it, or denies it, force conviction. In short, then, what is the meaning of 'Two things are different in representation,' other than 'They can as such be distinguished, belong to a particular class of distinguishable contents'? I know not in what other sense we can talk of the difference of colours. This criterion however is just as applicable to positions; nor do I know how difference of colours is distinguished from difference of positions [*Orte*]". James, *The Perception of Space*, cit., p. 27 (I have added Stumpf's original terms in square brackets), quoting from Stumpf, *Raumvorstellung*, pp. 121–122. James omitted the whole passage in the chapter on space of the *Principles of Psychology* [*Works* 10, p. 1434].
132 *Raumvorstellung*, p. 121. Stumpf defends his claim that "some sort of space is immediately given with the representation of a quality and in it" against the possible objection that since

this is what distinguishes them from tones; however, this compromises their *absolute* nature just as little as it would be the case with tones, if we were forced by some psychical arrangement to always hear all tones simultaneously.[133] – Couldn't "Ort" be translated as *locality* (or place)? – Best greetings!

Halle a/S. 18 February 1887   Your stalwart | C Stumpf

"the represented places [*Orte*] are all perfectly alike", we could not distinguish them from each other. He contends that the opponents' "represented places" are not points, but rather surfaces "which are distinguished as parts of a larger surface" (*Raumvorstellung*, pp. 115, 121). Even if one was able "to represent mathematical points", this would make no exception to his general theory (pp. 108–109). See also the following passage: "We divide mental contents, as far as the possibility of representing them together is concerned, into two main classes: autonomous contents and partial contents": the former occurs "where the element of a complex idea can be [...] represented separately", the latter, when this is impossible. Color (visual quality) and extension belong to the latter class. Accordingly, "space is no less originally and directly perceived than quality". *Raumvorstellung*, p. 115.

133 "That we can actually perceive several places [*Orte*] together (as parts of a larger place), but not many instants together, according to the nature of time, is irrelevant. If we recall a sensation we experienced yesterday, and at the same time we actually perceive the same content, then we can distinguish either of them, in the same way in which we distinguish the same quality in different places". *Raumvorstellung*, pp. 151–152.

[12, 1889]

NORTH WESTERN HOTEL, LIVERPOOL | Aug 15 1889

My dear Stumpf,
Your charming letter reached me six weeks ago,[134] and the only reason why I have not replied to it sooner is that my plans were still unsettled until 5 days since, and there was a bare possibility of my getting into your neighborhood after all. As things have turned out, I sail in 2 hours for *die liebe Heimath*,[135] having determined in Paris to cut short my travels and not to go any further East than that place. I have recovered my health and spent all my money, – what better *finale* can one desire to a vacation-tour? I should gladly stay longer in Paris, gladly go to Switzerland and Tyrol, but truly refined epicureanism always knows how to leave off when it is still hungry! Besides I long for the pleasant month of September in my New Hampshire hills with my babes and poor wife who only enjoys Europe *par ouie-dire*.

The Congress in Paris was delightful. I have written a very short account of it for Mind[136] (not entering into details) which you will see, so I say nothing of it now, except this, that the courtesy of the Frenchmen was beyond all praise, and that the sight of 120 men all actively interested in psychology has made me feel much less lonely in the world and ready to finish my book this year with a great deal more *entrain*. A book hanging so long on one's hands at last gets outgrown, and even disgusting to one. The Congress has remedied that. – The men who struck me most were Richet and Pierre Janet.[137] The former a beautiful moderate, gentlemanly fellow, the latter one from whom strong work will come, I feel sure. MM. Gley and Marillier seemed to me also very solid men.[138] The hypnotists were there in great force, Binet, Delboeuf, Bernheim, Liegeois, Forel etc etc. good fellows all.[139] I am sorry that there were only 2 germans, Münsterberg, and one

---

134 Stumpf's "charming letter" is not known. It is certainly not the postcard of February 18th 1887 [11, 1887], written two and a half years earlier.
135 "The beloved homeland".
136 W. James, "Report on the Congress of Physiological Psychology at Paris", Mind 14, 1889, pp. 614–615. The congress took place on 6–10 August 1889.
137 Charles Richet (1850–1935), see below, [40, 1900]; Pierre Janet (1859–1947), see below, [13, 1890].
138 Eugène Gley (1857–1930); Léon Marillier (1862–1901).
139 Alfred Binet (1857–1911); Joseph Delboeuf (see above, [2, 1882]); Hippolyte Bernheim (1840–1919); Jules Liegeois (1833–1908); Auguste Forel (1848–1931).

Schrenk-Notzing from Munich.¹⁴⁰ Münsterberg disappeared after the 1st day – I hope not because he succumbed to the temptations of the great Capital!

Well! good bye. Within three years I shall be back in Europe with Wife and Children, and then I promise to see you, wherever you are. I am indeed sorry to hear of your aural troubles¹⁴¹ continuing and hope that the danger is over. I am also very glad that your 2nd vol. is so forward. Being the musical barbarian that I am, I very much fear that I cannot assimilate it as well as I did the first.

Pray give my warm regards to Mrs. Stumpf and believe me

Ever truly yours | Wm James

---

140 Hugo Münsterberg (1863–1916); Albert Freiherr von Schrenck-Notzing (1862–1929). James met Münsterberg in Paris and started a correspondence which eventually led Münsterberg to Harvard. See the *Introduction*. Schrenck-Notzing is mentioned below: [13, 1890] and [30, 1896]. James wrongly spells his name as 'Schrenk-Notzing'.

141 James probably refers to a remark in Stumpf's lost letter. In the course of time, Stumpf had "three dangerous abscesses of the ear, with two trepanations of the right temporal bone". However, his "ear passed its rigorous test *magna cum laude*; each time it completely recovered its hearing". *Autobiography*, p. 409.

[13, 1890]

Munich 17 Nov 90.

Dear friend!
I have a very bad conscience. I was supposed to thank you long ago for your extensive work: but the semester had just begun, and such a beginning many duties. Even today, I can only briefly express to you my inner joy, my heartfelt thanks, my great admiration. I have only skimmed through your book,[142] but still enough to recognize that you have endowed us with the *best* psychology and that we Germans must be envious, if there ever were envy in these "hallowed halls". I am extraordinarily glad about the study and will write to you about it as soon as I can look closer into its main contents.

Hopefully you now have time to write me more than a card. In America, things are indeed going forward quite delightfully in psychological work. Here in Munich, the ground is still cultivated very little, and I can only slowly grasp the roots with my efforts. New circles are only created in the field of hypnotism, by Du Prel, Schrenck-Notzing, and now also by some private lecturer Schmidkunz, but unfortunately they use too many unreliable practices.[143] For my part, I find these things and, in particular, Janet's book[144] of great interest for the theory of *personality*; but the men around here seem not to think of this exact application. I liked your article on Janet very much.[145] Telepathy nevertheless is not yet apparent to me, let alone spiritism.

I see with satisfaction that you have forcefully expressed your opinion on Wundt's lack of clarity in the book.[146] Yesterday I corrected the proofs of an

---

142 W. James, *The Principles of Psychology*, 2 vols., New York, Holt, 1890.
143 Carl Freiherr du Prel (1839–1899); Hans Schmidkunz (1863–1934). On Schmidkunz see below, [16, 1891].
144 In his library, Stumpf had a copy of P. Janet, *L'automatisme psychologique. Essai de psychologie expérimentale sur les formes inférieures de l'activité humaine*, Paris, Alcan, 1889 [*Stumpf Collection*, p. 52]. As to Janet's *État mental des hystériques* see below: [26, 1894].
145 Most probably: W. James, "The Hidden Self", *Scribner's Magazine* 7, 1890, pp. 361–373, where James discusses Janet's *De l'automatisme psychologique*. Stumpf certainly had a copy of *The Hidden Self* [*Stumpf Collection*, p. 52].
146 For instance: "I must confess to finding all Wundt's utterances about 'apperception' both vacillating and obscure. I see no use whatsoever for the word as he employs it". *Principles of Psychology* 1, p. 89 [*Works* 8, p. 96]. See below, [18, 1891] for further reference.

article concerning an essay from his school,[147] where I severely fustigate their experimental methods. Of course, you will receive it in December.[148]

Things are going well personally for me and my family; we live happily in this beautiful and pleasant city of art. Best wishes also to you and your family. Sincerely

Your stalwart | C. Stumpf

---

[147] The reference is to Carl Lorenz's PhD Thesis at the University of Leipzig, published in the journal directed by Wundt. Lorenz repeatedly criticizes Stumpf: for providing "insufficient evidence", for confining himself to "general considerations" instead of systematic experiments, etc. C. Lorenz, "Untersuchungen über die Auffassung von Tondistanzen", *Philosophische Studien* 89, 1890, p. 92. See the *Introduction*.

[148] C. Stumpf, "Über Vergleichung von Tondistanzen", *Zeitschrift für Psychologie und Physiologie der Sinnesorgane* 1, 1890, pp. 419–462. See below [17, 1891] and the footnotes.

[14, 1890]

WILLIAM JAMES | 95 IRVING ST. | CAMBRIDGE, MASS. | Dec 1. 90

My dear Stumpf

It gave me the greatest pleasure to get your letter to day. There is a solidity of heartiness, so to call it, in the tone of your letters, of which you of course are not aware yourself as a peculiar quality, but which *is* altogether personal, and which makes me especially rejoice in the possession of you as a friend and correspondent. It is partly *deutsch*; but not all the *Deutschen* have it; so I make the most of it. Besides, so far off, you are the ideal *homo* or *vir*, and when you speak kindly, as now of my book, it is as if I were being approved by "the Absolute"! an Absolute moreover who can write a Tonpsychologie! The second volume is still on my shelf waiting to have it leaves cut. It is the great trial of my life to have to move so slowly from point to point, and postpone what I most want to do till the things I least want are finish. I know that I shall learn endless things from that volume, but as I am giving this year a course in metaphysics and one in the History of Phil., neither of which I have ever given before, all psychological reading is at a standstill.[149] – The publication of my two volumes has cleared my mind for *receiving*; and I feel now as if I might *learn* something about psychology, had I plenty of time to give to it. But life seems sometimes to consist of pure interruptions; and day after day often passes here without my finding an hour in which to *read*. *Sonst*,[150] things go well, wife, children & self all in good health etc, etc. – I am sending a card of introduction to you to an old pupil of mine, Dr. F. Coggeshall,[151] who has lately gone to Munich with his newly married bride, to continue his medical studies. They will be perfect strangers in Munich, and I thought that an acquaintance with your wife might possibly make a great difference to Mrs. C[oggeshall]. C[oggeshall] himself is a heroic fellow, widely cultivated, excessively conscientious, and who has had a hard struggle with poverty all his life. He lacks social ease somewhat, but is a good fellow through & through, and any kindness which you & Frau Stumpf may show them will be appreciated by me.

Best wishes for Christmas & the New Year!

Yours ever, | Wm James

---

149 On James's lectures, see the editor's notes in *Corr.* 7, p. 116.
150 "Other than that".
151 James had known Frederic Coggeshall since 1885. He defined him a "dreary-hearted student" [*Corr.* 6, p. 68].

[15, 1891]

95 Irving Street | Cambridge, Mass. | April 25. 91

My dear Stumpf
I am perplexed about translations of my book. Herr Cossmann, whom I imagine to have been inspired by you, has sent me a specimen of his ability in the shape of the first chapter.[152] There are two or three mistakes in the sense, but the German seems to me free and readable. Meanwhile Costenoble the Jena publisher wishes for my authority to publish a translation, and says that he is in correspondence with Prof. v. Giżycki on the subject.[153] I have written to Giżycki urging delay till the abridged edition[154] comes out, and also advising him to consult with you on the subject. I don't know whom he has in mind as translator; but I think (and have told him so) that Mr. Cossmann has the "right of way" in the matter, and should not be interfered with. His translation ought, however, to be looked over by someone completely familiar with english, as he *may* make mistakes in the sense. Will you kindly tell me something more about him. My book is so unclassic in form, that I confess it seems not altogether right to inflict the whole of it on a foreign nation with whom my country is at peace. Yet on the other hand I can see that the unconventionality and excursiveness of the style may have something to do with making it more readable than most of its rivals. I write with great difficulty, and aim at brevity, hating too many words. Yet although I may succeed with my *sentences*, I don't succeed with my *pages*, of which there are far too many. I send with this a letter to Herr Cossmann, which I wish you would kindly read before sending to him, and between yourself, Gizycki, him & Costenoble, come to some conclusion as to what is best to do. I will follow your advice.

---

[152] Paul Nikolaus Cossmann (1869–1942) studied natural science and philosophy in Munich, where he probably attended Stumpf's lectures. See below, [18, 1891]. In 1904 he co-founded and edited the journal *Süddeutsche Monatshefte*. As a Jew who had converted to Catholicism, Cossmann was deported in 1938 and died in Theresienstadt in 1942. K.A. Müller, "Cossmann, Paul", *Neue Deutsche Biographie* vol. 3, 1957, pp. 374–375.
[153] Georg von Giżycki (1851–1895) was a preeminent representative of the "ethical movement". He translated into German a book by William Salter, James's brother-in-law. See above, [7, 1886]. Spelled both 'Giżycki' and 'Gizycki' in the Ms.
[154] W. James, *Psychology (Briefer Course)*, New York, Holt, 1892.

Alas! I haven't yet had a chance to look into your second volume. But vacation comes in 2 months, and ere the summer is gone I shall have read every word. Next year, by way of variety, I am to be allowed to teach nothing but Psychology, and hope to be able to do some reading on that profoundly unsatisfactory subject.

Warm regards to both of you!

Yours ever | Wm James

[16, 1891]

Munich 14 May 91 | (Georgenstrasse)

My dear James!
Right after your letter, I received one from Gizycki, who told me more about the circumstances.

I do not have the merit of having directly encouraged the translation, I have done so only indirectly by praising your book in a lecture. Cossmann thereby came to the idea of the translation by himself, and I certainly encouraged him in it. In regard to the execution, he also did not ask me for advice and help straight away, but I offered it voluntarily out of interest in the matter. Now, however, an alteration in my personal relations to Cossmann occurred say two months ago, which unfortunately prevented me from going forward. I sent him your letter and only noted that, since the smaller edition is so closely impending, certainly waiting for it would seem more advisable to me (just like to Gizycki).

You need not decide to withdraw your trust in him – what I personally had against Cossmann only concerns me and him.[155]

If I can help *you* further regarding the matter in any way, you can count on me.

Don't let yourself get angered by the infamous article (Viertelj. Schr. f. Philos.) from our private docent here, Schmidkunz, about your book;[156] the man identifies psychology with hypnotism and is entirely wrapped up in it. *I* find your chapter on hypnotism splendid, and I think it completely meets the present demands both in its extent and in its content.

---

155 See below, [18, 1891].
156 The reference is to a review of James's *Principles of Psychology*. Schmidkunz complains that James is unable to subsume scattered facts about hypnosis under a general theory of "suggestion". H. Schmidkunz, "Der Hypnotismus in der neuesten 'Psychologie'", *Vierteljahrsschrift für wissenschaftliche Philosophie*, 1891, p. 214. Moreover, James allots too little space to hypnotisms in the *Principles of Psychology* (2, pp. 593–616 [*Works* 9, pp. 1194–1214]). In 1892, James reviews Schmidkunz's *Psychologie der Suggestion* for the *Philosophical Review*. He notes: "Qui trop embrasse peu étreint; and in seeking to extend the notion of 'suggestion' so as to find illustrations of it in every department of human life, the notion itself tends to lose all distinctness, and the author's results become most vague of outline". The book itself "is little else than a mass of mere 'suggestions'". W. James, "Review of H. Schmidkunz's Psychologie der Suggestion", *Philosophical Review* 1, 1892, p. 306 [*Works* 17, p. 419]. Having realized that James was indeed committed to psychical research, Schmidkunz subsequently softened his judgment: H. Schmidkunz, "Berichtigung", *Vierteljahrsschrift für wissenschaftliche Philosophie* 15, 1891, pp. 348–350. Upon receiving this "Correction", in August 1891 James wrote to Alice: "Another letter from Schmidkunz with a 'Berichtigung' in the 4teljhrschft [sic]. I send the *1st 2 pages* of the letter to amuse you. He *is* an amusing kind of an ass" [*Corr.* 7, p. 186].

Sully did not exactly greet my second volume kindly.[157] After going so much effort to produce a detailed analytical work, one would expect some gratitude rather than such a grumpy reprimand, even if it has taken a somewhat long time. *This* is certainly not the way to encourage me to deliver the third volume very quickly.

Things are going well otherwise, I agree with the climate in Munich, but I really need some rest from work and would like to recommend you do not work too much. With a thousand heartfelt greetings, also from my wife

Your | C Stumpf

Best thanks for the *Moral philosopher!*[158]

---

[157] "Professor Stumpf makes exceptional demands on his readers. To publish Section 3 of Part I of a treatise seven years after publishing Sections 1 and 2 (see *Mind* IX. 593) is to count on fidelity of interest and on tenacity of memory. Nor is this all. A book written in instalments with such intervals of years between them is pretty certain to suffer in its structure. The new accumulations of material, and the progress of speculation, in the writer's own mind as well as in the scientific world to which he belongs, render modifications of the original plan inevitable. This necessity is strikingly illustrated in the present case by the fact that the author is driven again and again back on points previously dealt with, adding to and correcting what has already been said. All this makes Prof. Stumpf's book difficult reading". Sully goes on: "Prof. Stumpf carries the estimable thoroughness of the German *savant* to a quite confusing point. His discussions of some matters, notably the various conceivable theories of fusion of tones, are prolonged to the point of wearisomeness. He appears to lack sense of proportion, and devotes as much space to a far-fetched supposition as to a quite reasonable and respectable hypothesis. To make matters still worse, the author seems indifferent to form, and frequently puts down his points, his queries and so on, in the rude manner of a memorandum book rather than in the cultivated style of a treatise. One cannot but wonder, indeed, after reading through a ponderous volume put together in this way, whether the science of the future is going to detach itself altogether from literature. It seems hardly unfair to suggest that Prof. Stumpf, in spite of his seven years' waiting, has hurried his workmanship. Indeed, the whole book makes on one the impression of a rich accumulation of material, but very imperfectly elaborated into the form required by a treatise". J. Sully, "Review of C. Stumpf, Tonpsychologie 2", *Mind* 16, 1891, pp. 274–275. However, Sully concludes: "In taking leave of Prof. Stumpf's volume I wish to say that its instructiveness resides to no small extent in a feature to which a review is unable to do justice; I mean in the number and variety of side-suggestions with which the exposition is enriched. Again and again the phenomenon specially dealt with is illustrated by a happy allusion to something analogous in other regions of sense. In this way the discussion becomes much more than a specialist's treatment of one group of psychical facts: it helps to elucidate and to render more precise the more general conditions of sensation and of mental experience as a whole. All serious students of psychology must pray that the author may be able to carry through, with as little delay as possible, the vast and important work he has planned out" (p. 280).

[158] W. James, "The Moral Philosopher and the Moral Life", *International Journal of Ethics* 1, 1891, pp. 330–354, reprinted in W. James, *The Will to Believe and Other Essays in Popular Philosophy*, New York and London, Longmans, Green & Co., 1897 [*Works* 6, pp. 161–142].

[17, 1891]

                        34 De Vere Gardens | London W | England | Sept 21. 1891
My dear Stumpf
Do not be too much surprised by this superscription[159] – I am only here for a week, having been suddenly called over by the alarming illness of my only sister, and being obliged to return on Tuesday[*][160] of next week to go on with my professorial duties. On the ship, coming over, I finished the second volume of your Tonpsychologie which one frustration after another has prevented my attacking at all until about three weeks ago. And truly it is not a morsel to be taken up when one's mind is occupied with other things, but a book to be studied with all the liberty of one's attention. You have done a monumental piece of work, which will be a model to all time of the way in which general views and the minute study of details can be combined. My interest in the reading lay more with the general views, for although I know a little more of music than I did when I was with you at Prag I am still an exiled spirit kept outside the walls of that paradise. Of course for you, & for such readers as are truly worthy of you, the culmination of the work will be the aesthetical part,[161] and as the only effects you can there treat will be simple effects, I do not despair, by the time the next volumes are out, of being able to some degree to "catch on" to their significance also. But my powers of "Analyse and heraushören"[162] will always, I fear, be minimal. The way in which you squeeze the last drops of formulable truth out of the facts is admirable but of course your strong point is your incorruptible critical clear headedness. It is certainly not the clear headedness of a purely and drily logical mind which always seems negative and shallow, but that of a mind whose dissatisfaction with vague and facile formulas proceeds from its own sense of the presence of profounder sources of truth. What a strange thing an intellectual *atmosphere* is! To many of your 'popular scientist' readers you must seem displeasingly cold-blooded, but it was a constant delight to me to feel the firm and close knit *texture* of your thought. It is a strange fact – for your positive and constructive ideas seem to have no great similarity to mine – that I feel you, perhaps more than any other psychologist whom I read

---

159 "34 De Vere Gardens" was the London address of William's illustrious brother Henry James from 1886 to 1902.
160 [*] is a mark added by James, which refers to a subsequent remark: "6 hours later – my departure is on Saturday Oct 3rd".
161 The reference is to the projected third volume of *Tonpsychologie*, which was never published. On Stumpf's aesthetics cf. Ch. Allesch, "Ästhetik als praktische Philosophie: Zur impliziten Ästhetik von Carl Stumpf", in *Essays on Stumpf*, pp. 293–313.
162 "Analysis and the analytical hearing".

to day, to be a *gleichgesinnter Mensch*[163] with myself. I am sure that if fate had allowed us to grow side by side we could have worked out many things together – a thing now probably impossible even if we *were* side by side, on account of the difficulties which increasing age brings to the irresponsible interchange of unmatured ideas. – Of one thing I am sure: the quality of your book will give it a *permanent* place in the history of Psychology.

I am so overwhelmed with the thought of all things to do during these few days – (I hope in the midst of it all to be able to run over to Paris for 24 hours) – that I am in no mood for going into details in regard to the book. Let me say that §28[164] particularly interested me, especially the part about klangfarbe.[165] After that, §22.[166] In the "Verschmelzung"[167] business you have no doubt struck a fertile new conception, and I am curious to see what its farther developments will be. The positive manner in which you have struck the *Räumlichkeit*-note,[168] is also something quite new, and naturally pleases me very much.[169] I confess that what worries me most is the sense of similarity[170] and the metaphysics thereto

---

163 "Like-minded man".
164 *Tonpsychologie* 2, pp. 497–549, § 28: *Geräusch und Klangfarbe* ("Noise and Timbre").
165 "Timbre". *Tonpsychologie* 2, p. 514 ff.
166 *Tonpsychologie* 2, p. 276, § 22: *Function der Aufmerksamkeit bei der Analyse und dem Heraushören* ("The function of attention in analysis and in analytical hearing"). For Stumpf, attention coincides with the faculty of analyzing a mental content in its parts, that is, both its elements and the relations between them (*Tonpsychologie* 2, pp. 278–279). In the *Principles of Psychology* James approvingly quotes Stumpf's doctrine of attention: "Weak impressions would, as Stumpf says, become stronger by the very fact of being observed". *Principles of Psychology* 1, p. 426 [*Works* 8, p. 403].
167 "Fusion". *Tonpsychologie* 2, p. 127, § 19: *Stufen der Tonverschmelzung* ("Degrees of Tonal Fusion"). As to tonal fusion, Sully notes that "The *piece de resistance* of the volume is undoubtedly the theory of tone-fusion and analysis, that is, the detection of a plurality of ingredients in a tone-complex. In truth, the whole book may be said to be the working out of a theory of this subject". Sully, *Review of Tonpsychologie* 2, cit., pp. 275–276.
168 "Spatiality-note".
169 On the spatiality of tones, see the *Introduction*.
170 One of the reasons for Stumpf to deal with the problem of similarity in the second vol. of *Tonpsychologie* was a polemic against Mach. Stumpf argues in favor of the existence of absolutely *simple* tones. Mach, one of the opponents of this view, claimed that all tones are made up of two "specific energies", called "dull" and "bright" (see above, [8, 1886] and the footnotes). Accordingly, for Mach there are no *absolutely simple* tones: rather, each tone is a mixture of "dull" and "bright" according to a certain proportion. Mach did not prove this hypothesis experimentally: rather, he argued that since tones form an ordered series, they must be somehow *similar*; and since *similarity* must ensue from the presence of common elements, there *must* be some common elements ("dull" and "bright") within them. Mach writes: "in accordance with the principle of investigation by which we are guided, we are obliged to assume in all tone-sensations common

appertaining,[171] concerning which I have found your previous writings[172] most instructive. It seems to me an almost irresistible *postulate* that resemblance should be analyzable into partial identity.[173] May we be here before one of the antinomies of the infinite – to be treated no differently from the others? Your whole doctrine of "Mehrheitslehre"[174] and of existent sensations not discriminated[175] is at variance with the formulas I have used in my book,[176] and seems to

---

factors". Mach, *Beiträge zur Analyse der Empfindungen*, Eng. trans. *Contributions to the Analysis of the Sensations*, Chicago, Open Court, 1897, p. 128. For Stumpf, then, defending the view that there are simple tones implies advocating the possibility that there are instances of simple similarity, independent of any common partial elements. *Tonpsychologie* 2, pp. 272–276.
171 Again, as to the "metaphysics thereto appertaining", one must consider Mach's philosophy. Neural processes – Mach argued – always correspond to our sensations: when I see e.g. two squares of different colors, there must be two corresponding spatial-sensations (of "square"), together with the correspondent equal neural processes. "If two figures are *similar* (that is, if they yield partly identical space-sensations) then the appurtenant nerve-processes contain partly identical components". Mach, *Contributions to the Analysis of the Sensations*, cit., p. 31. Stumpf insists (*Tonpsychologie* 2, pp. 272–273) that Mach's view of similarity as partial identity is a consequence of his psycho-physical parallelism, and of the related monistic metaphysics. The crucial argument against Mach is that similarity must not derive from identity of common parts, as already shown in *Tone Psychology* 1, p. 62 [*Tonpsychologie* 1, p. 111].
172 In the *Principles of Psychology*, James states that "equality [...] is thus nothing but the *extreme degree of likeness*". *Principles of Psychology* 1, p. 532 [*Works* 9, p. 502]. In a footnote, he credits Stumpf's *Tonpsychologie* 1, pp. 111–122 (cf. *Tone Psychology* 1, pp. 62–69) for this view. See the *Introduction* and below, [24, 1893].
173 See the *Introduction*.
174 "Multiplicity-theory". Stumpf lists all the thinkable solutions for the question of perceived multiplicity: we can perceive "many sensations at the same time, or just one sensation, or many sensations one after another". *Tonpsychologie* 2, p. 12. According to these three options, a perceived chord is either made up of many tone-sensations ("multiplicity-theory": *Mehrheitslehre*); or it is as a unitary sensation – let us say a "chord-sensation" ("unity-theory": *Einheitslehre*); or else, finally, the perceived chord results from a very fast alternation of the tones in the mind ("contrast-theory": *Wettstreitslehre*). It is interesting to note that Aristotle had already posed the same question in his *Parva Naturalia* (*De sensu* VII, 447a 12). Stumpf embraced the "multiplicity-theory". *Tonpsychologie* 2, p. 40 ff.
175 See above, [5, 1884].
176 See below, [18, 1891] and the *Introduction*. James notes that Stumpf occasionally allows "later knowledge of the things felt to be foisted into" his account "of the primitive way of feeling them"; that is, he commits the "psychologist's fallacy". *Principles of Psychology* 2, p. 522 [*Works* 8, p. 493]. In support of this criticism, James quotes a long passage from Stumpf: "Of coexistent sensations there are always a large number undiscriminated in consciousness. [...] They are, however, no fused into a simple quality. When, on entering a room, we receive sensations of odor and warmth together, without expressly attending to either, the two qualities of sensation are not, as it were, an entirely new simple quality, which first at the moment in which attention analytically steps in changes into smell and warmth. [...] In such cases we

me hard to keep clear of entanglement with psychic chemistry etc.[177] I believe that there will be no satisfactory solution of that whole matter except on some erkenntnistheoretische[178] Basis, which will succeed in clearing up the relations between the "state of mind" and its "object." This is an obscure matter about which I have aspirations to write something which shall do away with the contradictions which occur so much on the psychological plane. I mean no ontological theory of knowledge, but an analysis of the way in which we come to treat the *phenomenon* or datum of experience sometimes as a thing sometimes as a mental representation of a thing etc etc.[179] But this is unintelligible – ! – Cossman writes that he prefers the abridgement of my book. It will doubtless sell well, being only 1/3 (or less) of the size of the big book, and without polemic and other dry matter. Confidentially, is he a man to be trusted. He strikes me as energetic & pushing, and asks for various cooperations from me (such as a new preface etc) but I fear to give any pledges until I know more of his quality. Cordial greetings to Frau Stumpf! I hope that you both are well.

Always yours | Wm. James

---

find ourselves in presence of an indefinable, unnamable total of feeling. And when, after successfully analyzing this total, we call it back to memory, as it was in its unanalyzed state, and compare it with the elements we have found, the latter (as it seems to me) may be recognized as real parts contained in the former, and the former seen to be their sum. So, for example, when we clearly perceive that the content of our sensation of oil of peppermint is partly a sensation of taste and partly one of temperature". Stumpf *Tonpsychologie* 1, pp. 106–107, in James's translation [cf. also *Tone Psychology* 1, p. 59]. James comments: "I should prefer to say that we perceive that objective fact, known to us as the peppermint taste, to contain those other objective facts known as aromatic or sapid quality, and coldness, respectively. No ground to suppose that the vehicle of this last very complex perception has any identity with the earlier psychosis – least of all is contained in it". *Principles of Psychology* 1, p. 523 [*Works* 8, p. 494].
177 In spite of this divergence, Stumpf basically agreed with James on the unity of consciousness. In his lectures of 1906–1907, "Stumpf took a position similar to that of James against the atomistic theory. The unity of consciousness is not a sum of parts but a totality, the parts of which are recognized only through abstraction". H.S. Langfeld, "Stumpf's 'Introduction to Psychology'". *The American Journal of Psychology* 50, 1937, p. 55.
178 "Pertaining to the theory of knowledge".
179 James anticipates here his doctrine of radical empiricism, expounded in the preface to *The Will to Believe* (1897) and then, more decidedly, in "Does Consciousness Exist?", *Journal of Philosophy, Psychology and Scientific Methods*, 1904, pp. 477–491. W. James, *Essays in Radical Empiricism* ed. by R.B. Perry. New York and London, Longmans, Green & Co., 1912.

I haven't read your controversy with Wundt yet – I see it has reached the dangerous stage.[180] Poor Wundt – he is only a make-believe strong man in his powers of execution, but his *program* is so noble that I feel kindly towards him, & don't wonder at his having been irritated by the references in your book.

---

180 Wundt's reaction against Stumpf's review of Carl Lorenz (see above [13, 1890]) ignited a long series of polemic articles: W. Wundt, "Über Vergleichungen von Tondistanzen", *Philosophische Studien* 6, 1890, pp. 605–640; C. Stumpf, "Wundts Antikritik", *Zeitschrift für Psychologie und Physiologie der Sinnesorgane* 2, 1891, pp. 266–293; W. Wundt, "Eine Replik C. Stumpf's", *Philosophische Studien* 7, 1891, pp. 298–327; C. Stumpf, "Bemerkung zu S. 290 des vorigen Heftes", *Zeitschrift für Psychologie und Physiologie der Sinnesorgane* 2, 1891, p. 426; C. Stumpf, "Mein Schlusswort gegen Wundt", *Zeitschrift für Psychologie und Physiologie der Sinnesorgane* 2, 438–443; W. Wundt, "Auch ein Schlusswort", *Philosophische Studien* 7, 1891, pp. 633–636.

[18, 1891]

München, Georgenstr. 15 | 24 Oct. 91

My dear friend James!
Sorry I am only now answering your lovely, long letter from London, in which you said so many friendly and appreciative words, although you seemed to count on a swift reply. The letter found me in the middle of the preparations for a change of apartment, and numerous visits from colleagues returning from the mountains as well as the correction of minor works took away all my time. Now everything is fortunately over with, and I can entertain myself a little with you, which gives me more pleasure than entertainment with my colleague Wundt.

Thus, firstly I express my heartfelt thanks for your good words about my book. If they are partly due to your personal friendship with me, then this friendship is indeed a great source of happiness for me, but I daresay that they are partly due to the book itself. Sully reviewed it so dourly and Wundt has so maligned me in general, that I am highly receptive to your praise. What you say about the deeply heartfelt kinship of our spiritual tendencies comes from the soul. I also completely understand the objections you had to make against many specific points, and I can sufficiently sense their weight to empathize with you also on these points that divide us. This holds in particular for your opposition to unperceived sensations. I myself would have rejected them 12 years ago; however, the consequence of numerous individual observations appears to me to lead to the fact that we must distinguish between actual "unconscious" representations and unnoticed parts of a whole; I consider the first inadmissible, the latter necessary. I do not believe that it is the "psychologist's fallacy"[181] which carries the blame here, but rather only certain specific arguments. However, this matter requires a thorough investigation of principle, which will *necessarily* lead to an understanding. If I understand you correctly, according to you, there are in general no *parts* in the content of representation; each is an absolutely simple quality. All "analysis [*Zergliederung*]", instead of an actual analysis, is a discovery or production of entirely *new* simple qualities.

The consequence of this, I think, is that there is also no classification. *Nothing* then is common to individual appearances; every general concept is itself in turn a new simple quality sui generis. Is that your opinion?

I can also appreciate your opposition to "simple similarities," since this claim did not impose itself on me until lately, and since I still find certain

---

181 Stumpf had been charged with this fallacy in the *Principles of Psychology*. References in [17, 1891], footnotes, and in the *Introduction*.

difficulties in it. However, precisely from *your* standpoint, this assumption seems the least avoidable. For if in general there are no parts in sensations, how ought we then define "similarity" by "partial sameness or identity"?[182]

Perhaps we would discuss this better and definitely more easily in person. Your student Delabarre,[183] who visited me briefly, raised my hopes that you would have your big vacation year next year; and I hope that a small part of it will also be allotted to Munich. The brother-in-law that you visited in London is indeed Mr. Salter? I have the greatest esteem for him and shake his hand in spirit, although the conviction in an all-powerful *noûs* does not seem *so* irrelevant morally to me as it does to him. Certainly, every duty remains the same also for atheists. But for the whole *mood* of life, such a difference is like that between the representation of the firmament as a fixed ceiling and as an infinite space, or yet an even greater difference! – Your sister hopefully is feeling well again and you could return reassured?[184]

Concerning Cossmann, I want to share with you in *complete confidentiality* what prompted me to break off any interaction with him. A lecture notebook of his accidentally happened into my hands, in which he had accompanied the explanations of my psychology lecture immediately, while listening, with comments like "foolish argument" etc., instead of correctly copying the explanations down and then thinking about them. There was a number of reviling expressions in it that showed me that he had no respect for me whatsoever, though I had been personally instrumental to his work in every way. A *critical* student is very dear to me, yet I could no longer get over myself to communicate with a young person whose critique assumed such a form. I thus wrote to him that I saw myself compelled to break off any personal communication without making the motive known, in order to cut off any discussion.

This serves as a clarification *between us*; it need not influence you in any way. I believe that he will do a good job with the translation, even though I still have no idea about his *style* in German. But you will indeed review it yourself.

Unfortunately, I cannot share your sympathy for "poor Wundt" and am almost surprised about it, since you have treated him yet worse in various places in your book (e.g., ‡ 277).[185] And do you not also have sympathy for *me* in this

---

182 See the *Introduction* and below, [24, 1893].
183 Edmund Burke Delabarre (1863–1945). See e.g. James's letter of July 1890 to Münsterberg [*Corr.* 7, pp. 49–50].
184 Unfortunately, Alice's illness worsened. She died in March 1892. Cf. Simon, *Genuine Reality*, cit., p. 240.
185 After a quotation from Wundt (on local signs), James comments: "Now let no modest reader think that if this sounds obscure to him it is because he does not know the full context;

matter, as I was accused of the crassest ignorance and most outrageous tendencies? I do not regret taking up the fight with Wundt, especially given what I know now about him. What a fraud! But we do not want to become petty because of him. A thousand heartfelt greetings from your

C Stumpf

---

and that if a wise professor like Wundt can talk so fluently and plausibly about 'combination' and 'psychic synthesis,' it must surely be because those words convey a so much greater fulness of positive meaning to the scholarly than to the unlearned mind. Really it is quite the reverse; *all* the virtue of the phrase lies in its mere sound and skin. Learning does but make one the more sensible of its inward unintelligibility. Wundt's 'theory' is the flimsiest thing in the world. It starts by an untrue assumption, and then corrects it by an unmeaning phrase". *Principles of Psychology* 2, p. 227 [*Works* 9, p. 907].

[19, 1892]

Pension Stutz, Lucern, 24. 6. '92

My dear Stumpf

I have been in Europe with my whole family for nearly three weeks, but <u>so</u> LAZY[186] all the time that until this morning I have lacked energy to inform you of the fact. My purpose is to stay 15 months myself, and (if the boys' schooling goes well, and my wife is happy) to leave her with the Children for a second year. But *where*? – that is the question. I don't want a big city, on the children's account. I don't want a small dull place on our own. I don't think it makes much difference, as far as the children are concerned, whether they absorb french teaching or german teaching during the time of their stay – they cant get both, and either will be equally useful to them hereafter. I mean that they shall *live* at home with us, while at school. If my own taste were to decide, I should go to Munich – but my two youngest children have a terribly catarrhal tendency, and I hear such bad accounts of the Munich climate that I am afraid. I *suspect* that Versailles will be our destination, with Paris close at hand for the parents, and a certain amount of rusticity for the children. But I should be very grateful to you for *any* advice whatever – I feel quite lost sometimes, and wish I hadn't brought them at all. My eldest boy (*aet.* 13) [187] won't fit exactly into any German Gymnasium, I fear. I examined that at Freiburg i/B where we have spent 10 days. It has a good reputation, but the latin is begun so early in Germany and studied in so grammatical and practical a way, that whereas my boy is hardly up to the *quarta* in that; in other things, he is in the *ober tertia*, and I don't like to drop him into the *quarta* merely on account of the latin. He will fit into a *lycée* better, if he can only get far enough on with french before the 1st of October. Freiburg is a sweet little town, but I dread the narrow social life, and absence of Art etc. Is there any german place which you think perfect for a man like me? Not Berlin, not Dresden, not Leipzig!

But I ought not to trouble you with our perplexities. My main object in writing to you is to ask what your summer plans are, so that I may know whether it will be possible to meet you. My family will be here for at least 10 days longer, so you had better address me here. *I* go, however, in two or three days to the lake of Geneva to make a lot of inquiries, and we shall certainly be in Switzerland all summer. I *hope* that you may possibly be coming this way. Are you perhaps

---

186 Underlined 4 times.
187 Henry James 3rd, born in 1879. Often referred to as "Harry", also in this correspondence.

going to the Psychologists' Congress in London at the end of July.[188] I am *not*; the expense is too great; and although it will doubtless be amusing enough, it will do me more good after the cerebral fatigue of last year to stagnate intellectually and use my legs in the midst of this beautiful Nature, than to chatter and drink ale and wine for several days with a lot of exciting and stimulating companions. I hope all the same that the Congress will succeed; and since you were not at the last one in Paris, I should think that you might find it quite profitable to go to this one and see the psycho-zoo-logical garden.

You will have heard of our calling Münsterberg to Harvard University.[189] We have there now a first rate laboratory, and a lot of students, and we ought to have the best experimental teacher; and when all is said that be said against Münsterberg (and much has been said that is very unjust) it remains true that he is a great *force* in Psychology, a wonderfully active thinker who tries to test all his ideas by experiments, and a man so amiable and liberal minded that he is sure to grow riper with the years. I have seen a good deal of him and like him thoroughly, I should think one might grow to love him very much. Meanwhile he is, by the unanimous confession of all his students, a *teacher* whom it is impossible to surpass. My only doubt is as to his ability to master the english language sufficiently, in a limited number of years.[190] At present he is quite unprepared. – I also say a good deal of Riehl at Freiburg.[191] Both he and his wife treated us very kindly. He reads a lot, especially of english; but I fear he is a somewhat disappointed man, and his face wears a curious contraction which suggests melancholy or inner discord of some sort.

I have been too lazy to read Marty's review of my psychology until just now.[192] I shall write him a letter about it. It has been very instructive to me. Much of his criticism hits home; some of it (far the smaller part) is based on misunderstanding. My chief complaint is that he is too microscopic – *i.e.* doesn't

---

188 The International Congress of Experimental Psychology of August 1892 in London.

189 James had met Hugo Münsterberg at the Paris Congress of 1889: see above, [12, 1899]. See D.W. Bjork, *The Compromised Scientist: William James in the Development of American Psychology*, New York, Columbia University Press, 1983, pp. 39–72 (ch. 3: "The German Connection: James and Hugo Münsterberg").

190 James invited Münsterberg to Harvard notwithstanding his poor English. However, "learning English was not Münsterberg's fundamental qualm. Even the prospect of replacing America's most famous psychologist at America's best university could not obliterate a cultural distance that went beyond language". Bjork, *The Compromised Scientist*, cit., p. 49.

191 In 1905 Alois Riehl (1844–1924) would become Stumpf's colleague in Berlin. They cooperated to the establishment of the Berlin Philosophical Seminar. Stumpf, *Autobiography*, p. 409.

192 A. Marty, "Anzeige von William James' Werk 'Principles of Psychology'", *Zeitschrift für Psychologie und Physiologie der Sinnesorgane* 3, 1892, pp. 297–333.

sufficiently realize the general pedagogic attitude and intention of the book, and that he is too long. Who but *I* will care to read so long and minute a review? – I doubt whether *you* have read it all or ever will! But I feel honoured and touched that anyone should have studied the book so very seriously and thoroughly as to write such a review. Only germans are capable of such devotion!

Pray write soon, and say that you all are well, to yours always cordially

Wm James

[20, 1892]

Munich, Georgenstr. 18 | 30 June 92.

Dear James!
I have already heard from Münsterberg that you would be with family in Europe and wanted to spend the winter there – a great joy for me, since I now have the hope of also seeing you again some time and perhaps of meeting your dear wife and family. It would be superb if you decided on Munich, and do not doubt that I as well as my wife would make every effort in *every respect* in order to make your stay comfortable for you. The schools are good here, and if your oldest does not immediately fit into a particular class, then private instruction could soon be set up so *that* he does. As for you, Munich would be like a health resort; I know no other city that has such good and nerve-strengthening air. That's due to its relatively high elevation (520 m). And, which is equally wonderful, we could argue about all kinds of questions!

Unfortunately I cannot completely rebut the one reservation that you expressed. In winter, it's indeed occasionally harsh here, definitely around 2 degrees *colder* on average than in other cities in Germany. My oldest often had a sore throat in the first year, for which he has a great predisposition. However, in the second and third year, he got it more and more seldom and almost never gets it now. I think that the climate heals the very wounds that it inflicts, and finally even makes one immune to them. But since you do not want to stay here permanently, I do not know whether this hardening is as valuable for you as it is for us. I would be *very* sorry if you decided on Paris, but I ought not be guilty of denying its less advantageous aspects. However, *way too much* ill is certainly said of Munich's climate, it is *much better* than its reputation, you ought to discount generously half of what you hear. Earlier, Munich was in fact an *unhealthy* city; Typhus, Cholera, etc. reaped a rich harvest. That has *totally* changed since the canalization, water pipes, slaughter yards, etc. (mainly thanks to Pettenkofer); there is no more talk of the above diseases, at least not more than in any healthy city. I for myself, and also my wife, are essentially doing far better than before, here. Hopefully you will come!

Wouldn't you do best to take up residence simply for a time *to try it* here in one of the many family guesthouses? –

When he asked me for advice, I immediately advised Münsterberg to urgently accept the offer.[193] Like you, I also think of him more favorably than many

---

[193] The reference is to the offer from Harvard.

others. He surely has *talent* to a high degree. He is only too hasty for me and of incomprehensible flippancy in drawing conclusions. But that can change.

Marty is, on the contrary, nearly *too* conscientious, if one might say so. As you point out, his review must not be judged by the usual standard. It is a meticulous and detailed series of observations rather than an evaluation of the great inspiring force and general progress that come from your psychology work. But I am pleased that you were not hurt by it and appreciated the actual acumen and the objective manner of the man. Heartfelt greetings from house to house!

Your | C Stumpf

[21, 1892]

18 Piazza dell Indipendenza | Florence, Dec 20. 92

My dear Stumpf,

I really cannot remember now whether I ever wrote to you since leaving Luzern, whether in particular I ever told you that we were coming to Florence, or whether to all the other crimes which my vice of unpardonable laziness has piled up for me to expiate in purgatory, the omission to give you any more information about my whereabouts in Europe has been added. I can only assure you that there is no one in Europe of whom I have *thought* more often (I find two blank post cards *addressed* to you in my portfolio now as I seek your last letter) and there is no one the loss of whose neighborhood I have so much regretted in coming to Italy. My plan is now to go to Munich alone by the end of April, and see you and take counsel with you about many things. But may not you yourself be meditating an "Italiänische Reise" during the Easter vacation? I sometimes think that you may turn up in Florence before I do in Munich. If you did we could revisit the monuments together and soften Philosophy with Art. Doesn't the idea tempt you at all. We are settled here in a furnished apartment, with an ultra conscientious and cheap man-cook, and save that our rooms are uncomfortably cold, the winter is passing pleasantly away. We could devise no entirely satisfactory school-plan for our boys, so tired of the problem we said "Old age has its rights as well as youth, let's make sure of a light & entertaining winter for ourselves, which shall be a real holiday, and go to Florence!["][194] We have not regretted it. The city is both small and *important*, a very rare combination. You go from one end of it to another in an ordinary afternoon walk, and yet you feel as if in a *Weltstadt*. The streets are endlessly entertaining and the art-treasures divine. The boys are a school which, though english, seems really good, and are kept hard at work, and I, after months of absolute intellectual lethargy am beginning to wake up again, and feel as if there might be some powers of production left in me yet. I suppose the lethargy was a wholesome reaction upon the fatigue which made me leave home. I hear excellent news of the way in which Münsterberg is taking hold of the work at Harvard, and he in turn seems delighted with the place. I don't know whether you have yet looked into the 4th Heft of his Beiträge,[195] but they seem to me

---

194 As to the actual circumstances behind the sudden decision to go to Florence cf. Richardson, *William James: in the Maelstrom of American Modernism*, cit., pp. 326–327. Nothing had been adequately planned for the long European journey.
195 H. Münsterberg, *Beiträge zur experimentellen Psychologie*, 4 parts. Freiburg i.Br., Mohr, 1889–1892. In 1893 Stumpf reviewed the 4th part of Münsterberg's work: C. Stumpf,

charming, and I don't see what fault his worst enemy can find there. He *is* rash, oversweeping and shallow in his generalizations; – but who is not, in Psychology? A psychologist's merit seems to me, in the *present* condition of that science, to consist much less in the *definitiveness* of his conclusions, than in his suggestiveness and fertility. Creatures like G. E. Müller are up so high on horseback on their mathematical & logical criticism of experimental methods that they make experimentation simply impossible. They are sterile themselves [I confess, however, that I haven't read M's. Theorie der Muskelcontraction[196]]; and almost the entire upshot of the work of the exact school of Psychophysic experiment, including especially the work of Wundt's laboratory, tends to show that *no* experimentation can be exact enough to be of any value. The result will be to abandon experimentation altogether, as a false and fruitless direction of activity! I am now in the midst of Wundt's System der Philosophie,[197] which interests me a good deal, though he irritates more and more by his strange mania for appearing *smooth*. He oils his transitions and *soaps* all his conclusions on to you by plausible apriori introductions that make you sick. It is the subtlest sort of mental dishonesty, born rather in the sphere of an abominably false aesthetic ideal than in that of the will, but it is turning him fast into a humbug. Moreover, this everlasting search for *unoccupied ground* on which he may plant a new theory! – I went last week to Padua to a Galileo tercentenary at the University.[198] I represented Harvard, and it was great fun. There were 6 german professors there. How I wish that you had been among them!

I hope that you, Mrs. Stumpf, and the children are all well, and that the year's work is going bravely. How comes on Vol III of the T.psy.? We both send to both of you our heartiest Christmas wishes, and beg you to believe me your sincere and faithful friend

Wm James

"H. Münsterberg: Vergleichung von Tondistanzen. Münsterbergs *Beiträge zur experimentellen Psychologie*, Heft 4, 1892", *Zeitschrift für Psychologie und Physiologie der Sinnesorgane* 5, 1893, pp. 114–117.
196 G.E. Müller, *Theorie der Muskelcontraktion*, 1er Teil, Leipzig, Veit, 1891.
197 W. Wundt, *System der Philosophie*, Leipzig, Engelmann, 1889.
198 W. James, "The Galileo Festival at Padua", *Nation* 56, 1893, pp. 8–9.

[22, 1893]

Meggen, bei Luzern, April 24

My dear Stumpf,

I ought to have written to you some time since to tell you of our decisions, which were still inchoate when I was at Munich.[199] If you could have seen the confusion in which my last six weeks have been spent, however, you would excuse any derelictions on my part. *Incessant* sociability in florence, pushed to such an extreme that one pair of young American friends came and *had a baby (!!!)* in our appartment, there being no other convenient place for the event to take place in. Fortunately my wife came away three days ago, and left them in possession – "mother and child well." I have also done a little traveling in Italy, and for a week past have been in Switzerland putting my second boy in a family at Vevey, seeing some sick cousins at Geneva, and finding this paradise for the rest of the family here. When it became evident that Harry could not be fitted for the Gymnasium in April, we concluded that the whole family had better return together in the summer to America. It is the *comfortable* decision, and we have been happy in it ever since. I believe that from the point of view of education, the best possible thing for American boys would be to pass the years from *6 to 10* in German schools. At Harry's age, however, the advantages of only one single year are doubtful. But three or four months where he is will consolidate his german, so that when he gets home I think there will be little danger of its getting lost as far as the *reading* use of it goes.

We are going to spend most of the summer in England, and have taken the road through Switzerland rather than through Tyrol for economical reasons. This means that my wife, and possibly I will not have the chance of meeting you and Mrs. Stumpf this summer, which we both regret – but of regrets life seems to be made up! We are in this heavenly spot, with the trees all in bloom about us, and shall stay a fortnight at least, before going farther, but my safe address is always 34 De Vere Gardens, London W. I am glad to have said good bye to the sweet rottenness of Italy, of which I shall always preserve the tenderest memories but in which I shall always feel a foreigner. The ugly swiss faces, costume and speech seem to me delicious, primeval, pure, and full of human soundness and moral good. And the air! the air! there can be nothing like it in the world. I was hardly able to read a line in the past 6 weeks in Italy; but in the last few days in Switzerland I have read 250 of Paulsen's Einleitung die

---

199 The second and last meeting of the two friends had taken place in Munich.

Philosophie.²⁰⁰ I don't know on what account you spoke so disparagingly of it in Munich – but our tone about a book always depends on what we *expect* of it. To me it seems a wonderful book for the human sympathy that is in it, for the fairness and candor that it breathes, and for its admirable artistic composition. It will probably be a classic translated into all languages,²⁰¹ a means of enlarging the narrowness of mind of many scientific materialists, and an adequate expression of the naturalistic pantheism that is in the air to day.²⁰² It the work of a thoroughly cultivated man; and although I am not satisfied with the standpoint that satisfies Paulsen, I have learned much both morally and intellectually from the pages wh[ich] I have read, expect to learn much more from those that remain. It seems to me that if there ever is a *true* philosophy it must be susceptible of expressions as popular and untechnical as this. The man is a *good* man, through and through!

I am sorry that those days those not easily to be forgotten days that I spent in dear old Munich, are likely to be the last ones of our seeing each other for a long time to come. My boy has enjoyed much his visits to your house, and I thank you for inviting him. My love to you both (Mrs James is so sorry not to make the acquaintance of "the Stumpf's,") –

Yours ever | Wm James

---

200 F. Paulsen, *Einleitung in die Philosophie*, Berlin, Hertz, 1892.
201 James wrote the Preface for the English edition of Paulsen's book, which was published by Holt. W. James, "Preface", in F. Paulsen, *Introduction to Philosophy*, New York, Holt, 1895. The "immense merit of Paulsen's work" is "his perfect candor and his abandonment of scholasticism". Paulsen, in turn, prefaced the German translation of James's *Will to Believe*. W. James, *Der Wille zum Glauben und andere popularphilosophische Essays*, m. e. Geleitwort von Fr. Paulsen, Stuttgart, Frommann, 1899.
202 Paulsen defends the point of view of "idealistic monism" against "supernatural dualism" and "atomistic materialism". Paulsen, *Einleitung in die Philosophie*, cit., p. iii-iv. Accordingly, reality is the "appearance of a spiritual whole-life" which is the "realization of a single sensibility" and the action of "a will that realizes the Ideas" (p. vii). In this way, Paulsen believes, scientific and religious aspirations can be reconciled.

[23, 1893]

Munich 17 Mai 93

Dear James,

I am infinitely sorry that we did not see your dear wife more at all, and that *I* did not get acquainted with her at all! My wife and sister-in-law were so delighted by her that I have to view it as a great loss. But they must already have told you that, as we wanted to visit each other at exactly the same time; if this occurred due to some telepathic attraction, then I curse telepathy. The days before and afterwards I was just so completely engaged that I could not repeat my visit, but cherished the faint hope that she would still be able to accept our invitation for noon on Monday with Harry. She appears, however, to have travelled back before that. And that I now should also not see you, dear friend, "for a long time", as you write, is no less sorrowful for me: for I saw less of you in your presence around here than I had hoped because of your multiple business engagements. You are in Europe for a full year – a year I have been looking forward to for 10 years – and of this year, few hours were allotted to seeing each other again, hours in which your thoughts and feelings were still occupied by urgent matters! I cannot reproach you for this, of course, but I am sad about it; so sad that – to say it openly – I have the uncertain feeling that your friendship has lost some of its liveliness through the years, that you perhaps have not found in it what you promised yourself initially, or that something about me has proven alien or unpleasant to you. Perhaps my demeanor against Wundt?[203] We have indeed both become *more honest*, much more honest in these 10 years; also, life is so short and the world in which we live so small! But so much the firmer I would like to hold on to what I love and appreciate sincerely.

Your enthusiastic judgment of Paulsen's writing makes me eager to read more of it soon; my own judgment rests only on a rather fleeting glance and will very likely come nearer to yours, if I become acquainted with the book more closely. I have always estimated this man very highly even before this, and I admire the popular writer and the knower of life he is.[204]

The experimental exercises I have begun have found much appeal among my students, but take away an inhuman amount of time and effort on my part, as you correctly predicted – time and effort that should actually belong to scientific work. I am downright assaulted by it and will definitely be able to focus

---

203 See above, [9, 1887].
204 Paulsen and Stumpf would later be colleagues in Berlin. Stumpf recalls that he maintained the "most cordial and harmonious relations with Dilthey, Paulsen, and their successors". *Autobiography*, p. 402.

on the matter *alone* in the future only on a rather small scale, but perhaps I should find an assistant.

Wundt's Psychologie, Vol. 1 has just now come out in its 4th edition.[205]

I would like to still note one thing on what we were discussing[206] regarding the question of simple similarities. If you find that my argument would be avoided by thinking the final elements[207] tiered neither qualitatively nor quantitatively,

---

205 W. Wundt, *Grundzüge der physiologischen Psychologie*, Leipzig, Engelmann, 1893^4. In this edition, Wundt changed his mind about innervation feelings. Wundt's failure to make this point clear and to acknowledge his previous critics is stigmatized in W. James, "Professor Wundt and Feelings of Innervation", *The Psychological Review* 1, 1894, pp. 70–73.

206 Perhaps a reference to their conversation in Munich.

207 The reference is to a discussion that runs through both *Tonpsychologie* 1 and James's *Principles of Psychology*. The problem of simple similarity had been discussed by James in chapter 13 ("Discrimination and Comparison") of the *Principles of Psychology* where Stumpf is repeatedly referred to. James incorporates a long passage from Stumpf, advocating his view on identity: "When we compare a deep, middle, and a high note, e.g., C, f sharp, a^{iii}, we remark immediately that the first is less like the third than the second is. The same would be true of c d e in the same region of the scale. Our very calling one of the notes a 'middle' note is the expression of a judgment of this sort. But where here is the identical and where the non-identical part? We cannot think of the overtones; for the first-named three notes have none in common, at least not on musical instruments. Moreover, we might take simple tones, and still our judgment would be unhesitatingly the same, provided the tones were not chosen too close together [...] Neither can it be said that the identity consists in their all being sounds, and not a sound, a smell, and a color, respectively. For this identical attribute comes to each of them in equal measure, whereas the first, being less like the third than the second is, ought, on the terms of the theory we are criticising, to have less of the identical quality [...] It thus appears impracticable to define all possible cases of likeness as partial identity *plus* partial disparity; and it is vain to seek in all cases for identical elements". Stumpf, *Tonpsychologie* 1, pp. 115–116 (corresponding to *Tone Psychology* 1, p. 64), translated and quoted by James in *Principles of Psychology* 1, pp. 532–533 [*Works* 9, pp. 502–503]. So far, James agrees with Stumpf. However, James adds: "I have omitted, so as not to make my text too intricate, an extremely acute and conclusive paragraph [*scil.* from Stumpf], which I reproduce here: 'We may generalize: Wherever a number of sensible impressions are apprehended as a series, there in the last instance must perceptions of simple likeness be found. Proof: Assume that all the terms of a series, e.g. the qualities of tone, c d e f g, have something in common, – no matter what it is, call it X; then I say that the differing parts of each of these terms must not only be differently constituted in each, but must themselves form a series, whose existence is the ground for our apprehending the original terms in serial form. We thus get instead of the original series a b c d e f ... the equivalent series Xa, Xb, Xg, ... etc. What is gained? The question immediately arises: How is a b g known as a series? According to the theory, these elements must themselves be made up of a part common to all, and of parts differing in each, which latter parts form a new series, and so on ad infinitum, which is absurd'". *Tonpsychologie* 1, p. 116 (corresponding to *Tone Psychology* 1, pp. 64–65), translated and quoted by James in *Principles of Psychology* 1, p. 533 [*Works* 9, p. 503]. Now, James does not share this generalization unconditionally:

but rather solely *numerically*,²⁰⁸ then I cannot regard this as an actual solution to the difficulty, since it indeed is generally agreed that it is impossible for several qualitatively completely similar (and also spatially not differently localized) sensations to exist simultaneously in consciousness.²⁰⁹ Thus, one would have to give up this principle and hence contradict all experience.

Enough for today – I have to get some air in order to get some sleep again. Live well and may you and your wife be greeted with the best from us.

Your stalwart | C. Stumpf

"Stumpf (Tonpsychologie, I. 116 ff.) tries to prove that the theory that all differences are differences of composition leads necessarily to an infinite regression when we try to determine the unit. It seems to me that in his particular reasoning he forgets the ultimate units of the mindstuff theory. I cannot find the completed infinite to be one of the obstacles to belief in this theory, although I fully accept Stumpf's general reasoning, and am only too happy to find myself on the same side with such an exceptionally clear thinker". *Principles of Psychology* 1, p. 493 [*Works* 8, p. 467].

208 In the *Principles of Psychology* James agrees with Stumpf's definition of similarity and identity (see above). On closer inspection, however, he introduced a limitation: the vanishing "of all perceptible difference – James wrote – between two numerically distinct things makes them *qualitatively the same or equal*. Equality, or *qualitative* (as distinguished from numerical) *identity*, is thus nothing but the *extreme degree of likeness*". *Principles of Psychology* 1, p. 532 [*Works* 9, p. 502]. Remarkably, James insists twice on *qualitative* identity, considered "as distinguished from numerical" identity.

209 Stumpf argues that you cannot have the *same* sensation twice simultaneously, unless there is a spatial difference between the two. Accordingly, James cannot escape Stumpf's argument on similarity in [18, 1891] by assuming such different sensations.

[24 1893]

Meggen, bei Luzern, Schweiz | May 26. 93

My dear Stumpf;
Your letter of the 17th.,[210] just received, touches me very much, and confirms me in my habitual belief that your heart is as strong and active an organ as your head. But how *could* I have conveyed to you the impression that my feeling of personal affection for you, and satisfaction in being able to count you as a friend, had grown less in the past ten years? Older I am indeed, and probably much duller, but I speak sincerely when I say that during my last visit I felt more intimately and closely the charm of your character and our intellectual kinship than when we were together ten years ago in Prag. That was relatively superficial. I only wish it were possible for my wife to repeat to you all the things I said about the impression I had of you, when I got back to Florence. I was, as I now see, a little too afraid, when in Munich, of encroaching on your time and appealing to your hospitality. My own experience of the visits of English people to Cambridge who expect entertainment when I am hard pressed with work, has perhaps made me too sensitive, in that regard, towards others. You were busy & I was relatively idle; I didn't wish to make it possible that you should think me a bore. But with *you*, I see now that the thought of such possibilities ought to have been absent from my mind. Over and above that, however, most men's friendships are too inarticulate. As our Emerson says: "There is more kindness than is ever spoken."[211] And in the beautiful verses of an old friend and neighbor of mine,

> Thought is deeper than all speech,
> Feeling deeper than all thought.
> Heart to heart can never teach
> What unto itself was taught.
> Like the stars that gem the sky,
> Far apart, though *seeming* near
> - - - -
> We are spirits clad in veils,
> Soul with soul can never meet;
> We are columns left alone,
> Of a temple once complete – .[212]

---

210 [23, 1893].
211 R.W. Emerson, "Friendship", in *Essays*, Boston, Houghton Mifflin, 1884, p. 183.
212 James liberally quotes form Christopher Pearse Cranch, "Enosis", in *Poems*, Philadelphia, Carey and Hart, 1844, p. 51.

Alas! I find that I have forgotten the words, which sadly express the "dialectic contradictoriness" that is to be found in finite individuality. – Will a "higher synthesis" ever come to give relief? Your letter meanwhile shall be one of my most cherished possessions, and makes me feel freer with you than ever before. I feel free now to express my amusement at your suggestion that the tone of your polemics with Wundt should have made my love turn cold. I confess that that sentence gave me a good long laugh, and makes me laugh again now! Wundt seems to be "getting himself generally disliked." In this pension we have had a Herr Carl Hauptmann author of a book called "die Metaphysik in die Physiologie"[213] (which you perhaps know) and his friend Prof. Avenarius,[214] both with their wives. Hauptmann is a charming modest man, and his wife an angel, and Avenarius a very good natured creature (superficially, at any rate), but they both seem to have Wundt "on the brain," and can hardly talk for five minutes about any subject without some groaning reference to him. Victor Hugo says of Bonaparte that he fell because *"il gênait Dieu."*[215] Is that to be also Wundt's fate? He certainly begins to encroach on God's omniscience. If only he could show a spark of creative genius *dabei!*[216] – As for Hauptmann, the book does not seem to me as good as the man. I have not yet read a page of Avenarius's books,[217] but have an *apriori* distrust of all attempts at making philosophy systematically exact just now. The frequency with which a man loves to use the words "streng wissenschaftlich"[218] is beginning to be for me a measure of the shallowness of his sense of the truth. Altogether, the less we have to say about "strenge"[219] the better, I think, in the present condition or our speculations. That is one reason for which I enjoy Paulsen's book.[220] There is no pretense of "strenge" about it; and yet the most pedantically written works have no *more* solid *stuff* to give you than he gives in this absolutely popular and unpretending way. To me the stuff is theoretically quite unsatisfying; but it is so fundamental and uncomplicated that it admits of addition, possibly without much alteration; and I cannot but esteem it a great gain for the truth to

---

213 C. Hauptmann, *Die Metaphysik in der modernen Physiologie. Eine kritische Untersuchung*, Dresden, Ehlermann, 1893.
214 Richard Avenarius [1843–1896] taught at Zurich University. Mentioned above [8, 1886] as publisher of the *Vierteljahrsschrift für Wissenschaftliche Philosophie* (together with Wundt and Heinze).
215 See above, [10, 1887].
216 "Thereby".
217 R. Avenarius, *Kritik der reinen Erfahrung*, 2 vols., Leipzig, Reisland, 1888–1890.
218 "Strictly scientific".
219 "Rigor".
220 Paulsen, *Einleitung in die Philosophie*, cit., 1892. See above, [22, 1893].

have such deep matters treated so absolutely-without technical apparatus.[221] It makes one realize the alternatives in their natural nakedness, unveiled by what I must call the humbug which a would-be "streng wissenschaftlich" treatment generally disguises them in. On the matter of resemblance,[222] there is a reply from me to Bradley in the April *Mind*,[223] I don't know whether you have seen it. I agree with you that a multitude of qualitatively identical coexistent elements of consciousness is an unintelligible conception;[224] but still, *if* one chooses to adopt it (as Spencer & Taine, *e.g.* adopt it) it affords a refuge from the infinite regress of composition, it seems to me.

The dinner bell rings, and I must stop. My wife has been saying all the morning that we *must* come over to the Munich "Congress" in 1895,[225] we two

---

221 See also W. James, *A Pluralistic Universe. Hibbert Lectures at Manchester College on the Present Situation in Philosophy*, New York and London, Longmans, Green & Co., 1909, p. 18 ff. Paulsen's popular tone, and the content of his book, aiming at a mediation between materialism and spiritualism, are in line with James's writings on pragmatism.
222 See above, [18, 1891].
223 James's doctrine of resemblance (see above, [17, 1891]) had been targeted by F.H. Bradley in "Professor James's Doctrine of Simple Resemblance", *Mind* n.s. 2, 1893, pp. 83–88. James answers arguing that the problem leads to "one of two conclusions, either to (1) The postulation of point after point, encapsulated within each other in infinitum, as the constitutive condition of the resemblance of any two objects; or to (2) A last kind of element (if one could then say "kind") of whose self-compoundings all the objects, and of whose diverse numbers in the objects, all the likeness and unlikeness in the world are made. Of these two views of resemblance the former leads to a sort of Leibnitzian metaphysics, and the latter to what I call the Mind-dust theory". Now, James goes on, "My solution, or rather Stumpf's (for in my book I am but the humble follower of the eminent Munich psychologist), was to take neither of these objectionable alternatives, but (challenging the hasty hypothesis that composition must explain all) to admit (3) That the last elements of things may differ variously, and that their 'kinds' and bare unmediated resemblances and contrasts may be ultimate data of our world as well as provisional categories of our perception". W. James, "Mr Bradley on Immediate Resemblance", *Mind* n.s. 2, 1893, p. 208. In the same issue of *Mind*, Bradley replies that simple resemblance without identity is "sheer nonsense" (F.H. Bradley, "Professor James on Simple Resemblance", *Mind* n.s. 2, 1893, p. 509). James counter-argues that every "act of reasoning, every bit of analysis, proves the practical utility and the psychological necessity of the assumption that identical characters may be "encapsulated" in different things. But I say that there must be some things whose resemblance is not based on such discernible and abstractable identity". W. James, "Immediate Resemblance", *Mind*, n.s. 2, 1893, p. 509. As Sprigge notes, the "main thing at issue" is of sheer metaphysical nature: the "existence or being of generic universals as opposed to purely specific ones", the latter view being the one endorsed by James. T.L.S. Sprigge, *James and Bradley. American Truth and British Reality*, Chicago and La Salle, Open Court, 1993, p. 391.
224 Stumpf's objection is in [23, 1893].
225 Stumpf was one of the organizers of the Congress, which took place in 1896.

without the children! *Perhaps* the gods will provide the means! but I have no very strong hopes. Meanwhile I enclose a sheet from her,[226] written yesterday, and am with warmest regards to you all, your faithful friend,

Wm James

---

226 Not preserved.

[25, 1893]

Cambridge (Mass) Sept. 12. 93

My dear Stumpf

Let me announce to you that we have arrived safely at home after an admirably smooth voyage, and that after 15 months of pensions & hotels the comforts of our own house are most enjoyable. It has been a costly, but on the whole a profitable year to all, especially to the children who have been made much more perceptive and intelligent than they would have been without all the travel they have had.

I also have a business matter to propound to you. The American Journal of Psychology edited by G. Stanley Hall[227] has always left much to be desired. Its field is very narrow and much of its work ill done. During the past year Profs. Baldwin, Cattell and Munsterberg have been negotiating with Hall to see if some arrangement might not be made for improving the Journal, but everything has failed, and the result is that a new Journal is to be started, under the title (probably) of "the Psychological Review,"[228] with Baldwin and Cattell as chief editors, and all the Professors of Psychology in the american universities (except Jastrow and Hall)[229] as co-operating editors. Such names as Ladd, Münsterberg, Donaldson, James, Scripture etc etc.[230] I cannot but hope that the new Review will prove good. It will be published by the great house of Macmillan in both countries.

The Editorial Committee now request you (through my hand) to permit your name to be placed on the title-page as co-operating editor. Binet has already allowed his name to be so used for France. I feel quite sure that the *character* of the Review will be such that you need have no mistrust about your name being connected with it. On the other hand what the editors particularly desire is that your name figuring on the title should be a guarantee to other Germans of your own confidence in the capacity of the other editors. We do not expect that you should take your *duties* very seriously, but should be exceedingly grateful for any thing you may be able to send in the way of

---

227 Granville Stanley Hall (1846–1924), professor at Johns Hopkins University, founder of the *American Journal of Psychology* in 1887.
228 *The Psychological Review*, ed. by J. McKeen Cattell and J. Mark Baldwin, New York, Macmillan (1st issue 1894). Stumpf contributed to the second issue with an essay on Helmholtz, who had died in 1894: C. Stumpf, "Hermann von Helmholtz and the New Psychology", *Psychological Review* 2, 1895, pp. 1–12.
229 Joseph Jastrow (1863–1944).
230 George Trumbull Ladd (1842–1921); Henry Herbert Donaldson (1857–1938); Edward Wheeler Scripture (1864–1945).

1.) Articles;
2.) Reviews or bibliographic abstracts;
3.) Suggestions as to articles, information about books of which we ought to give a prompt account, etc.
4.) Items of "news" from the German psychological world which might interest our readers.

I will undertake either myself to translate or to guarantee a good translation of any MS., long or short, which you may send for publication.

Pray think favorably of this. We all, including Münsterberg, think that there is no German psychologist whose name would so honour and adorn the new Journal, as yours. And I earnestly hope that you may yield to our desire.

I hope that you are having a good vacation in the Tyrol. Nothing agrees with *me* as well as the mountains. With affectionate regards to all your family, I am as ever yours faithfully

Wm James

[26, 1894]

95 Irving St. Cambridge, Mass. | Jan. 24. 94

My dear Stumpf,

I had been promising myself the pleasure of writing you a letter of New Year's greeting on January 1st, but Jan. 1st found me in bed with influenza and I have regained my strength so slowly that with all the arrears of duty I had to attend to as soon as I began to get well, this letter has been postponed to this day. – First of all, let me congratulate you on the Berlin Professorship,[231] for which you were of course the most suitable candidate, and your appointment to which made Baldwin, Cattell Münsterberg and myself all very glad. I only feared that Berlin might prove a rasping, fatiguing, and *ungemüthlich*[232] place to live in, and that you might be buying honour, if you accepted the appointment, at the price of peace of soul. But Münsterberg tells me that they have exempted you from responsibility about a laboratory, and that is a great point gained.[233] I may say that I myself enjoy inward peace and a good professorial conscience for the first time, now that Münsterberg has taken charge of the entire experimental field. Needless to say that if I had lived 1000 years I should not have done what he has been doing in the past two years here. He is a wonderful organizer, methodical to the last degree, our laboratory being a picture to look upon since he has taken hold; and he is moreover a most high minded and lovable human being, so that I can only be thankful for the inspiration that led me to tempt him away from Freiburg. My only fear now is that his stay with us may be short, for although he likes America so far, and perhaps sees it in too ideal a light, his ambition of course would be better fulfilled by a German Professorship. But the future will decide. We have a three weeks' holiday from lecturing at present, and with characteristic energy he has gone to California in

---

231 Stumpf moved to Berlin in 1894. "I never imagined that I could leave Munich again, but, after five years, as in Prague and Halle, temptation approached me once more. Althoff tendered me an invitation to Berlin, where they wanted an experimental psychologist, when Zeller resigned, and Dilthey represented the historical approach. Although the call was a distinct honor, I had never felt any love for Berlin, and feared especially that there I should not be able to carry out my scientific life-work as I had planned it, so I declined. But, after a few weeks, I began to realize that Munich, after all, was not the right place to realize my ambitions". *Autobiography*, p. 401. As Langfeld puts it, in 1894 Stumpf gained "the most coveted chair of philosophy in Germany". Langfeld, *Carl Stumpf*, cit., p. 318.
232 "Uncomfortable".
233 Stumpf preferred to begin humbly, with a "psychological seminary, which started in three dark back rooms" before developing it "into a large institute". *Autobiography*, p. 402. See also Ash, *Gestalt Psychology*, cit., p. 33 ff.; Sprung, *Carl Stumpf. Eine Biographie*, cit., p. 132 ff.

order to visit the educational institutions there, and the principal colleges on the way. Some 13,000 kilometers of railroad in 3 weeks seems to me a bit too much! – We had a rare passage home, the Ocean like a lake, and we found our own clean house just as we had left it, and very comfortable after our fifteen months of pension-life. But I found it very hard to begin teaching again. I had been rather melancholy all summer, but it grew acute with my lectures. *I shrank to nothing, psychology shrank to nothing* – etc. It passed away, however, and now not a trace of it is left. But it has taught me the lesson that 15 months is too long a vacation for a man like me to take. Teaching is such an artificial discipline, that one loses the habit of it almost immediately, and seems to forget all that one ever knew. At present I have "Cosmology" and "Mental Pathology" (taken in a wide sense), 3 + 2 hours a week throughout the year, and "psychology" (3 hours a week) until the middle of march. – Our new Psychological review, of which your name adorns the cover,[234] promises well. I think that B. & C.[235] will be good editors, and if you will only occasionally write a few pages, or give them timely advice about German books or news, the thing will succeed. It is a bad time to start such an enterprise, for the country is groaning under the worst financial depression it has ever known. With the passage of the bill reducing the tariff, & with the beginning of the Spring, business will probably revive. Meanwhile every one is trying to save money, and the poor are in a sad condition of distress. Fortunately the winter so far has been a mild one. – Our university has even had to dismiss instructors; but our *own* income is, so far, not reduced, altho' we are trying to spend as little as possible in order to repair the frightful ravages left by our European year. – Ladd is just out with a new and heavy-looking "psychology".[236] From all the new psychologies either published or about to appear, there *ought* to be *some* sedimentary deposit of truth – I devoutly hope that it may be clearly discernible by all! To me the sort of thing that Pierre Janet has just done in his "Etat Mental des hystériques"[237] seems to outweigh in importance all the "exact" laboratory

---

234 Stumpf's name is included in the list of co-operators until vol. 13 of 1906.
235 Baldwin and Cattell. See above, [25, 1893].
236 G.T. Ladd, *Psychology: Descriptive and Explanatory. A Treatise of the Phenomena, Laws and Development of Human Mental Life*, New York, Scribner, 1894. James's claim that "there can be no science of psychology except a cerebral psychology" is considered by Ladd "highly prejudicial to the interests of scientific psychology" (pp. 11–12). See also W. James, "Review of G.T. Ladds Psychology: Descriptive and Explanatory", *Psychological Review* 1, 1894, p. 286, where James critically highlights the preponderance of the "descriptive" over the "explanatory" part.
237 P. Janet, *État mental des hystériques*, 2 vols., Paris, Rueff et Cie, 1892–1894; 2nd edition Paris, Alcan, 1911.

measurements put together. For of what laboratory experiments made with brass instruments can one say that they have opened an entirely new chapter in human nature, an led to a new method of relieving human suffering? Not even of the ophthalmoscope[238] can *all* that be said. – We had Helmholtz here, by the bye, in the autumn. A fine looking old fellow, but with formidable powers of holding his tongue, and answering you by a friendly inclination of the head. His wife was a *femme du monde*, however, and fully made up for his lack of conversation. Another countryman of yours, Hagen from Konigsberg, for many years Professor of Entomology at Harvard,[239] died here this winter after a sad illness of nearly three years. Also a *herrlicher Mensch*.[240] – I think of the strong good air, the horizontal spaces, the noble architecture both German and Greek, of Munich, the beer, the picture, the whole civilization there, as an *el Dorado* to which I wish I could return.[241] I should think that you and Mrs. Stumpf would hate to leave so good a dwelling place. I fear I never may return. One should not be a cosmopolitan, one's soul becomes "disaggregated" as Janet would say. Parts of it remain in different places, and the whole of it is nowhere. One's native land seems foreign. It is not a wholly good thing, and I think I suffer from it. But it is a danger that menaces not *you*. Please take the heartiest wishes from both of us for your continued prosperity in 1874. Harry too sends Gluckwünsche[242] and regards to Rudi and the younger boy. I am as ever,

your most affectionate | Wm James

---

238 The ophthalmoscope was invented by Helmholtz in 1851. See A. Tuchman, "Helmholtz and the German Medical Community" in *Hermann von Helmholtz and the Foundations of Nineteenth-Century Science*, ed. by D. Cahan, Berkeley, University of California Press, 1993, pp. 50–108.
239 Hermann August Hagen (1817–1893).
240 "Lovely person".
241 James had previously seen Munich quite differently. He didn't even consider Stumpf's advice of a trial period in Munich for his European stay: see above, [20, 1892].
242 "Good wishes".

[27, 1894]

Cambridge, April 1 1894

My dear Stumpf

My former pupil Mr. Arthur H. Pierce,[243] who has been assistant in our Psychological Laboratory for a year (two years practically) is going to Germany to study psychology and philosophy. I venture to recommend him to you, as a man of the highest character as well as intelligence, to whom your advice may be precious. He will not ask you for more – at any rate at first.

Heartiest greetings to you all from yours faithfully

Wm James

---

243 As for his Berlin stay, Arthur Henry Pierce frankly voices frustration and disappointment in a letter to James: "Stumpf has fitted up two rooms to be used as a Lab. but so far he has begun no independent researches with his students. It has been all demonstrations up to now, a couple of courses of this kind being given by Dr. Schumann, while Stumpf himself gives a course in systematic psychology and a seminar". He goes on: "Stumpf's idea, as he once expressed it to me, is that in the future each Lab. will have its own narrow specialty and remain true to that. He is evidently doing what he can to bring about this condition of things. They have now very little apparatus and only a small library, and about twenty-five men are attending the Seminar and laboratory courses. Stumpf is, as you know, a very pleasing person to meet personally, but in the lecture-room he is unutterably dry and tedious, illustrates everything by some experiment in sound, and the last semester had only about forty students to listen to him. I cannot really see why Berlin should have called such a man to be at the head of what ought to be a delightfully attractive department. I suppose 'politics' was somewhere underneath it all" [*Corr.* 8, pp. 13–14].

[28, 1895]

95, Irving Street | Cambridge | April 12. 95

My dear Stumpf

I fear that it may be too late for me actually to *introduce* to you my friend George M. Stratton, psychologist from California.[244] But I should like to send you a word of *recommendation* of him. He is an excellent man intellectually and morally, who is preparing to teach psychology in the California State university, and who is worthy of any special favour that it may be in your power to extend.

Our correspondence languishes, my dear friend, but we can both understand the reason. I am always overworked, and I hope that on your part Berlin is not proving too terrible a taskmistress. The multiplication of one[']s relations to life in a place like that is destructive to all inner peace and harmony.

Believe me, with best greetings to yourself and to dear Mrs. Stumpf, as well as the boys,

yours always truly | Wm James

---

244 George Malcolm Stratton (1865–1957). On the same day of this letter, James wrote to Stratton: "I am a sinful creature to have left you all winter without a line either of friendliness or of introduction to Stumpf [...] I suppose that by this time you are beyond the need of any introduction to Stumpf, to whom I nevertheless send you a brief line of recommendation. I am sorry to hear so many Americans write of his lectures as very dry. But he is clear and a born analyst, and a true hearted man" [*Corr.* 8, p. 24]. Stratton had probably also complained about Stumpf's lectures.

[29, 1895]

Cambridge | Mass. | Dec. 18. 1895.

My dear Stumpf,

It did my eyes good to see our handwriting once more and I was gladder still to hear the pleasant words in which you urge me not to be absent from Munich next summer.[245]

I wish for many reasons I could go. Such things keep one from fossilizing and prolong one's possibilities of "Adaptation". Nevertheless I have little hope. I ruined myself financially by my last excursion *en famille* to Europe, and nothing but the need of foreign travel for my health could justify so speedy a repetition of the process. Moreover, it unsettles my americanism (that tender plant) to go too often abroad, and that must be weighed against the intellectual and social advantages of the Congress. It is no light matter to feel foreign in one's native land. I am just beginning to feel american again, when this temptation comes! I should like to see you, and a very few others. I should like to see Munich, and then spend a month in Tyrol, but I don't think I can or shall, and *my name must on no account be announced*. I am heavily worked this year, but doing nothing original. As I grow older I get impatient (and incompetent) of details and turn to broad abstractions. I wish to get relieved of psychology as soon as possible, but am trying at present to keep Münsterbergs nest warm for him ere his return,[246] which we all pray for, for he proved an efficient, and in fact an invaluable man here. There are many valuable attributes, even in a professor, beside infallibility and taking one man with another, M[ünsterber]g. is about as infallible as any one who takes as broad a field. I am glad Dr. Schumann has charge of most of your laboratory operations.[247] There are two classes of men, and the regular routine of the lab. can only be well carried on those trained from youth *ad hoc*.[248] I also re-echo your groans about Berlin.

---

245 The reference is to Stumpf's lost letter of invitation to the Congress of psychology in Munich. James did not attend the congress. A letter to Sidgwick concerning psychical research was read in Munich by Sidgwick's wife: W. James, "Final American Report: Letter to Henry Sidgwick", in *Dritter International Congress für Psychologie in München vom 4–7 August 1896*, München, Lehmann, 1897.
246 See below, [30, 1896] and the footnotes.
247 Friedrich Schumann (1863–1940), Stumpf's assistant in Berlin in 1894.
248 Langfeld notes: "Stumpf discovered early in his career that he lacked manual dexterity and he left all the details of the experimental set-up, including his own, to his assistants. It was a rare occasion when he appeared in the students' research room. For example, he only once made an observation in my visual experiment and then it was a hurried five-minute visit motivated by anxiety over the unorthodox results I was obtaining. Yet one realized that he felt

Your going there was a case of obedience to the army maxim of accepting promotion "though it lead to hell." And meanwhile you are publishing hardly at all. Does the Aesthetik come on?[249]

But enough. I am much pressed for time these days. Accept both for Frau S. and yourself my most affectionate regards. I suppose that "Rudi" is in the University.[250] My Harry entered this fall. We are all well.

Always truly yours | Wm. James.

How finely you are *organizing* the Congress! Of Cossman or his translation I know nothing.[251] I withdrew my authorization 3 years ago.

---

his responsibility for the work of his laboratory, especially when he began to criticize the final thesis". Langfeld, *Carl Stumpf*, cit., p. 318.
249 James refers to the 3rd volume of *Tonpsychologie*, which was never completed.
250 Born in 1881, Rudolf was only 14 years old.
251 See above, [15, 1891].

[30, 1896]

BERLIN W. | NÜRNBERGERSTRASSE 14 | 13 Oct. 1896

Dear friend,

I have let a long pause arise in our correspondence. But you have certainly pardoned me given the extraordinary work that was to be done for the congress; and this was in fact the primary reason for my silence. I had unending correspondence with foreign scholars and with the general secretary.[252] The latter proved himself all-too independent in his arrangements. I was – said in confidence – at the point of resigning several times, but I let myself be swayed by my colleagues to endure the situation for the sake of the affair.

I feel the congress has nevertheless succeeded as much as it was possible under the given circumstances. I certainly share with others the impression that too many talks have been accepted, including some very insignificant ones. However, since I was not in the local committee,[253] I could only exercise a slight influence on this; one also has to admit that it is difficult to find the limits and to make judgments on the sole basis of the subject matter.

Yesterday I received a report from Baldwin in the "Nation", from which I see that he gave expression to his dissatisfaction with the organization.[254] I must objectively admit that he is mostly correct. Mind you, his sharp criticism is very odd coming from Baldwin (who had also called on you the most to represent America, whom I had already asked a year before to give a talk and who still otherwise is so productive), since he did not contribute *a single word* to our scientific discussions – he must have intervened perhaps at some point in the discussion when I did not notice.[255] I am sorry now that America, where a rich

---

[252] Stumpf presided the Munich Congress along with Theodor Lipps. The secretary was Schrenk-Notzing.

[253] Stumpf had moved from Munich to Berlin in 1884.

[254] J.M. Baldwin, "The Third Congress of Psychology", *The Nation. A Weekly Journal Devoted to Politics, Literature, Science and Art* 63, No 1628, 1896, pp. 192–193. "The tendency to allow the popular attendance upon the meetings to swamp the scientific proceedings was more marked in Munich, and it is not too much to say that this constituted a very great defect in the arrangements" (p. 192).

[255] However, Baldwin describes the "crowded condition of the programme" as follows: "besides the general meetings, which came in the forenoon sessions, the committee arranged for five sections all running simultaneously [...]. Besides the constant interruptions and great confusion which this produced, it practically prevented a person from hearing any reader whom he especially desired to hear. Since the time limits were not enforced upon the papers or discussions, one could never tell how far on this section or that had progressed, and so could not time his presence for any particular reader". Baldwin, *The Third Congress of Psychology*, cit., p. 192.

development is cropping up, was not represented at all in the talks.[256] It is not our fault![257]

Meanwhile, I have picked up the most pleasant memories of the contact with the scholars of various countries, and now regret not having interacted more amply with some of them; e.g., with Mr. Strong,[258] who I thought was an acute mind. We briefly covered his controversy with you in the seminar, along with some chapters from your Psychology.

If you wanted to do me a favor, it would be this: that you monitor a little the English translation of my speech, which, if I remember correctly, is supposed to appear in the Psychol. Review.[259] I no longer know exactly whether it was Mr. Baldwin or Mr. Buchner[260] who sought approval from me for it. In the French translation (Revue scientif.) [261] there are dire misunderstandings.

Am I fooling myself, or was there a bit of resentment about German psychologists in your last letter to me? You seem dissatisfied that we do not show Münsterberg an equally unconditional appreciation as we do for you, and you fear "losing too much of your Americanism" in a new trip to Europe.[262] I was a little taken aback by this, and I suspect it was Münsterberg who painted you the picture of Germany as a Philistine country, on account of his discontent over the scant appreciation that he finds here. Gradual differences in the appraisal of certain qualities in third parties could indeed pull us apart in a way: but I don't see how this should give rise to resentment among us. Anyway,

---

[256] "When we take into account the fact that Germany is to-day the country where psychology is most vigorously and successfully pursued, it follows that this Congress is, up-to-date, the greatest gatherings of eminent psychologists ever seen. As to France, the attendance was disappointing in numbers [...] the same is true of the British contingent. The other countries, except America, where adequately represented; the small attendance on our side of the water being a matter of more surprise in view of the tendency of our professors to take their vacations abroad [...]". Baldwin, *The Third Congress of Psychology*, cit., p. 192.

[257] Münsterberg also complained about the absence of "Stanley Hall, Sully, Binet and many others who announced papers". Bjork, *The Compromised Scientist*, cit., p. 54.

[258] Charles Augustus Strong (1862–1940). On September 2nd, 1896 James wrote to Münsterberg: "I have just had a few words about the Congress from Wadsworth, Strong and Baldwin" [*Corr.* 8, p. 197].

[259] No English edition of Stumpf's opening speech could be found. C. Stumpf, "Eröffnungsrede des Präsidenten, Prof. Dr Carl Stumpf", *Dritter International Congress für Psychologie in München vom 4–7 August 1896*, München, Lehmann, pp. 3–16; published (with modifications) as "Leib und Seele" in C. Stumpf, *Philosophische Reden und Vorträge*, Leipzig, Barth, 1910, pp. 65–93.

[260] Edward Franklin Buchner (1868–1929).

[261] C. Stumpf, "L'âme et le corps". *La Revue Scientifique* 6, 11, 1896, pp. 321–326.

[262] [29, 1895].

perhaps I am closer to you regarding Münsterberg more than most of my colleagues, but for external reasons it was entirely impossible to admit him here as a private lecturer [*Privatdozent*] according to his wishes. We are over-full with faculty members and had to reject about *10* similar petitions in this *one* year! An exception could not be made here without harming the others, even if Münsterberg had the greatest claim due to his previous positions. At any rate, he has now gladly obtained a professorship in Zürich.[263]

Enclosed is my photography for friendly memories. Of course, please do not let Baldwin become aware of any of my statements above; on a personal level, we have understood each other very well, and he held a nice speech during the banquet in the town hall. Hopefully you will not repay me tit for tat for my silence – I hope to hear from you soon! I now look forward again to the work to come. Heartfelt greetings from house to house!

PS. Did you receive my speech?[264]   Your true C Stumpf

---

[263] Bjork, *The Compromised Scientist*, cit., p. 54. Münsterberg would eventually go back to Harvard in 1897.

[264] Probably Stumpf, *Eröffnungsrede des Präsidenten*, previously mentioned in this letter.

[31, 1896]

Cambridge, Mass., Nov. 24, 1896.

My dear Stumpf:
Your long and friendly letter was an extreme satisfaction to me. I trust you will pardon my sending you a typed answer. I have so much work that I have lately found it necessary to dictate my correspondence, and the luxury is so great that I cannot bear to go back to autographic script. Your account of the congress was highly interesting, and the most complete account I had received except from Sidgwick.[265] I should think that both you and von Schrenck would have been *aufgerieben*[266] by the vast amount of business. The criticism by Baldwin in the Nation didn't seem to me anything to feel badly about, – I took it as so much reflection on how to manage a future congress so as to get the best possible results.[267] Many of the leaflets which were sent to me were full of interest, and I confess that the quantity of material astonished me. As for myself, I have given up trying to keep abreast of the progress of experimental psychology. Communications succeed each other so abundantly, and what they contain is usually so much a matter of hair splitting, that the experimental ones make no impression upon my memory at all; though this, I know, is, in part, a symptom of senile degeneration. I feel (though) as if I had bought the right to say good-bye to Psychology for the present, and turn myself to more speculative directions. For instance, as long as I have been teaching, I have never had an opportunity until this year to teach Kant, and you may imagine that I enjoy it very much. Next year I have some hopes of a course in Hegel, and who knows if I live long enough whether I may not get out a system of metaphysics before you have finished your Tonpsychologie?[268] I should think that from the hardness and confusion of Berlin, you would look back with occasional

---

265 Henry Sidgwick (1838–1900), professor at Cambridge and first president of the Society for Psychical Research. See above [7, 1886].
266 "Worn down".
267 "The membership was over four hundred. There was a constant flow from hall to hall, and the corridors were filled with bewildered people. Some limit must be put on the popular membership at the next congress, or the scientific people will yield the field to the sightseers and amateurs". Baldwin, *The Third Congress of Psychology*, cit., p. 192.
268 "Towards the end of his career, James made repeated allusions to the metaphysics which he was about to write. He was not spared to accomplish his purpose with that completeness and technical rigor for which he hoped. Some will say that he found the difficulties insuperable, but the perpetual freshness and fecundity of his mind up to the year of his death must cast doubt upon such a judgment". *Thought and Character* 1, p. 462.

regrets to the relative simplicity of Munich. I found Munich so sympathetic, that if three years hence I take another sabbatical year, I imagine that I shall spend the winter in that place.[269] If so, I shall trust to a summer in Tyrol with your family close by, and some walks through the mountains with you and one or two other chosen spirits, such as Flournoy of Geneva.[270]

I am really amused at what you say of my "Verstimmung uber die deutschen Psychologen".[271] I did not know that I had expressed any, and can't now remember the passage in my letter to which you refer. It must have been some general pessimism. But I am still more amused that you should describe it to Munsterberg's influence. My fear of losing my Americanism if I went abroad again was entirely complimentary to your side of the Atlantic. Civilization is so much more advanced in many ways with you, and the American so quickly catches the European tone, that when he comes back he finds his own country in many ways foreign and displeasing, and it takes him a long time to resume his old, simple minded relations with it. I have suffered from this discord many times, particularly after my last return home; I am now on thoroughly good terms with my native land, and dread very much to throw myself out of tune again. Like all ideal things, harmony of this kind must be worked for and bought by certain renunciations. We have many ideal things here, and the best thing an American can do is to stay at home as much as possible, and try to increase them. Therefore, I am making an effort not to go to Europe again until 1900, when my regular leave of absence from the University falls due. Munsterberg, so far from appearing "disgruntled," at not being able to go to Berlin, explained to me the situation as you have just explained it, agreeing entirely with its reasonableness. The rumor about him and Zurich was premature, & although they have sounded him, it doesn't seem yet to be quite a practical question. We are still hoping to hear that he may return to us next year, whether he goes to Zürich or not. He has organized our laboratory instruction most admirably, and is the most valuable man for our purposes whom I know.

---

269 See above, [26, 1894].
270 James had met Théodore Flournoy (1854–1920) at the Paris Congress of 1889. They kept an intense correspondence: *The Letters of William James and Théodore Flournoy*, ed. by R. Le Clair, Madison, Milwaukee and London, The University of Wisconsin Press, 1966. In 1910 James accepted an invitation from the *Association chrétienne d'Etudiants* to deliver a conference in Swiss. After James's death, Flournoy considered it a "sacred duty" to substitute him and take the "opportunity of evoking for my young hearers the memory of the man of genius, the rare spirit and the true friend who had been so suddenly taken from us". Th. Flournoy, *La Philosophie de William James*, Eng. trans. *The Philosophy of William James*, New York, Holt & Co., 1917 (p. iv).
271 "Resentment about German psychologists": see above, [30, 1896].

Thank you for your photograph, which shows you very little changed. I will send you the next one I get taken. As for your presidential address, I will add something to-morrow.

Nov. 28, 1896.

I read the address with extreme satisfaction. I think it is high time that someone in such an authoritative position should raise a voice against the excessively shallow dogmatism of the parallelists, who simply affirm the truth of a conception that they conceive as neat and pretty. You did the business in a perfectly masterly way. I especially admired the breadth of the treatment and the skill with which you avoided entering into any minute or secondary considerations. I can't help thinking that the day of the cruder parallelism, as the last word of scientific philosophy, is passed. That thistle needs only to be firmly grasped to show its feebleness! I have written to Baldwin to send me the translation of address, and will carefully look over it before it goes to press.[272]

I am glad that you say such kind words of Strong, who is an extremely honest and accurate minded fellow, and of Miller,[273] who is one of the most delightful beings I ever knew. From him I hope good things for philosophy.

I am putting a book through the press now, a collection of essays, of which I will send you a copy as soon as it appears.[274] I suppose Rudi is now a student in the University, belonging to a corps, and inviting and accepting duels. My wife sends her best regards, and I am, as always dear Stumpf,

Yours affectionately

---

[272] See above, [30, 1896]. No evidence could be found that James and Baldwin touched upon the translation of Stumpf's speech. See *Corr.* 8, p. 186, 206.

[273] The reference is to Dickinson Sergeant Miller (1868–1963). However, in his letter [30, 1896] Stumpf mentioned only Strong, not Miller. James wrote to Miller: "I wish I could have been with you at Munich and heard the deep-lunged Germans roar at each other. I care not for the matters uttered, if I only could hear the voice" [*Corr.* 8, p. 195, Aug. 30]. On Strong and Miller, *Corr.* 9, pp. 221–222.

[274] W. James, *The Will to Believe, and Other Essays in Popular Philosophy*, New York and London, Longmans, Green & Co., 1897.

[32, 1898]

BERLIN W. | NÜRNBERGERSTRASSE 14 | 30 Oct. 1898

Dear friend!
How long we have not written to one another! But my allegiance to you is always the same; only the burden of working shortens the correspondence. I have to thank you heartily, however, for your booklet on immortality.[275] It is good that representatives of scientific psychology are taking this issue of the human heart into hand once again, instead of always investigating mere reaction times. I can say that this has occupied me all my life more than anything else, and lately I have also learned to consider the influence of the belief in immortality on ethical intuitions ever more highly. I believe the *value* of life sinks nearly to nothing without such an assumption. But time and again I see around me honorable and optimistic [*lebensmutig*] people that slog through without these beliefs and carry their heads higher than me. And so I wait to see whether my own views will clear up a bit more.

Yesterday I received an article by H.T. Lukens from the "Ped. Sem". Oct. 1898,[276] in which he made a highly superficial and inappropriately humorous[277]

---

[275] W. James, *Human Immortality: Two Supposed Objections to the Doctrine*, Boston and New York, Houghton Mifflin, 1898.

[276] Hermann Tyson Lukens (1865–1949) published a report in Stanley Hall's pedagogical journal. Lukens explains the origin of his text: "During the past academic year the writer has made a pedagogic trip through Germany, France, and Great Britain. His attention was directed mainly to university courses bearing on psychology and pedagogy, and the aim was to meet men and get ideas". H.T. Lukens, "Notes Abroad", *The Pedagogical Seminary* 6, No 1, Oct. 1898, p. 114. As to Stumpf's Institute, Lukens notes: "Stumpf is a wonderful man in his field and he keeps pretty close to it, thoroughly German in his specialistic ideas, and with no interest for anything else. His assistant, Dr. Schumann, is an able, industrious and obliging worker, who is sure to rise to eminence in his subject. The laboratory occupies four rooms, dark and cramped for space, but containing several pieces of apparatus of much interest and adapted to the special investigations under way on sound. Some new work on the tendency to group similar objects into units and the influence of this on the formation of judgments of differences is in progress". Stumpf probably took more offense at the inclement comparison with Wundt's Leipzig: "Berlin is badly off for a satisfactory university building, and after being's accustomed to the commodious and hygienic Leipzig palaces, one is painfully impressed with the poor lighting and bad ventilation at Berlin" (p. 118). Langfeld gives a similar account of the Institute in Dorotheenstraße 5: in 1920, "the laboratory was moved from the rather gloomy and malodorous apartment to twenty-five rooms in the imperial palace". Langfeld, *Carl Stumpf*, cit., p. 318.

[277] "Dilthey gives a clear, good note book, as the German student says, and pounds it in with a ridiculously monotonous left-handed gesture. Indeed the automatisms of the professors are extremely interesting. Paulsen carries a pencil, which he places carefully on the desk when he begins to speak. In about five minutes or less he picks it up as he would have a new thought

travel report. Since such reports have now appeared already several times in American written work, in the future we will receive less accommodatingly men who stick their nose into our institute only for half an hour, or deign to visit a lecture in order then to publish a disparaging judgment about the people and the matter.

In contrast, Fullerton, who was here a few days in the summer, was very pleasant to me, and I was sorry we couldn't talk longer.

I pass along with zeal the studies on tone, in order to finally get to other and higher things; but my hands are slow, since my nerves have long been ruined. My family is well and the children are growing satisfactorily. A thousand greetings from house to house!

Your true Stumpf

---

and plays awhile with it in his hands, and then as carefully places it on the desk again just as he finishes one topic and is about to go over to another. Wundt makes only one gesture, an ambidextral outward movement with his hands as he leans on his elbows. Eucken looks at the ceiling. Richet makes a continuous double-handed gesture of depreciation, as much as to say: 'This is all very trifling and trite, I know.'" Lukens, *Notes Abroad*, cit., p. 119.

[33, 1899]

Villa Luise, Bad-Nauheim, Hessen | Aug. 30. 1899

My dear Stumpf

It will doubtless surprise you to get a letter from me with the above dating – but here I am, and have been here for a month. *Leider als Curgast!*[278] I discovered last November that I had a slight mitral insufficiency with some dilatation of the heart, though the symptoms were but slightly troublesome. Last June I went to my beloved Adirondack hills, and got lost in the woods one day, converting what was to have been a walk of a few hours into a 13 hours scramble, etc.[279] This produced a bad dilatation, with severe chest-symptoms, & for that I am now under treatment! I suppose I shall have to stay three weeks longer, and only after that shall I know subjectively that I am better, for the baths arouse all sorts of queer cardiac feelings in me. Meanwhile my doctor expresses himself as satisfied with my progress as revealed to the stethoscope. We are all mortal! and the trees don't grow into the sky. I hope that you have no similar tale of misfortune to send me in return for mine. In any case my mountain climbing days (such as they were) are over. To continue on the chapter of the Ego, I have leave of absence from work for the next academic year, and have also an appointment to give the "Gifford lectures" for this year and next, at the University of Edinburg. These are two courses, of ten lectures each, on "Natural Religion," public, and very well paid, so that it is both an honour and a profit to receive the appointment. But I am terribly unprepared. This Kur will knock out two months from the time I expected to have to devote to their composition, so I am in no small degree anxious about this first course. I shall go immediately after I am released from Nauheim, to England and settle in some quiet place (very possibly near Cambridge) and begin to work, losing as little time as possible. I shall certainly have to return to Nauheim next summer, and it may be that we shall then meet. I may possibly be at the Paris "Congress."[280] Is it likely that you shall be there? I detest congresses, but the american Psych. Ass appointed me as delegate, and I didn't like to say no.

---

278 "Unfortunately, as a patient!"
279 Simon, *Genuine Reality*, cit., pp. 290–291; Richardson, *William James: in the Maelstrom of American Modernism*, cit., p. 388.
280 *Quatrième Congrès International de Psychologie*, Tenu à Paris, du 20 au 26 Août 1900 [...]. *Compte rendu des séances et texte des mémoires publiés par les soins de P. Janet*, Paris, Alcan, 1901. James would eventually not go to this Congress.

It seems impossible injustice that Dreyfuss[281] should not be acquitted. If he is acquitted, France will have turned a very bad corner, and everything will probably go well. If not, no one knows what will happen! – Does Berlin better agree with you? – or is the life there still too *aufreibend*? Have you got a new book, or some more Tonpsychologie in preparation? – I find myself growing less psychological – – I have now-a-days a perfect horror of experimental psychology, for which fortunately Münsterberg is exclusively responsible, – and more metaphysical. I have certain glimmerings of new ideas, but they are very hard to make clear, and nothing will ever come of them, probably. The writing and printing of these Gifford lectures will fully occupy me for the next 3 years.[282] Write and give me good news of yourself, of Mrs. Stumpf and of all the family!

Always faithfully yours | Wm James

---

281 Sic, here and elsewhere. The reference is to the notorious Dreyfus Affair.
282 W. James, *The Varieties of Religious Experience. A Study in Human Nature,* New York and London, Longmans, Green & Co., 1902.

[34, 1899]

Wengen in Bernese Oberland | 8 Sept. 1899

Dear friend!

I am certainly surprised by your letter, and I would otherwise look so much forward to your stay in Germany – *this* stay grieves me without end. I put my confidence in the baths in Nauheim, which have done many of my acquaintances well, and I hope that you come out of them newly invigorated. But these Gifford Lectures! Can they not be postponed for a year in light of such an impediment? Does the financial gain justify the sacrifice in health? Would you not do better, in this important moment so decisive for your further lifetime, to put aside everything that hinders bodily invigoration? – True friendship and concern are the cause of these questions; I will not answer them, [for] you surely know best all the circumstances involved and are in a position to weigh them objectively against one another. Moreover, you have your revered wife as the most trusted advisor at your side, if she also, as it seems, is not with you in person at the moment.

In any case, I beg you urgently not to rush with your work!

You mention nothing at all of a personal gathering on German soil. Would you perhaps fear a disruption of your healing? In this case, of course, I have to suppress my wishes. But how easy it would have been to visit you in Nauheim for a couple of hours a few weeks ago, since the way to Switzerland goes through Nauheim, and I spent a day in Frankfurt anyway. Had I had an inkling of your stay, then nothing but your decisive veto would have hindered me from seeing you. Now, the way things stand is more difficult in that I only have a limited time before me. I must be in Berlin on the 18th or 19th, but will spend 1–2 days in Würzburg with my sisters, 17–18 Sept. If you could come there, then you would also meet Külpe. But I would gladly travel towards you, say to *Aschaffenburg*, so that we would both only have to make a daytrip without spending the night. My ticket takes me from Würzburg to Berlin, not via Frankfurt. Please write to me in complete honestly whether it is possible for you and desirable under the present circumstances to make such an excursion. My Würzburg address is: Friedenstrasse 37/3. If you answer immediately, your letter will still meet me in *Luzern*, poste restante, from where I depart on the 15th.

I will likely *not* come to Paris in 1900. I am indeed much less cut out for congresses than you are and would prefer to view Paris once without the congress. In addition to that, there is still the turmoil of a world fair – the thought is already making me nervous.²⁸³ Concerning the French, I must unfortunately say that for me, that nation – abstracting of course from particular people – inspires less and less respect. If the truth about Dreyfuss also comes to light – is it not already sad beyond all measure, that one should place so many hindrances to the truth? I am reading today that Germany and Italy have agreed to Labori's request to bring Schwartzkoppen and Panizzardi to testify, that even the advocate of the indictment, Carrière, objected to nothing in this proposal – and the president equally rejected it!!²⁸⁴ Could one show any more clearly that one does not *want* the truth? –

Dear James, we are better men in that we *want* the truth. Whether we find it is another question. And I say this especially with regard to a rivalry that has arisen between us, whether you (as it seems) know of it or not. You probably have not yet received my last essay "Über den Begriff der Gemütsbewegung"²⁸⁵?

Since I have taken a position against your theory²⁸⁶ in it, I initially meant to send you a letter as an accompaniment to it, but I did not make it before my departure and took comfort in the fact that you would be in a position, more than any other living philosopher, to unite personal friendship with scientific rivalry, and that no words would be required in order to secure the continuation of our personal relationship. Anyway, at our get-together, if it were possible, I would best avoid any discussion so as not to hinder in any way the rest that you need.

Things went strangely with Brentano about my essay. I thought that I quite agreed with him regarding emotions [*Affecte*], but then I received a 7-sheet long letter²⁸⁷ from him in which he declared himself decisively for *your* view and

---

283 Presided by Théodule Ribot, the Fourth International Congress of Psychology took place on 20–26 August, simultaneously with the 1900 Paris Exposition (April-November).
284 Stumpf refers to some controversial aspects of the Dreyfus trial.
285 In this essay, Stumpf criticizes James among others: if emotions are organic sensations, every organic sensation (stomach-ache, etc.) must be regarded as an emotion too. C. Stumpf, "Über den Begriff der Gemüthsbewegung", *Zeitschrift für Psychologie und Physiologie der Sinnesorgane* 21, 1899, p. 84. However, emotions differ from organic sensations as to their quality, intensity and temporal progression (p. 85 ff.).
286 W. James, "What is an Emotion?", *Mind* 9, 1884, pp. 188–205.
287 Brentano reacted to Stumpf's essay *Über den Begriff der Gemüthsbewegung* with a long letter on 18 August 1889, where Stumpf is charged of adopting an unorthodox standpoint: above all, for Brentano, Stumpf fails to adopt the "distinction of the intentional in-existence of the object as an important principle of classification". F. Brentano, *Briefe an Carl Stumpf 1867–1917*, ed. by G. Oberkofler. Graz, Akademische Druck- und Verlagsanstalt, 1989, p. 115. Brentano does not exactly endorse James's doctrine of emotions; rather, he considers his own theory a better arrangement of a "sensualistic" point of view (p. 122) somehow analogous to James's. Brentano expresses his disappointment for the scarce attention paid by Stumpf to his

against mine. A somewhat embarrassing effect of my argumentation! If he someday goes to publication with his work, you will have in him a pillar for your doctrine of emotions that is not to be scorned. But what is the truth? I know one thing for sure: that it would cost me no inner negotiation at all, if I convinced myself of the opposite, also to *admit* it and to revoke earlier explanations, sans phrase, following your noble example in other cases.

I can only report good things, thank God, about me and my family. Berlin suits me completely, there is a big amount of splendid and industrious people there, including the students. My wife certainly preferred *life* in Munich, and she is not completely used to the new home, although she had already lived there for 5 years before. As for our children, Rudi is already 18 years old. I have now taken him out of high school because he displayed an expressed talent and inclination towards *painting* – strangely enough; he is going to art school in Stuttgart on 1 October. Precisely for this reason, I have to be home soon in order to be with him for 8–10 days, and tell him this and that before his entrance into the world. How is your good Harry doing? Greet your very adored wife and your Harry, and heartfelt greetings to you from your stalwart

Stumpf

---

new doctrine of sensory phenomena, expounded by him at the Munich congress of 1896: F. Brentano, "Über Individuation, multiple Qualität und Intensität sinnlicher Erscheinungen", in *Untersuchungen zur Sinnespsychologie*, Hamburg, Meiner, 1979^2, pp. 66–89.

[35, 1899]

Villa Luise, Bad-Nauheim | 10 Sept. 1899

My dear Stumpf,
Your letter, so full of the truest sympathy and friendship, gave both me and my wife acute pleasure. Affectionate recognition by men like you is surely to be counted among the prizes of life. Friendships of personal intimacy grow up in youth, through propinquity. A friendship like ours based on higher mental affinities and sympathy of character is the fruit of years and of work. I greatly repent now that I didn't write to you earlier, for I have been here now for just six weeks. But I was tired, dispirited, and consequently unsociable – I wished no one to see or know me in that state. I am now close to the termination of my bath-course; and it is even possible that we may get away from here on Wednesday night. If so we may yet meet in Luzern – best of all places for a meeting! It was our intention to go for 10 days to a place on the Jura above Lausanne where we spent a summer seven years ago. The D^r. has just insisted that I must not go straight to England, as I at first proposed, but spend a couple of weeks in high air as a "Nachcur,"[288] first. So we were going over Basel to Vevay, where my daughter now is, thence to Lausanne and then via Paris to England. We can go as well, or better, through Luzern, if there is only a chance of meeting you there. So let me know *immediately* your address at Luzern, and I will telegraf you as soon as the Doctor fixes the date of my last bath. I must stay till the very last. I suppose that they are doing my heart good, though it is impossible to judge by one's subjective feelings. They perturb the innervation; and both weaken & excite one, generally, so the immediate effect is on the whole disagreeable in many cases (certainly in my case) and the results only become apparent after one gets away.

In case I have to stay here longer, I think we must put off the meeting till next summer. I shall unconditionally return here next April and very likely once more next August, and a *zusammenkunft*[289] with plenty of time to arrange it will be easily brought about. And who knows? We may both yield to the temptations of the Devil and find ourselves in Paris, in spite of all our good resolutions!

No! I have not received your Essay on the Emotions,[290] and shall be too delighted to read it, whatever its conclusions may be. I think the question is introspectively an exceedingly difficult one to solve, as soon as one takes the less

---

[288] "Convalescence".
[289] "Gathering".
[290] Stumpf, *Über den Begriff der Gemütsbewegung*. See [34, 1899].

excited *stimmungen*²⁹¹ as the object of investigation. Everyone seems to admit that the feeling is from the body so far as there is violent affect. Pray send me another copy of the Essay, when you get home. Have you received a little volume of mine, called Talks to Teachers, etc. very popular.²⁹² The only thing I care to have you read in it is the last 2 articles, especially the one before the last.²⁹³

I fear I am ceasing to be a psychologist and becoming exclusively a moralist & metaphysician. I have surrendered all psychological teaching to Munsterberg and his assistant, and the thought of psychophysical experimentation, and altogether of brass-instrument and algebraic-formula psychology fills me with horror. All my future activity will probably be metaphysical – that is if I have any future activity, of which I sometimes doubt. The Gifford lectures (which have to result in 2 vols. of 300 each) ²⁹⁴ are a fine opportunity, were I only able to meet it. Don't be afraid, I shall not risk my life: the conditions are fortunately elastic enough to permit of postponement in case my health should imperatively require it. Are you not also growing cold towards the details of psychology, and turning more and more towards those widest views of life which seem the proper occupation of ones latter years?

What dreadful news is this from Rennes! It *did* seem as if the french republic were about to turn successfully round the most dangerous corner in her history; and that after this crisis a new evolution might slowly begin. It will do so yet, I believe. "Les intellectuels" have not become militant in france for nothing. But meanwhile all the difficulties are 100-fold increased by this slip into the hell-ward direction. This verdict proves that the spirit of caste is the strongest force in Society. I am glad I belong to a republic. The most grotesque thing in the trial to me has been the treatment of the diplomatic etiquette as something half divine, in spite of the fact that the diplomatic function here was one of absolute crime. If Germany and Italy do not now publish the full *corpus delicti*, with all details and names of guilty persons, they will, it seems to me be morally exactly on a par with Esterhazy – or else it will be that Dreyfuss is really guilty. But I don't believe he is: and it will be the mere insanity of etiquette

---

291 "Tempers". James discussed "subtler" emotions in *What is an Emotion?*, p. 201 ff. [*Works* 13, p. 181 ff]; and *Principles of Psychology* 2, p. 468 ff. [*Works* 9, p. 1082].
292 W. James, *Talks to Teachers on Psychology: and to Students on Some of Life's Ideals*, New York, Holt, 1899.
293 The last two chapters (XIV-XV) of *Talks to Teachers on Psychology* touch upon apperception and the will. James defines apperception "nothing more than the act of taking a thing into the mind" [*Works* 12, p. 95]. The "fate of every impression" is to "fall into a mind preoccupied with memories, ideas, and interests, and by these it is taken in"; accordingly, we "never get an experience that remains for us completely nondescript" [*Works* 12, p. 95].
294 James, *Varieties*.

and pride, if they keep silent any longer. They, and Esterhazy their faithful servant and ally, their fellow criminal, together will be cold bloodedly allowing an innocent man vicariously to suffer. It is impossible to say that their faithfulness to Esterh[azy] (or whoever the real criminal may be) will keep their tongues tied. Esterhazy is safe, and so will anyone else be safe before they speak, safe in foreign parts, & then they must give them a brilliant pension to make them happy for the rest of their days. If Esterhazy was the traitor, of course the german government owes him the largest possible pension. It is a horrible business. – But no more! I hope we shall meet. Write or telegraph. Best regards from both myself and wife to you both. Affectionately yours,

Wm James

[36, 1899]

Villa Luise Nauheim | 12. Sept. 1899

My dear Stumpf,
your telegram arrives at the very moment when I am about beginning to write to you. The doctor tells me yesterday that I have to take more baths – so I am here at least through this week. And although I might agree now to go to Aschaffenburg to meet you (say on Sunday) I think on the whole that I will not do so, but rather postpone the whole business until next summer. The truth is that the effect of the baths on my nervous system is very strong, both exhausting and exciting me. I lose sleep, my eyes are bad, I am aphasic, irritable etc. I can hardly speak german at all. In short I am not in a favorable condition to make a journey expressly to see even my dearest friend, and carry on a conversation of several hours actively. This is why I have to take a fortnight of higher air in Switzerland to tone my nerves a little before I go to England. I aspire towards solitude until I get better. Therefore we will not speak of a meeting at Aschaffenburg now, but hope for a much better meeting somewhere next summer. I shall doubtless find that my health symptoms are much better after a few weeks. The doctor is guided entirely by percussion and auscultation, and not at all by the patient's report of his subjective symptoms; and he assume[s] that I am much better than when I came. – So for the present, dear Stumpf, good bye! I will write to you from England, and hope I can give you a better account of myself when I do so. I am to settle either in London or in Cambridge, I do not yet know which. My permanent address so long I am in Europe is my bankers': Brown, Shipley & Co, London. Auf wiedersehen!

Yours always | Wm James

My two elder boys have been spending the summer as day laborers on the U.S. forestry commission in the Olympic mountains off Puget Sound, on the Pacific Ocean. It is a great opportunity for them to see their native land, and to escape the corruptions of stacked shirt civilization. Both will be in the University next year. Harry is always bachelor of Arts, and will study law. He is an extremely judicious, conscientious & healthy boy. I hope your Rudy will be a great artist.[295] From the pecuniary point of view it is a terrible profession. My wife sends her great regrets that she is not to see Mrs Stumpf and hopes for next year.

---

295 See above, [34, 1899].

[37, 1899]

Weggis, Hôt. Köhler, Tuesday 12 Sept 1899

Dear James,

I only just received your letter that was sent to me from Lucerne. As my telegram already told you, I am here until Thursday evening, but can come to Lucerne anytime. Early Friday, in any case, I am going there and want to continue on to Stuttgart on Wednesday at 1 o'clock. But if you telegraph me or write me a letter *poste restante Lucerne*, I can spare a day and spend time with you there, which I would look forward to tremendously, especially since I would also meet your revered wife. A thousand thanks for your dear letter. From my heart

Your | C Stumpf

In any case, I request your address if your stay somewhere longer.

[38, 1899]

BERLIN W. | NÜRNBERGERSTRASSE 14 | 30 Dec. 1899

Dear friend,

How are you doing? I think of you often and would be very pleased to have news from you (hopefully good news). It is a certain occasion besides this, however, that leads me to write to you today. For the 200-year jubilee of our Academy of Sciences, a number of corresponding members are supposed to be appointed. For philosophy, Dilthey has proposed Messrs. Wundt and Heinze – I did not partake in this proposal nor in the election of Wundt. On the contrary, I have proposed *you*. In the philosophical-historical category, all three are already chosen, and I do not doubt that the plenary assembly will perform the selections. If this occurs – the election happens in the first half of January – then the selections will be submitted to the Kaiser for confirmation. The pronouncement happens on 19 March, the jubilee day.

Now, a few years ago it happened that Herbert Spencer, who was appointed a Knight of the Order "pour le merite" by the Kaiser, rejected this distinction as a matter of principle. With the French, we also tend to privately ensure in advance that no rejection will occur in the case of academy selections. But no one had thought of that with Spencer. An *academic* position is now something other than an Order, and someone can be against Orders in principle, and yet accept academic dignities.

However, just in case, I wanted to hereby direct the *completely confidential* enquiry to you, whether you would accept our homage offered to you; and I would like to ask you to send me your approving answer *as soon as possible*.

I ask you to keep everything that I have shared with you here secret, with the exception of your revered wife, of course.

Things are going quite well for us, only I always suffer from lack of sleep, and for this reason I also progress slowly with my work. We send to you both the best greetings and wishes for the turn of the year – may the year bring good health and vitality for you! Wholeheartedly

Your | C Stumpf

[39, 1900]

Lamb House | RYE | 2 January, 1900.

My dear Stumpf,

Your letter was a most agreeable surprise to me this morning, both as a reminder of you, and for its interesting content. The United States Constitution forbids citizens to receive titles of nobility and orders from foreign powers, but there is nothing against the reception of academic honours; so, although I feel myself quite unworthy of so great a distinction, I shall only be too happy to accept it if conferred.

My health has run down very much since I wrote you last September; in fact I am in a deplorable condition of imbecility, and unable to make the slightest effort – even dictate this letter – without cardiac distress. I have given up my Edinburgh lectures and shall probably not be able to do any more teaching at Harvard.[296] If I can live long enough to get a couple of things written I shall only be too thankful. Under these circumstances the compliment of the Berlin Academy is unusually valuable to me. If I never write anything more, it may be my children's chief title to hereditary respectability, to be able to point to their father as a correspondent of the Academy of Sciences of Berlin!

I am glad to hear good news of yourself, though I commiserate your wakefulness. It seems a law of nature that philosophers should have bad nerves. A happy new year to you and yours, all the same; and may the next century be better than the last one – though I confess there are few signs of it at present. A real wave of barbarity seems to be flooding the world.

My address is always: c/o Brown Shipley & Co., Founders' Court
London, E.C.
With warmest thanks for your interest in my undeserving person,

I am, ever faithfully yours, | [hand] Wm James

---

296 James delivered the Gifford Lectures in 1901–1902; he resigned from Harvard in 1907.

[40, 1900]

Carqueiranne (Var) France | March 17. 1900

My dear Friend,

It is a long time since I have given you any account of myself, and in the meantime I have received your address on the Entwickelungsgedanke[297] and an invitation from Prof(?) Auwers to be present at the festival of the Academy.[298] As that takes place in a few days, I feel a certain enlivening of the Berlin department of my soul, and it seems natural to take my pen and write a little to you. First, as regards my own condition, I have good news to report. We left England the 10th. of January, and came straight down to Costebelle near Hyères. After a week at a hotel we got a cook and chambermaid and took possession of Charles Richet's empty Chateau, where we have been very comfortable ever since, our fellow occupiers during one month being F.W.H. Myers (of Cambridge, England) & his wife and two children, (he also sent to the Mediterranean with a "heart.").[299] Richet's hospitality just at this crisis has been a most extraordinarily friendly and beneficent thing for us both, and in particular exactly the kind of abode that my condition required. I feel in November into an acute and profound condition of nervous prostration, with extreme development of the cardiac sensibility. There was no visible relief till about 5 weeks ago when quite suddenly I began to feel that I was better. I am now *much* better in point of nervous and am, as you see, able to do each day a little writing. I have finished *one* (!) lecture for Edinburgh, and hope to begin the second tomorrow. [They have postponed my appointment, so my first course of ten is not due till next winter, and I feel quite sure now of getting them out in time.] I still am unable to walk except for a *very* short distance once daily; but I am mending fast, and despair has give[n] way to hope and new aggressive projects upon life. Early in May I shall go to Nauheim again & see what D^r. Schott advises. The climate here is simply superb, and the whole country between Toulon & Hyères, exquisitely beautiful. How nice it would be if I could take some drives here with *you*! In 10 days we shall proceed northwards, gradually to Lake Leman, etc. reaching Nauheim early in May.

I read your Rede[300] with great interest [The paper on Gemüthsbewegungen was left, with most of my books, in England, and I haven't read it yet] You have a roman severity of style, in all this kind of work, which makes you very

---

[297] C. Stumpf, *Der Entwicklungsgedanke in der gegenwärtigen Philosophie*, Berlin, Lange, 1899.
[298] Arthur Julius von Auwers (1838–1915), professor of Astronomy and head of the *Akademie der Wissenschaften*.
[299] Myers also suffered from a heart disease. He would die soon after, in January 1901.
[300] Stumpf, *Der Entwicklungsgedanke in der gegenwärtigen Philosophie*.

impressive – monumental, as it were – and one can make use of you for "texts." I got much *Anregung*[301] from this address. But I won't tire myself with commenting upon it now, except to call your attention to the logical possibility that out of a world of *complete* chance at the or[i]gin, during infinite time, systems of coherent order were sure to have developed, of which our world may be one, all the chance facts disconnected and ununified with that world, having long since disappeared, either from existence, or from observation from that world's point of view.[302] In my second Course of Gifford lectures, I am going to defend *radical* pluralism and tych-ism, and I hope to make a convert of you.

You don't know how pleased I feel at this honour from Berlin. The world at large will never know that it is really an honour from Professor Carl Stumpf! I suppose that Herr Auwers (what and who is he, by the way?) will send me the official programs, etc., but perhaps you will send me some newspaper with a report. It is a *tremendous* disappointment to me not to be able to go in person – not my only disappointment this year! I hope the year has gone well with you, & not too much fatigue. Pray let me know. – With best regards, in which my wife joins, to both of you, I am always faithfully yours

Wm James

---

301 "Stimulation".
302 In the speech under discussion, Stumpf introduces his cosmology: he subscribes to a form of non-theistic finalism in accordance with physical-mathematical laws. Stumpf, *Der Entwicklungsgedanke in der gegenwärtigen Philosophie*, pp. 114–115. Stumpf's self-professed "cosmological Ideas" are: the incessant mutation of the world, the reciprocal action between things, the world's progress towards higher stages and its infinity in time (p. 118 ff.).

[41, 1900]

Berlin, 23 March 1900

Dear friend!
I am quickly notifying you that you should address your notification and your thanks to the *Sekretar der the K. Akad. d. Wiss. zu Best., Geheimen Oberregierungsrat Prof. Dr. Auwers.* Anyway, I ought to say to you that you do not owe the honor to me alone, but that Dilthey was most gladly in agreement with it.[303] The celebration is now over, it brought us all rich stimulation and cheerful hours, in which the only thing I was sorely missing was you. But *how glad I am* about the better news! May it continue in this direction; we send you and your revered wife the most heartfelt wishes. I am going away in the next few days, probably to Bozen, but my address is always the local one. – The non-resident philosophers here were Höffding, von Wyk (Utrecht), Ziegler, Heinze u. Kuno Fischer.[304] Live well and a thousand greetings from your academic colleagues

Stumpf

---

[303] Dilthey praised James in "Ideas for a Descriptive and Analytic Philosophy", Eng. trans. in *Selected Works*, vol. 2, ed. by R.A. Makkreel and F. Rodi, Princeton and Oxford, Princeton University Press, 2010, p. 142, 151. In fact, "Dilthey had good reason to cite James in support of the dynamic and holistic conception of consciousness he presented in his 1894 essay, 'Ideas on Descriptive and Analytical Psychology.' For him, as for James, conscious experience is not a collection of simple sensations and their corresponding "ideas", but "a structured whole" combining intellect, feeling, and will. This whole is not static but dynamic, a 'living, unitary activity within us.' The 'dominant psychology' cannot grasp this reality, Dilthey argued, because its representatives persist in reducing 'all phenomena of consciousness to elements imagined to be atom-like'" Ash, *Gestalt* Psychology, cit., p. 72.
[304] Harald Höffding (1843–1931); Bernard H.C. van der Wijck (1836–1925); Theobald Ziegler (1846–1918); Max Heinze (see above); Kuno Fischer (1824–1907).

[42, 1900]

Costebelle, (Var) April 16. 1900
– I suppose that about this time you are returning to and to work. In a week we shall be going first to Geneva, then to Heidelberg to consult Erb, and after that probably to Nauheim for another course of baths. My nervous strength continues to get better, and this morning I wrote the last page of the 3rd lecture of my course of 10, to be given at Edinburgh next winter. I don't learn a single detail of the Akademie celebration. You forgot to send me a newspaper, and Prof. Auwers sends me nothing. What I want chiefly to know is *who the other corresponding members were*. I know only of Wundt & Heinze, of whom you wrote me in the winter. One's joy in such vanities is in inverse proportion of the number of the participants! I fear that in this case there were many. – Ought I to make any other acknowledgement that the note of thanks I sent to Auwers' invitation to come? And ought I to order my printed books sent to the library of the Academy? Address me at Prof. Fournoy's | 9. Flourissant | Geneva, Switzerland

Wm James

[43, 1900]

Bei Prof. Flournoy, in Genf. April 30. 1900 – Many thanks for your letter & enclosed list of persons honored. My diploma arrived, *via* America, by the same post. I had already thanked Auwers, from Carqueiranne, but I have just repeated it a little more formally, perhaps. It is a fine list; and as I say, I am glad of it particularly for my children's sake. The world takes these things objectively; and they won't know that the whole thing is only a sign of Prof. Stumpf's friendship! Shall I order my opera omnia sent to the library? – Are these correspondentships a newly created set of places? Or do they fill vacancies in old places? Thanks & best regards.

W.J.

c/o Brown, Shipley & Co, London.

[44, 1900]

Berlin, 20 May 1900

Dear friend!

You are now probably already sitting in Nauheim, but I am sending these lines through London to be safe. May your healing constantly progress! The beginning of spring would certainly be desirable for that – we are still freezing here. Your works will be very welcome at the library of the Academy; it is not required, however, to donate them. Correspondent positions [*Correspondentenstellen*] are not new positions, but old ones that, however, were not occupied; we had 8 free places for philosophy, and 5 are still to be awarded. By the way, I can repeat to you that Dilthey (Paulsen is not in the Academy) was in *immediate* agreement with your selection and had already spoken of it once early in the year even without my suggestion.[305] So, it is not a matter of personal friendship! A thousand greetings and wishes.

Your true | Stumpf

---

305 See above, [41, 1900].

[45, 1900]

Montreux, June 8. 1900

My dear Stumpf,

Your card reached me duly at Nauheim a fortnight ago. I should probably have written to you earlier but the baths, although four doctors conspired in recommending me to go at them again, threw me once more into such a formidable state of nervous prostration that all letter-writing had to stop and the only thing left to me for a couple of weeks seemed to be the contemplation of the vanity of human wishes. Evidently Nauheim is not meant for *me*! And I don't think I shall ever return there again. I am slowly getting back to my condition of a month ago under the influence of this higher air and shall remain in this region for some weeks longer, though I am ruminating a plan which may take me out of Switzerland in July, and of which I will give you news if it ever is carried into effect. I am disgusted with the fallibility and superficiality of doctors; and with what I have learned in the past year fancy I can now take care of myself better without their help than with it – at any rate, without the help of any more specialists.

Of course philosophy is at a stand-still and so are my Edinburgh lectures. But I don't despair of attacking the latter very slowly after a few weeks. One so quickly adapts himself to new conditions that my active life of only a year ago seems almost as if it were a fiction. I hope that you will be able to keep up yours for many a long year to come. Will you kindly send me the exact address under which my immortal works may best reach the library of the Kgl. Pr. Acad. d. Wiss.

I was much interested to learn from you that these recent three elections are the only three "correspondents" yet named in Philosophy. I don't exactly understand why the Academy should preserve so many places vacant. Is the world so unworthy. To tell the unvarnished truth, it seems to me that if any one living foreign philosopher be entitled to such an honor, it is the veteran Ch. Renouvier.[306] He is a "Chef d'École" in the complete sense of the term (as very few philosophers now-a-days are) although he holds no Academic place and hardly ever leaves his country house near Avignon; his technical equipment and erudition are immense; the moral and civic aspects both of his system and of his life are elevated and influential and now at the age of 80 his activity as a writer is undiminished. It seems to me there have been few such careers and that the Academy would honor itself in honoring him, whilst at the same time it

---

[306] Charles Bernard Renouvier (1815–1903) strongly influenced James. See the *Introduction*.

would be a graceful international act. You see I am already taking seriously my privileges and duties as "Corresponding member"!

If you wish me to nominate an English Correspondent I am also ready to do that! Cuba and the Philippine Islands I will hold in reserve.[307]

How are you feeling about all this war and international savagery? Yet the world does advance, but oh! how slowly. I am afraid of what the French people may do during the Katzenjammer[308] which will inevitably succeed the exhibition.

Keep well, dear Stumpf and pray just send me a post-card telling me of the proper manner in which to address the Academy library. This letter needs no prompt reply. With best regards to all of you, in which my wife joins, I am ever affectionately yours

Wm James

---

[307] As a consequence of the Spanish-American war and of the Philippine-American war, the U.S. government occupied Cuba (from 1898 to 1902) and annexed the Philippines (until 1946). James distanced himself from American Imperialism in a series of public writings (1898–1904). See A. Livingstone, *Damn Great Empires! William James and the Politics of Pragmatism*, Oxford, Oxford University Press, 2016.
[308] "Hangover".

[46, 1900]

Berlin, 11 June 1900

Dear friend!
I am very saddened that you had a negative result in Nauheim and sincerely wish you a speedy recovery. As addr. for your work it suffices to write: "An die k. pr. Ak. d. Wiss". Also send a letter "an den vorsitzenden Sekretar der k. pr. Ak. d. W"., wherein you communicate the transmission. Greeting in the letter: "Hochgeehrter Herr Secretar!" Then *under* the text and your signature: "An den vorsitzenden Sekr. d. k. pr. Ak. d. W". (You *could* also add: "Herrn Geheimrat Professor Dr. Vahlen" – who has now taken over then presidency[)].[309] – I want to discuss your suggestion concerning Renouvier with Dilthey and I thank you for it. Incidentally, *Sigwart*[310] as well is also a correspondent in Tübingen.

Your C Stumpf

---

[309] Johannes Vahlen (1830–1911).
[310] Christoph von Sigwart (1830–1904), professor in Tübingen.

[47, 1901]

Bad-Nauheim | Villa Luise, | July 10. 1901

My dear Stumpf – It is high time that I should once more send you *de mes nouvelles*. You see where I am for the 4th., or rather for the 3 1/4th time, – since the 3rd time, last May, was too short to count. I have come back more as a routine precaution than anything, for although the doctors tell me each time that the baths are making my thoracic organs better, my sensations don't ever corroborate what they say, and the really great improvement which I have experienced in the last 3 months is certainly due to my acute neurasthenia having worn away in great part, leaving me less sensitive.

My wife and I spent the winter very happily in Rome. If you ever gain a winter of holiday or have [to] take an Urlaub,[311] I recommend that place. Its climate is excellent, and its intellectual climate wonderfully tranquillizing and yet nourishing. In April we went to my brother's in England, and in May I went, with some trembling, to give my lectures on "The Varieties of Religious Experience" at Edinburgh. They turned out a perfect success, both as regards the size & interest of the audience, and as regards their effect on my health. They made me tougher. And of course the effect on my *moral* of being able to earn my bread again is unspeakably good. Next year I give 10 more lectures on the same subject,[312] which completes my appointment there, and I hope to publish the two courses together, soon after. The matter is treated psychologically and descriptively, and illustrated by as many documents as possible, and will doubtless be a popular book – too biological for the religious, too religious for the biologists, I fear! Our son Harry has come over to see us and is now here, reading my big psychology. I am sorry to say, out of pure filial piety. Is your son Rudolph a practising artist? and pray where is he now? Next year Harry begins his law studies in the Harvard School. We sail for home on the 31st. of August, and shall feel like kissing the walls of our own house, etc. Two years is too long a time away. I shall only keep up a half nominal connexion with my university duties, giving but one hour a week of instruction (Psychology of Religion) next year, until I find out whether or not my aorta will permit me to give more.

So much for ourselves. Now how goes it with you all? I hope the University year is not grinding you to powder. I hope too that when you leave Berlin for

---

311 "Holiday".
312 James had planned a second, more philosophical series of lectures. However, he later changed his mind and worked on the surplus material emerging from the first series. This letter confirms his intention. See Lamberth, *William James and the Metaphysics of Experience*, cit., pp. 105–106.

your vacation, it may be possible for us to meet. Two summers ago here, I was in such bad condition that it would have been unsatisfactory for you or anyone to see me. Now, it is very different indeed. What are your plans of travel, if you have any? I suppose that in 4 weeks from now, or less, we shall go into the Hartz mountains for 10 days of *nachcur*,[313] and then make straight for England. It need not be the Hartz mountains – it might be somewhere else.

Have you any book in gestation? The aesthetic part of your music? The professor of music at Edinburgh, Nieck, is a german;[314] he told me he was writing a musical psychology. Do you know him? Do you feel as sad, as I do, at the savagery of "empire" that is pouring itself over the world? The good ancient soul of my own native country is, I fear, dead beyond resurrection. Man is essentially an[315] adventurous and warlike animal, and one might as well preach against the intercourse of the sexes as against national aggrandisement by piracy. – I hope to get good news of you. With affectionate regards both to yourself and Mrs. Stumpf, in which my wife joins, I am ever faithfully yours,

Wm James

James Sully asks me if I know of a good family, in the country anywhere, where he might bring his son and leave him a couple of months, to talk german. Can you name anyone? The youth is, *I think* about 18. Have you looked into Münsterberg's big Grundzüge?[316]

---

313 "Convalescence".
314 Since 1891 Friedrich Maternus Niecks (1845–1924) had been Reid Professor in Music at the University of Edinburgh.
315 The manuscript reads 'and'.
316 H. Münsterberg, *Grundzüge der Psychologie*, 1st vol., Leipzig, Barth, 1900.

[48, 1901]

Bad-Nauheim, Aug 6. 1901

My dear Stumpf

My fate is at last decided: We leave here on Saturday next in all probability, and take the after cure in the Vosges, starting from Strassburg. I have decided on this instead of the Hartz because our time is getting very short and the Vosges region lies more directly on the way through Paris to Folkestone, and my brother where we must first go in England to pick up our daughter, lives at Rye, near Folkestone. We have a certain amount of business to do in London which will take several days, a visit of a couple more days in England, besides a week with my brother, so that the after cure will have to be cut pretty short, since we sail from Liverpool on the 31st of this month. As your destination is Munich Bayreuth and Tyrol, I begin to fear that we must put off the date of our meeting to some watering place in "another and a better world".[317] Yet, in spite of a very *marked* improvement in my pectoral condition during this course of baths (a much greater improvement than I felt last year) I may have to come back to Nauheim again some future summer or summers, and we need not quite abandon hope. I confess that after my next Spring's course of Edinburgh lectures (which finishes my engagement there) I should like to return to America with the certainty that I must finish my days there and never be obliged to leave it again. These absences from one's native country break up the adhesions of the rootlets of one's being in the soil, and I have made too many absences, first and last. I should like to stay at home, and see my children grow up successfully & establish themselves in life, and *write*, myself, in a way which if possible might slightly help to influence American ideals. But successfully to do so one must live very close to them. Otherwise one's voice sounds foreign. There are splendid things about America, but the old human leaven of national adventure and aggrandizement is threatening to substitute i[t]s brute instinctive power for our historic and hereditary principles, and liberal Americans will have a hard fight to keep the country on the happier and more beneficent traditional track. Munsterberg is to publish next year in German – a book on the Americans, which will be brilliant certainly and contain much true observation.[318] I shall be very curious to see it. I think M. has by various articles of

---

317 The reference is to *Varieties*, p. 87 [*Works* 15, p. 78], where James quotes from a successful play by August Kotzebue, *Menschenhass und Reue*, translated into English as *The Stranger* [see *Works* 15, p. 440].
318 H. Münsterberg, *Die Amerikaner*, Berlin, Mittler u. Sohn, 1904.

his done a good deal towards helping the two Nations towards mutual understanding.³¹⁹ After my lectures on religious experience are published, I hope to write a more systematic attempt at a *Weltanschauung* on a radical empiricist and pluralist basis, seeking to destroy the notion of a monistic Absolute of any sort.³²⁰ Of course I shall fail; but I can say a few things differently from others, and I am sure that in the general organization of philosophical literature some far more radical expression than pluralism has yet received will be useful, even though in the end pluralism were not the true philosophy. Just try *seriously* to conceive the world as a finite collection of many original facts – I think you will lose some of your prejudices in favor of an Absolute. But few people ever try seriously enough! Good bye! my dear Friend. That you may remain active & well, and as productive of truth as ever, is my wish. My wife and I both send our love to you & yours. I will write to you again within the year.

Affectionately | Wm. James

---

319 H. Münsterberg, *American Traits from the Point of View of a German*, Boston & New York, Houghton Mifflin, 1901.
320 Though James failed to deal systematically with that, the problem is tackled in many of his later popular works. For further reference, see the *Introduction*.

[49, 1902]

My dear Stumpf
Permit this note to serve as a personal introduction to you to my old friend, Miss Mary W. Calkins,[321] Professor of Philosophy and Psychology at Wellesley, one of our best femal Colleges. You probably know some of her monographic contributions to psychology, and may have seen her "Introduction" of 500 pp. to Psychology[322] published a few months ago. She is admirable, both in intellect & character, and if you can *orientieren* her a little in Berlin, I shall feel most grateful.

Sincerely yours, as ever. | Wm James

Cambridge, Feb. 11.1902

---

321 Mary Whiton Calkins (1863–1930).
322 In her *Introduction to Psychology* Calkins writes: "My greatest indebtedness is to Professors William James and Hugo Münsterberg. One of the distinctive theories of the book – the existence of elements of consciousness which are neither sensational nor affective – is simply a developed and systematized statement of the teaching of James, and the frequent quotations from the 'Principles of Psychology' are better reading than any original paragraph in the book". Mary W. Calkins, *An Introduction to Psychology,* New York and London, Macmillan, 1901, p. iv. Yet Calkins also criticized James for oscillating "without explanation" (p. 445) between a definition of conscience in terms of subsequent states determined by physiological conditions, and one in terms of the conscious self. James ironically answered in a letter to her of 9 October 1901: "I think I can easily remedy the "oscillation without explanation" of which you complain [...] since my return, I've gone to *smash! – absolute* nerve prostration!" [*Corr.* 9, p. 550].

[50, 1904]

Cambridge, Mass., Jan. 1, 1904.

My dear Stumpf, –

It is years, it seems to me, since a word has passed between us in either direction. I sent you my "Varieties of Religious Experience" when it appeared, but did not get from you any acknowledgment of reception. I hope you got it all the same. I have heard of you occasionally from passing students; but I have read nothing from your pen for two or three years, and I feel that, if I let the year 1904 begin without anything in the way an electric current passing, the way from your heart to mine is in danger of becoming obliterated by the growth of distance and time.

For the last two years I have been regaining my health which is now, although not exactly vigorous, satisfactory enough. At the same time I am letting go of much of my academic work. As one grows older one is appealed to in so many different ways to write articles, make speeches and the like, that it becomes a terrible *corvée* and I am thinking very seriously of withdrawing entirely from teaching and spending the rest of my life more or less in the country and as a free man. I ought to be writing a big book on metaphysics; but with my abridged working power and the interruptions I speak of, it does not get ahead at all. I don't know whether you saw Münsterberg this summer, who seems to have had great success in enlisting German lecturers for his great scheme at the St. Louis Exhibition.[323] I confess I felt relieved at not seeing your name. It will be frightfully hot and fatiguing, and I personally take no interest either in the form or the content of the whole enterprise. But Münsterberg has the most extraordinary power of schematization and programme-making and so far has succeeded, as he always does succeed, in a remarkable way. For his sake I trust that the thing will not be a failure. It will give me, I hope, an opportunity of seeing at own little country place some of the foreigners who come here, among whom Bergson[324] of Paris, Ostwald,[325] Windelband,[326] and Lipps[327] are perhaps the

---

[323] The "Louisiana Purchase Exhibition" of 1904 celebrated the centennial of the purchase of Louisiana by the U.S. from the French (1803). It coincided with the Olympic Games.

[324] On James's relation with Henri Bergson see S. *Bergson et James, cent ans après*, ed. by Madelrieux, Paris, Presses Universitaires de France, 2011.

[325] Friedrich Wilhelm Ostwald (1853–1932), a chemist awarded with the Nobel prize in 1909.

[326] Wilhelm Windelband (1848–1915).

[327] On Lipps, see above [7, 1886]. A meeting with Lipps took place at the Fifth International Congress of Psychology at Rome in 1905, yet it wasn't terribly exciting. On 24 March 1905 James wrote to Pauline Goldmark: "I tell it to you to illustrate the caprices of fame, that I, who have never had anything to do with Italy, should have really so much more to 'do' there than

more exciting to my imagination. I wish that you were coming merely as a visitor, although I confess that America does not offer the *agréments* to a tourist which almost any part of Europe offers. I suppose that by this time you feel like one of the aboriginal Berliners; but life in a capital, unless a man is made of iron and India rubber (and you are not!) is too *aufreibend* for any one whose main interest is contemplation and the pursuit of truth. I wish you would write to me soon after receiving this and tell me just how it is with yourself and all your family. Please take our best New Year wishes for yourself, Mrs. Stumpf, and the two children, who are now children no longer, and believe me, with sincerest regards, in which my wife joins,

Yours ever affectionately | [*hand*] Wm.James

Professor C. Stumpf[328]

---

in Germany, which has occupied so large a share of my life. I think that my name is almost unknown in G[ermany]. Prof Lipps of Munich, after my rigmarole at the Congress, rose to express his radical dissent. When I shook hands with him after wards, he said (good naturedly enough) 'Ich bin kein Vermittlungsmensch, ich bin vielmehr ein Mann des Kampfes' etc. You see why I think Italy a greater, stronger, nobler country than I ever did before!" [*Corr.* 11, p. 46].

328 Typewritten indication of the addressee.

[51, 1904]

Baden-Baden 26 March 1904

My dear friend James!
Now finally, far from Berlin, I can finally respond to your dear letter from 1 January, and I must above all tell you *how glad* and moved I was that you think of me in old and true loyalty. As for me, I must also say that bond between us is completely unbreakable in my heart. It is actually only the hydra of daily work that has made me dawdle so much over writing; with every year, that hydra seems to grow new heads, even without the old ones being chopped off. My desire then tends to be the same as yours – the furthest valley would be the dearest residence for me. I would like to – and indeed I must – finally reap what I sowed sometime – but for now I see no possibility of escape, except in vacation, and I will likely have to hold my post in Berlin so long as my bodily powers suffice.[329]

I had initially said yes to Münsterberg, since the adventure tempted me, but last summer I wrote to him again; my nerves could not withstand it. The whole enterprise is actually not pleasant in general, nothing will come of it. Everyone will talk about the relationship between his science and other sciences – I imagine there must be about 20 volumes filled with such merely methodological observations!

However, let me move now to your lovely book.[330] It is in fact quite wrong of me to have written nothing to you about it besides the card that you must not have gotten. Forgive my wretched soul! I do not lack interest in it. Indeed, in my youth, for years I harbored the plan of becoming a Catholic priest and burying myself in theology, until the inner contradictions of the dogmas drove me away under the heavy agony of my heart.[331] I have experienced in my own

---

329 "Thus, at Easter of the year 1894, I went to Berlin, and now, after thirty years, I still believe that my decision was for the best. My fear that I might not be able to finish the Tonpsychologie and other greater works I had planned, unfortunately, proved well founded. But the psychological seminary, which started in three dark back rooms, developed into a large institute; and I have been able to pursue every kind of work, often fully, in every direction that interested me. Berlin's genius loci, the all-pervading spirit of work, had caught me. Inspirations came a-plenty, and there was no question, however remote, on which one could not find an expert opinion. Berlin was, moreover, musically the foremost city of the world, and Joachim, that noblest of performing artists whom I had known for some time as a friend, was still in his prime". *Autobiography*, p. 402.
330 James, *Varieties*.
331 "In the fall of 1869, I entered the ecclesiastical seminary in Würzburg where I was initiated into the liturgical ceremonies of the Church, the ascetic regulations, which I observed most

life most of what you report about religious experiences. I have certainly become afterwards all the more strict in the mastery and criticism of all of these feelings, and so now I have to say that I find anything sentimental, enrapturing, cutesy, and unctuous about these things extremely repugnant in grown people, and that only what turns into active altruism appears valuable to me.

I also cannot muster this contrite consciousness of sins on which religion should rest according to the devout, despite my knowledge of my deficiencies and mistakes. There is "something wrong about us"[332]: certainly, but *outside* us there is yet much more evil than inside us, and we need salvation not merely from our sins but rather from all of the infinite terrible things in the world, which precisely *the* God from whom one hopes to receive salvation is supposed to have created. In all of these aspects, the religion of the religious seems perverse and unnatural to me.

But I completely agree with what you say about religion in the further and actual sense (p. 485),[333] and in every moment of my life, I feel this cohesion with the invisible spirit realm that surrounds us, and the power that it emits.

---

conscientiously, and all the details of religious exercises. The theological lectures gave me no pleasure, except those of the genial old commentator Schegg, who had traveled through the Holy Land and could describe it most vividly. Besides, I studied most diligently Thomas Aquinas and other scholastics; and Hebrew, on account of the Bible. The fact that I now know only the first letter of the alphabet of this language is a striking example of the effect of disuse on memory. Within the walls of the seminary, however, even in the spring of 1870, the second, still more fundamental regeneration overtook me, and again under Brentano's influence. The whole structure of the Catholic-Christian dogmatic theology and Weltanschauung crumbled to dust before my eyes. In terrible agony of soul I had to give up my chosen life work, my ideal. In July, I took off the black robe. I had not been ordained as yet, so there were no serious complications. But I had to find my way back to the world, and many favorable, as well as unfavorable, after-effects of this year I was to feel for a long time to come". *Autobiography*, pp. 393–394.

332 Here and below, Stumpf quotes from James's *Varieties*. James wrote that the "common nucleus" of all religious creeds consists of "an uneasiness" and "its solution", the former being "a sense that there is something wrong about us as we naturally stand". *Varieties*, p. 508 [*Works* 15, p. 400].

333 "Summing up in the broadest possible way the characteristics of the religious life, as we have found them, it includes the following beliefs: 1. That the visible world is part of a more spiritual universe from which it draws its chief significance; 2. That union or harmonious relation with that higher universe is our true end; 3. That prayer or inner communion with the spirit thereof be that spirit 'God' or 'law' is a process wherein work is really done, and spiritual energy flows in and produces effects, psychological or material, within the phenomenal world". *Varieties*, p. 485 [*Works* 15, p. 382].

Should I now tell you something about my "over-belief"?[334] I do not know whether I will decide to publish such thoughts, which occupy me every day of my life. However, I will gladly share them with you confidentially. Personal immortality stands in the foreground for me. Your sentence "if our ideals" (p. 524) [335] seems to me to contain a kind of inner contradiction. Indeed, the actualization of ideals is only possible under the presupposition of individual immortality. Psychic values do not add up. Even if new individuals are born, then the newer ones might well be better than the older, but they still vanish into nothingness, and it is absurd to sum up the values which exist only within one personality. If the congealment of the earth occurs, and therefore no more new individuals arise, where does the actualization of ideals reside, if what is spiritual does not endure?[336] For me, this is the first condition, if life is not to be absolutely bleak and meaningless. This is not *egoism*: what is spiritual must last not because it is me, but rather because it is a bearer of values; and I certainly would be prepared to relinquish my own continued existence if the continued existence of what is spiritually valuable outside me were tied to this condition.

However, that which is perpetuated of us will only be what is morally valuable, that which a good will has drawn into its sphere and has adhered to. In a certain sense, individuality will indeed disappear, not merely bodily individuality but also spiritual individuality, even though people see the essence of individuality in the contingent trifles that our "individual psychology" uses as a characteristic mark. As for how it will be for us one day, the best analogy for that, I think, is the state of high pleasure in front of art or of an ethically great representation that is very fulfilling to us; our "I" is present, but freed from

---

334 James notes that "high-flying speculations like those of either dogmatic or idealistic theology", must "be classed as over-beliefs, buildings-out performed by the intellect into directions of which feeling originally supplied the hint". *Varieties*, p. 431. Furthermore: "I shall add my own over-belief (which will be, I confess, of a somewhat pallid kind, as befits a critical philosopher), and you will, I hope, also add your over-beliefs, and we shall soon be in the varied world of concrete religious constructions once more". *Varieties*, p. 504 [*Works* 15, p. 341].

335 "I have said nothing in my lectures about immortality or the belief therein, for to me it seems a secondary point. If our ideals are only cared for in 'eternity,' I do not see why we might not be willing to resign their care to other hands than ours. Yet I sympathize with the urgent impulse to be present ourselves, and in the conflict of impulses, both of them so vague yet both of them noble, I know not how to decide". *Varieties*, p. 524 [*Works* 15, p. 412].

336 "God's existence is the guarantee of an ideal order that shall be permanently preserved. This world may indeed, as science assures us, some day burn up or freeze; but if it is part of his order, the old ideals are sure to be brought elsewhere to fruition, so that where God is, tragedy is only provisional and partial, and shipwreck and dissolution are not the absolutely final things". *Varieties*, p. 517 [*Works* 15, p. 407].

those contingent trifles, elevated into a higher sphere, and accompanied by the blissful feelings of being-one [*Eins-Seins*] with all the good and high spirits of all times. For me, in such moments and hours, it is as if I felt the living presence of my loved ones, of all of those who preceded me; they seem to be around me and to speak to my soul just like those who sit next to me in the empirical present, mutely indulging in the same feelings.

These are my two articles of faith, which both appear at the end the Athanasian Creed – "communion of saints and an eternal life"[337] – whereas all remaining articles have fallen, including the existence of the Christian God. The dreadful evil of the course of nature and the wickedness of people, which is part of it, exclude this assumption. However, if we want a pantheistic god, then we can very likely take this communion of the blessed as a part of it – a communion that grows every day and at the same time forms an inner unity.

I do not want to explain in further detail how I make these thoughts work with my psychological and natural philosophical views. Anyway, you will easily detect some lines of connection with my short essays on the body and the soul and with my thoughts on evolution.[338]

According to this, our views are close in many respects. Even your pluralism is not so alien to me as it probably is to most of our colleagues (although I believe that you underestimate the value of the feeling of unity of what is highest [*des Höchsten*]). Only I would not like to associate the concept of God with the subconscious. What I know about it seems not to point in this direction; rather, I would believe that these states themselves belong to the non-eternal parts of us that eventually fall away with the body.

Now, dear friend, enough with philosophy! You also asked about my family. My wife is doing well again; after a few bad years, she is not with me but at home with our little daughter, Elizabeth, who was born in Munich. Rudi, our oldest, now 22 years old, is a painter, has studied 2 years in Paris and several semesters in Stuttgart and Munich, and now lives in Weimar, which promises to become the center of our German "Secessions", that is, of the non-official, independent trends. He makes us glad for his honesty and firmness, and is

---

[337] The Creed referred to by Stumpf is rather the "Apostle's Creed", whose final lines read: "Credo in Spiritum Sanctum, sanctam Ecclesiam catholicam, *sanctorum communionem*, remissionem peccatorum, carnis resurrectionem, *vitam aeternam*" (emphasis added). Together with the Athanasian and the Nicene Creed, the Apostle's Creed belongs to the so-called "Ecumenical Creeds", adopted by both Catholics and Reformed Churches. James refers to the Athanasian Creed as a source of mystic experience for Saint Teresa. *Varieties*, p. 411 [*Works* 15, p. 326].

[338] Stumpf, *Leib und Seele* (1896) and *Der Entwicklungsgedanke in der gegenwärtigen Philosophie* (1899). See the *Introduction*.

valued by his teachers. Felix is still in high school, but for the past 2 years not in Berlin but in the calm and healthy Wernigerode am Harz. He will hopefully go to university next Easter, his abilities seem to point towards physics, yet of course nothing final can be known yet. He is also a good lad.

And what about your Harry, and, above all, how is your highly adored wife? I need not tell you that your own continual recovery pleases me beyond all measure. Would you not come over here again sometime? We definitely want to make room to see you again! Heartfelt greetings to your family and the truest wishes to you

Your *old* | C. Stumpf

I would be very thankful if you confirmed the reception of this letter, even if only with a word.

[52, 1904]

Chocorua (New Hampshire) | July 17. 1904

My dear Stumpf,
I got your delightfully cordial and deeply interesting letter last March, and acknowledged it by a post-card. Now that the fatigues of the Cambridge year are over, and that we are all together on our little country place in the Mountains, I have repose enough of body and mind to write to you at greater length. First, I congratulate you at not being at Saint Louis. The heat in September there will be exterminating, and to my mind the empty immensity of the whole affair is repugnant. Like yourself, I can only see in these 24 volumes of methodological considerations in 3 languages (for such, I believe, is the hoped for outcome of the whole scheme) one of those enormities which our present-day civilization abounds in and which add to the burdens of humanity. Surely there is enough thought in the world that spontaneously publishes itself, without getting all this mass of it published to order! Nevertheless Münsterberg's organizing genius is very great. His *philosophy* seems to me thoroughly artificial.

Your own confidences as to your religious state of mind interest me deeply. I agree that a God *of the totality* must be an inacceptable religious object. But I do not see why there may not be superhuman consciousness of *ideals* of ours, and *that* would be *our* God. It is all very dark. I never felt the *rational* need of immortality as you seem to feel it; but as I grow older I confess that I feel the practical need of it much more than I ever did before; and that combines with reasons, not exactly the same as your own, to give me a growing faith in its reality. I wish that you, some day, anonymously or over your name, would expand and publish these reflections. I think that these states of mind, which are what people live by, are thoroughly normal; but the artificial rationalistic conscience of professional *Gelehrten*,[339] makes them so often ashamed of the public expression of these inner faiths, that the literature of the world is getting too much weighted the other way; and, lacking examples of faith in minds whose intellects they respect, common people grow ashamed to have any faith of their own.[340] You will probably have seen already Stanley Hall's new American Journal of Religion,[341] etc. I wish that there might be many such documents as

---
339 "Pundits".
340 In 1912, Stumpf added two square brackets in red pencil onto James's manuscript letter. He bracketed the words from the beginning of the paragraph ("Your own confidence ... ") to "of their own". His reasons to do so are illustrated below: [63, 1912].
341 *The American Journal of Religious Psychology and Education* (1904–1911). Stanley Hall explained: "Scrupulously refraining from interfering with any characterization of superhuman

yours published therein. – I do not suppose that it will continue for many years; but I imagine that for five or six years there will be abundant good material to publish.

My nervous condition is a miserable one for work. I don't know whether or not it is connected with a high degree of arterio-sclerosis, with which I am afflicted, but whenever I begin to write anything serious my sleep goes, and I have to stop. I ought to be writing a book; but at Cambridge last year I succeeded in writing just 32 pages! Pity me! I have become much interested of late in the philosophy of John Dewey of Chicago. Have you seen his "Logical Studies.["][342] I have just written an article for the October number of Mind[343] (Bradley having attacked the point of view in this July number[344]) in which you may possibly be interested. Bradley is a man of great subtlety, but *perverse*, in my opinion; so that the importance of his writings is not at all commensurate with their originality.

I have just read the "Memoires" of H. Berlioz.[345] As a musician, you must have read them long ago, but if by accident you have not done so, I can warmly recommend them. I am glad that the account you give of your family, is so good a one. I also have nothing but good news to impart. Harry who has developed into a really splendid character for practical affairs and general perfection, enters upon his professional career as a lawyer in Boston tomorrow. William, the second, now just 22 has had two years of medical study – tentatively, for I never could believe him born to be a doctor. He has himself now decided against it: but what else? – God only knows! The wife is well and excellent. She joins me in warm regards to you & Mrs. Stumpf.

Your ever affectionate | Wm James

---

agencies or transcendental provisions for, or aims and results of, this change, psychology limits itself solely to the study of its phenomena in the human soul with a view to determining their chief forms, sequences and laws. What has been done here is probably only a beginning and the best is yet to be accomplished". G. Stanley Hall, "Editorial", *The American Journal of Religious Psychology and Education* 1, 1904, p. 1.
342 J. Dewey, *Studies in Logical Theory*, Chicago, The University of Chicago Press, 1903.
343 W. James, "Humanism and Truth", *Mind* n.s. 13, 1904, pp. 457–475.
344 F. Bradley, "On Truth and Practice", *Mind* n.s. 13, 1904, p. 315. Bradley tackled Dewey's ideas along with the volume *Personal Idealism* edited by Henry Sturt, which had already been reviewed by James (W. James, "Reviewed Work[s]: Personal Idealism. Philosophical Essays by Eight Members of the University of Oxford, by Henry Sturt", *Mind* n.s. 12, 1903, pp. 93–97). In his discussion, Bradley critically refers to James's review.
345 *Mémoires de H. Berlioz, comprenant ses voyages en Italie, en Allemagne, en Russie et en Angleterre (1803–1865)*, Paris, Calmann-Lévy, 1878.

[53, 1907]

BERLIN W. 50, | AUGSBURGERSTR. 61 | 8 Mai 07

Dear friend,

I am finally getting to answer your dear card from January that has long lain on my desk. It is indeed true that "We lead a life of non-communication",[346] and I am no less sorry for this than you are. But how can this be otherwise, so long as this Berlin machine holds me in chains? You are giving up your teaching activities to lead a life of science only. I cannot resolve myself to do that yet; partially for the sake of my family, for whom I cannot relinquish the considerable revenues of the lectures here, since the three children need much, but partially for the sake of the thing itself, since I am just now perceiving extensive and growing success in my teaching activity and still feel powerful enough to continue with it. My nerves have even gotten better with age. It is only the organization of time that is an unsolvable problem in Berlin. The vast distances and the many official functions, exams, etc. devour the better part of my time.

A growing divergence appears to be occurring in our views, dear and revered friend. I cannot befriend pragmatism and humanism. The positivistic theory of knowledge, in which you agree with Mach, seems to me impossible, or barren.[347] In both essays that you receive together with this letter, I try to justify this.[348] You will label this a standpoint that you have *abandoned*; I agree with the earlier James more than with the present one. But at the same time, James the *person* stands as near to me as before, and I hope that you will say the same of me.

Have I also sent you the "Gefühlsempfindungen"?[349] This essay is more likely able to hope for your approval than the two academic ones.

My family is doing well. Rudi has growing success as a portraitist, particularly in etchings. Felix studies physics in Göttingen. Elisabeth is about to turn to her high school studies, following the course of time, and she is a fresh, life-loving, and powerful girl. And how are things with your revered wife and your children, especially Harry? Give heartfelt greetings to everyone from us and be well

Your devoted | C. Stumpf

---

346 English in the original.
347 See the *Introduction*.
348 C. Stumpf, "Erscheinungen und psychische Funktionen", *Abhandlungen der Königlich-Preußischen Akademie der Wissenschaften, Philosophisch-historische Classe* 6, 1906, pp. 3–40; "Zur Einteilung der Wissenschaften", *Abhandlungen der Königlich-Preußischen Akademie der Wissenschaften, Philosophisch-historische Classe* 5, 1906, pp. 1–94.
349 C. Stumpf. "Über Gefühlsempfindungen", *Zeitschrift für Psychologie und Physiologie der Sinnesorgane* 44, 1907, pp. 1–49.

[54, 1907

95 Irving St. | Cambridge, Mass. | May 20. 1907

My dear Stumpf;

You have enriched me in three days with 2 Abhandlungen,[350] with the horse of Herrn von. Osten,[351] and with your most welcome letter of the 8th. All these things find me in a rather fatigued state with the work of the year, so that I cannot attack the Abhandlungen immediately, as I should like to, but I shall devour them in a month's time, & let you know of my reaction. They both look *exciting*; and it rejoices me that you too are working more and more into metaphysics, which is the only study worthy of Man! Music & metaphysics! You will receive from me in a week or two the sole product of *my* Muse this winter, namely a little popular book called "Pragmatism".[352] In spite of what you say so gravely and even sorrowfully in this letter, I shall be surprised if, when I have read your quarto pages, and you my much smaller ones, we seem to each other as far apart in our thinking as you now suppose us to be. What staggers me in the recent controversial literature of pragmatism and humanism is the colossal amount of mutual *misunderstanding* that can exist in men brought up in the same language and with almost identical educations. It is hard to believe! Language is the most imperfect and expensive means yet discovered for communicating thought. – I see, dear Stumpf, from the way in which you speak of Berlin, that you are one of the victims of life in a modern "great capital." *Simplification* is the summum bonum for a certain type of man, to which I, and (I fancy) you belong. Great capitals make it impossible. I, having resigned my professorship, shall be able from next Autumn onwards to simplify *my* life far more than heretofore, and the thought of being free from all those "adaptations" to other human beings, unintelligible and unassimilable as most of them are, fills me with extraordinary elation. Alone with

---

350 "Essays". See above, [53, 1907].
351 The reference is to the volume O. Pfungst, *Das Pferd des Herrn von Osten. Der Kluge Hans*. Leipzig, Barth, 1907. Stumpf authored the "Einleitung" (pp. 7–15) and the essay "Der Rechenunterricht des Herrn v. Osten" (pp. 175–180). Stumpf and his assistant Pfungst cleared up the case of a horse, nicknamed Kluge Hans (*smart Hans*), allegedly able to perform elementary arithmetical operations. The case raised sensation at the time. Stumpf and Pfungst showed that the horse was able to perceive some inadvertent movement of the head of his master, Mr. Osten.
352 W. James, *Pragmatism: A New Name for Some Old Ways of Thinking*, New York and London, Longmans, Green & Co., 1907.

God! with truth! what a prospect!!! Join me!! – My family flourishes. Harry *very* satisfactory: a lawyer and good man of affairs. Can't you send me one of Rudi's etchings? as a sample? M 2nd son, Wm., is also going to be a portrait painter – is now working in Paris. Warmest regards "von Haus zu Haus".[353]

Yours affectionately | Wm. James

---

[353] "From house to house".

[55, 1909]

Berlin, 20 Mai 09

Dearest friend!
I ought not procrastinate any longer to express to you the most heartfelt thanks for your latest book.[354] It has excited me, and I now also want to consider more closely your Bergson.[355] Regarding the "final things", I think I stand closer to you than in respect to the pragmatic concept of truth, although I also do not underrate what is true in it.[356] Couldn't we see each other again sometime? This interaction with the quill is indeed too tenuous, and I am a bad letter writer. My wife and I send our best wishes to you both and to your Harry, if he still remembers us.

Your true | C. Stumpf

---

354 W. James, *A Pluralistic Universe. Hibbert Lectures at Manchester College on the Present Situation in Philosophy*, New York and London, Longmans, Green & Co., 1909.
355 James, *A Pluralistic Universe*, chapter 6: "Bergson and his Critique of Intellectualism".
356 See the *Introduction*.

[56, 1909]

Berlin W. 50, Augsburger Str. 45 | 26 Oct. 09

Dear friend and colleague!

I sincerely thank you for your new book[357] and will attempt to further penetrate the essence of pragmatism, to which I cannot yet confer the importance that you attribute to it. I would like to believe that the treatment *of singular great problems* from this standpoint could alone demonstrate its significance persuasively. However, I have read much in your writings about it with approval and enjoyment.

Today I would like to recommend to you a young American psychologist, Mr. *Langfeld*,[358] who studied here for a number of years and finally obtained his doctorate with me with his experimental study on brightness comparisons.[359] He has now traveled over again with his wife, also an American, and will seek you since he wishes to continue to work there.[360] He is a very capable and highly amiable person; we also liked his wife very much.

Things are well with us, we can be satisfied with our health, and also with the children and life in general, even if I always sigh somewhat under the burdens of excessive work, and would gladly have more time for the development of my general philosophical thoughts. Accept heartfelt wishes for you and your family

from your devoted | C. Stumpf

---

[357] W. James, *The Meaning of Truth: A Sequel to "Pragmatism"*, New York and London, Longmans, Green & Co., 1909.
[358] Herbert Sidney Langfeld (1879–1958) earned his doctorate in Berlin in 1909. In his 1936 obituary, Langfeld (*Carl Stumpf*, cit.) gave a short, but singularly vivid and rigorous description of Stumpf's main ideas and of his personality.
[359] H.S. Langfeld, *Über die heterochrome Helligkeitsvergleichung*. Inaugural-Dissertation zur Erlangung der Doktorwürde, Universität zu Berlin, Leipzig, Barth, 1909.
[360] Langfeld taught psychology at Harvard (1910) and subsequently at Princeton (1924).

[57, 1910]

95 Irving St. | Cambridge (Mass.) | Jan. 6.1910

My dear Stumpf,
I thank you heartily for your new book.[361] I shall be glad to read some of the essays a second time.[362] We seem to be growing asunder in our pursuits; the various finite minds, buried under the infinite mountain of problems to follow and books to be read, cannot follow the same directions and get out of sight of one another's operations. I believe that if you and I [could] be near each other, and could see each other frequently, we should work very well together, but at present we inhabit somewhat different fields of view. The thing of yours that has most interested me of late is the Erscheinungen und Psychische Funktionen[363] wherein you differ from things that I have printed in a way to make my take notice and revise. I have got very far away from psychology in my recent work, but I hope to get back again and to pick at the dropped threads. My health permits of only an hour and a half a day of application, but I have no duties to anything but my own "genius" at present, so that that hour and a half ought to be enough. Mr. (or Dr.?) Langfeld was here the other day, and talked very gratefully and admiringly about you. He confirmed my idea that Berlin was overworking you. The moth and the candle! A country College, like those in America or a small university-town with good professors is the ideal. L[angfeld] gave me a fine account of your son's career as an artist. My second son is also trying to become a portrait painter – I think he will succeed. A happy new year, dear Carl Stumpf, to you, to Mrs. Stumpf and all your family, from your affectionately

Wm.James

---

361 Stumpf, *Reden und Vorträge*.
362 The reference is to *Leib und Seele* and *Entwicklungsgedanke*. Besides, Stumpf's volume includes: "Die Lust am Trauerspiel", "Zur Methodik der Kinderpsychologie", "Die Wiedergeburt der Philosophie", "Vom ethischen Skeptizismus", "Die Anfänge der Musik".
363 See above, [53, 1907].

Family Letters

William James to Alice Howe (Gibbens) James

[58, 1882]

Aussig, Nov 2. 82

Dearest Alice, I came as far as this last night on my way to Dresden in order to catch the morning boat and see the handsome part of the river. Yesterday was in Prag one of the few fine days of the year and it looked last night as if it would last. But this A.M. the dirtiest and lowest of brown clouds are crawling over the river, and though the hotel keeper says he thinks it will clear before noon I at this hour of 9.45 still doubt it.

As for Prag, veni, vidi, vici. I went there with much trepidation to my social scientific duty. The mighty Hering in especial intimidated me beforehand; but having taken the plunge, the cutaneous glow and "euphoria" (vide Dictionary) succeeded, and I have rarely enjoyed a 48 hours better, in spite of the fact that the good & sharp nosed Stumpf, (whose book über die Raumvorstellungen[364] I verily believe thou art capable of never have noticed even the cover of!) insisted on trotting me about, day & night, over the whole length & breadth of Prague, and that Mach, Professor of Physics, & genius of all trades, simply took Stumpf's place to do the same.

I heard Hering give a very poor physiology lecture and Mach a beautiful physical one. I presented them with my visiting card saying that I was with their Schriften sehr vertraut u. wollte nicht eher Prag verlassen als bis ich wenigstens ein Paar worte mit Ihnen umtauschte etc.[365] They received me with open arms. I had an hour & half's talk with Hering which cleared up some things for me. He asked me to come to his house that evening, but I gave an evasive reply being fearful of boring him. Meanwhile Mach came to my Hotel and I spent 4 hours walking & supping with him at his Club – an unforgettable conversation. I don't think any one ever gave me so strong an impression of pure intellectual genius. He apparently has read everything & thought about everything, and has an absolute simplicity of manner and winningness of smile when his face lights up that are charming. With Stumpf I spent 5 hours on Monday evening, (This is Thursday) 3 on Wednesday morning, and 4 more in

---

364 Stumpf, *Raumvorstellung*.
365 "I am well acquainted with [your] works, and I would preferably not leave Prague without a talk with you".

the afternoon, so I feel rather intimate. A clear headed and just-minded, though pale and anxious looking man in poor health. He had another philosopher named Marty to dine with me yesterday, a jolly young fellow. My native Geschwatzigkeit[366] triumphed even over even the difficulties of the german tongue, I careered over the field, taking the pitfalls and breastworks at full run, and was fairly astounded myself at coming in alive. I learned a good many things from them, both in the way of theory and fact, and shall probably keep up a correspondence with Stumpf. They are not so different from us as we think. Their greater thoroughness is largely the result of circumstances. I found that I had a more *cosmopolitan* knowledge of modern philosophic literature than any of them, and shall on the whole feel much less intimidated by the thought of their like than hitherto!

My letters will hereafter I feel sure have a more jocund tone. D – n Italy! It isn't a good thing to stay with one's inferiors. With the nourishing breath of the german air, and the sort of smoky and leathery German smell, vigor and good spirits have set in. I've walked well, & slept well & eaten well and read well, and in short begin to feel as I expected I should when I decided upon this arduous pilgrimage. Prag is a – city, the adjective is hard to find – not "magnificent" for every thing about it is too honest and homely, – we have in fact no English word for the peculiar quality that good German things have, of depth, solidity, picturesqueness, magnitude and homely goodness combined. They have worked out a really great civilization. "*Dienst ist Dienst!*"[367] said the gateman of a certain garden yesterday afternoon whom Stumpf was trying to persuade to let me as an American in to see the view five minutes after the closing hour had struck. "*Dienst ist dienst*". That is really the german motto everywhere and I should like to know what American would ever think of justifying himself by just that formula. I say German of Prag for it seems to me in spite of the feverish nationalism of the natives to be outwardly a pure german city.

---

366 "Loquaciousness".
367 "Duty is duty!"

Hotel de Saxe Neumarkt, Dresden Nov. 3. Dearest Alice, sure enough the sun feebly showed itself before 11 yesterday but I wisely took the train instead of the boat and got here before 2. A pleasant, correct, cheerful little town, which the-greater-strength in-the same-line of Prague makes to seem a little insignificant. I spent the afternoon in sauntering about, looking into the bookstores, and at my old haunts, from whence all the human beings I knew here have passed away or are now unfindable, and in which ignorant strangers must be dwelling as if there lay no human history back of their own upstart presence, – doing this, I say, and longing that thou wert by my side to show me your old haunts and tell me of many a little incident of your lives here that sensible sight would quicken into remembrance. To day is a beautiful day, I have had a first rate Bouillon mit Ei, and the old delicious Dresden bread and butter, I find the Gemälde Gallerie is closed for repairs but will open to morrow so I decide to stay one more night for the sight of it. At the Hof-Theatre they play Richard II to night, and I will take a ticket. I went last night to the "Residenz Theatrer["] in the Circus Strasse & saw an intensely German farce, wobei I was förmlich ausser mich[368] that you 3 sisters couldn't be there to enjoy mit. The pale smoky sunshine floods the rather bleak Neumarkt, with its mighty and steep roofed Houses. A tramway with handsome cars runs through it, the Schulstrasse (or Moritz Str. I forget wh.) to the Zoological Garden. I will mitfahren and visit my friends the beasts, I would that Culturmensch were mit.

A propos of Prague, I mustn't forget to say that Frau Stumpf sent you a cordial Gruss. She is a nice little German professor's wife, with many ach Gotts & Herrjeses'es, mother of a little Rudolf or Rudi, 14 months old, with a sharp aquiline nose like his father's and a large white forehead on which one might draw the plan of the city. She reads lots of english novels. I promised to send her some of Harry's. Haven't we an extra copy of the P. of a L.?[369] I will send her from London the American, and if you can send her the other, it will make 2.[370] I wish you would also send me *all* the copies of the Feeling of Effort, of the Sentiment of Rationality, of my J. of Spec. Phil. articles, and a dozen each of the Atlantic and of the Unitarian Review article.[371] Swapping one's articles is the great way to get

---

368 "Whereby I was totally disappointed".
369 Henry James, *The Portrait of a Lady*, Boston, Houghton, Mifflin and Co., 1881.
370 Henry James, *The American*, Boston, Osgood & Co., 1877.
371 The essays referred to are: W. James, "The Sentiment of Rationality", Mind 4, 1879, pp. 317–346; *The Feeling of Effort. Anniversary Memoirs of the Boston Society of Natural History*, Boston, 1880; "The Spatial Quale", *Journal of Speculative Philosophy* 13, 1879, pp. 64–87; "Brute and Human Intellect", *Journal of Speculative Philosophy* 12, 1878, pp. 236–276; "Great Men, Great Thoughts and their Environment", *Atlantic Monthly* 46, 1880, pp. 441–459; "Reflex Action

things early & surely from other men. The number of the atlantic was October 1880,[372] nicht wahr?[373] You'll have to write a card to Houghton and Mifflin asking them to send a dozen copies out by Sawin C.O.D. You should the wholesale price, as the order is from a contributor. Do the same by Ellis, in Franklin St, pretty low down, or send Sawin directly there. He is publisher of Unitarian Review. *Cut out* my articles and throw the rest away. Send also the Princeton Review reprints.[374] Write or go to Appleton's Agent in Hawley St. Boston just out of Milk & (left hand side as you enter) get a dozen copies of the number that contains my Assocn. of Ideas article,[375] which treat in the same way. You'll have to make one or two bundles of all this, and mail them to me, care of Messieurs Hottinguer & Cie, Banquiers, à Paris. I'm afraid the postage will exhaust your small stipend. I was foolish to have tried so hard to keep the bulk of my books down. Since the trunk has but to make one journey to Paris and pay but freight rates, I might have enlarged it with no extra cost or risk to speak of. Don't forget your photograph!

And now dearest, with oceans of love, to Father & Alice, to your mother sisters aunts, self & children, Good bye

Your Wm. J

---

and Theism", *Unitarian Review* 16, 1881, pp. 389–416. Except for *Brute and Human Intellect* Stumpf had all of these essays in his library [*Stumpf Collection*, pp. 51–52].

372 W. James, "Great Men, Great Thoughts and their Environment", *Atlantic Monthly* 46, 1880, pp. 441–459.
373 "Isn't it?"
374 W. James, "Rationality, Activity and Faith", *Princeton Review* 2, 1882, pp. 58–86.
375 W. James, "The Association of Ideas", *Popular Science Monthly* 16, 1880, pp. 577–593.

William James to Hermine (Biedermann) Stumpf

[59, 1893]

16 Piazza Indipendenza | March 14. 1893

My dear Mrs Stumpf,
you flattered me by asking for my photograph, which I promised to send. Here it is! – found at last in the bottom of a trunk, and far from being good. If I ever get a better one I promised to send it to your address. I also promise to send you in a couple of weeks a photograph of my wife, which we must have taken in Florence before we leave.

My trip to Munich has left the most delightful series of Gedächtnisbilder[376] in my mind. On the whole the pleasantest of all are those of the dinners at your house. But Florence also looked delightful on my return. The two weeks had made a sudden step toward spring, and the look of the streets in the warm light and shadow was charming. I wish you could come on to enjoy it in the Easter vacation. *Change* is the thing most necessary to man!

Harry[377] writes that he spent saturday very pleasantly at your house. You are very kind, but you must not have you "on your mind." He seems very contented in Munich.

Pray give my best greetings to your husband and sister, and believe me, with affectionate regards from both of us, yours faithfully

Wm James

---

376 "Memory images".
377 William's eldest son Henry.

Carl Stumpf to Alice Howe (Gibbens) James

[60, 1911]

Dearest Mrs. James!
I give you my best thanks for your kind submission of the final work of your husband,[378] my unforgettable and cherished friend and colleague. I expect rich stimulation and instruction from it and will study it with special love, as if I heard his living voice. My wife joins me in sending our best greetings to you and to the editor, your son Henry. Your always loyal

C. Stumpf

Berlin W, Augsburger Str. 45, 7 June 1911

---

378 Probably W. James, *Some Problems of Philosophy. A Beginning of an Introduction to Philosophy*, New York and London, Longmans, Green & Co., 1911. The book is included in Stumpf's library [*Stumpf Collection*, p. 52].

Carl Stumpf to Henry James, 3rd

[61, 1911]

Dear Mr. James,
I sincerely thank you for sending me the "Memories and Studies"[379] of your revered father, my unforgettable colleague and friend. Although I possess very many essays by him, these were all still new to me. I will shortly pick out all of your father's letters to me and send them to you. With heartfelt greetings and with regards to your mother

Your loyal | C. Stumpf

Berlin 11 Nov. 1911

---

[379] W. James, *Memories and Studies*, ed. by H. James Jr., New York and London, Longmans, Green & Co., 1911.

[62, 1911]

Berlin W. Ausburger Str. 45, 3 Dec. 1911

Dear Mr. James,

A card from me to you must have gone missing; I have thanked you long ago for the "Memories and Studies", which are a very dear remembrance of my deceased friend and colleague, and I have promised to transfer his letters to you. But I was so glutted with work that I have not yet gotten around to gather them up from the bundles of the previous years (our acquaintance reaches back to 1884).[380] Nevertheless, I will do it as soon as possible. We were very glad that you still remembered Munich and our family. Hopefully we will see you here sometime! With my best regards to your revered mother.

Your | C. Stumpf

---

380 Should be 1882.

[63, 1912]

Berlin, 3 March 1912

Dear Mr. James!
What you must think of me, that I have let the whole winter elapse without having fulfilled my promise! But believe me when I say that it was physically impossible: I was uninterruptedly engaged with ongoing duties. My collection of letters is unfortunately not ordered alphabetically in the later years. For this reason, I first came to review them in the past few days, at the beginning of my vacation. I have found 31 letters and cards. The majority are attached here, the rest will follow in a separate letter. I had committed two letters to the autograph collection of the Königlichen Bibliothek at its request; I am sending you transcripts of these, which were made at the K. Bibliothek.[381]

In the letter from *17.VII.04*,[382] I have bracketed with "[]"[383] a long piece of text. If you publish this letter, I ask you to leave out this piece of text.[384] It refers to a letter of mine to your father[385] about my religious views at the time. However, I do not wish to share any of them with the public, until these views do not appear completely matured to me. It is not bashfulness before the public

---

381 See the *Introduction*.
382 [52, 1904].
383 The brackets are red.
384 The bracketed passage in James's letter is the following: "[Your own confidences as to your religious state of mind interest me deeply. I agree that a God of the totality must be an inacceptable religious object. But I do not see why there may not be superhuman consciousness of ideals of ours, and that would be our God. It is all very dark. I never felt the rational need of immortality as you seem to feel it; but as I grow older I confess that I feel the practical need of it much more than I ever did before; and that combines with reasons, not exactly the same as your own, to give me a growing faith in its reality. I wish that you, some day, anonymously or over your name, would expand and publish these reflections. I think that these states of mind, which are what people live by, are thoroughly normal; but the artificial rationalistic conscience of professional Gelehrten, makes them so often ashamed of the public expression of these inner faiths, that the literature of the world is getting too much weighted the other way; and, lacking examples of faith in minds whose intellects they respect, common people grow ashamed to have any faith of their own]". See above, [52, 1904].
385 In [52, 1904] James commented on Stumpf's previous letter [51, 1904]. Accordingly, Stumpf is afraid that from that passage of James's letter [52, 1904], the reader could guess Stumpf's own opinions. In his edition of his father's correspondence, Henry did not publish the letter [52, 1904] at all.

that determines me to this, but rather, on the contrary, my own bashfulness with myself, since I sense a particularly heavy responsibility in these things.[386]

Should my letter from March 1904[387] still be found in the papers of your father, then I would ask you to send it back to me;[388] it was meant only for him.

Otherwise, there ought to be nothing in your father's letters that appears unfit for publication. If you do not require them any longer, I would like to ask for them back, since they are a cherished keepsake of a friend and colleague with whom I was joined for so long in the warmest sympathy. With my most heartfelt regards to your revered mother

Your loyal | C. Stumpf

My wife and our son Rudolf enclose their greetings also. Have you already asked Schrenck-Notzing in Munich for letters? Prof. Lipps in Munich could also have letters. I will also ask other gentlemen at the congress on 16–19 April.[389]

---

386 Stumpf concludes his *Autobiography* with these words: "I cannot close this sketch of my life without mentioning that in 1921 I severed my connection with the Catholic Church. Although estranged for over fifty years, I had never formally withdrawn, being too well aware of the blessings our Church bestowed, nor had I any inclination to exchange my old confession of faith for any other. But the behavior of the officiating priest at the funeral of one of my brothers (he considered it necessary to apologize for standing at this grave, because the deceased, whose noble human qualities he later on felt constrained to praise duly, had not lived up to the regulations of the Church) induced me to take the decisive step. Though I am now non-denominational, as it were, I still confess myself with all my heart a disciple of Christianity as the religion of love and mercy – which needs no revaluation, but rather a higher appreciation – and I hope that in some time to come the different denominations will meet in this spirit, if not for a complete reunion, at least for a closer approach, a reconciliation". *Autobiography*, p. 413.
387 [51, 1904].
388 Henry did not send back the letter: the manuscript is still at the Houghton Library.
389 The 5th Congress of experimental psychology in Berlin (April 16–20, 1912). See *Bericht über den fünften Kongreß für experimentelle Psychologie in Berlin vom 16. bis 20. April 1912*, ed. by F. Schumann, Leipzig, Barth, 1912.

[64, 1912]

Berlin 13 March 1912

Dear Mr. James,

I have subsequently found another letter. You will probably receive my two shipments at the same time with this one. Best wishes

Your | C. Stumpf

You have probably written to Flournoy in Geneva; he ought to have a number of letters.[390]

---

[390] *The Letters of William James and Théodore Flournoy*, ed. by R. Le Clair, Madison, Milwaukee and London, The University of Wisconsin Press, 1966.

Henry James 3rd to Carl Stumpf

[65, 1921]

February 16, 1921 | Professor Carl Stumpff[391] | Berlin

Dear Professor Stumpff: –

The war has produced many false rumors; one of them reached me to the effect that you had died two or three years ago, and as a result, I took no steps about sending you the collection of my father's correspondence which I published in December. Recently I instituted an inquiry to learn the whereabouts of other members of your family, with a view to writing them about the manuscript of my father's letters to you which are still in my possession, and the result is that have just learned that the report of your death was false. Needless to say, I am very glad indeed to hear this.

As I have not yet received any word giving me your present address, I send this to you through the American Mission in Berlin. By reason of the same uncertainty, I am not ordering the publishers to send you the two volumes of letters,[392] but am enclosing to you a note which you can forward to them with further proper instructions.

You were kind enough to send me the manuscript of a number of my father's letters, and I am now ready to return these to you by whatever channel you advise. I hope you will believe that I have been most grateful to you for these letters; some of them you will see are among the best that have included in the book.[393] There are a good many letters and papers which have not been published, but which are so interesting that they deserve to be preserved. If you do not care to have the manuscript of your letters returned to you, or if at any later time you have no other disposition that you care to make of them, I shall always be glad to place them with the collection that is being preserved in Cambridge, but hope you will understand that in informing you of this possibility, I am not pressing you to do anything with the manuscripts that really belong to you, except what you may prefer to do with them.

---

[391] Sic, here and below.
[392] *Letters of William James*. 2 vols. ed. by his son H. James, Boston, Atlantic Monthly Press and London, Longmans, Green & Co., 1920.
[393] Henry included two letters to Stumpf: [7, 1886] and [10, 1887]. Cf. *The Letters of William James*, vol. 1, pp. 247–249 and 262–267.

I hope that you and your family, especially the two sons whom I remember when we were boys in Munich, are well. I am happy to say that all goes well with my mother who still lives in Cambridge, and with my brothers and sister.

With regards, | Yours truly,

[66, 1922]

July 25, 1922.
Professor Carl Stumpf | 45, Ausbergerstrasse, | Berlin, W. Germany.
Dear professor Stumpf: –
I have lately been in Cambridge, and got this package of letters out of the file,[394] and send them to you in accordance with your request to have them back in order that you may take such of them as you want to have in manuscript. Some had been copied a few years ago, but copies do not exist in duplicate. I have just had the remainder re-copied, and of these send you duplicate copies for your convenience. Of course, I should be glad to have any manuscripts that you don't care to keep instead of copies, but I quite appreciate your desire to have some of the manuscripts, and it is your right to.

My mother begged me to send her best regards to you and your Frau Stumpf. Please believe me with best wishes and regards,

Yours sincerely, | [hand] HJ[3]

---

394 See the *Introduction*.

Appendices

I Overview of Correspondence

Table 1: W. James – C. Stumpf. Correspondence.

Serial	W. James – C. Stumpf. Correspondence				Source	
	William James	Carl Stumpf	Type	Place	William James Papers. Houghton Library, Harvard University. Series I: bMS Am 1092.9	Berlin, Staatsbibliothek – Preussischer Kulturbesitz
[1, 1882]	26/11/1882		autograph letter	Paris		3778
[2, 1882]		8/12/1882	autograph letter	Prague	620	
[3, 1884]	9/1/1884		dictated	Cambridge		3779
[4, 1884]		4/2/1884	autograph letter	Prague	621	
[5, 1884]	15/11/1884		autograph letter	Cambridge		3780
[6, 1885]		12/2/1885	autograph letter	Halle	622	
[7, 1886]	1/1/1886		autograph letter	Cambridge		3781
[8, 1886]		8/9/1886	autograph letter	Sassnitz	623	
[9, 1887]		2/1/1887	autograph letter	Halle	624	
[10, 1887]	6/2/1887		autograph letter	Cambridge		3782
[11, 1887]		18/2/1887	postcard	Halle	625	
[12, 1889]	15/8/1889		autograph letter	Liverpool		3783
[13, 1890]		17/11/1890	autograph letter	München	626	

I Overview of correspondence — 201

[14, 1890]	1/12/1890		autograph letter	Cambridge	3784
[15, 1891]	25/4/1891		autograph letter	Cambridge	3785
[16, 1891]		14/5/1891	autograph letter	München	627
[17, 1891]	21/9/1891		autograph letter	London	3786
[18, 1891]		24/10/1891	autograph letter	München	628
[19, 1892]	24/6/1892		autograph letter	Lucerne	3787
[20, 1892]		30/6/1892	autograph letter	München	629
[21, 1892]	20/12/1892		autograph letter	Florence	3788
[22, 1893]	24/4/1893		autograph letter	Meggen	3789
[23, 1893]		17/5/1893	autograph letter	München	630
[24, 1893]	26/5/1893		autograph letter	Meggen	3790
[25, 1893]	12/9/1893		autograph letter	Cambridge	3791
[26, 1894]	24/1/1894		autograph letter	Cambridge	3792
[27, 1894]	1/4/1894		autograph letter	Cambridge	3793
[28, 1895]	12/4/1895		autograph letter	Cambridge	3794
[29, 1895]	18/12/1895		autograph letter (copy)	Cambridge	3795
[30, 1896]		13/10/1896	autograph letter	Berlin	631
[31, 1896]	24–28 Nov 1896		dictated; typed	Cambridge	3796

(continued)

Table 1 (continued)

Serial	W. James – C. Stumpf. Correspondence				Source		
	William James	Carl Stumpf	Type	Place	William James Papers. Houghton Library, Harvard University. Series I: bMS Am 1092.9	Berlin, Staatsbibliothek – Preussischer Kulturbesitz
[32, 1898]		30/10/1898	autograph letter	Berlin	632	
[33, 1899]	30/8/1899		autograph letter	Bad-Nauheim		3797
[34, 1899]		8/9/1899	autograph letter	Wengen	633	
[35, 1899]	10/9/1899		autograph letter	Bad-Nauheim		3798
[36, 1899]	12/9/1899		autograph letter	Bad-Nauheim		3799
[37, 1899]		12/9/1899	postcard	Weggis	634	
[38, 1899]		30/12/1899	autograph letter	Berlin	635	
[39, 1900]	2/1/1900		dictated; typed	Rye		3800
[40, 1900]	17/3/1900		autograph letter	Carqueiranne		3801
[41, 1900]		23/3/1900	postcard	Berlin	636	
[42, 1900]	16/4/1900		postcard	Costebelle		3802
[43, 1900]	30/4/1900		postcard	Geneva		3803

I Overview of correspondence — 203

[44, 1900]		Berlin	postcard		637	
[45, 1900]	20/5/1900	Montreux	dictated		3804	
[46, 1900]	8/6/1900	Berlin	postcard		638	
[47, 1901]	11/6/1900	Bad-Nauheim	autograph letter	[3805, copy]		Samml. Darmstaedter 2a 1890: James, William (D3589.10)
[48, 1901]	10/7/1901	Bad-Nauheim	autograph letter		3806	
[49, 1902]	6/8/1901	Cambridge	autograph letter	[3807, copy]		Samml. Darmstaedter 2a 1890: James, William (D3589.10)
[50, 1904]	11/2/1902	Cambridge	typed		3808	
[51, 1904]	1/1/1904	Baden Baden	autograph letter		639	
[52, 1904]	26/3/1904	Chocorua	autograph letter		3809	
[53, 1907]	17/7/1904	Berlin	autograph letter		640	
[54, 1907]	8/5/1907	Cambridge	autograph letter		3810	
[55, 1909]	20/5/1907	Berlin	postcard		641	
[56, 1909]	20/5/1909	Berlin	autograph letter		642	
[57, 1910]	26/10/1909	Cambridge	autograph letter		3811	
	6/1/1910					

Table 2: Previous publication.

Serial	Previous publication		
	The Letters of William James (1920)	The Correspondence of William James (1992–2004)	Perry, Thought and Character, vol. 2 (1935)
[1, 1882]		[calendared, 5: 561]	
[2, 1882]		[calendared, 5: 561]	
[3, 1884]		5: 480–482	
[4, 1884]		[calendared, 5:568]	
[5, 1884]		5: 532–534	
[6, 1885]		[calendared, 6: 562]	
[7, 1886]	part., 1: 247–249	6: 104–106	
[8, 1886]		[calendared, 6:574]	English transl.: part., pp. 66–67; German original: part., pp. 738–739
[9, 1887]		[calendared, 6: 579]	part., p. 739
[10, 1887]	part., 1: 262–267	6: 202–205	
[11, 1887]		[calendared, 6, 580]	
[12, 1889]		6: 525–526	
[13, 1890]		[calendared, 7: 577]	
[14, 1890]		7: 115–116	
[15, 1891]		7: 155–156	
[16, 1891]		[calendared, 7: 582]	
[17, 1891]		7: 200–202	
[18, 1891]		7: 209–211	
[19, 1892]		7: 285–287	
[20, 1892]		[calendared, 7: 591]	
[21, 1892]		7: 352–354	
[22, 1893]		7: 410–411	
[23, 1893]		7: 422–424	part., pp. 739–740

Table 2 (continued)

Serial	Previous publication		
	The Letters of William James (1920)	The Correspondence of William James (1992–2004)	Perry, *Thought and Character*, vol. 2 (1935)
[24, 1893]		7: 424–427	
[25, 1893]		7: 460–461	
[26, 1894]		7: 484–486	
[27, 1894]		[calendared, 7: 610]	
[28, 1895]		[calendared, 8: 566]	
[29, 1895]		8: 106–107	
[30, 1896]		[calendared, 8: 588]	
[31, 1896]		8: 209–211	
[32, 1898]		[calendared, 8: 621–622]	
[33, 1899]		9: 33–34	
[34, 1899]		[calendared, 9: 575]	part., pp. 740–741
[35, 1899]		9: 37–39	
[36, 1899]		[calendared, 9: 575]	
[37, 1899]		[calendared, 9: 576]	
[38, 1899]		[calendared, 9: 585]	
[39, 1900]		[calendared, 9: 586]	
[40, 1900]		9: 165–166	
[41, 1900]		[calendared, 9: 592]	
[42, 1900]		[calendared, 9: 594–595]	
[43, 1900]		9: 196	
[44, 1900]		[calendared, 9: 598]	
[45, 1900]		9: 223–224	
[46, 1900]		[calendared, 9: 599]	
[47, 1901]		9: 516–517	
[48, 1901]		9: 525–527	

Table 2 (continued)

Serial	Previous publication		
	The Letters of William James (1920)	The Correspondence of William James (1992–2004)	Perry, *Thought and Character*, vol. 2 (1935)
[49, 1902]		[calendared, 10: 581]	
[50, 1904]		10: 355–356	
[51, 1904]		[calendared, 10: 616]	part., pp. 741–744
[52, 1904]		10: 435–436	
[53, 1907]		[calendared, 10: 611]	part., p. 744
[54, 1907]		10: 367–368	
[55, 1909]		[calendared, 10: 624]	part., p. 744
[56, 1909]		[calendared, 10: 626]	
[57, 1910]		11: 410	

Table 3: Family Letters.

Serial	Date	William James	Carl Stumpf	Henry James 3rd	Type	Place	Source: The William James Papers, Houghton Library (1092.9)	Source: Adolph-Wurth Archive – Würzburg
[58, 1882]	2/11/1882	to Alice Howe James			autograph letter	Aussig	1299	
[59, 1893]	14/3/1893	to Hermine Stumpf			autograph letter	Florence		Carl Stumpf (1848 – 1936). Expansion 2014 (K2).
[60, 1911]	7/6/1911		to Alice Howe James		postcard	Berlin	4336	
[61, 1911]	11/11/1911		to Henry James 3rd		postcard	Berlin	172	
[62, 1911]	3/12/1911		to Henry James 3rd		autograph letter	Berlin	172	
[63, 1912]	3/3/1912		to Henry James 3rd		autograph letter	Berlin	172	
[64, 1912]	13/3/1912		to Henry James 3rd		autograph letter	Berlin	172	
[65, 1921]	16/2/1921			to Carl Stumpf	typed	Cambridge, MA	256	
[66, 1922]	25/7/1922			to Carl Stumpf	typed	Cambridge, MA	256	

II German letters of Carl Stumpf

Briefe an William James (1882–1909)

[2, 1882]

Smichov-Prag 8. Dez 82

Lieber James!
Mit aufrichtiger Freude erwidere ich Ihre Anrede in gleicher Weise. Denn ich habe bei Ihrem nur allzu kurzen Besuche doch den festen Eindruck gewonnen, dass wir nicht blos in unseren wissenschaftlichen Ansichten und Absichten in einer seltenen Weise harmonieren, sondern auch allzeit gute persönliche Freunde sein werden.

Für die Zurücksendung meiner kleinen Aufsätze, weit mehr aber für die Zusendung Ihrer beiden Abhandlungen bin ich Ihnen zu Dank verpflichtet. Von den letzteren habe ich, da ich mit dem Drucke meiner Tonpsychologie jetzt alle Hände voll zu thun habe, erst eine, „The Feeling of Effort" gelesen und bin mit Ihren gründlichen Ausführungen fast völlig einverstanden; freue mich auch, in der Tonpsychologie einmal zur Bestätigung darauf hinweisen zu können (die „Innervationsgefühle" spielen nämlich da auch ihre zweifelhafte Rolle).

Mein Aufsatz über die 4te Dimension erschien in den Philosoph. Monatsheften v. Schaarschmidt 1878.

Ich hoffe, dass dieser Brief Sie noch in London antreffen wird, und zwar in besserer Gesundheit. Ob nicht doch die unstete Lebensweise, welcher Sie in Europa huldigen, einen ungünstigen Einfluss auf Ihre Nerven hat? Ich wenigstens wäre dadurch längst ruiniert. Doch Sie müssen sich besser kennen als ich.
Ihre Notizen über Helmholtz, Delboeuf u. A. waren mir von Interesse. Ich hoffe sehr, dass wir auch künftig *wenigstens einmal* im Jahre von einander hören. Das nächste Zeichen von mir wird allerdings etwas lange auf sich warten lassen, da ich jetzt und voraussichtlich während des ganzen Jahres 83 mich ohne Athem holen „unter der Presse" befinden werde.

Die herzlichsten Grüsse sowohl von mir als meiner Frau und Marty, welche die Ihrigen dankend und mit Freude empfangen haben.
Alles Gute!

Ihr getreuer | C Stumpf

[4, 1884]

Prag, Smichov 4.II.84

Mein lieber James!

Haben Sie besten Dank für Ihren lieben Brief und Ihre verehrte Frau für das Schreiben derselben! Es wundert mich, dass Sie mein Buch so spät erhielten, da ich bereits in der 2. Hälfte Oktober Hirzel den Auftrag gab, es Ihnen zuzusenden und die übrigen Sendungen auch damals in der That effektuirt wurden. Es muss lange auf dem Wege gelegen haben. Für die freundlichen Worte, welche Sie mir darüber sagen, bin ich von Herzen dankbar; bis jetzt ist die Anerkennung, die ich gefunden, äusserst gering und beschränkt sich auf 2–3 Briefe. Ich kann auch nicht hoffen, dass das Buch viele Leser finden werde; es geht zu sehr in's Detail. „Mind" brachte eine Notiz, in welcher die Vermutung ausgesprochen war, dass mir Gurney unbekannt geblieben. Dies ist, Dank Ihrer Erinnerung, nicht der Fall, ich kenne das Werk seit mehr als einem Jahre (das meinige war etwa bis § 11 gedruckt), fand aber darin leider nicht so viel als ich hoffte. Mit dem I und II Bande des meinigen berührt es sich so gut wie gar nicht; erst für den III werde ich es benutzen können. Ich bin jetzt am II Bande, der aber nicht vor Ostern 85 erscheinen wird, da meine Nerven keine grössere Anstrengung vertragen; darin werde ich eine neue Theorie der Consonanz bringen.

Ihre „Courses of Study" erhielt ich bereits und habe mit Interesse davon Kenntnis genommen. Die Einrichtungen scheinen allerdings von unseren sehr verschieden, mehr schulmässig, aber gewiss praktisch. Wir haben jetzt übrigens in Prag auch ein philosophisches Seminar, 2 Stunden in der Woche, von mir und Marty geleitet, das erste in Österreich.

Ihren I. Aufsatz im Mind sah ich in der Universitätsbibliothek und las einstweilen die ersten Seiten, welche mich auf das Weitere begierig machen. Brentano thun Sie jedoch Unrecht, wenn Sie ihm die extreme Ansicht zuschreiben; er betont ja, dass die Psychologie wesentlich auf Beobachtung in der *Erinnerung* angewiesen u. dass diese keineswegs unfehlbar sei. Marty wird Ihnen einen Aufsatz über „Subjektlose Sätze" zusenden.

Haben Sie im vorigen Jahre unsere Photographien erhalten? Meine Frau sandte Ihnen dieselben zugleich mit dem besten Dank für die schönen Bücher Ihres Hrn Bruders, welche sie mit vielem Genusse gelesen hat.

Ihre Aufsätze studirte ich noch nicht vollständig, aber zum grösseren Teile, und freute mich sehr, in wesentlichen Puncten der Psychologie mit Ihnen übereinzustimmen. Ihre ausgezeichnete Arbeit über Innervationsgefühle werden Sie in der Tonpsychologie s. 167 bereits zitiert finden. Inzwischen ersah ich aus dem grossen Handbuch der Psychologie von Hermann, dass auch Hering (Raumsinn S. 547) und Funke (Tastsinn S. 363 f) sich in unserem Sinne ausgesprochen. Ganz vorzüglich interessierten mich Ihre Ausführungen über den philosophischen Glauben; doch muss ich gestehen, dass ich meine Zustimmung, wie in der Sache selbst, so auch in der Theorie der Sache noch zurückhalte. Zuviel ist schon durch den Glauben auch in der Philosophie gesündigt und verdorben worden, als dass wir nicht mit dieser Neigung streng umgehen sollten. Ich selbst habe damit zu schmerzliche Erfahrungen gemacht, die mich Jahre der Entwicklung kosteten. Aber Sie haben Recht, dass die Frage zur Sprache gebracht werden muss, während sie bisher beinahe todgeschwiegen ist; und ich achte all die Detailarbeit, die ich treibe, für sehr gering gegen jene grossen Fragen, die den Kern und die Seele der Philosophie allzeit ausmachen werden. Darüber hoffentlich einmal mündlich! Dann müssen Sie aber nicht Tage sondern Wochen bleiben und auch Ihre verehrte Frau mitbringen. Herzlichen Gruss!

Ihr | C Stumpf

[6, 1885]

Halle a/S. den 12 II 85

Lieber James!

Ihren Brief vom 15.XI.84, sowie die Sendung des Literar. Nachlasses Ihres Vaters, die beide noch nach Prag adressiert waren, erhielt ich hierher nachgesandt. Den Aufsatz „On the Function of Cognition" adressirten Sie bereits hierher, haben also inzwischen vernommen, dass wir umgezogen sind. Ich erhielt im August einen Ruf hierher und nahm denselben sogleich an, zumal auch die materiellen Bedingungen günstig waren. Wir beide empfinden die Rückkehr in's deutsche Reich wie eine Erlösung; denn es war uns in Prag immer unbehaglicher geworden; es deprimirt fortwährend die eigene Nation beschimpft und unterdrückt zu sehen. Nur von meinem lieben Freunde Marty schied ich mit Schmerzen; ich werde nirgends wieder einen so treuen und zugleich wissenschaftlich anregenden Gefährten finden. Hier haben wir uns seit dem Ende des Oktober gut eingelebt und sind in jeder Hinsicht zufrieden, besonders aber mit den collegialen Kreise. Vor 8 Tagen ist unser Glück noch verdoppelt worden, indem meine Frau mich mit einem zweiten Knaben beschenkte und sowohl die Mutter als das Kind wol und munter sind.

Mit Betrübnis vernahm ich hingegen aus Ihrem Brief, dass Sie keine gute Zeit durchgemacht haben und immer mit Ihren Augen kämpfen müssen. Arbeiten Sie nicht zu viel, lieber Freund! Sie schreiben ja ununterbrochen. Freilich ist alles so woldurchdacht und anregend, dass ich den Wunsch sogleich wieder zurücknehmen möchte. Unsere Wissenschaft bedarf so sehr neuer Kräfte, die in *unbefangener* Weise die alten Probleme in Angriff nehmen, dass es mir unendlich leid thut eine der besten unter ihnen durch schlechte Gesundheit am Wirken gehindert zu sehen. Aber ohne frische Nerven geht es nun einmal nicht auf die Dauer! Ich sage mir dies ebenfalls, und hüte mich jetzt sehr vor Überarbeitung.

Das Buch Ihres Vaters mit Ihrer ausführlichen Einleitung konnte ich bis jetzt ebenso wenig näher kennen lernen wie Ihren letzten Aufsatz; es fehlte mir die Zeit, nicht das Interesse. Wie die Religionsphilosophie, so ist auch das Verhältnis der Religion zur Moralität für mich eine der wichtigsten Fragen und ich bin begierig, die Anschauung Ihres Vaters u. die Ihrige genauer kennen zu lernen; hoffentlich bringen mir die Ferien die nötige Musse, um die Abende dazu zu verwenden, während die Tage meinem Buch gehören müssen. Jetzt bin ich Abends entweder zu müde oder muss Gesellschaften mitmachen, die hier auch leider einen grossen Teil der Zeit und Kraft wegnehmen und doch im Anfange nicht zu vermeiden sind.

Für Ihre gute Meinung von meiner Tonpsychologie sage ich den herzlichsten Dank; Ihre Anerkennung ist mir mehr wert als die der meisten meiner deutschen

Collegen. Wundt hat im Literar. Centralblatt eine ganz perfide Rezension *anonym* geschrieben, welche auf den Leser den Eindruck machen muss als ob ein *Dritter* sich gerade in den Puncten, in denen ich Wundt angegriffen habe, auf dessen Seite stellte. Sonst bin ich allerdings durch eine ziemliche Zahl freundlicher Rezensionen überrascht worden; die Sully's war recht sachverständig, nur mein S. 33 gebrachtes Argument hat er total misverstanden, sein Einwand dagegen ist offenbar hinfällig. Die Bemerkungen Ihres Briefes, welche mit einem Hauptpuncte bei Sully, wie Sie selbst sagen, nahezu zusammentreffen, und für welche ich sehr dankbar bin, muss ich überlegen; vielleicht gibt der II Band Gelegenheit darauf zurückzukommen. Ich erinnere mich, eine ähnliche Ansicht von der Sache selbst früher gehabt zu haben; aber die Theorie wollte sich nicht durchführen lassen. Vielleicht ist irgend ein Mittelweg zu finden. Mit dem II. Bd. hoffe ich in diesem Jahre fertig zu werden. Der Umzug u. die neue Stellung hat mich in der Arbeit zurückgeschlagen. Ich habe seit dem November nur eine Abhandlung „Über englische Musikpsychologie oder über Sprachmusik u. Thiermusik" nahezu vollendet, welche in die neue Vierteljahrsschrift für Musikwissenschaft kommen soll, doch erst im Juli erscheinen wird. Sie enthält zugleich Studien für den II und III. Band und gibt Einiges ausführlich, was dann im Buch kürzer behandelt wird. Spencer, Sully, Darwin, Gurney, Pole werden kritisiert. Sind Ihnen noch neuere Arbeiten über Musikpsychologie in England bekannt? Gurney habe ich bereits im Dezember 1881 auf Ihre Anregung hin angesehen, konnte aber für den I. Band nichts damit anfangen; Sully bemerkt daher mit Unrecht, dass mir „oddly enough" dieses Werk unbekannt scheine. Leider werde ich auch in den folgendem Bänden wenig Positives daraus benützen können; die Berufung auf einen musical sense ist keine Erklärung.

Im vorigen Jahre sandte meine Frau Ihnen unsre Photographien und später schrieb ich Ihnen einen Brief, worin u. A. von Ihren Arbeiten über Religionsphilosophie kurz die Rede war (an den sonstigen Inhalt erinnere ich mich nicht). Haben Sie beides erhalten? Bitte mir in dem nächsten Brief darüber zu antworten. Es wird überhaupt gut sein, wenn wir regelmässig den Empfang des letzten Briefes u. der etwaigen Sendungen erwähnen, meinen Sie nicht? Nun leben sie wol, lieber Freund, und nehmen Sie mit Ihrer verehrten Frau und Familie von uns beiden, die wir mit wahrer Freude an Ihre Anwesenheit zurückdenken, die herzlichsten u. besten Wünsche. Möge es Ihnen im neuen Jahre gut gehen!

Ihr | C Stumpf

[8, 1886]

Sassnitz (auf der Insel Rügen) am 8. Sept. 86

Lieber James!

Verzeihung, dass ich Ihren lieben langen Brief vom 1. Januar noch nicht beantwortet! Ich verschob es auf die grossen Ferien, nebst so manchem Andern, was liegen geblieben. Jetzt sitze ich hier, am schönsten Puncte Rügen's, geniesse mit Frau u. Kindern die Bäder u. die Luft und gedenke der Freunde in den Ferne, und nicht am wenigstens dessen, der am weitesten entfernt. Ihr Brief hat durch mancherlei Nachrichten unsre Teilnahme erweckt; vor allem unser schmerzliches Mitgefühl an dem Verlust Ihres jüngsten Kindes. Möchte die Zeit Ihnen ein guter Arzt und die Philosophie ein guter Prediger gewesen sein, deren Lehren, so wie *Sie* dieselben verstehen, ja auch Ihrer verehrten Frau nicht unzugänglich sind. Und möchte auch der letzteren Sorge um die Mutter durch die italienische Reise gehoben sein. Sehr erfreut waren wir durch die Nachricht Ihrer Beförderung zum Ordinarius, die Sie nach meiner Überzeugung viel früher verdient hatten; auch die bessere äussere Lage, die bequemere Wohnung, die kräftigeren Augen sind alles Dinge, von denen ich gerne höre. Wir unsrerseits dürfen ebenfalls nicht klagen. Halle, die Collegen, die Studienverhältnisse behagen mir; man lebt ruhig und in gutem Einvernehmen. Wir fühlen uns wie aus dem unruhigen Meer in den stillen Hafen versetzt. Die Studenten sind fleissig, meine Vorlesungen gut besucht (etwa 70 in der Logik diesen Sommer). Die Luft ist zwar in Halle auch wie in Prag durch Fabriken verunreinigt doch bei weitem nicht in demselben Masse. Die Wohnung äusserst bequem. Man ist in einem *cultivirten* Land, während ich Böhmen und speziell Prag nur zu den halbcultivirten Gegenden zählen möchte. Unsere Kinder (Rudolf jetzt 5 ¼, Felix 1 2/3 Jahre) gedeihen im Ganzen, sodass wir nur vorübergehende und kleine Sorgen und daneben viele Freuden mit ihnen haben. Mir selbst fehlt es immer noch an einem dauernd und gleichmässig guten Schlaf; auf 7 mangelhafte kommt nur 1 wirklich gute Nacht. Das hemmt die Thätigkeit und beeinträchtigt oft die Freudigkeit; aber man muss sich eben hineinfinden und die Hoffnung nicht sinken lassen. So hoffe ich jetzt wieder besonders durch diese Seebadecur mir einen guten Winter zu erwerben, u. hoffentlich wird die Hoffnung nicht trügen. Unter dieser Voraussetzung hoffe ich dann auch endlich mit dem II. Band der Tonpsychologie fertig zu werden, an dem ich in den letzten Jahren nur äusserst langsam u. mit fortwährenden Unterbrechungen arbeiten konnte; teils wegen der üblen Nerven, teils wegen der akademischen Pflichten. Dem II. wird, so Gott will, noch ein III. Band folgen, dessen Grundzüge ebenfalls längst feststehen. Dann will ich grosses Fest feiern und die Töne auf sich beruhen lassen, um so vieles Andere, das mir auf dem Herzen u. im Sinne liegt, zur Reife zu bringen. Aber wie kurz ist das

Leben! Man sieht dies ein, wenn man über die erste Hälfte hinaus ist; vorher liegt es wie ein Ocean, ohne absehbare Grenzen, u. jetzt – muss man für jeden neuen Tag, jede Stunde frischer Arbeit, jeden Augenblick des Sonnenscheins danken wie für ein unerwartetes Geschenk.

Über *Lipps* denke ich vielleicht nicht ganz so günstig wie Sie; er erscheint mir zwar talentvoll, aber noch recht unreif. Es wäre ihm nützlich, wenn er einige Jahre mit Schriftstellern pausirte u. nicht seine Studien vor dem Publicum machte. Aber unsre junge Generation ist gar ehrgeizig. Die Schrift von *Mach* hat mir viel Vergnügen bereitet; aber wenn man näher zusieht, löst sich doch Vieles in mehr geistreiche als wahre Aperçu's auf. Ich erlaubte mir dies so höflich als möglich in meiner Recension in der „Deutschen Litt. Ztg" anzudeuten u. erfuhr zu meiner Freude, dass Mach den Widerspruch nicht übel genommen. Vielmehr sprach er mir seinen Dank aus. Neuerdings habe ich auch Spencers Psychology in derselben Ztg. recensirt u. bin mir dabei über Spencer's eigentliches Wesen recht Klar geworden; er ist im Grunde ein modernisirter Hegel, scheint's Ihnen nicht auch so? Wenn Sie gern Abdrücke der Recensionen haben, sende ich sie. Zwei andre Arbeiten haben mir viel Zeit gekostet: ein Referat über Ellis' Untersuchungen exotischer Tonleiter, die sehr schwierig zu studiren waren, u. ein Bericht über meine Untersuchung der Gesänge der Bellacula-Indianer, die sich im vorigen Herbst in Halle sehen u. hören liessen; beides werden Sie in den nächsten Monaten wol erhalten. Den Aufsatz über „englische Musikpsychologie" habe ich Ihnen doch gesandt? – Kennen Sie einen Prof. *Grafe* in Leyden? Er besuchte mich im Sommer u. erzählte, dass er über Innervationsempfindungen arbeite. Ihre Schrift darüber war ihm bekannt. Er schien aber ein *Anhänger* der Inn = Empf. zu sein. Besonders wurde ich an sie erinnert durch den Besuch eines Ihrer amerikanischen Collegen, *Fullerton* aus Philadelphia. Er brachte einige Wochen in Halle zu. Wir philosophirten etliche Male, und zwar besonders über den Idealismus (Phänomenalism), zu dem er sich bekennt, während ich denselben für undurchführbar halte. Naturwissenschaft ist nicht möglich als Wissenschaft der Phänomene, da diese als solche keine Gesetzmässigkeit zeigen, sondern erst dann, wenn wir vom Bewusstsein unabhängige Realitäten hinzuergänzen, die unter sich und mit dem Empfindungsobjekte in gesetzlicher Wechselwirkung stehen. Die Aussenwelt ist die allgemeinste Hypothese, von welcher alle anderen Hypothesen u. Gesetze der Naturwissenschaft nur Spezialisirungen sind. Mehr als die gesetzlichen *Beziehungen* unter den Realitäten erkennen wir freilich nicht, also *nicht* ihre absoluten Qualitäten. Natürlich sind wir aber nicht einig geworden. Fullerton schien mir ein scharfer Kopf, aber (unter uns gesagt) mit etwas zu starkem Selbstvertrauen und zu wenig Information über die philosophische Litteratur. Er ist noch sehr jung, und so mag er wol diese Mängel noch überwinden. Mit Ihnen, lieber James, habe ich in kürzerer Zeit weit engere Fühlung gewonnen, sowol wissenschaftlich als persönlich; wir standen uns offenbar bereits vorher, ohne es zu wissen, unserer geistiger Organisation und unserer Gesinnung zufolge besonders nahe.

Durch Fullerton erhielt ich auch ausführlichen Bericht über die Thätigkeit Ihrer „psychical Society", von der Ihr Brief vom 1./I spricht. Full.[erton] geht ja fast ganz darin auf und scheint dieselbe als Hauptzweck seiner ganzen Reise zu betrachten. Da Sie mich über meine Auffassung dieser Forschungen fragen, so bekenne ich wol meine Übereinstimmung mit den allgemeinen Prinzipien, die Sie in dem Briefe darüber aussprechen, und glaube von dem Vorurteil frei zu sein, welches das Ungewöhnliche für unmöglich hält. Aber eine actuelle Bedeutung scheint mir dergleichen erst dann zu erlangen, wenn sich zugleich einige Aussicht darbietet, es mit dem bereits Erklärten in Zusammenhang zu bringen. Nun bieten uns im psychischen Leben schon die alltäglichen Erscheinungen noch so viele Räthsel, dass es mir nicht Recht dünken will, wenn wir unsere beste Kraft jenen aussergewöhnlichen zuwenden wollten. Ich glaube auch nicht, dass *Sie* dies thun oder zu thun gedenken. Fullerton hingegen schien mir mehr als gebührlich von dieser Sache eingenommen.

Man muss ja allerdings auch der individuellen Neigung hierin einen Spielraum lassen, und will ich über ihn in dieser Hinsicht nicht absprechen, obschon es mich verwunderte, wie er trotz der immer und überall durch seine eigenen Nachforschungen bestätigten Unsolidität der Beobachtung noch Lust am weiteren Nachfragen empfinden konnte. Nun, er wird Ihnen ja selbst Bericht erstatten über das, was ihm Fechner und Andere gestanden haben. Besser als die *spiritistischen* Manifestationen stehen die *hypnotischen* da, und besitzen ohne Zweifel schon jetzt einen wissenschaftl. Wert durch die Analogien mit so manchen bekannten Erscheinungen. Der Anschluss an diese wird gewiss über kurz oder lang gefunden; und Jeder, der Neues darüber bringt, vermehrt die Chancen dazu. Ich beglückwünsche Sie daher zu dem, was Sie nach Ihrem Briefe durch eigene Versuche hierüber gefunden. Wenn ich als Freund, wie sich's gebührt, *ganz* offen reden soll und Sie es mir darum auch nicht übel nehmen wollen, muss ich nur meinen Zweifel aussprechen, ob es rätlich sei, *Studenten* in höherem Masse zu solchen Versuchen heranzuziehen. Leicht gewinnen diese doch dadurch die Meinung, als seien die Seltsamkeiten die Hauptsache in der Wissenschaft. Fullerton scheint auch in dieser Beziehung ausserordentlich weit zu gehen; hat er doch nach seiner Erzählung gegen 10000 Versuche über Gedankenlesen mit Studenten gemacht! Nochmals aber: wir sind gewiss auch in diesen Dingen prinzipiell einig u. Sie denken's mir nicht als Anmassung.

Diese Einigkeit in den Principien und den Zielen der Forschung wird mir immer wertvoller, je mehr ich sehe, dass Männer, die man früher glaubte der gleichen Richtung und Gesinnung zuzählen zu dürfen, sich von derselben entfernen. Fast scheint es mir z. B., dass Sully von seinen grossen Talenten nicht mehr ganz den richtigen Gebrauch macht; er scheint mir mehr auf Vielschreiberei und Popularisirung auszugehen. Seine „Sensation and Intuition" enthält meinem Dafürhalten nach mehr Anregendes, als die späteren Schriften; jede neue geht mehr in's Breite als in die Tiefe. Vielleicht bietet seine Stellung als Examinator dazu die Veranlassung. Aber die Wissenschaft muss trauern, wenn die Studenten lachen.

Ganz gewiss gilt das Gesagte von *Wundt*. Seine Grossmannssucht und seine Confusion wachsen in gleichem Verhältnis. Er macht die Studenten und einige andere Leute glauben, dass mit den immer wiederholten Messungen der Reactionszeiten der Anfang zu einer ganz neuen „experimentellen Psychologie" gemacht sei, von welcher aus man nur mit Hohn und Spott auf die alte Psychologie zurückblicken könne. Sehen Sie seine Essays darüber, sehen Sie die Äusserungen seiner Schüler im Literar. Centralblatt. Als ob aus jenen Zeitmessungen überhaupt etwas Wichtiges zu folgern wäre, als ob sie nicht selbst nur durch die innere Beobachtung interpretirt werden müssten, als ob endlich Zahlen und nicht vielmehr klare Begriffe die Hauptsache wären! Und welch' schlechtes Beispiel gibt in Hinsicht des klaren und scharfen Denkens der Lehrer den Schülern! Wie seine Relativitätslehre, so steckt auch die Apperceptionslehre u. fast alles Allgemeinere voll von Mehrdeutigkeit und Widerspruch. Keiner versteht heutzutage besser die Kunst den Leuten mit volltönenden Worten und unter dem Schein der Exactheit Sand in die Augen zu streuen. Mein lieber Marty hat in Wundts eigener Vierteljahrsschrift dessen Apperceptionslehre jetzt einer schneidigen Kritik unterzogen, und dies scheint W. so verstimmt zu haben, dass der Herausgeber Avenarius die Fortsetzung einstweilen sistirt hat. Aber W. wird nichts Triftiges dagegen erwidern können; er wird versuchen, von oben herab dagegen wieder einige allgemeine Phrasen in's Feld zu senden, um sich wenigstens bei seinen blinden Verehrern zu rehabilitiren.

Meine Neigung geht zu wenig auf blosse Polemik, sonst würde ich in der That einmal das ganze Sündenregister W.'s zusammenstellen, und versuchen, die Augen wieder auf das wahrhaft Wertvolle in aller Forschung hinzulenken, über welchen die jüngere Generation durch W.[undt] vielfach getäuscht wird. Doch wird man von selbst wieder darauf zurückkommen. Wie oft ist schon die Psychologie in solcher Weise „exact" gemacht worden, um nachher doch wieder in die alten Bahnen, in die *psychologische Psychologie* zurückzulenken!

Genug, mein lieber James, der Klagen, ja zu viel davon! Lassen Sie uns lieber freudig das Erfreuliche hervorsuchen in Welt und Menschen und es vor allem in uns selbst verwirklichen.

Und damit bleiben Sie gut Ihrem Carl Stumpf, der mit Frau Sie und die Ihrige von Herzen grüsst.

[9, 1887]

Halle a/S. 2 Jan. 1887

Lieber James!

Dieses Mal ist an mir die Reihe, zum neuen Jahr zu gratuliren (das vorige Mal thaten Sie's); und so sende ich Ihnen denn über den Ocean die allerherzlichsten Wünsche für Ihr eigenes Wolsein und das Ihrer Familie. Von Woche zu Woche, und manchmal von Tag zu Tag, verschob ich es, Ihnen für die letzten Karten und die Zusendung der „Proceedings" zu danken, da ich doch noch etwas Mehr schreiben wollte und dazu sich die Zeit schwer finden liess. Nun, bevor die Vorlesungen wieder beginnen, sei alles dieses nachgeholt! Auch mit meinen Glückwünschen zum Jubiläum Ihrer Universität, wovon in unseren Zeitungen mit vieler Teilnahme gesprochen wurde, komme ich nun viel zu spät. Es freute mich, so vieles Rühmliche und Hoffnungsreiche von der Universität zu lesen, welcher Sie angehören und zur Zierde gereichen.

Nach meinem letzten Brief hatte ich ein Gefühl, welches wir als „Kater-Gefühl" zu bezeichnen pflegen (Sie kennen doch diesen studentischen Ausdruck); das Gefühl, dass ich darin fast nur Andere getadelt und meiner Erbitterung über so manche Unsolidität bei berühmten Schriftstellern oder sonstigen Collegen freien Lauf gelassen hatte; wodurch der Anschein der Selbst-Überhebung entstehen konnte, die mir im Grunde des Herzens ferne liegt und als schlimmste Eigenschaft verhasst ist. Darum war ich durch Ihre Karte wahrhaft beruhigt, da sie zeigte, dass Sie den Brief nicht in diesem gefürchteten Sinne gedeutet hatte. Ihr Urteil über Spencer interessirte mich; da man selten ein so scharfes Wort über diesen Denker, namentlich von englischen oder amerikan. Philosophen, aussprechen hört. Jeder von uns beiden sieht eben die Mängel und die Unsolidität des ihm näher Stehenden deutlicher: Sie diejenigen Spencer's, ich diejenige Wundt's. Das Treiben des Letzteren ist in der That für Solche, die es näher durchschauen, Ärgernis erregend. Von allen Fachmännern, deren originelle Gedanken er benutzt – Mathematikern, Physiologen, Sprachphilosophen u. sw. – hört man klagen, dass er ihre Gedanken wie eigene behandelt, ohne den Leser hinreichend über deren Ursprung zu orientiren. Allerdings gibt er diesen Ideen immer eine etwas andere Façon. Aber nicht blos ist er unglücklich in der Auswahl der Ideen selbst (indem er einen besonderen Instinct für das Falsche u. Confuse besitzt z. B. Relativitätsgesetz!), sondern er verschlechtert sie regelmässig noch durch seine Bearbeitung. Dazu diese unerträgliche Vielschreiberei – schon wieder ein dickleibiges Product, die „Ethik"! Nichts als Völkerpsychologie und dunklen Reden über Allgemeinheiten. Dieser „Gesamtwille", auf den die Ethik bei ihm hinausläuft, ist ja eitel Mystik, aufgewärmter Schopenhauer! Aber genug, ich komme ja wieder in denselben Ton. Man muss sich bei solchen Jeremiaden doch

immer vergegenwärtigen, dass wir Einiges vor der Hegelschen Zeit vorausha-
ben, dass doch die Isolirung der Fragen, die aufmerksame Analyse im Ganzen
zunimmt; sonst könnte man verzagen.

In den „Proceedings" ist Ihr Beitrag entschieden das Beste, ja, wie mir
scheint, das einzig Gute; es hat mich sehr interessirt. Besonders scheint mir die
Bemerkung S. 99 über die vereinigte Wirkung einer unanalysirten Summe von
Merkmalen und die Anwendung auf die Tiere lehrreich und nicht minder neu als
wahr. Dagegen kann mich der sonstige Inhalt dieses Heftes nicht von der Nütz-
lichkeit dieses so grossen Apparates für „psychische Untersuchung" (müsste heis-
sen: für Untersuchung *aussergewöhnlicher* psych. Thatsachen) überzeugen. Die
einzigen zwei Thatsachen, welche der Präsident in seiner langen Rede vorbringt
(S. 75–76) sind doch äusserst schwach beglaubigt im Verhältnis zu der Sicherheit, die man für solche Dinge haben müsste. Und dieses Pseudo-„Gesetz", mit
physikalischen Ausdrücken ausstaffirt, aber in sich selbst von kläglicher Unbe-
stimmtheit und noch kläglicheren Begründung, S. 82! Nun, Sie selbst haben sich
ja in dem 2. Aufsatz „Report" zurückhaltend und verständig ausgesprochen und
noch offener in Ihrer Karte. Aber ich danke Ihnen doch, dass Sie mich durch Zusendung des ganzen Heftes über diese Bewegung besser orientirt haben, als es
bisher der Fall war.

Fullerton sandte mir auch seinen Aufsatz über das Unendliche. Über die
abstracten Begriffe spricht er gut, über das Unendliche selbst aber sehr ungenügend. Meine beiden Kinder haben Scharlach, doch geht es wieder besser. Wir
Eltern sind gesund. Ich teile meine Zeit zwischen Buch u. Colleg. Nochmals
alles Gute für 1887!

Ihr | C Stumpf

Ich sende Ihnen eine Studie über *Indianer-Lieder*. Wenn Sie mir ähnliches
Material oder Literatur angeben können, oder wenn Sie musikalisch Begabte
veranlassen könnten, ähnliche Untersuchungen anzustellen, würde Ihnen die
„Tonpsychologie" Dank wissen. Sully erfreute mich durch seine Recension der
„Musikpsych. in England". So objektiv würde ein *Angegriffener* in Deutschland
selten referiren.

[11, 1887]

L.J.
Damit Sie nicht an meinem Brief einen neuen Anstoss nehmen, füge ich nachträglich bei, dass ich nicht etwa Puncte (oder gar *mathematische* Puncte) für *isoliert* wahrnehmbar halte, sondern (wie auch in meinem Buche) nur als Teile des ganzen Sehfeldes. Dadurch unterscheiden sie sich allerdings von den Tönen; aber dies beeinträchtigt ihre *absolute* Natur ebensowenig als es bei den Tönen der Fall wäre, wenn wir durch eine physische Einrichtung gezwungen wären, immer sämtliche Töne zugleich zu hören. – Sollte „Ort" nicht durch *locality* (oder *place*) übersetzt werden können? – Herzl. Grüsse!

Ihr treuergebener | C Stumpf

Halle a./S. 18/II 87

[13, 1890]

München 17 Nov 90.

Lieber Freund!
ich habe ein sehr schlechtes Gewissen. Längst hätte ich Ihnen danken müssen für Ihr grosses Werk: aber das Semester hatte eben begonnen und solcher Anfang bringt jedesmal viele Geschäfte. Auch heute kann ich Ihnen nur kurz meine innige Freude, meinen herzlichen Dank, meine hohe Bewunderung aussprechen. Noch habe ich wenig in dem Buche geblättert, aber doch soviel, um erkannt zu haben, dass Sie uns mit der *besten* Psychologie beschenkt haben und dass wir Deutsche neidisch sein müssten, wenn es in diesen „heiligen Hallen" überhaupt Neid gäbe. Ich freue mich ausserordentlich auf das Studium und werde Ihnen darüber schreiben, sobald ich den Hauptinhalt übersehen kann.

Hoffentlich erlaubt es jetzt Ihre Zeit, mir auch wieder einmal mehr als eine Karte zu schreiben. In Amerika geht es ja höchst erfreulich mit den psychologischen Arbeiten vorwärts. Hier in München ist der Boden noch sehr wenig cultivirt und ich kann nur langsam Wurzel fassen mit meinen Bestrebungen. Nur in der Richtung des Hypnotismus ist durch Du Prel, Schrenck-Notzing und jetzt auch durch einen Privatdozenten Schmidkunz die Teilnahme weiterer Kreise erregt, aber leider mischt sich da zu viel unsolider Gebahren ein. Ich meinerseits finde diese Dinge und besonders das Buch Janet's von grossem Interesse für die Theorie der *Persönlichkeit*; aber gerade an diese Verwertung scheinen die hiesigen Herren nicht zu denken. Ihr Artikel über Janet hat mir sehr gefallen. Die Telepathie jedoch will mir noch nicht einleuchten, und noch weniger der Spiritismus.

Mit Genugthuung sehe ich, dass Sie Ihre Meinung über Wundt's Unklarheiten kräftig in dem Buche ausgesprochen haben. Ich habe gestern einen Artikel über eine Arbeit aus seiner Schule corrigirt, der die Art des Experimentirens in derselben scharf geisselt. Sie werden ihn im Dezember wol erhalten.

Persönlich geht es mir u. den Meinigen gut; wir leben gerne in dieser schönen u. angenehmen Stadt der Künste. Beste Wünsche auch für Sie u. die Ihrigen. Von Herzen

Ihr treuergebener | C. Stumpf

[16, 1891]

München 14 Mai 91 | (Georgenstrasse)

Mein lieber James!
Sogleich nach Ihrem Briefe erhielt ich einen von Gizycki, der mir Weiteres über die Sachlage erzählte.

Ich habe nicht das Verdienst, die Übersetzung direct angeregt zu haben, nur indirect, indem ich im Colleg Ihr Buch rühmte. Cossmann kam dadurch von selbst auf die Idee der Übersetzung, in welcher ich ihn dann allerdings bestärkte. In Bezug auf die Durchführung hat er mich auch nicht geradezu um Rat und Hilfe gebeten, doch habe ich mich aus freien Stücken, aus Interesse an der Sache dazu angeboten. Nun aber ist eine Änderung meiner persönlichen Beziehungen zu Cossmann seit etwa 2 Monaten eingetreten, welche mich leider daran verhindert. Ich sandte ihm Ihren Brief und bemerkte nur, dass mir, nachdem die kleinere Ausgabe so nahe bevorsteht, allerdings (ebenso wie Gizycki) das Abwarten derselben rätlicher erscheinen würde. Cossmann führt nun selbst die Verhandlung mit Gizycki weiter.

Was ich persönlich mit Cossmann hatte, braucht Sie nicht zu bestimmen, ihm Ihr Vertrauen zu entziehen, es betrifft nur mich und ihn.

Kann ich *Ihnen* in Bezug auf die Angelegenheit in irgend einer Weise weiter raten, so zählen Sie auf mich.

Lassen Sie sich durch den infamen Artikel (Viertelj. Schr. f. Philos.) unseres hiesigen Privatdozenten Schmidkunz über Ihr Buch nicht ärgern; der Mensch identifiziert Psychologie mit Hypnotismus und geht ganz darin auf. *Ich* finde gerade Ihr Kapitel über Hypnotismus vorzüglich und sowol nach Ausdehnung als Inhalt den gegenwärtigen Anforderungen vollkommen entsprechend.

Meinen II Bd. hat Sully auch nicht gerade freundlich begrüsst. Wenn man sich solche Mühe gegeben hat, Detailarbeit zu verrichten, so erwartet man eher Dank als eine so mürrische Abkanzelung, auch wenn es etwas lange gedauert hat. *Dadurch* wird er mich nicht ermuntern, den III Band nun sehr schnell zu liefern.

Sonst gehts gut, mir bekommt das Münchener Klima, aber ich bedarf wirklich einiger Ruhe vom Arbeiten und möchte Ihnen auch empfehlen, es nicht allzu toll zu treiben. Mit tausend herzlichen Grüssen, auch von meiner Frau

Ihr | C Stumpf

Besten Dank für den *Moral philosopher*!

[18, 1891]

München, Georgenstr. *15* | 24. Oct. 91.

Mein lieber Freund James!

Verzeihen Sie, dass ich Ihren lieben langen Brief aus London, worin Sie mir so viele freundschaftliche und anerkennende Worte sagen, erst jetzt beantworte, obschon Sie auf eine rasche Antwort zu rechnen schienen. Der Brief traf mich in den Vorbereitungen zu einem Wohnungswechsel, während zugleich zahlreiche Besuche der aus dem Gebirg heimkehrenden Collegen und die Correctur kleiner Arbeiten meine Zeit wegnahmen. Nun ist dies alles glücklich überstanden und ich kann mich ein wenig mit Ihnen unterhalten, was mir viel mehr Vergnügen macht als die Unterhaltung mit dem Collegen Wundt.

Also vorerst meinen innigen Dank für Ihre guten Worte über mein Buch. Wenn ich auch einen Teil davon auf Ihre persönliche Freundschaft zu mir schieben muss, so ist mir doch eben diese Freundschaft selbst ein hohes Gut, und Einiges bleibt doch auch für das Buch übrig. Sully hat es so verdrießlich recensirt und Wundt mich überhaupt so schlecht gemacht, dass ich für ein Lob aus solchem Munde heute doppelt empfänglich bin. Was Sie über die tiefinnere Verwandtschaft unserer geistigen Tendenzen sagen, ist mir aus der Seele gesprochen. Ich verstehe auch vollkommen die Einwendungen, die Sie gegen viele meiner Ansichten im Einzelnen zu machen haben, und empfinde deren Gewicht hinreichend, um mich auch in diesen Puncten, die uns trennen, in Sie hineinversetzen zu können. So besonders die Opposition gegen die unwahrgenommen Empfindungen. Ich selbst würde sie vor 12 Jahren geleugnet haben; aber die Consequenz zahlreicher Einzelbetrachtungen scheint mir dahin zu führen, dass wir zwischen den eigentlich „unbewussten" Vorstellungen und den unbemerkten Teilen eines Complexes unterscheiden; die ersteren scheinen mir unanerkennbar, die letzteren notwendig. Ich glaube nicht, dass es der „psychologische Fehlschluss" ist der hieran die Schuld trägt, sondern nur bestimmte Argumente im Einzelnen. Aber gewiss bedarf diese Sache einmal einer eingehenden prinzipiellen Untersuchung, die zu einer Verständigung führen *muss*. Wenn ich Sie recht verstehe, gibt es nach Ihnen überhaupt keine *Teile* in dem Vorstellungsinhalt; jeder ist eine absolut einfache Qualität. Alle „Zergliederung" ist statt einer wirklichen Zergliederung eine Entdeckung oder Production gänzlich *neuer* einfacher Qualitäten.

Die Consequenz davon scheint mir zu sein, dass es auch keine Classification gibt. *Nichts* wäre den einzelnen Erscheinungen gemeinsam; jeder allgemeine Begriff wäre selbst wieder eine neue einfache Qualität sui generis. Ist dies Ihre Meinung?

Auch Ihre Opposition gegen die „einfachen Ähnlichkeiten" kann ich würdigen, da auch diese Behauptung sich mir erst spät aufgedrängt hat, und da ich gewisse

Schwierigkeiten selbst noch immer darin finde. Aber gerade von *Ihrem* Standpuncte scheint mir diese Annahme am wenigsten vermeidlich. Denn wenn es überhaupt keine Teile in den Empfindungen gibt, wie dürften wir dann „Ähnlichkeit" durch „teilweise Gleichheit oder Identität" definieren? –

Vielleicht würden wir mündlich besser und jedenfalls leichter hierüber discutiren. Ihr Schüler Delabarre, der mich kürzlich besuchte, machte mir Hoffnung, dass Sie im nächsten Jahre Ihre grossen Jahresferien halten würden; und davon wird, hoffe ich, auch ein Teilchen auf München entfallen. Der Schwager, den Sie in London besuchten, ist wol Herr Salter? Ich habe von ihm die allergrösste Hochachtung und drücke ihm im Geiste die Hand, obschon mir die Überzeugung von einem allwaltenden νοῦς moralisch nicht *so* irrelevant scheint wie ihm. Gewiss bleibt jede Pflicht auch für den Atheisten die nämliche. Aber für die ganze Lebens*stimmung* ist doch ein Unterschied wie zwischen der Vorstellung des Firmaments als einer festen Decke und als eines unendlichen Raums, oder noch viel mehr Unterschied! – Ihrer Frau Schwester geht es hoffentlich wieder gut und Sie konnten beruhigt zurückkehren?

Cossmann betreffend, will ich Ihnen *ganz vertraulich* mitteilen, was mich veranlasste, den Verkehr mit ihm abzubrechen. Es fiel mir zufällig ein Collegienheft von ihm in die Hand, worin er die Ausführungen meiner Psychologie-Vorlesung, statt sie correct niederzuschreiben und dann darüber nachzudenken, sogleich während des Hörens mit Bemerkungen wie „läppisches Argument" u. dgl. begleitet hatte. Es war eine Anzahl beschimpfender Ausdrücke darin, die mir zeigten, dass ihm jede Pietät gegen mich, der ich ihm persönlich in jeder Weise zu seinen Arbeiten behilflich gewesen, fehlte. So lieb mir ein *kritischer* Schüler ist, so konnte ich es doch nicht mehr über mich gewinnen, mit einem jungen Menschen, dessen Kritik solche Formen annahm, persönlich zu verkehren. Ich schrieb ihm deshalb, dass ich mich gezwungen sehe, den persönl. Verkehr abzubrechen, ohne jedoch das Motiv namhaft zu machen, um jede Discussion abzuschneiden.

Dies zur Aufklärung *unter uns*; für Sie braucht es ja in keiner Weise bestimmen zu werden. Ich glaube, dass es die Übersetzung gut besorgen wird, wenn ich auch über seinen deutschen *Stil* noch keine Ansicht habe. Aber Sie werden sie ja selbst durchsehen.

Ihr Mitgefühl mit dem „poor Wundt" kann ich leider nicht teilen und wundere mich fast darüber, da Sie ihn doch an verschiedenen Stellen Ihres Buches noch schlechter behandelt haben (z. B. ǂ 277). Und haben Sie nicht auch mit *mir* in dieser Sache Mitgefühl, dem die crasseste Unwissenheit und die abscheulichsten Tendenzen vorgeworfen werden? So wie ich Wundt *jetzt* kenne, reut es mich „erst recht" nicht, den Kampf mit ihm aufgenommen zu haben. Schwindel! Aber wir wollen uns darob nicht böse werden. Tausend herzl. Grüsse v. Ihrem

C Stumpf

[20, 1892]

München, Georgenstr. 18 | 30.VI 92.

Lieber James!
Bereits durch Münsterberg hörte ich, dass Sie mit Familie in Europa seien und den Winter da zubringen wollten – eine grosse Freude für mich, da ich doch nun Hoffnung habe, Sie auch einmal wiederzusehen und vielleicht auch Ihre liebe Frau und Familie kennen zu lernen. Herrlich wäre es, wenn Sie sich zu München entschlössen, und Sie werden nicht zweifeln, dass sowol ich als meine Frau in *jeder Beziehung* alles aufbieten würden, um Ihnen den Aufenthalt bequem zu machen. Die Schulen sind gut hier, und wenn Ihr Ältester nicht sofort in eine bestimmte Classe passt, so lässt sich's durch Privatunterricht bald so einrichten, *dass* er passt. Für Sie selbst wäre München als Luftkurort ausgezeichnet; ich kenne keine Stadt, die bei gleicher Grösse so gute und nervenstärkende Luft hat. Das macht die relativ hohe Lage (520 m). Und wie schön könnten wir über alle möglichen Fragen uns aussprechen!

Nur das Eine Bedenken, das Sie äussern, kann ich leider nicht ganz entkräften. Im Winter ists hier wol gelegentlich rauh, jedenfalls um durchschnittlich 2° R. *kälter* als in anderen Städten Deutschlands. Mein eigener ältester hatte in dem ersten Jahr öfters Halsentzündung, zu der er grosse Neigung hat. Aber im 2. und 3. Jahr ist sie immer seltener geworden und fast ganz verschwunden. Ich denke, dass das Klima die Wunden selbst heilt, die es schlägt, und zuletzt sogar dagegen gefeit macht. Aber da Sie nicht dauernd hier bleiben wollen, weiss ich nicht, ob Ihnen diese Abhärtung so viel wert ist wie uns. Es wäre mir *sehr leid*, wenn Sie sich für Paris entschlössen, aber ich darf nicht durch Ableugnung der nachteiligen Seiten eine Verantwortung auf mich laden. Jedenfalls wird indessen dem Münchner Klima auswärts *viel zu viel* Schlimmes nachgesagt, es ist *viel besser* als sein Ruf, Sie dürfen von dem was Sie hören reichlich die Hälfte abrechnen. Früher war ja München in der That eine *ungesunde* Stadt; Typhus, Cholera u.s.f. hielten reiche Ernte. Das ist seit der Kanalisation, Wasserleitung, Schlachthof etc. (hauptsächlich durch Pettenkofers Thätigkeit) *total* anders; von obigen Krankheiten ist keine Rede mehr, wenigstens nicht mehr als in jeder noch so gesunden Stadt. Ich selbst, ebenso meine Frau, befinden uns hier ganz wesentlich besser als vorher. Hoffentlich kommen Sie!

Sollten Sie nicht am besten thun, sich einfach eine Zeitlang *auf Probe* hier in einer von den vielen Familienpensionen niederzulassen? –

Münsterberg habe ich sofort als er mich um Rat fragte, dringend zur Annahme des Rufes geraten. Ich denke von ihm gleichfalls günstiger als manch' Anderer. *Talent* hat er sicherlich in hohem Masse. Er ist mir nur zu voreilig und oft von unbegreiflicher Flüchtigkeit in den Schlussfolgerungen. Aber das kann sich ändern.

Marty ist im Gegenteil beinah *zu* gewissenhaft, wenn man so sagen darf. An seine Rezension darf man, wie Sie ja selbst andeuten, nicht den Massstab gewöhnlicher Rezensionen legen. Sie ist mehr eine minutiöse Auseinandersetzung im Detail als eine Würdigung der grossen anregenden Kraft und des Fortschrittes im Ganzen, der durch Ihre Arbeite der Psychol. zu Teil geworden. Aber es freut mich, dass Sie dadurch nicht gekränkt sind und den wirklichen Scharfsinn u. die sachliche Art des Mannes schätzen. Die herzlichsten Grüsse von Haus zu Haus!

Ihr | C.Stumpf

[23, 1893]

München 17 Mai 93

Lieber James!

Es ist mir unendlich leid, dass wir Ihre liebe Frau nun gar nicht mehr gesehen haben, und dass *ich* sie überhaupt nicht kennen gelernt habe! Meine Frau und Schwägerin waren so entzückt von ihr, dass ich es als einen grossen Verlust betrachten muss. Aber sie wird Ihnen bereits erzählt haben, wie wir zu genau gleicher Zeit uns gegenseitig besuchen wollten; wenn dies auf Grund einer telepathischen Anziehung geschah, so verwünsche ich die Telepathie. Die Tage vorher wie nachher war ich gerade so vollständig in Anspruch genommen, dass ich meinen Besuch nicht wiederholen konnte, hegte aber doch die leise Hoffnung, dass sie mit Harry unserer Einladung auf Montag Mittag noch folgen könne. Sie scheint aber bereits vorher zurückgereist zu sein. Und dass ich nun auch Sie selbst, lieber Freund, „auf lange Zeit", wie Sie schreiben, nicht mehr sehen soll, ist mir nicht minder leid: denn ich hatte bei Ihrer hiesigen Anwesenheit infolge Ihrer vielfachen Geschäfte weniger von Ihnen als ich gehofft hatte. Sie sind ein volles Jahr in Europa – ein Jahr auf das ich mich seit 10 Jahren gefreut hatte – : und von diesem Jahr entfallen auf unser Wiedersehen wenige Stunden, in denen noch dazu Ihr Denken und Fühlen durch dringende Angelegenheiten in Anspruch genommen ist! Ich kann Ihnen dies natürlich nicht zum Vorwurf machen, aber ich bin traurig darüber; und um so traurig, als ich – um es offen zu sagen – das unbestimmte Gefühl habe, dass Ihre Freundschaft zu mir in den Jahren doch etwas an Lebendigkeit eingebüsst habe, dass Sie vielleicht darin nicht gefunden, was Sie anfangs sich versprachen, oder dass irgend etwas an mir Ihnen direct befremdlich oder unsympathisch erschien. Etwa das Auftreten gegen Wundt? *Ernster*, viel ernster sind wir ja alle beide seit diesen 10 Jahren geworden; das Leben ist auch so kurz u. die Welt so klein, in der wir leben. Aber um so fester möchte ich an denen halten, die ich von Herzen hochschätze und liebe.

Ihr begeistertes Urteil über Paulsen's Schrift macht mich begierig, bald mehr darin zu lesen; mein eigenes Urteil ruhte ja nur auf ganz flüchtigem Einblick und wird sich sehr wahrscheinlich dem Ihrigen nähern, wenn ich das Buch näher kennen lerne. Den Menschen schätze ich ja ohne dies von jeher sehr hoch, und bewundere den populären Schriftsteller und den Kenner des Lebens.

Die experimentellen Übungen, die ich begonnen, haben unter den Studirenden viel Anklang gefunden, nehmen mir aber, wie Sie richtig voraussagten, unmenschlich viel Zeit und Mühe weg, die eigentlich wissenschaftlichen Arbeiten gehören sollten. Ich bin geradezu angegriffen davon und werde jedenfalls *allein* die Sache künftig nur in ganz kleinem Massstab treiben können, aber vielleicht findet sich ein Assistent.

Wundts Psychologie I Band ist soeben in 4. Aufl. erschienen.

Zu dem, was wir über die Frage der einfachen Ähnlichkeiten besprachen, möchte ich noch Eins bemerken. Wenn Sie finden, dass meinem Argument dadurch zu entgehen wäre, dass man die letzten Elemente weder qualitativ noch quantitativ sondern lediglich *numerisch* abgestuft denkt: so kann ich dies doch nicht für eine wirkliche Lösung der Schwierigkeit anerkennen, da es doch nach allgemeiner Ansicht unmöglich ist, dass mehrere qualitativ völlig gleiche (und auch räumlich nicht verschieden localisirte) Empfindungen im Bewusstsein gleichzeitig existiren. Dieses Prinzip also müsste man aufgeben u. damit aller Erfahrung widersprechen.

Genug für heute – ich muss noch an die Luft, um mir den nächtlichen Schlaf wieder zu erwerben. Leben Sie wol und seien Sie und Ihre liebe Frau Gemahlin aufs Beste von uns gegrüsst.

Ihr getreuer | C. Stumpf

[30, 1896]

BERLIN W. | NÜRNBERGERSTRASSE 14 | 13 Okt 1896

Lieber Freund!
ich habe eine lange Pause in unserer Correspondenz entstehen lassen. Aber Sie haben mich gewiss entschuldigt mit der ausserordentlichen Arbeit, die für den Congress zu leisten war; und dies war in der That der Hauptgrund meines Schweigens. Ich hatte unendliche Corresponenz, mit auswärtigen Gelehrten und mit dem Generalsacretär. Letzterer erwies sich als allzu selbständig in seinen Arrangements. Ich war – im Vertrauen gesagt – mehrmals auf dem Puncte abzudanken, habe mich aber von Collegen der Sache halber bestimmen lassen, auszuhalten.

Meinem Gefühl nach ist nun doch der Congress so gut gelungen, als es nach der Anlage der ganzen Sache möglich war. Freilich habe ich mit Anderen den Eindruck, dass man *zu viel* Vorträge zugelassen hatte, darunter auch recht unbedeutende. Aber da ich nicht im Localcomité war, konnte ich hierauf nur geringen Einfluss üben; auch muss man zugeben, dass es schwer ist, die Grenze zu finden und auf Grund des blossen Thema's sich ein Urteil zu bilden.

Gestern erhielt ich einen Bericht von Baldwin in der „Nation", woraus ich sehe, dass er seiner Unzufriedenheit mit den Einrichtungen sehr kräftigen Ausdruck gibt. Sachlich muss ich ihm ja zumeist Recht geben. Immerhin berührt die scharfe Kritik gerade von seiner Seite insofern etwas seltsam, als Baldwin, der auch Ihnen am meisten berufen gewesen wäre Amerika zu vertreten, den ich schon vor einem Jahr um einen Vortrag gebeten hatte und der doch sonst so productiv ist, *nicht ein Wort* zu unseren wissenschaftlichen Verhandlungen beigetragen hat – es müsste denn sein, dass er vielleicht irgendeinmal in die Discussion eingegriffen hätte, wovon ich indessen nichts bemerkte. Es thut mir sehr leid, dass nun Amerika, wo eine reiche Entwicklung empor blüht, in den Vorträgen so gut wie gar nicht vertreten war. Es ist nicht unsre Schuld!

Persönlich habe ich indessen die angenehmsten Erinnerungen an den Umgang mit den Gelehrten der verschiedenen Länder mitgenommen, und bedaure nun, mit Einigen nicht noch ausgiebiger verkehrt zu haben; z. B. mit Herrn Strong, der mir ein scharfsinniger Kopf zu sein scheint. Wir haben seine Controverse mit Ihnen kürzlich im Seminar durchgenommen, nebst einigen Kapiteln aus Ihrer Psychologie.

Wenn Sie mir einen Gefallen thun wollen, wäre es dieser, dass Sie die englische Übersetzung meiner Rede, die, wenn ich mich recht erinnere, in der Psychol. Review erscheinen soll, ein wenig überwachen. Ich weiss nicht mehr genau, ob es Hr. Baldwin oder Hr. Buchner war, der mich um die Bewilligung dazu ersuchte. In der französischen Übersetzung (Revue scientif.) sind arge Misverständnisse.

Täusche ich mich oder klang aus Ihrem letzten Brief an mich nicht ein bisschen Verstimmung über die deutschen Psychologen heraus? Sie schienen unzufrieden, dass wir Münsterberg nicht eine ebenso unbedingte Schätzung entgegenbringen, wie Sie selbst, und Sie fürchteten, durch eine neue Reise nach Europa „zuviel von Ihrem Amerikanismus einzubüssen". Ich habe dies wenigstens als einen leisen Stich empfunden, und hege die Vermutung, es möchte vielleicht Münsterberg in seinem Unmute über das geringe Entgegenkommen, das er in Deutschland findet, Ihnen einen scharfen Bericht über die hier herrschende Philister-Wirtschaft gesandt haben. Es mögen nun wol graduelle Unterschiede in der Wertschätzung gewisser Eigenschaften an dritten Personen uns von einander trennen: aber ich sehe nicht ein, inwiefern dies zu einer Verstimmung unter uns Anlass geben könnte. Übrigens nähere ich mich Ihnen in Hinsicht Münsterbergs vielleicht mehr als die meisten meiner Collegen, aber es war in der Taht schon aus äusseren Gründen ganz unmöglich, ihn seinem Wunsche gemäss hier als Privatdozent aufzunehmen. Wir haben eine Überfüllung mit Lehrkräften und mussten in diesem *einen* Jahr etwa *10* ähnliche Gesuche ablehnen! Hierin ließ sich nicht eine Ausnahme machen, ohne andere zu verletzen, wenn auch Münst. infolge seiner bisherigen Stellungen unter allen das grösste Anrecht hatte. Übrigens ist er ja nun glücklich in Zürich zur Professur gelangt.

Anbei meine Photographie zur freundlichen Erinnerung. Bitte natürlich Baldwin nichts von meinen obigen Auslassungen merken zu lassen; persönlich haben wir uns ja auch recht gut verstanden und bei dem Banquet im Rathaus hat er eine nette Rede gehalten. Hoffentlich vergelten Sie mir nun nicht Gleiches mit Gleichem, sondern lassen bald von sich hören! Ich freue mich nun wieder an's Arbeiten zu kommen. Herzliche Grüsse von Haus zu Haus!

Ihr treuer C Stumpf

PS. Haben Sie meine Rede erhalten?

[32, 1898]

BERLIN W. | NÜRNBERGERSTRASSE 14 | 30 X 1898

Lieber Freund!
Wie lange haben wir uns nicht geschrieben! Aber meine Anhänglichkeit an Sie ist immer die nämliche; nur die Last der Arbeiten verkürzt die Correspondenz. Für Ihr Büchlein über Unsterblichkeit muss ich Ihnen aber herzlich danken. Es ist gut, dass die Vertreter der wissenschaftlichen Psychologie diese Angelegenheit des menschlichen Herzens auch wieder in die Hand nehmen, und nicht immer blos Reactionszeiten untersuchen. Ich kann sagen, dass sie mich zeitlebens mehr als alles andere beschäftigt hat und dass ich in den letzten Jahren auch den Einfluss des Unsterblichkeitsglaubens auf die ethischen Anschauungen immer höher anzuschlagen gelernt habe. Der *Werth* des Lebens scheint mir ohne solche Annahme fast auf Null zu sinken. Aber immer wieder sehe ich um mich herum ehrenfeste und lebensmutige Menschen, die ohne diesen Glauben sich durchschlagen und den Kopf aufrechter tragen als ich selbst. Und so warte ich zu, ob nicht die eigenen Anschauungen sich noch besser abklären.

Gestern erhielt ich einen Artikel von H.T. Lukens aus dem „Ped. Sem." Oct. 1898, worin er einen höchst oberflächlichen und unpassend-scherzhaften Reisebericht abstattet. Da solche Berichte nun schon mehrmals in amerikanischen Blättern erschienen, so werden wir die Herren, die nur auf ½ Stunde ihre Nase in unsre Institute stecken oder einer Vorlesung anzuwohnen geruhen, um dann ein absprechendes Urteil über den Menschen und die Sache drucken zu lassen, künftig weniger entgegenkommend empfangen.

Fullerton, der im Sommer einige Tage hier war, ist mir dagegen sehr sympathisch gewesen und es hat mir leid gethan, dass wir uns nicht länger aussprechen konnten.

Ich wälze nun mit Eifer die Tonstudien ab, um endlich zu anderen und höheren Dingen zu gelangen; aber es geht mir so langsam von der Hand, die Nerven sind eben längst ruinirt. Den Meinigen geht es gut u. die Kinder entwickeln sich befriedigend. Tausend Grüsse von Haus zu Haus!

Ihr treuer Stumpf

[34, 1899]

Wengen im Berner Oberland, | 8. Sept. 1899.
Lieber Freund!
Allerdings bin ich überrascht durch Ihren Brief, und so sehr ich mich sonst über Ihren Aufenthalt in Deutschland freuen würde – *dieser* Aufenthalt betrübt mich unendlich. Ich setze Vertrauen in die Bäder von Nauheim, die schon manchem Bekannten gut gethan haben, und hoffe, dass Sie neugestärkt daraus hervorgehen. Aber diese Gifford-Lectures! Lassen sie sich nicht angesichts eines solchen Hinderungsgrundes um ein Jahr verschieben? Rechtfertigt das was Sie pecuniär dabei gewinnen das Opfer an Gesundheit? Würden Sie nicht besser thun, jetzt in diesem wichtigen, für Ihre weitere Lebenszeit so entscheidenden Moment alles andere gegen die körperliche Kräftigung hintanzusetzen? – Treue Freundschaft und Sorge gibt mir diese Fragen ein; beantworten will ich sie nicht, da Sie selbst doch am besten alle Umstände übersehen und objektiv gegen einander abzuwägen im Stande sind, überdies Ihre verehrte Gattin als treueste Ratgeberin zur Seite haben, wenn sie auch, wie es scheint, augenblicklich nicht in Person bei Ihnen ist.

In allen Fällen bitte ich Sie dringend sich mit der Arbeit nicht zu überstürzen!

Sie erwähnen gar nichts von einer persönlichen Zusammenkunft auf deutschem Boden. Würden Sie etwa eine Störung Ihrer Kur befürchten? In diesem Fall müsste ich natürlich meine Wünsche unterdrücken. Aber wie leicht wäre es mir vor einigen Wochen gewesen, Sie in Nauheim ein paar Stunden zu besuchen, da mich der Weg in die Schweiz über Nauheim führte und ich in Frankfurt ohnedies einen Tag verbrachte. Hätte ich eine Ahnung von Ihrem Aufenthalt gehabt, so würde nichts als Ihr entschiedenes Veto mich daran gehindert haben, Sie aufzusuchen. Jetzt liegen die Dinge schwieriger insofern als ich nur beschränkte Zeit vor mir habe. Ich muss am 18. oder 19. im Berlin sein, werde aber in Würzburg bei meinen Schwestern 1–2 Tage verbringen, 17–18 Sept. Könnten Sie dahin kommen, so würden Sie ausser mir auch Külpe treffen. Aber ich würde Ihnen gern auch entgegenreisen, etwa nach *Aschaffenburg*, sodass wir beide nur eine Tagespartie ohne Übernachtung zu machen hätten. Mein Billet führt mich von Würzburg nach Berlin nicht über Frankfurt. Bitte schreiben Sie mir ganz offen, ob es Ihnen möglich und unter den gegenwärtigen Umständen erwünscht ist, eine solche Excursion zu machen. Meine Würzburger Adresse ist: Friedenstrasse 37/3. Wenn Sie sogleich antworten, trifft mich Ihr Brief auch noch in *Luzern* poste rest., von wo ich am 15. abreise.

Nach Paris werde ich 1900 wahrscheinlich *nicht* kommen. Ich bin wol noch viel weniger als Sie für Congresse geschaffen und würde mir Paris lieber einmal ohne Congress ansehen. Dazu noch das Getümmel einer Weltausstellung – schon der Gedanke macht mich nervös. Was die Franzosen betrifft, so muss ich leider sagen, dass mir die Nation – von Einzelnen natürlich abgesehen – immer weniger Respect einflösst. Wenn auch die Wahrheit über Dreyfuss an den Tag kommt – ist es nicht schon über die Massen traurig, dass man ihr solche Hindernisse bereitet? Heute lese ich, dass Deutschland u. Italien auf Labori's Ansinnen, Schwartzkoppen und Panizzardi zu einer Aussage zu veranlassen, *eingegangen* sind, dass selbst der Vertreter der Anklage, Carrière, gegen diesen Antrag nichts einwendete – und der Vorsitzende lehnt ihn gleichwol ab!! Kann man deutlicher zeigen, dass man die Wahrheit nicht *will*? –

Darin, lieber James, sind wir bessere Menschen, dass wir sie *wollen*. Ob wir sie finden, ist die andre Frage. Und dies sage ich speziell mit Bezug auf eine Gegnerschaft, die zwischen uns beiden entstanden ist, ohne dass Sie, wie es scheint davon wissen. Sie haben wol meine letzte Zusendung „Über den Begriff der Gemütsbewegung " noch nicht bekommen?

Da ich darin gegen Ihre Theorie Stellung genommen habe, so wollte ich anfänglich einen Brief als Begleitung mitschicken, kam aber vor der Abreise nicht mehr dazu und tröstete mich damit, dass Sie mehr als irgendeiner unter den lebenden Philosophen im Stande sein werden, persönliche Freundschaft mit wissenschaftlicher Gegnerschaft zu vereinigen u. dass es keiner Worte bedarf, um die Fortdauer unsres persönlichen Verhältnisses sicher zu stellen. Bei unserer Zusammenkunft, wenn eine solche möglich wäre, würde ich übrigens am besten jede Discussion vermeiden, um die Ihnen notwendige Ruhe in keiner Weise zu beeinträchtigen.

Merkwürdig ists mir mit Brentano gegangen. Ich dachte, mit ihm in Hinsicht der Affecte ziemlich einstimmig zu sein und erhalte nun von ihm einen 7 Bogen langen Brief, worin er sich entschieden für *Ihre* Auffassung und gegen die Meinige erklärt. Eine etwas beschämende Wirkung meiner Argumentationen! Wenn er einmal an das Veröffentlichen seiner Arbeiten geht, werden Sie an ihm für die Affectlehre eine nicht zu verachtende Stütze haben. Aber was ist Wahrheit? Das Eine weiss ich sicher, dass es mir gar keine innere Überwindung kosten würde, falls ich mich vom Gegenteil überzeuge, mich auch dazu zu *bekennen* und frühere Ausführungen zu widerrufen, sans phrase, Ihren edlen Beispiel in andren Fällen nachfolgend.

Von meinem u. der Meinigen Befinden kann ich gottlob nur Gutes melden. Mir behagt Berlin durchaus, es ist eine Menge trefflicher arbeitsamer Menschen da beisammen u. die Studenten gehören auch dazu. Meiner Frau war das *Leben* in München allerdings lieber u. sie gewöhnt sich nicht ganz an die neue Heimat, obschon sie früher schon 5 Jahre dort gelebt hatte. Von unsren Kindern ist Rudi nun schon 18 Jahre. Ich habe ihn jetzt vom Gymnasium genommen, da er ausgesprochene Begabung u. Neigung zur *Malerei* zeigte – merkwürdigerweise; er kommt 1. October in die Kunstschule zu Stuttgart. Eben darum muss ich bald zu Hause sein, um noch 8–10 Tage mit ihm zusammenzusein u. ihm vor dem Eintritt in die Welt dies u. jenes zu sagen. Was ist denn mit Ihrem guten Harry geworden? Grüssen Sie Ihre hochverehrte Frau u. Ihren Harry u. seien Sie selbst herzlich gegrüsst von Ihrem getreuen

Stumpf

[37, 1899]

Weggis, Hôt. Köhler Dienstag 12 Sept 99

Lieber James,
Eben erst erhielt ich Ihren Brief, der mir von Luzern aus nachgesandt wurde. Wie mein Telegramm Ihnen bereits sagte, bin ich hier bis Donnerst. Abends, kann aber natürlich jederzeit nach Luzern kommen. Freitag früh fahre ich ohnedies dahin und will Mittags 1 Uhr nach Stuttgart weiterfahren. Aber wenn Sie mir telegraphieren oder einen Brief *poste rest. Luzern* schreiben, kann ich einen Tag zugeben und dort mit Ihnen verleben, was mich ungeheuer freuen würde, zumal ich auch Ihre verehrte Frau treffen würde. Tausend Dank für Ihren lieben Brief. Von Herzen

Ihr | C Stumpf

Jedenfalls bitte ich Ihre Adresse, wenn Sie irgendwo länger bleiben.

[38, 1899]

BERLIN W. | NÜRNBERGERSTRASSE 14 | 30 XII 1899.

Lieber Freund!
Wie mag's Ihnen gehen? Ich denke oft an Sie und würde mich sehr freuen, einmal wieder Nachricht und gute Nachricht zu haben.

Eine besondere Veranlassung ists aber ausserdem, die mich heute zum Schreiben führt. Beim 200jährigen Jubiläum unserer Akademie der Wissenschaften sollen eine Anzahl von correspondirenden Mitgliedern ernannt werden. Für die Philosophie hat Dilthey die Herren Wundt und Heinze vorgeschlagen – ich habe mich bei diesem Vorschlag nicht beteiligt, sowie auch der Abstimmung über Wundt enthalten. Dagegen habe ich *Sie* vorgeschlagen. In der philosophisch-historischen Classe sind nun alle drei bereits gewählt, und ich zweifle nicht, dass auch das Plenum diese Wahlen vollziehen wird. Ist dies geschehen – die Abstimmung erfolgt in der ersten Januarhälfte – dann werden die Wahlen dem Kaiser zur Bestätigung vorgelegt. Die Verkündigung erfolgt am 19. März, dem Jubiläumstage.

Nur ereignete es sich von einigen Jahren, dass Herbert Spencer, der zum Ritter des Ordens „pour le merite" vom Kaiser ernannt worden war, diese Auszeichnung aus prinzipiellen Gründen zurückwies. Bei Franzosen pflegen wir auch im Falle von Akademiewahlen uns vorher privatim zu versichern, dass keine Ablehnung erfolgt. Aber bei Spencer hatte man nicht daran gedacht. Nun ist ja eine *Akademiker*-Stellung etwas anderes als ein *Orden*, und es kann Jemand prinzipiell gegen Orden sein, während er akademische Würden billigt.

Ich wollte aber für alle Fälle hiermit an Sie die *ganz vertrauliche* Anfrage richten, ob Sie unsre Ihnen dargebrachte Huldigung annehmen würden; und möchte Sie bitten, mir *sobald als möglich* Ihre zusagende Antwort zu schicken.

Alles, was ich Ihnen hier mitgeteilt habe, bitte ich geheim zu halten. Ihre verehrte Frau ist natürlich ausgenommen.

Uns gehts ziemlich gut, nur leide ich immer an Schlafmangel, und komme darum auch mit Arbeiten nur langsam voran. Wir senden Ihnen beiden zum Jahreswechsel die allerbesten Grüsse und Wünsche – Möchte Ihnen das Jahr gute Gesundheit und Lebensfreude bringen! Von ganzem Herzen

Ihr | C Stumpf

[41, 1900]

Berlin 23/3 00.

Lieber Freund!
In Eile teile ich mit, dass Sie Anzeige und Dank zu adressiren haben an den *Secretar der K. Akad. d. Wiss. zu Berl., Geheimen Oberregierungsrat Prof. Dr. Auwers*. Übrigens darf ich Ihnen sagen, dass Sie die Ehre nicht mir allein verdanken, sondern dass Dilthey freudigst damit einverstanden war. Das Fest ist nun vorüber, es hat uns allen reiche Anregung und frohe Stunden gebracht, bei denen nur Sie mir schmerzlich gefehlt haben. Aber *wie sehr* ich mich über die besseren Nachrichten freue! Möge es in dieser Richtung weitergehen; wir senden Ihnen u Ihrer verehrten Frau die herzlichsten Wünsche. Ich verreise in den nächsten Tagen, wol nach Bozen, meine Adresse ist aber immer die hiesige. – Von auswärtigen Philosophen waren hier Höffding, von Wyk (Utrecht), Ziegler, Heinze u. Kuno Fischer. Leben Sie wol und seien Sie tausendmal gegrüsst von Ihrem akademischen Collegen

Stumpf

[44, 1900]

Berlin, 20. V. 00

Lieber Freund!
Sie werden jetzt wol schon in Nauheim sitzen, ich sende diese Zeilen aber der Sicherheit wegen über London. Möchte Ihre Gesundung stetig fortschreiten! Dazu wäre freilich auch ein endlicher Beginn des Frühlings erwünscht – wir frieren hier noch immer. Ihre Werke werden der Bibliothek der Akademie sehr willkommen sein; Pflicht ist es jedoch nicht, sie zu stiften. Die Correspondentenstellen sind keine neuen, sondern alte, die aber nicht besetzt waren; wir hatten für Philosophie 8 freie Plätze, 5 sind immer noch zu vergeben. Übrigens kann ich Ihnen wiederholen, dass Dilthey (Paulsen ist nicht in der Akademie) *sofort* mit Ihrer Wahl freudig einverstanden war und in früheren Jahren auch ohne meine Anregung einmal schon davon gesprochen hatte. Also ist's nicht Sache persönlicher Freundschaft! Tausend Grüsse u. Wünsche Ihres treuen

Stumpf

[46, 1900]

Berlin, 11/VI 00.

Lieber Freund!
ich bin sehr betrübt, dass Sie in Nauheim negativen Erfolg hatten und wünsche von Herzen baldige Besserung. Als Adr. für Ihre Werke genügt: „An die k. pr. Ak. d. Wiss." Gleichzeitig senden Sie dann einen Brief „an den vorsitzenden Sekretar der k. pr. Ak. d. W.", worin Sie die Übersendung mitteilen. Anrede in dem Briefe: „Hochgeehrter Herr Secretar!" Dann *unter* dem Text und Ihrer Unterschrift: „An den vorsitzenden Sekr. d. k. pr. Ak. d. W." (Sie *können* hier auch noch beifügen „Herrn Geheimrat Professor Dr. Vahlen" – der jetzt den Vorsitz übernommen hat. – Ihre Anregung wegen Renouvier will ich mit Dilthey besprechen u. danke dafür. Übrigens ist doch auch noch *Sigwart* in Tübingen Correspondent.

Ihr C Stumpf

[51, 1904]

Baden-Baden 26. März 1904

Mein lieber Freund James!
Jetzt endlich, fern von Berlin, komme ich zur Beantwortung Ihres lieben Briefes vom 1. Januar und muss Ihnen vor allem sagen, *wie sehr* es mich gefreut und gerührt hat, dass Sie in alter treuer Anhänglichkeit meiner denken. Von mir darf ich es aber auch sagen, dass Bünde, wie sie zwischen uns bestehen, völlig unzerreissbar in meinem Herzen fortdauern. Es ist wirklich nur die Hydra der täglichen Arbeiten, die mich so saumselig im Schreiben gemacht hat; mit jedem Jahr scheinen ihr neue Köpfe zu wachsen, auch ohne das man die alten abschneidet. Meine Sehnsucht geht denn auch dieselben Wege wie die Ihrigen – das fernste Thal wäre mir der liebste Aufenthalt. Ich möchte und müsste endlich auch einmal meine Garben binden – aber ich sehe vorläufig keine Möglichkeit zu fliehen, ausser in den Ferien, und werde es wol so lange auf meinem Posten in Berlin aushalten müssen, als die körperlichen Kräfte reichen.

Münsterberg hatte ich zuerst zugesagt, weil mich das Abenteuer reizte, aber schon im letzten Sommer schrieb ich ihm wieder ab; meine Nerven hätten es nicht ausgehalten. Das ganze Unternehmen ist eigentlich überhaupt nicht erfreulich, es wird nichts herauskommen. Alle sollen über das Verhältnis ihrer Wissenschaft zu anderen Wissenschaften reden – man denke sich nun etwa 20 Bände mit solchen blos methodologischen Betrachtungen angefüllt!

Nun aber zu Ihrem schönen Buch. Es ist in der That sehr unrecht von mir, dass ich Ihnen ausser der Karte, die Sie nicht bekommen haben müssen, nichts darüber geschrieben habe. Verzeihen Sie es dem Vielgeplagten! An Interesse dafür fehlte es mir nicht. Habe ich doch in meiner frühen Jugend jahrelang den Plan gehegt, katholischer Priester zu werden und mich thatsächlich in die Theologie vergraben, bis die inneren Widersprüche der Dogmen mich unter schweren Herzensqualen hinwegtrieben. Was Sie über die Religiösen Erlebnisse berichten, davon habe ich das Meiste am eigenen Leibe erfahren. Freilich bin ich nachher um so strenger in der Beherrschung und Kritik all dieser Gefühle geworden, und so muss ich auch jetzt sagen, dass mir alles Sentimentale, Verzückte, Süssliche, Salbungsvolle in diesen Dingen beim erwachsenen Menschen aufs ausserste zuwider ist und dass mir nur das als wertvoll erscheint was sich in thätige Nächstenliebe umsetzt.

Auch kann ich trotz der Erkenntnis meiner Mängel und Fehler jenes zerknirschte Sündenbewusstsein nicht aufbringen, auf welchem die Religion nach den Frommen ruhen soll. „Something wrong about us" – ja freilich! Aber *ausser* uns ist noch viel mehr schlecht als in uns, und wir brauchen Erlösung nicht bloss von unseren Sünden sondern von all dem unendlich Entsetzlichen in der

Welt, die eben *der* Gott geschaffen haben soll, von dem man Erlösung hofft. In allem diesem erscheint mir die Religion der Religiösen verkehrt und unnatürlich.

Aber vollkommen stimme ich dem zu, was Sie über die Religion im weiteren und eigentlichen Sinne sagen (p. 485) und in jedem Augenblick meines Lebens fühle ich diesen Zusammenhang mit dem unsichtbaren Geisterreich das uns umgibt, und die Kraft die von da ausströmt.

Soll ich Ihnen nun auch etwas von meinem „over-belief" sagen? Ich weiss nicht ob ich während meines Lebens jemals solche mich täglich beschäftigende Gedanken zu veröffentlichen mich entschliessen werde. Ihnen aber teile ich sie gern vertraulich mit. Die persönliche Unsterblichkeit steht mir im Vordergrund. Ihr Satz „if our ideals ... " (p. 524) scheint mir eine Art von innerem Widerspruch zu enthalten. Die Verwirklichung der Ideale *ist* eben nur möglich unter Voraussetzung der individuellen Unsterblichkeit. Psychische Werthe addiren sich nicht. Wenn immer neue Individuen sich ablösen, so mag das folgende besser sein als das frühere, aber es vergeht ebenso in Nichts, und eine Summirung von Werthen, die nur innerhalb einer Persönlichkeit Existenz haben, ist absurd. Tritt die Erstarrung der Erde ein, entstehen also keine neuen Individuen mehr, wo bleibt dann die Verwirklichung der Ideale, wenn Geistiges nicht fortdauert? Dies ist fur mich die erste Bedingung, wenn das Leben nicht absolut trost- und sinnlos sein soll. Nicht *Egoismus* ist dies; nicht weil ich es bin, sondern weil es ein Träger von Werten ist, muss das Geistige dauern; und gewiss, ich würde bereit sein, auf die eigene Weiterexistenz zu verzichten, wenn die des geistig Wertvollen ausser mir an diese Bedingung geknüpft wäre.

Das was von uns fortbesteht wird aber nur das moralisch Wertvolle sein, das, was ein guter Wille in seine Sphäre hineingezogen und da festgehalten hat. In gewissem Sinne wird so allerdings die Individualität schwinden, nicht bloss die körperliche sondern auch die geistige: wenn anders man die zufälligen Kleinigkeiten, die unsere „Individualpsychologie" als Merkmale benützt, für das Wesen der Individualität ansieht. Wie uns dereinst sein wird, dafür scheint mir die beste Analogie der Zustand während eines hohen Kunstgenusses oder während einer uns ganz erfüllenden ethisch-grossen Vorstellung: auch dann ist unser „Ich" vorhanden, aber befreit von jenen zufälligen Kleinigkeiten, in eine höhere Sphäre gehoben und von den beseligendsten Gefühlen des Eins-Seins mit allen guten und hohen Geistern aller Zeiten begleitet. Mir ist es in solchen Augenblicken und Stunden in der That wie eine lebendige Gegenwart meiner Lieben, aller derer die mir vorausgegangen sind; sie scheinen mir in gleicher Weise um mich zu sein und zu meiner Seele zu reden, wie die, welche in empirischer Gegenwart, den gleichen Gefühlen stumm hingegeben, neben mir sitzen.

Dies sind meine zwei Glaubensartikel, die beiden am Schlusse das athanasianischen Credo „Gemeinschaft der Heiligen und ein ewiges Leben" – während alle übrigen Artikel dahingefallen sind, auch das Dasein des christlichen Gottes. Die fürchterlichen Übel des Naturlaufes und die doch auch dazu gehörige Schlechtigkeit der Menschen schliessen diese Annahme aus. Wollen wir aber einen pantheistischen Gott, so können wir sehr wohl eben diese Gemeinschaft der Seligen dafür einsetzen, die täglich wächst und doch zugleich eine innere Einheit bildet.

Wie ich diese Gedanken mit meinen psychologischen und naturphilosophischen Anschauungen im Einzelnen zusammenreime, will ich Ihnen nicht weiter erklären, Sie werden ja ohnedies auch leicht manche Verbindungslinien mit den kleinen Aufsätzen über Leib und Seele und den Entwicklungsgedanken herausfinden.

Unsere Anschauungen stehen sich hiernach in vieler Beziehung nahe. Selbst Ihr Pluralismus ist mir nicht so fremdartig, wie wohl den meisten Fachgenossen (obschon ich meine, dass Sie den Gefühlswert der „Einheit" des Höchsten unterschätzen). Nur mit dem Unterbewusstsein möchte ich den Gottesbegriff nicht in Zusammenhang bringen. Was mir darüber bekannt ist, scheint mir nicht nach dieser Richtung zu deuten; eher würde ich glauben, dass diese Zustande zu den mit dem Körper hinwegfallenden, nicht ewigen, Teilen unseres selbst gehören.

Nun, lieber Freund, genug der Philosophie! Sie fragen auch nach den Meinigen. Meiner Frau geht es wieder gut, nachdem sie einige schlechte Jahre hatte, sie ist nicht bei mir sondern mit unsrem Töchterchen, der in München geborenen Elisabeth, zu Hause geblieben. Rudi, unser Ältester, jetzt 22jähriger, ist Maler, hat 2 Jahre in Paris, mehrere Semester in Stuttgart u. München studiert und lebt jetzt in Weimar, das ein Centrum unsrer deutschen „Sezessionen" d. h. der nicht-offiziellen selbstständigen Richtungen zu werden verspricht. Er macht uns Freude durch sein ernstes, festes Wesen und wird von seinen Lehrern geschätzt. Felix ist noch auf dem Gymnasium, aber seit 2 Jahren nicht in Berlin sondern in dem stillen und gesunden Wernigerode am Harz, er wird hoffentlich nächste Ostern die Universität beziehen, seine Anlagen scheinen ihn etwa nach Seite der Physik zu weisen, doch lässt sich noch nicht Festes erkennen. Auch er ist ein braver Kerl.

Und was ist mit Ihrem Harry und vor allem, wie geht es Ihrer hochverehrten Gattin? Dass Ihre fortdauernde eigene Besserung mich über die Massen freut, brauche ich Ihnen nicht zu sagen. Ob Sie nicht doch einmal wieder herüber kommen? Dann wollen wir aber ganz gewiss ein Wiedersehen herbeiführen!

Herzliche Grüsse den Ihrigen und Ihnen selbst die treuesten Wünsche

Ihres *alten* | C. Stumpf

Wenn Sie mir, wenn auch nur mit einem Wort, den Empfang dieses Briefes anzeigten, wäre ich Ihnen dankbar.

[53, 1907]

BERLIN W. 50, | AUGSBURGERSTR. 61 | 8.V. 07

Lieber Freund!
Endlich komme ich dazu, Ihre liebe Karte vom Januar, die immer auf meinem Schreibtisch lag, zu beantworten. Ja es ist wahr „We lead a life of non-communication" und mir tut dies nicht minder leid wie Ihnen. Aber wie soll dies anders werden, solange mich diese Berliner Maschine gefesselt hält? Sie geben Ihre Lehrtätigkeit auf, um ganz der Wissenschaft zu leben. Dazu kann ich mich noch nicht entschliessen; teils der Familie halber, für die ich auf die erheblichen Einnahmen der hiesigen Vorlesungen gerade jetzt am wenigsten verzichten kann, da die drei Kinder viel gebrauchen, teils aber auch der Sache halber, da ich gerade jetzt ausgiebige und wachsende Erfolge meiner Lehrtätigkeit wahrnehme und mich noch kräftig genug fühle, sie fortzusetzen. Die Nerven sind sogar mit dem Alter besser geworden. Nur die Zeiteinteilung bildet in Berlin ein unlösbares Problem. Die gewaltigen Entfernungen und die vielen verschiedenen amtlichen Funktionen, Prüfungen u. sf. verschlingen die beste Zeit. Damit muss ich mich eben abfinden.

In unseren Anschauungen, lieber und verehrter Freund, scheint leider eine eine wachsende Divergenz einzutreten. Ich kann mich mit Pragmatismus und Humanismus nicht befreunden. Die positivistische Erkenntnisstheorie, in der Sie sich mit Mach berühren, scheint mir unmöglich, resp. unfruchtbar. In den beiden Abhandlungen, die Sie etwa zugleich mit diesem Briefe erhalten, versuche ich dies zu begründen. Sie werden dies als einen Standpunkt bezeichnen, den Sie *verlassen* haben; ich stimme mit dem früheren James mehr als mit den heutigen überein. Aber der *Mensch* steht mir dabei innerlich so nahe wie früher, und das, hoffe ich, sagen Sie auch mir gegenüber.

Habe ich Ihnen auch die „Gefühlsempfindungen" geschickt? Diese Abhandlung dürfte eher auf Ihre Zustimmung hoffen können, als die beiden akademischen.

Den Meinigen geht es gut, Rudi hat wachsende Erfolge als Porträtist, namentlich in Radierungen. Felix studiert Physik in Göttingen. Elisabeth ist im Begriffe, sich gymnasialen Studien zuzuwenden, dem Zuge der Zeit folgend, sonst aber ein frisches lebenslustiges und kräftiges Mädchen. Und wie geht es Ihrer verehrten Frau und den Kindern, besonders Harry? Grüssen Sie alle von uns herzlichst und bleiben Sie gut

Ihrem treuergebenen | C. Stumpf

[55, 1909]

Berlin, 20 V 09

Verehrtester Freund !

ich darf nicht länger zögern Ihnen für Ihr letztes Buch den herzlichsten Dank auszusprechen. Es hat mich wieder stark angeregt, u. ich will mich nun auch mit Ihrem Bergson naher befassen. In Bezug auf die „letzten Dinge" glaube ich Ihnen näher zu stehen als in Hinsicht der pragmatischen Wahrheitsbegriffe, obgleich ich Wahres darin auch nicht verkenne. Könnten wir uns nicht einmal wiedersehen? Es ist doch ein zu dürftiger Verkehr mit der Feder, und ich bin ein schlechter Briefschreiber. Meine Frau und ich senden Ihnen beiden u. Ihrem Harry, wenn er sich noch an uns erinnert, beste Grüsse.

Ihr getreuer | C. Stumpf

[56, 1909]

Berlin W. 50, Augsburger Str. 45 | 26 / X 09

Lieber Freund und Kollege!
ich danke Ihnen herzlich für das neue Buch und werde mich bemühen, an Ihrer Hand noch weiter in das Wesen des Pragmatismus einzudringen, dem ich bisher noch nicht die Wichtigkeit zuerkennen kann, die Sie ihm zuschreiben. Ich möchte glauben, dass die Behandlung *einzelner grosser Probleme* von diesem Standpunkte seine Bedeutung allein überzeugend dartun könnte. Vieles in Ihren Schriften darüber habe ich aber mit Zustimmung und Genuss gelesen.

Ich möchte Ihnen heute einen jungen amerikanischen Psychologen empfehlen, Mr. *Langfeld*, der hier eine Anzahl von Jahren studiert und zuletzt mit einer experimentellen Studie über Helligkeitsvergleichungen bei mir promoviert hat. Er ist jetzt mit seiner Gattin, auch einer Amerikanerin, wieder hinübergereist und wird Sie aufsuchen, da er dort weiterzuarbeiten gedenkt. Er ist ein sehr tüchtiger und höchst liebenswürdiger Mensch; auch seine Frau hat uns sehr gefallen.

Uns geht es gut, wir können mit der Gesundheit, auch mit den Kindern und dem ganzen Leben zufrieden sein, wenn ich auch immer etwas unter der Bürde allzuvieler amtlicher Arbeiten seufze und gern mehr Zeit für die Ausbildung allgemein philosophischer Gedanken übrig hätte. Nehmen Sie die herzlichsten Wünsche für sich und die Ihrigen

von Ihrem treuergebenen | C. Stumpf

Carl Stumpf
Briefe an die Familie James

An Alice Howe (Gibbens) James

[60, 1911]

Hochgeehrte Frau James!
Ich sage Ihnen den besten Dank für die gütige Einsendung des letzten Werkes Ihres Gatten, meines unvergesslichen teuren Freundes und Kollegen. Ich erwarte mir davon reiche Anregung und Belehrung und werde es mit besonderer Liebe, als hörte ich seine lebendige Stimme, studieren. Meine Frau sendet mit mir Ihnen und dem Herausgeber, Ihrem Herrn Sohn Henry, die besten Grüsse.
    Ihr stets ergebener

C. Stumpf

Berlin W, Augsburger Str 45, den 7.VI.11

An Henry James 3rd

[61, 1911]

Sehr geehrter Herr James!
Ich danke Ihnen herzlich für die Zusendung der „Memories and Studies" Ihres verehrten Vaters, meines unvergesslichen Kollegen und Freundes. Obgleich ich sehr viele Aufsätze von ihm besitze, waren diese mir noch alle neu. Die Briefe Ihres Vaters an mich werde ich demnächst alle heraussuchen und Ihnen zusenden. Mit herzlichen Grüssen und mit Empfehlungen an Ihre Frau Mutter

Ihr ergebener | C. Stumpf

Berlin | 11/XI 11

[62, 1911]

Berlin W. Ausburger Str. 45, 3/XII 11

Lieber Herr James!

Es muss eine Karte von mir an Sie verloren gegangen sein; ich habe Ihnen längst für die „Memories and Studies", die mir eine sehr liebe Erinnerung an den verstorbenen Freund u. Kollegen sind, gedankt und die Übersendung seiner Briefe versprochen. Aber ich war so überhäuft mit der Arbeit, dass ich noch nicht dazu gekommen war, sie aus den Faszikeln der vergangenen Jahre (unsere Bekanntschaft reichte bis 1884 zurück) zusammenzusuchen. Ich werde es jedoch baldmöglichst tun. Es freut uns sehr, dass Sie sich noch an München und unsere Familie erinnern. Hoffentlich sehen wir Sie einmal hier! Mit besten Empfehlungen an Ihre verehrte Frau Mutter.

Ihr | C. Stumpf.

[62, 1912]

Berlin 13/3. 12

Lieber Herr James!
Was müssen Sie von mir denken, dass ich den ganzen Winter verstreichen liess, ohne mein Versprechen zu erfüllen! Aber glauben Sie mir, dass es physisch unmöglich war: so ununterbrochen war ich durch die laufenden Pflichten in Anspruch genommen. Meine Briefsammlung ist leider in den älteren Jahren nicht alphabetisch geordnet. Daher bin ich erst in den letzten Tagen, nach Beginn der Ferien, zur Durchsicht gekommen. Es sind 31 Briefe und Karten, die ich so gefunden habe. Die Mehrzahl liegt hier bei, der Rest folgt gleichzeitig in einem besonderen Brief.

2 Briefe hatte ich der Autographen-Sammlung der Königlichen Bibliothek auf ihr Ansuchen hin übergeben; von diesen sende ich Ihnen Abschriften, die in der K. Bibliothek gemacht sind.

In dem Briefe vom *17.VII.04* ist von mir eine längere Stelle mit [] eingeklammert. Wenn Sie diesen Brief publizieren, bitte ich diese Stelle auszulassen. Sie bezieht sich auf einen Brief von mir an Ihren Vater über meine damaligen religiösen Anschauungen. Ich wünsche aber nicht eher etwas davon der Öffentlichkeit mitzuteilen, ehe diese Anschauungen mir nicht *völlig gereift* erscheinen. Es ist nicht die Scheu vor der Öffentlichkeit, die mich hierin bestimmt, sondern im Gegenteil die Scheu vor mir selbst, da ich die Verantwortung in diesen Dingen als eine besonders schwere empfinde.

Sollte sich mein Brief aus dem März 1904 noch in den Papieren Ihres Vaters finden, so würde ich bitten, ihn mir zurückzusenden; er war nur für ihn bestimmt.

Sonst dürfte wohl nichts in den Briefen Ihres Vaters stehen, was mir nicht publikationsfähig erschiene. Wenn Sie sie nicht mehr brauchen, möchte ich sie mir zurückerbitten, da sie mir ein teures Andenken an den Freund und Kollegen bilden, mit dem ich so lange in wärmster Sympathie verbunden war.

Mit herzlichen Empfehlungen an Ihre verehrte Frau Mutter

Ihr ergebener | C. Stumpf

Auch meine Frau und unser Sohn Rudolf schliessen sich den Grüssen an.
Haben Sie v. Schrenck-Notzing in München schon nach Briefen gefragt? Auch Prof. Lipps in München könnte Briefe haben. Ich werde bei dem Kongress 16–19 IV auch noch andere Herren fragen.

[63, 1912]

Berlin 13/3 12

Sehr geehrter Hr James,
diesen Brief fand ich noch nachträglich. Meine 2 Sendungen werden Sie wohl gleichzeitig mit diesem erhalten.
    Bestens grüssend

Ihr | C. Stumpf

An Flournoy in Genf haben Sie wohl geschrieben; er dürfte wohl eine Anzahl von Briefen haben.

III Carl Stumpf, "William James nach seinen Briefen" (1927)

Die von Henry James in zwei Bänden veröffentlichten Briefe seines Vaters[1] verdienen die größte Aufmerksamkeit der Philosophiehistoriker und Philosophen, werden aber auch dem Freunde solcher biographischen Urkunden, die das Lebensbild eines bedeutenden Menschen und wundervollen Charakters anschaulich aufbauen, großen Genuß bereiten. Da sie in Deutschland noch wenig bekannt scheinen, möchte ich im folgenden einiges daraus mitteilen, was mir für das Verständnis seiner Philosophie und seines damit sehr eng verknüpften menschlichen Wesens besonders wichtig erscheint. Des öfteren werden wir dabei auch erläuternde oder ergänzende Stellen aus seinen Werken heranziehen.

Die Ausgabe beruht auf intimster Personen- und Sachkenntnis, ist aber auch technisch musterhaft eingerichtet. Den einzelnen Abschnitten, in welche die chronologisch angeordneten Briefe eingeteilt werden, sind biographische Einleitungen vorausgeschickt, die über den jeweiligen Lebensabschnitt und, soweit als nötig, über die Adressaten und die Veranlassungen der Briefe orientieren. Wo man aufschlägt, findet man oben die entsprechende Jahreszahl und James' Lebensalter angegeben: eine für alle ähnlichen Sammlungen und alle Biographien höchst empfehlenswerte Maßregel. Die mitgeteilten Briefe sind nicht bloß an Gelehrte gerichtet, sondern auch an die Familienmitglieder, an gute Freunde und Freundinnen, und geben dadurch einen tiefen Einblick in das persönliche äußere und innere Leben des Verfassers. Zuweilen vermißt man allerdings die Briefe seiner Korrespondenten oder die Äußerungen, auf die James in seinen Antworten Bezug nimmt. Sie scheinen nicht mehr vorhanden zu sein, hätten freilich auch mit Rücksicht auf den Umfang des Ganzen nur in sehr beschränkter Auswahl eingefügt werden können. Im folgenden sind sowohl die Briefe selbst als die Einleitungen des Herausgebers benützt, aber auch gelegentlich Bemerkungen aus 32 an mich gerichteten Briefen beigefügt, von denen zwei in die Sammlung aufgenommen sind. James muß, obgleich er sich einmal als Graphophoben bezeichnet, eine gewaltige Korrespondenz geführt haben. Seine Handschrift war trotz aller Flüchtigkeit immer deutlich und ungewöhnlich [206] schön, ein Ausdruck seines freien, großzügigen Charakters. Sie

---

[1] The Letters of William James. Edited by his Son Henry James. London 1920.

Note: "William James nach seinen Briefen. Leben. Charakter. Lehre". Von Prof. Dr. Carl Stumpf, Berlin. Originally published in *Kant-Studien* 32 (1927), pp. 205–241.

hat sich, wie der Herausgeber bemerkt, seit seiner Jugend kaum verändert. Nur in der Zeit seiner ersten schweren Herzerkrankung, um 1900, wird sie in den Briefen an mich vorübergehend unansehnlicher. Die in Faksimile beigegebene Probe gibt kein richtiges Bild, sie zeigt nur, wieviel James auf den Raum einer Postkarte zusammenzudrängen vermochte.

William James wurde 1842 in New-York als Sohn des religiösen Schriftstellers Henry James geboren. Die Vorfahren waren im 18. Jahrhundert zumeist aus Schottland oder Irland herübergekommen, der väterliche Großvater erst 1798 aus Irland eingewandert. Der Vater, dessen literarischen Nachlaß James 1884 mit einer biographischen Einleitung herausgegeben hat, war durch Swedenborg stark angeregt, aber nicht eigentlich Swedenborgianer. Er war ganz erfüllt von religiösen Interessen und liebte es, darüber zu diskutieren. Seine, vielleicht im irischen Blute wurzelnde außerordentliche Lebhaftigkeit, sein Humor und seine sprudelnd geistvolle Schreibweise sind auf den Sohn übergegangen, der ihn gelegentlich den „weisesten der Menschen" nennt und mit Carlyle vergleicht, sich aber auch ein andermal scharfe Kritik an den wenig klaren Ausführungen des Vaters erlaubt. Williams Bruder Henry, der nach London übersiedelte, ist als Romanschriftsteller berühmt geworden. An ihn sind viele Briefe der Sammlung gerichtet.

Die Familie wechselte oft ihren Wohnort, und so empfing der junge William seine Ausbildung an den verschiedensten Orten, in Newport, New-York, Paris, London, Genf, Boulogne, Bonn. Den lückenhaften und unregelmäßigen Bildungsgang, der die Folge war, hat er später beklagt, aber es entsprang daraus als Nebenerfolg eine große Übung in drei lebenden Hauptsprachen, die ihm bei seinem unbegrenzten Lesebedürfnis und den späteren vielfachen Reisen zugute kam, sowie eine lebhafte Empfindung für die nationalen Unterschiede, die sich bis zu seinem Ende in den Briefen geltend macht.

Noch als Schüler hatte James eine Periode, in der er Maler werden wollte und unaufhörlich zeichnete. Er erhielt dann in Paris auch guten Unterricht in dieser Kunst. Aus Bonn schreibt er einem Freunde, er habe sich entschieden, es mit diesem Beruf zu versuchen. Die Proben, die der Briefsammlung an verschiedenen Stellen eingefügt sind, zeigen ihn dafür in der Tat ungemein begabt. Dennoch gab er nach etwa einem Jahre die künstlerische Laufbahn wieder auf, und hat auch später merkwürdigerweise von diesem großen Talent niemals wieder Gebrauch gemacht. Zwei seiner Söhne sind aber Maler geworden. Das Beispiel zeigt wieder, wie eng Religion und Kunst der Philosophie verwandt sind, mit der sie ja auch in Hegels Dialektik zu einer göttlichen Trias vereinigt werden.

Als Universitätsstudium trieb James zuerst Chemie, dann verglei-[207] chende Anatomie und aus Brotrücksichten Medizin. Nur vorübergehend dachte er auch an Theologie als Lebensberuf. Die darwinistische Bewegung der 60er Jahre und der Einfluß von Agassiz trieben ihn zu naturgeschichtlichen Studien. Von diesem großen Forscher, den er auch persönlich sehr verehrte, wurde er auf seine Reise an den Amazonenstrom mitgenommen, wobei er freilich die Gegenden mehr mit den Augen des Malers als des Naturforschers betrachtete. Aber er erkrankte schwer und wurde sich in dieser Arbeitspause klar, daß das Sammeln von Objekten nicht sein Beruf und daß er mehr für ein spekulatives als ein aktives Leben geschaffen sei. Nach der Rückkehr setzte er seine medizinischen Studien an der Harvard-Universität fort. Die blutigen Demonstrationen stießen ihn zwar ab, aber die Fundamentierung der Medizin auf Physiologie in den Händen der Claude Bernard, Helmholtz, Virchow, Ludwig machte ihm großen Eindruck. Diese Bestrebungen waren es denn auch die in Verbindung mit dem durch Agassiz und Wyman gelegten Grund an tatsächlichen Kenntnissen zuerst seine philosophischen Neigungen weckten.

Eine neue Erkrankung und der Trieb, die deutsche Wissenschaft an Ort und Stelle kennenzulernen, führten ihn als Fünfundzwanzigjährigen 1867–68 für 18 Monate nach Deutschland (Dresden, Teplitz, im Wintersemester Berlin). Er war physisch äußerst heruntergekommen und probierte alle möglichen Kuren; sein Geist wandte sich aber nach innen, zur Philosophie. Er liest jetzt Hegels Ästhetik und Kuno Fischer, aber auch die deutschen Klassiker. Preußens Sieg in Böhmen und seine Oberherrschaft in Deutschland erscheinen ihm als ein Schritt vorwärts in der Zivilisation. Deutschland scheint ihm eine gewisse Verwandtschaft mit Amerika zu haben. Er hört in Berlin, „einem unfreundlichen Ort", mit dessen Bewohnern er auch nicht warm werden kann, bei Virchow und Du Bois Reymond (an irascible man). Herman Grimm, dem er empfohlen ist, und seine Frau Gisela nehmen ihn freundschaftlich auf. Bei ihnen trifft er am 17.10.1867 mit Dilthey zusammen, der nicht genannt, aber als Verfasser eines Buches über Schleiermacher (S.'s Leben in Briefen) bezeichnet und interessant charakterisiert wird. Er liest in diesem Winter auch Psychologisches und hält die Zeit für eine exakte Psychologie für gekommen. „Es ist viel geschehen in der Sinnesphysiologie, besonders der Wahrnehmungslehre, was auch der Psychologie zugute kommt. Mein Weg geht in dieser Richtung." In Heidelberg seien Helmholtz und ein Mann namens Wundt am Werke. Er will im Sommer dahin. Trotz seiner höchst deprimierten Stimmung, die sogar Selbstmordgedanken aufkommen läßt, schreibt er an den Freund Ward, der noch verzweifelter war, einen rührenden Trostbrief, ruft ihm die Schönheit der Welt ins Gedächtnis, in der jederzeit irgendwo erhöhtes Leben pulsiere, vor allem aber das Edle im Menschen, in welchem [208] alles Gute beschlossen sei. Er empfiehlt ihm das geduldige Warten auf den Erfolg, das das Geheimnis des deutschen Heldenmuts zu sein scheine, ihm selbst aber fehle. Später hat er in der tiefernsten Betrachtung: „Ist das Leben wert, gelebt zu werden?" (1895), einer der schönsten Ansprachen eines väterlichen Freundes an die Jugend, solche Erwägungen seinen Hörern ans Herz gelegt. Nach einer vergeblichen Kur in Teplitz hört er bei Helmholtz in Heidelberg, reist aber plötzlich nach Berlin zurück, dann nach der Schweiz. Hier liest er zum ersten Male Kants Kritik der reinen Vernunft, die ihm großen Eindruck macht, und Renouvier, der ihm ein Führer werden sollte. Ohne gesund geworden zu sein, kehrt er im November 1868 nach Amerika zurück, enttäuscht in seinen Hoffnungen, aber reifer im Charakter wie im Denken und entschlossen, seine Gesundheit und seine Laufbahn in der Heimat zu suchen.

Es folgen nun vier äußerlich ruhige Jahre in körperlicher Schwäche, aber geistiger Regsamkeit. Er liest trotz schlechter Augen, die nur einige Tagesstunden zu gebrauchen sind, enorm viel Deutsches, die ganze klassische und romantische Literatur, mehr als die meisten von uns gelesen haben, aber auch Comte und seine Anhänger. In diese Zeit fällt ein furchtbares Halluzinationserlebnis, von dem wir unten hören werden. Im April 1870 rafft er sich unter dem Einflusse von Renouviers Freiheitslehre zu einem neuen Leben auf. „Ich will leben, dulden, schaffen". Diese innere Katastrophe bringt ihm die Psychologie noch näher. Aber auch das metaphysische Problem des Übels taucht in seiner ganzen Größe vor ihm auf. „Das Übel ist so real wie das Gute, es muß getragen, gehaßt, bekämpft werden, solange Atem in uns ist". Das ist schon der Grundgedanke seines Pluralismus und war ja auch bereits Renouviers Lösung. Mit diesem tritt er jetzt als dankbarer Schüler in Schriftwechsel. In dem Kriege zwischen Deutschland und Frankreich sind aber seine Sympathien wieder auf Deutschlands Seite.

1872 beginnt nun seine Lehrtätigkeit. Er wird Instruktor in Physiologie, dann auch in vergleichender Anatomie für die Undergraduates an der Harvard-Universität. Er empfindet es als heilsam, von seiner philosophischen Hypochondrie durch die Bindung an eine äußere Tätigkeit befreit zu werden. Aber sein Interesse gilt doch mehr der Philosophie als den Disziplinen, die er lehrt. Diese Tätigkeit wird während eines Winters (1873–74) durch eine Reise nach Italien unterbrochen. 1876 fügt er seinen Vorlesungen auch eine über physiologische Psychologie hinzu und richtet ein psychologisches Laboratorium ein, mit welchem er die nächsten Jahre in das Department für Philosophie übergeht. So hat er gleichzeitig mit Wundt die experimentelle Psychologie in den Universitätsbetrieb eingeführt.

Von nun an beginnt James' Wirksamkeit für eine Erneuerung der amerikanischen Psychologie, aber auch der amerikanischen Philosophie [209] überhaupt, deren zurückgebliebenen Zustand Stanley Hall und er selbst 1876 geschildert haben. Es galt vor allem, die Philosophie von der Theologie zu lösen, mit der sie durch die eigentümliche Geistesverfassung der Stifter und der Präsidenten der Universitäten verknüpft war, und als Hauptziel des philosophischen Unterrichts das vorurteilslose Denken zu pflegen.

In den Anfang dieser Vita nuova fällt auch seine Verheiratung (1878). Mit dem häuslichen Glücke ging Hand in Hand eine zunehmende Beliebtheit als Lehrer und eine schaffensfrohe schriftstellerische Tätigkeit. Er begann die Ausarbeitung der *großen Psychologie*, für die er 2 Jahre ins Auge faßte, die sich aber über 12 Jahre erstreckte. Er zog *Josiah Royce*, dessen Scharfsinn er überaus hochstellte, obgleich er seiner Metaphysik keineswegs beistimmte, als Kollegen heran und veröffentlichte die drei ersten seiner originellen erkenntnistheoretischen und psychologischen Spezialuntersuchungen (Sentiment of Rationality, Spatial Quale, Feeling of Effort). In der ersten untersucht er die emotionellen Motive des wissenschaftlichen, speziell philosophischen Denkens.[2] In der zweiten tritt er gegen den damals fast allgemein herrschenden Empirismus auf, in der dritten gegen die damit zusammenhängende, nicht nur bei Wundt, Exner, Mach, Stricker, sondern auch bei Helmholtz so ausgiebig verwertete Lehre von den zentralen Innervationsempfindungen. An der Harvard-Universität kämpft er gegen die Invasion des in Deutschland damals fast ausgestorbenen, aber nach Amerika aus England importierten Hegelianismus. Wenn er schon 1876 und später mit immer größerem Nachdruck gegen das „Absolute" und gegen den „Monismus" streitet, so ist immer Hegels Pantheismus gemeint, wie er in Oxford durch Caird und in Harvard selbst in modernisierter Form durch Royce und andere vertreten wurde. Im August 1882 unterbricht er diese akademische Tätigkeit durch eine neue Europareise. Er war (nach dem Herausgeber) stets für Europa eingenommen, solange er in Amerika war, aber auch umgekehrt. Er besucht Venedig, Wien, Prag, Leipzig. In Prag lernten wir uns kennen und verstanden uns sogleich aufs beste. Er hatte mein Raumbuch mit Zustimmung gelesen. In den Briefen erzählt er seiner Gattin von unserem Zusammensein, wie auch von Marty, Hering und Mach. [210]

---

[2] Man kann hier auch schon die Grundgedanken des Pragmatismus und des Pluralismus finden. „Was ist denn ein Begriff? Es ist ein *teleologisches* Werkzeug." „Der richtige Begriff für den Philosophen hängt ab von seinen Interessen". „Das Streben nach Sparsamkeit, nach Ökonomie in den Denkmitteln ist das philosophische Streben par excellence" (vgl. Mach, der denn auch diese Abhandlung beifällig zitiert). „Die einzige Tugend einer theoretischen Konzeption ist Einfachheit, und eine einfache Konzeption ist nur insoweit ein Äquivalent der Welt, als die Welt einfach ist; indessen ist die Welt, wieviel Einfachheit sie beherbergen mag, eine mächtig komplizierte Sache" (in den „Collected Essays" S. 86 ff., 123).

Die Jahre 1883–90 sind ausgefüllt durch anhaltende Arbeit an der „Psychologie". 1885 begründet er ein größeres psychologisches Laboratorium. Aber eigene experimentelle Betätigung reizt ihn nicht. Einmal schreibt er sogar: „Ich hasse von Natur aus experimentelle Arbeit". Er hielt sich dazu auch nicht für befähigt, urteilte aber in dieser Beziehung zu ungünstig. Das zeigen z. B. die Versuche über Raumtäuschungen, über den Drehschwindel bei Taubstummen (die in Machs Analyse der Empfindungen verwertet sind), über die Übertragung der an einem Stoff erworbenen Memorierfähigkeit auf andere Stoffe (Princ. of Psych. I, 666 ff.). Einmal machte er sogar einen recht gefährlichen Versuch über Halluzinationen nach Meskal-Genuß an sich selbst (Briefe II, 35, 37). Die damals in der Leipziger Schule überwiegenden Schwellenuntersuchungen schienen ihm allerdings ohne nachhaltigen Wert. Dagegen schenkte er schon seit 1869 der „Psychical Research", die ja auch eine Art experimenteller Psychologie ist, seine Aufmerksamkeit, trat 1884 der englischen Gesellschaft bei, gründete eine amerikanische Gesellschaft von gleicher Tendenz, die mit der englischen verschmolz, wurde 1890 Vizepräsident, für einige Jahre Präsident, veranstaltete selbst Sitzungen mit Miss Piper und veröffentlichte Verschiedenes in der Zeitschrift der Gesellschaft. Den Extremen gegenüber war er kritisch, lachte über gelegentlich nachgewiesene Betrügereien, begann auch das Interesse daran zu verlieren,[3] blieb aber bei der Überzeugung, daß Kenntnisse vorliegen, die nicht durch die Sinne gewonnen werden. 1889 veranstaltete er einen „Census der Halluzinationen" in Amerika, d. h. der abnormen Erscheinungen des Stimmenhörens, des Empfindens körperlicher Berührung u. dgl. bei guter Gesundheit und wachem Zustand, wobei etwa 7000 Antworten einliefen, aus denen er schloß, daß solche Erscheinungen 400 mal öfter auftreten, als nach der Wahrscheinlichkeitsrechnung bei zufälligen Koinzidenzen zu erwarten wäre. Er hat immer ein besonderes Interesse für das Abnorme und Pathologische bewahrt und solche Studien namentlich in dem religionspsychologischen Buche verwertet.

Aber die allgemeinphilosophischen Fragen traten dabei nicht zurück. Er korrespondierte auch in diesen Jahren über Optimismus, Determinismus, Mo-

---

[3] An Flournoy über Eusapia Palladino 30. IV. 03: „Forever baffling is all this subject, and I confess that I begin to lose my interest. Believe me, in whatever difficulties your review of Myers may have occasioned you, you have my fullest sympathy!" – 1909, ein Jahr vor seinem Tode, faßte er seine Eindrücke noch einmal zusammen in „Final Impressions of a Psychical Researcher", abgedr. in „Memoirs and Studies". Der Ton ist hier stark elegisch. „Ich finde mich in dem Glauben, daß,etwas daran ist' an diesen immer wiederholten Berichten über physikalische Erscheinungen, obgleich ich nicht den geringsten Begriff habe, was dieses Etwas ist" (S. 108). Er hält verschiedene Hypothesen für möglich, deren jede aber wieder viele Fragen nach sich zöge. Positiv weitergekommen sei man in der Sache nicht.

nismus und veröffentlichte Einzelnes darüber. Seine Vorlesungen [211] erstreckten sich 1888 auch auf Ethik und Religionsphilosophie, 1890 auf Metaphysik und Geschichte der Philosophie.

Durch diese anhaltende scharfe Arbeit erkrankt, gedachte er im Sommer 1889 die Schweiz aufzusuchen, nahm aber statt dessen an dem 1. internationalen Psychologenkongreß in Paris teil, wo ihm, wie er mir schrieb, die gemeinsamen Interessen so vieler Gleichstrebenden einen aufmunternden Eindruck machten, und kehrte sofort in die Heimat zurück. Hier hatte er schon seit seiner Verheiratung in Keen Valley in den Adirondack-Bergen Erholung gefunden und sich 1887 in Chocorua, einer lieblichen Landschaft, ein eigenes Landhäuschen erbaut, aus dem viele seiner Briefe datieren.

Den Abschluß der Psychologie mit ihren zwei mächtigen Bänden empfand er zuletzt als Befreiung von einer schweren Last. Er hatte nicht nur auf den Inhalt, sondern auch auf die Form, den Stil große Sorgfalt verwandt. So fließend und unmittelbar zum Leser redend sein Stil erscheint, er bekennt doch: „Wenn etwas Gutes darin ist, ist es Produkt vieler Arbeit, alles ist 4-5mal umgeschrieben." Und an mich 1889: „Ich schreibe mit großen Schwierigkeiten." Das mag manchen trösten.

Zu Beginn der neunziger Jahre trennt er sich ganz von der experimentellen Psychologie und dem Laboratorium durch die Berufung von Münsterberg, den er schon auf dem Pariser Kongreß getroffen hatte und dessen Arbeiten er außerordentlich schätzte, da er der Meinung war, daß es in diesem Gebiete zunächst mehr auf originelle und kühne Konzeptionen und auf experimentelle Problemstellungen, in denen Münsterberg ja wirklich Überraschendes leistete, als auf absolut exakte methodische Arbeit ankomme. Er nennt ihn gelegentlich den „Kipling der experimentellen Psychologie". Er tröstet ihn auch (schon vor der Berufung) in überaus freundlicher Weise über den scharfen Angriff G. E. Müllers.

Im Sommer 1892 trat James mit seiner Familie eine Reise nach dem Schwarzwald und der Schweiz an, um dort sein „Sabbathjahr" zu verbringen. Die Schweiz preist er als das ideale Land der Erholung. „Deutschland ist gut, die Schweiz ist besser." Hier lernte er am Genfer See Théodore Flournoy kennen und schloß mit ihm eine Freundschaft, die bis an sein Ende nur immer wärmer wurde. An ihn sind besonders viele Briefe der Folgezeit gerichtet. Gleich im ersten der mitgeteilten Briefe (19. IX. 1892) mahnt er ihn, lieber zu philosophieren als zu experimentieren; es entspreche besser seiner natürlichen Anlage. Ähnlich hat er auch mir geschrieben. Den Winter verbrachte er in Florenz und schwärmte nun auch für Italien, das seinem Malerauge unerschöpfliche Genüsse bieten mußte. Auf der Rückreise weilte er mit seiner Frau einige Zeit in München, wo der älteste Sohn zur Schule gebracht wurde. Wir erfreuten uns des Wiedersehens nach zehn arbeitsreichen Jahren. [212]

Die Reise hatte ihm wieder viele Gelegenheit zu Völkervergleichungen gegeben. Unter anderem schreibt er aus London:[4] „The cheery, active English temperament beats the world, I believe, the deutschers included. But so cartilaginous and unsentimental as to the *Gemüth*! The girls like boys and the men like horses!"

Aber er hatte nun das Reisen satt und glaubte sogar eine gewisse Schädigung der Seele als Folge davon zu bemerken. „Man sollte nicht Kosmopolit sein. Die Seele wird desintegriert, wie Janet sagen würde. Teile von ihr bleiben an verschiedenen Orten, und das Ganze ist nirgends. Das eigene Land erscheint fremd. Es ist keine gute Sache, und ich glaube, darunter zu leiden." (An mich 24. I. 94, ähnlich an den Bruder, Sept. 93.)

Zu Hause angelangt, konnte er im Herbst 1893 den 72jährigen Helmholtz mit seiner Frau im eigenen Hause begrüßen, „a fine looking old fellow with formidable powers of holding the tongue and answering you by a friendly inclination of the head". Seine Frau aber, eine Weltdame, komme voll auf für die Lücken seiner Konversation (an mich, ähnlich an den Bruder). Ein Jahr darauf starb Helmholtz. Übrigens war er auch im letzten Jahre nicht ganz so wortkarg. Wahrscheinlich hatte er James' Schriften noch nicht gelesen und fand nicht sogleich Anknüpfungspunkte.

Man kann die Zeit von etwa 1877 (dem Erscheinen der ersten psychologischen Abhandlungen) bis 1893 James' psychologische, genauer allgemein-psychologische, Phase nennen. Ihr folgte nunmehr die zweite, die religions-psychologische und philosophische. Das Zentrum seines Denkens waren im Grunde stets Religion und Philosophie gewesen. Jetzt nehmen diese beiden seine ganze Geisteskraft in Anspruch. Wir bemerken sogar eine starke Geringschätzung der gewöhnlichen Psychologie („a nasty little subject" II, S. 2). Auch die Vorlesungen gehen nach der metaphysischen Seite. Nur in den Übungen kommt auch die Psychologie zu ihrem Rechte, doch stehen dabei die allgemeinsten Fragen, zumal der Kampf gegen die Assoziationspsychologie und für die einheitliche Natur des Bewußtseins im Vordergrund. Über abnorme psychische Zustände hält er auch einmal eine öffentliche Vorlesung vor 1000 Hörern. Seine Lehr- und Unterrichtsmethode wird als höchst lebendig und persönlich geschildert, während sein Kollege Royce darin mehr den rein-sachlichen und in der Form pedantischen deutschen Typus repräsentierte. Mit Royce beginnt sich James nun

---

4 Wir geben Äußerungen, die zugleich für den Stil bezeichnend scheinen, im Original wieder. Deutsche und sonstige fremdsprachige Ausdrücke, die James in seine Briefe einflicht, sind, wie im Buche selbst, in Kursivdruck gesetzt.

immer ernsthafter auseinanderzusetzen. Er schwebt ihm trotz persönlicher Freundschaft als „zu überwindender Gegner" vor. Einer von beiden muß siegen. [213]

Aber dabei bildet er sich selbst zu größerer Klarheit fort. Es beginnen jetzt auch die Forschungen zu den „Varieties of Religious Experience". Seine allezeit sehr ausgebreitete Lektüre dehnt sich weiter nach dieser Richtung hin aus, auch auf die Lebensläufe der Heiligen, die Bekehrungsgeschichten usw. Zugleich wird er in seinem Pluralismus und Pragmatismus immer fester, fast möchte man sagen dogmatischer. Er schließt mit Schiller (Oxford) einen förmlichen Bund zum Eintreten für diese Anschauungen. Auch hält er von jetzt an vielfach Vorlesungszyklen an verschiedenen Universitäten Amerikas und Englands. Das Motiv war teilweise ein äußeres: er mußte bei dem geringen Professorengehalt für seine Familie sorgen. Diese Vorlesungen wurden jedesmal gedruckt und sind in seinen Werken seit den neunziger Jahren veröffentlicht. Ihrem Ursprunge gemäß sind sie für weitere Kreise berechnet. Den ersten Zyklus eröffnete er an der Berkeley-Universität in Kalifornien 1898 mit der für seine pragmatistische Einstellung hochbedeutsamen Antrittsrede „Philosophical Conceptions and Practical Results" (Coll. Essays, S. 406 ff).

In den Juli 1898 fällt eine zweitägige Fußwanderung in den geliebten Adirondack-Bergen, die ihm tiefste innere Erlebnisse, aber auch eine Überanstrengung brachte, welche in Verbindung mit einer zweiten im folgenden Jahre den Grund zu seinem Herzleiden legte. Die inneren Erlebnisse kann ich hier nur mit seinen eigenen unübersetzten Worten beschreiben, Worten, wie sie nur ein Meister der Introspektion finden konnte, obgleich er gerade, und gewiß auch mit Recht, die Unzulänglichkeit der Sprache für solche Geheimnisse betont, die „durch das Labyrinth der Brust wandeln in der Nacht". Sie zeigen wieder, wie sehr seine philosophischen Lehren – hier sein Pluralismus und sein Gottesbegriff – in den Tiefen seines Gemütslebens verankert sind.

> The temperature was perfect either inside or outside the cabin, the moon rose and hung above the scene before midnight, leaving only a few of the larger stars visible, and I got into a state of spiritual alertness of the most vital description. The influences of Nature, the wholesomeness of the people round me, especially the good Pauline, the thought of you and the children, dear Harry on the wave, the problem of the Edinburgh lectures, all fermented within me till it became a regular Walpurgis Nacht. I spent a good deal of it in the woods, where the streaming moonlight lit up things in a magical checkered play, and it seemed as if the Gods of all the nature-mythologies were holding an indescribable meeting in my breast with the moral Gods of the inner life. The two kinds of Gods have nothing in common – the Edinburgh lectures made quite a hitch ahead. The intense significance of some sort, of the whole scene, if one could only *tell* the significance; the intense in human remoteness of its inner life, and yet the intense *appeal* of it; its everlasting freshness and its immemorial antiquity and decay; its utter Americanism, and every sort

of patriotic suggestiveness, and you, and my relation to you part and parcel of it all, and beaten up with it, so that memory and sensation all whirled inexplicably together; it was indeed worth coming for, and worth repeating year by year, if repetition could only procure what in its nature I suppose must be all unplanned for and unexpected. It was one of the happiest lonesome nights of my existence, and I understand now what a poet is. He is a person who can feel the immense complexity of influences that I felt, and [214] make some partial tracks in them for verbal statement. In point of fact, I can't find a single word for all that significance, and don't know what it was significant of, so there it remains, a mere boulder of *impression*. Doubtless in more ways than one, though, things in the Edinburgh lectures will be traceable to it.

Infolge des Herzleidens mußte James die für Edinburg versprochenen Gifford-Vorlesungen über religiöse Erfahrung verschieben. Er suchte in Nauheim, in der Schweiz und in Italien (Rom) Genesung. Aus Nauheim schreibt er, seine einzige Gesellschaft seien jetzt die Heiligen. Nur Royce bleibt ihm als Gegner vor Augen. Ihm schreibt er, bei der Ausarbeitung seiner Vorlesungen blicke er immer mit einem Auge auf das Manuskript, mit dem anderen auf ihn. So stark war der zum Widerspruch herausfordernde Einfluß dieses rationalistischen Monisten. Sehr lebhaft ist James in dieser Krankheitszeit, wo er sich viel mit Zeitunglesen beschäftigte, an politischen Tagesfragen interessiert, die seinen ethischen Widerspruch hervorrufen. Die Kriege der Vereinigten Staaten gegen die Philippinen und der Engländer gegen die Buren reizen ihn zu scharfer Kritik im Sinne liberaler, menschenfreundlicher Gesinnung.

In einem Brief an mich aus Nauheim um dieselbe Zeit (10. IX. 1899), auf den Tränen gefallen zu sein scheinen, schreibt er: „Alle meine zukünftige Betätigung wird wahrscheinlich metaphysischer Art sein – d. h. wenn ich eine zukünftige Betätigung habe, woran ich manchmal zweifle. Die Gifford-Vorlesungen ... sind eine gute Gelegenheit, wenn ich nur imstande bin, sie zu nützen." Im Mai und Juni 1901 hält er dann in Edinburg die erste Serie seiner Vorlesungen vor dreihundert Hörern, meist Geistlichen, erfreut über den großen Erfolg, aber zwischen den Vorlesungen fast immer im Bette. Das Gelingen hebt ihn moralisch und sogar körperlich. Nach einem neuen Kuraufenthalt in Nauheim kehrt er gebessert im Herbst 1901 nach Amerika zurück, reduziert aber seine Vorlesungen, arbeitet an der zweiten Serie, die im April 1902 abgehalten wird. Das unter so schweren Leiden geborene Werk erschien in zwei Bänden 1902 und trug seinen Namen in noch viel weitere Kreise als die große Psychologie. Nun seien, meint er mit Humor, die protestantischen Prediger mit Reden für ein ganzes Jahr versorgt. Wie lebhaft aber auch die gelehrtesten Theologen die Förderung ihrer Wissenschaft empfanden, zeigt u. a. Troeltsch' Besprechung in seinem Vortrage „Psychologie und Erkenntnistheorie in der Religionswissenschaft" zu St. Louis 1904 und Wobbermins Einleitung zu seiner deutschen Übersetzung des Werkes. Da James sich selbst als „protestantischsten Protestanten" fühlt, freut es ihn noch besonders, auch in den katholischen Zeitschriften Anerkennung zu finden. Der ursprüngliche Plan des Werkes ging dahin, daß der zweite Band seine eigene Religionsphilosophie enthalten sollte; aber die Fülle des Materials drängte diese letztere in einen kurzen Anhang (den Wobbermin weggelassen hat). [215]

Seinen Standpunkt hatte er alsbald gegen Orthodoxe ebenso wie gegen Atheisten zu verteidigen. Schon während der ersten Vorlesungsserie beantwortete er zwischen zwei Vorlesungen die mehrfachen brieflichen Mahnungen eines ihm unbekannten rechtgläubigen Mr. Rankin mit einer sehr präzisen Formulierung. Er könne nicht an die christliche Erlösungslehre glauben. Der Urquell aller Religion liege für ihn in den mystischen Erfahrungen, mystisch im weitesten Sinne genommen. Alles Theologische und Kirchliche sei Zutat. Die Erfahrungen selbst aber träten in so biegsame Verbindungen mit dem intellektuellen Vorbesitz der Individuen ein, daß man sie nicht für sich in ein intellektuelles System fassen könne, sondern einer tieferen, mehr vitalen und praktischen Region zuschreiben müsse, weswegen sie aber auch durch keinerlei intellektuelle Argumente zerstört werden könnten. Dieses mystische oder religiöse Bewußtsein leitet er aus der Verbindung mit einem unterbewußten (subliminal) Ich her, das seine Botschaften dem Bewußtsein übermittle. „Wir überzeugen uns so von der Gegenwart einer viel weiteren und mächtigeren Sphäre ... Die Eindrücke, Antriebe, Gemütsbewegungen, die uns von da zukommen, helfen uns zum Leben, geben die unüberwindliche Überzeugung von einer Welt jenseits der Sinne, sie schmelzen unsere Herzen, verleihen jedem Ding Bedeutung und Wert und machen uns glücklich. Sie tun dies für alle, die sie [die mystischen Erfahrungen] haben, und andere folgen ihnen."

Das Gegenstück hierzu bildet der Brief an den Atheisten 1904: „Meine persönliche Stellung ist einfach. Ich habe keine lebendige Empfindung eines Verkehrs mit Gott. Ich beneide die, die eine solche haben, da ich weiß, daß sie mir unendlich helfen würde. Das Göttliche ist für mein aktives Leben auf abstrakte Begriffe beschränkt, die als Ideale mich interessieren und beeinflussen, aber sie tun es nur schwach im Vergleich mit dem Gottesgefühl, wenn ich ein solches hätte. Es ist nur ein Intensitätsunterschied, aber Intensitätsunterschiede können unser ganzes Energiezentrum verschieben. Immerhin ... es ist etwas in mir, das antwortet, wenn ich von Äußerungen des Gottesbewußtseins bei anderen höre. Ich erkenne die tiefere Stimme. Etwas sagt mir: dort liegt Wahrheit, und ich bin sicher, daß es sich nicht bloß um alte theistische Gewohnheiten und Kindheitsvorurteile handelt. Diese sind christlicher Art, und ich bin aus dem Christentum herausgewachsen ... Nennen Sie dies, wenn Sie wollen, meinen mystischen Keim, es ist aber ein sehr verbreiteter Keim. Er erzeugt die Heerschar der Gläubigen ... Geben Sie mir nur den Einfluß dieses mystischen Keimes auf unser Fürwahrhalten zu, so sind wir, denk' ich, auf meinem Standpunkt. Natürlich ist die Unterbewußtseinstheorie eine unwesentliche Hypothese, und die Frage nach Pluralismus oder Monismus gleich unwesentlich." Bei dem Gewicht, das James als Metaphysiker auf diese beiden Punkte legt, sind die letzten Einräumungen bedeutungsvoll. Sie zeigen, daß ihm, wenn es sich um die Definition der Religion handelte, an den mystischen Erlebnissen weitaus am meisten gelegen war, mehr als an jenen theoretischen Positionen.

Er hat nun aber auch die Vortragsreisen, ja selbst die Ehrungen, wie sie ihm in zunehmender Anzahl von amerikanischen und europäischen Universitäten und Akademien zuteil wurden, gründlich satt und scherzt öfters darüber in seiner anspruchslosen Art. Aber die Mitgliedschaft der Akademien von Berlin, Paris und Rom hat ihm doch Freude gemacht.

In unserer Korrespondenz war nach 1901 eine Lücke entstanden. Er hatte mir die „Varieties" gesandt, aber keinen Dank erhalten, was sicher nur ein postalischer Zufall war. Freilich muß ich auch gestehen, daß es mir schwer wurde, der Entwickelung seiner erkenntnistheoretischen und metaphysischen Gedanken zu folgen, und daß mir briefliche Auseinandersetzungen darüber wenig aussichtsvoll erschienen. Zu Neujahr 1904 nahm er gleichwohl den Briefwechsel in alter Herzlichkeit wieder auf.

Im Dezember 1902 beginnt die Korrespondenz mit Bergson, zu dessen Anschauungen sich James immer mehr hingezogen fühlt, und dessen Einfluß in seinen späteren Werken auch klar hervortritt. Er überhäuft ihn mit enthusiastischen Lobsprüchen, auch über seinen Stil.

Von 1903 an zieht er sich von dem Getriebe des akademischen Lebens mehr und mehr zurück. „Simplification" scheint ihm das einzige, was nottut, was er auch Flournoy wie mir immer wieder ans Herz legt. Dem Bruder schreibt er am 3. V. 1903: „Ich sehe jetzt mit absoluter Klarheit, daß, wie sehr ich auch durch meine Universitätstätigkeit bis heute gefördert und bereichert wurde, die Zeit gekommen ist, wo ich den übrigen Teil meines Lebens in anderer Weise verbringen muß, nämlich kontemplativ und mit Muße und mit Vereinfachung zugunsten der einzigen verbleibenden Aufgabe: mindestens in einem Buche den Eindruck wiederzugeben, den mein eigenes Denken vom Universum empfangen hat." Mir hatte er schon 1896 nach Berlin geschrieben: „Die Vervielfältigung der Lebensbeziehungen wirkt destruktiv auf alle innere Ruhe und Harmonie." Und nun wieder zu Neujahr 1904: „Ich nehme an, daß Sie sich wie ein geborener Berliner fühlen; aber das Leben vom Kapital ist, wenn man nicht von Eisen oder Kautschuk ist (und Sie sind es nicht), zu *aufreibend* für einen, dessen Hauptinteresse Kontemplation und Streben nach der Wahrheit ist."

Erholungsbedürfnis führte ihn 1905 doch wieder nach Europa. Er besuchte Athen und wohnte dann dem internationalen Philosophenkongreß in Rom bei, wo er, umgeben von einem Kreise junger Pragmatisten, unter denen er Papini besonders rühmt, außerordentlich gefeiert wurde. Freilich klagt er in den Briefen, daß sein Vortrag von keinem der Hörer richtig verstanden worden sei. Anfang 1906 reist er nach San Francisco, um an der Stanford-Universität in Berkeley Vorträge [217] und Übungen zu halten. Aber das Erdbeben vom 18. April, über dessen psychologische Wirkungen er interessante Beobachtungen mitteilt, veranlaßt den vorzeitigen Schluß der Universität und seine Rückkehr nach Cambridge. Einen Ruf als Austauschprofessor nach Berlin lehnt er ab. Hätte ich von diesem Ruf etwas vorher gewußt, so würde ich alles versucht haben, ihn zum Kommen zu bewegen. Es scheint aber nach dem Ton, in welchem diese Sache erwähnt wird („never"), daß ihm Berlin von früher her nicht im besten Andenken war.

November 1906 hält er Vorlesungen über den Pragmatismus in Boston und wiederholt sie Januar 1907 in New-York. Sie wurden unter demselben Titel gedruckt. Die Tage in New-York nennt er einmal „the high tide of my existence". Er wird gefeiert, lebt im Vollbewußtsein seines Wirkens und schwelgt sogar auch einigermaßen in dem Getümmel der Riesenstadt.

Unmittelbar darauf aber, Februar 1907, reicht er seine Demission an der Harvard-Universität ein, und ist glücklich, sich endlich frei zu finden. An die Tochter, 20. I. 1907: „Ich verwendete den ganzen Tag zur Vorbereitung der Vorlesung am nächsten Dienstag, die meine letzte an der Harvard-Universität sein soll, so helfe mir Gott, Amen!" An Schiller 18. V. 1907: er erwache jeden Morgen mit dem Gefühl der Freiheit. „Was ! Ich muß mich nicht der Menge fremder und widerstrebender Menschheit anpassen, nicht unter Widerständen denken, nicht bei jedem Schritt, den ich mache, mich anderen fügen – hurra! Es ist zu gut, um wahr zu sein. Allein sein mit der Wahrheit und mit Gott! *Es ist nicht zu glauben.*" Zwei Tage später an mich: „Vereinfachung ist das *summum bonum* für eine gewisse Menschenklasse, zu der ich und, wie ich denke, auch Sie gehören. Große Hauptstädte machen sie unmöglich. Ich kann nach Niederlegung meiner Professur mein Leben weit mehr als früher vereinfachen ... Allein mit Gott! Mit der Wahrheit! Welch eine Aussicht!!! Folgen Sie mir!!" – Er hatte mir, wie schon früher, aus dem Herzen gesprochen. Aber ich konnte die einmal übernommenen Aufgaben nicht im Stiche lassen, und gerade in diesem Jahre stand mir noch die schwerste Belastung mit akademischen und gesellschaftlichen Pflichten bevor, die dem deutschen Professor beschieden sein kann. Ein Jahr vorher hatte James die körperlich-geistige Verfassung, die den Großstädter vom Landbewohner unterscheidet, in der Kongreßrede „The Energies of Men", einem meisterhaften Beitrag zur Typenpsychologie (wiederabgedruckt in den Memories and Studies), geschildert. Da heißt es: „Wir sind samt und sonders in einem gewissen Grade Opfer einer erworbenen Neurose. Aber es wird dann auch eine erhöhte Leistungsfähigkeit in bestimmten Richtungen als Folge der Anpassung an eine solche Umgebung hervorgerufen."

Merkwürdig ist, daß James jetzt anfängt, Stoffe für eine Militär-[218]psychologie zu sammeln, die ein Gegenstück zur Religionspsychologie werden sollte. Auch dies zeigt, daß der Psychologe in ihm doch nicht abgestorben war. Die Briefe enthalten hier einiges über seine Stellung zum Militarismus und zum Pazifismus.[5]

Seine Briefe an Bergson werden immer wärmer, zumal nach dem Erscheinen der „Évolution créatrice", in der er einen Todesstreich gegen den Intellektualismus begrüßt. Der Pragmatismus erscheint ihm mehr und mehr als das erlösende definitive erkenntnistheoretische System.

Im Herbst 1907 kann er in dem geliebten Keen Valley ohne Beschwerde und mit Genuß, wenn auch langsam, wandern und sogar steigen. Es regt sich aber auch wieder Appetit nach Europa. Er läßt sich überreden, Vorträge in Oxford zu versprechen, obschon er vorhatte, in diesem Winter „etwas äußerst Trockenes, Unpersönliches und formell Exaktes" zu schreiben. Er hält dann in der Tat im Sommer 1908 in Oxford die Hibbert-Lectures über „pluralistische Mystik", die ein Jahr darauf unter dem Titel „The Pluralistic Universe" erschienen und 1914 ins Deutsche übertragen wurden. Rechtes Verständnis scheint er aber auch in Oxford nicht gefunden zu haben. An dem für dieses Jahr angekündigten Philosophenkongreß in Heidelberg teilzunehmen, verspürte er keine Lust. Über solche Kongresse schreibt er an Flournoy – meines Erachtens sehr richtig –:„Ich zweifle, ob Philosophen durch gegenseitige Besprechung so viel gewinnen wie andere Klassen von Gelehrten. Man muß mit einem Kollegen einen Monat lang täglich umgehen, ehe man ihn zu verstehen beginnt. Mir scheint, daß das Zusammenleben (collective life) von Philosophen wenig mehr ist als eine Organisation von Mißverständnissen. Ich hielt acht Vorlesungen in Oxford, aber außer Schiller und einem anderen Dozenten haben nur zwei Personen sie mir gegenüber überhaupt erwähnt, und das waren die zwei Vorsteher des Manchester-College, bei denen ich eingeladen war. Philosophische Arbeit, scheint mir, gedeiht ausschließlich in der Stille und in Druckschriften."

Sein körperliches Befinden hat sich wieder verschlechtert und färbt manche Stellen der Briefe aus dieser Zeit wehmütig, ja tieftraurig. Ein Stimmungsbild aus einem Brief an den Bruder (19. XII. 1908) möge wieder im Original hier stehen, gewissermaßen als düsteres Gegenstück zu dem von der Höhenwanderung (oben S. 213):

---

5 Weiteres in den Varieties S. 365 ff. und in zwei Aufsätzen 1904 und 1910 (Memories and Studies S. 265 ff., besonders 286, 304).

I write this at 6.30 [A. M.], in the library, which the blessed hard-coal fire has kept warm all night. The night has been still, thermometer 20°, and the dawn is breaking in a pure red line behind Grace Norton's house, into a sky empty save for a big morning star and the crescent of the waning moon. Not a cloud – a true American winter effect. But somehow ‚le grand puits de l'aurore' does n't appeal to my sense of life, or challenge my spirits as formerly. It suggests no more enterprises to the decrepitude of age, which vegetates along, drawing interest merely on the investment of its earlier enterprises. The accursed »thoracic symptom« is a killer of enter-[219]prise with me, and I dare say that it is little better with you. But the less said of it the better – it does n't diminish!

Flournoy hat ihn zum Genfer Universitätsjubiläum 1909, mit dem auch ein Philosophenkongreß verbunden werden soll, eingeladen. Er ist gesundheitlich verhindert, gibt ihm aber gute Ratschläge für die Schonung seiner Kraft bei dieser Gelegenheit, die nicht des alten Humors entbehren: „Geh hindurch wie ein Automat – das ist der beste Rat, den ich Ihnen geben kann. Ich finde es möglich, bei so anstrengenden Gelegenheiten vorwärts zu kommen durch Aufgeben aller Willensbetätigung. Nichts tun – und es wird schon etwas sich selbst machen, und nicht einmal so dumm in den Augen der anderen wie in den eigenen."

Er hält sich auf dem laufenden über Neuerscheinungen, äußert sich über „Funktionspsychologie", von der ihm Flournoy erzählt hatte, über Driesch, an dem er nur die unnötige gelehrte Aufmachung tadelt, über Freud und Jung. Er hofft, daß diese ihre Ideen auf die Spitze trieben, so daß man sähe, was daran ist. „Sie werden gewiß Licht werfen auf die menschliche Natur; aber ich gestehe, Freud hat auf mich persönlich den Eindruck eines Mannes gemacht, der von fixen Ideen besessen ist. Für meinen Teil kann ich nichts mit seinen Traumtheorien anfangen, und der ‚Symbolismus' ist offenbar eine sehr gefährliche Methode."

Es erscheint zu seinen Lebzeiten (1909) noch ein Band gesammelter Aufsätze: „The Meaning of Truth". Sie sollen den pragmatistischen Wahrheitsbegriff näher erläutern. Im Frühjahr 1910 reist James über Paris wieder nach Nauheim, wohin ihm später Frau und Sohn folgen. Im Juni richtet er noch zwei längere Briefe an einen gewissen Henry Adams über den zweiten Hauptsatz der mechanischen Wärmelehre und den daraus gefolgerten allgemeinen Wärmetod. Es findet sich sonst in den Briefen fast nichts über naturphilosophische Gegenstände. Aber offenbar lag ihm daran, gegenüber Adams, der einen offenen Brief an die amerikanische Lehrerschaft gerichtet hatte, seine Überzeugung von der Wertsteigerung trotz des Herabsinkens der freien Energie auszudrücken. Das Gehirn eines Dinosaurus, meint er, ist zwar physikalisch, der Masse nach, dem des Menschen überlegen, aber der Mensch kann unendlich mehr mit dem seinigen anfangen; er kann Geschichte machen. Der letzte Zustand des Universums mag völliges Erlöschen der Lebens- und Geistesfunktionen sein; der vorletzte könnte gleichwohl ein Millenniumszustand sein, in welchem ein Minimum von Energie aufwand ein Maximum von Glücks- und Kraftbewußtsein erzeugte. (Also gewissermaßen ein faustisches Weltende.) „Sie werden das nicht glauben, und ich will nicht behaupten, daß ich es glaube. Aber in der Energielehre ist kein Punkt, der einem solchen Glauben widerspräche."

Wir planten eine Zusammenkunft im Harz nach beendigter Badekur. [220] Aber zunehmende Atemnot veranlaßte ihn, südwärts zu reisen. Aus Genf ist der letzte Brief der Sammlung geschrieben, an den abwesenden Flournoy gerichtet, noch besonders warm, aber auch resigniert. Gehen, Sprechen und Schreiben wurden ihm schmerzhaft oder unmöglich. Er reiste mit seinen Angehörigen über London zurück nach Chocorua. Dort angekommen sank er in seinen Lehnstuhl mit den Worten: „It's so good to get home!" Wenige Tage darauf, am 26. August 1910, ist er schmerzlos verschieden.

Im folgenden Jahr erschienen, nach dem hinterlassenen unvollendeten Manuskript von seinem Sohn herausgegeben, Teile des von James schon seit Jahren beabsichtigten trocken-systematischen Werkes unter dem Titel „Some Problems of Philosophy". Er hatte noch aufgetragen, den fragmentarischen und unfertigen Zustand des Werkes hervorzuheben und es zu nennen: „A Beginning of an Introduction to Philosophy". Dies ist denn auch als Untertitel beigefügt. Bescheidener kann man sich nicht ausdrücken. In Wirklichkeit aber enthält dies Buch wohl die gründlichsten unter seinen metaphysischen Untersuchungen. Die letzten Kapitel betreffen den Unendlichkeits- und den Kausalbegriff. Letzteren leitet James aus dem Bewußtsein der psychischen Kausalität ab, die er (gegenüber Hume) als wahrnehmbare Bewußtseinstatsache betrachtet und näher beschreibt: eine Lösung, die auch bei uns von Beneke (Metaphysik) und Brentano (Vorlesungen) vorgetragen wurde und meines Erachtens das Richtige trifft, wenn sie auch nicht ganz leicht einwandfrei zu formulieren ist (vgl. dazu Martys Einwendungen, Raum und Zeit, S. 100 ff.). Es ist klar, daß James damit auch wieder das Gebiet der Psychologie betreten hat, und so liegen gerade auf diesem Gebiete seine letzten ebenso wie seine ersten Leistungen. Man versteht nun auch, warum er es öfters mit so viel Nachdruck als eine Forderung, ja als das Wesen des „radikalen Empirismus" bezeichnet, daß nicht nur die absoluten Inhalte unseres Denkens, sondern auch die Beziehungen zwischen ihnen aus der Wahrnehmung (einschließlich der inneren Wahrnehmung) hergeleitet werden müssen.

Später erschienen dann noch mehrere Bände von Einzelabhandlungen, aus früher erschienenen zusammengestellt.[6] Eine Liste der in Buchform erschienenen

---

[6] Memories and Studies 1911. Essays an Radical Empiricism 1912. Collected Essays and Reviews 1910. Die beiden letzten, von R. B. Perry herausgegebenen Sammlungen enthalten neben wichtigen älteren Abhandlungen auch mehrere Arbeiten aus seinem letzten Lebensjahre.

Schriften von James mit Inhaltsverzeichnissen findet sich am Schlusse der Briefsammlung. Eine chronologische Übersicht seiner, gegen das Ende des Lebens an Zahl außerordentlich zunehmenden Veröffentlichungen in „Psychological Review", Bd. 18, 1911. Ein noch vollständigeres Verzeichnis mit Inhaltsangaben hat R. B. Perry 1920 herausgegeben. [221]

Unter William James' persönlichen Eigenschaften seien hier nur diejenigen hervorgehoben, die bei der Lektüre der Briefe am meisten in die Augen fallen und auch bei der Beurteilung und dem Verständnis seiner Schriften besonders in Betracht kommen. Es ist vor allem die überquellende Herzlichkeit seines Wesens und die Neigung, überall das Gute zu sehen, ja es bei anderen in weit vergrößertem Maßstabe zu sehen. Seine Anerkennung fremder Leistungen und Fähigkeiten steigert sich leicht zur Bewunderung und zum Enthusiasmus, der zuweilen das objektiv berechtigte Maß bedeutend überschreiten dürfte. Er hielt es eben für richtig, befreundeten Menschen möglichst viel Gutes zu sagen, sie dadurch zu erfreuen und ihren Glauben an sich selbst zu stärken; was freilich nur denen gut ist, die an Verzagtheit und Selbstunterschätzung leiden. James war aber auch tatkräftig hilfreich, wo er nur konnte. Es sind in den Briefen einige rührende Beispiele dafür gegeben, selbst wo es sich um einen armen Skribenten handelte, von dem nichts Ordentliches mehr zu erwarten war. „Es gibt keine Entschuldigung für ihn, das gebe ich zu. Aber Gott hat ihn gemacht, und nachdem ich ihn zwanzig Jahre lang geschlagen, gestoßen, getreten habe, bin ich jetzt zu der Überzeugung gekommen, daß er rein und einfach mit Liebe behandelt werden muß, selbst wenn das ein Fehler wäre." Es ist sehr dankenswert, daß der Herausgeber auch bloße Familienbriefe nicht ausgeschlossen hat. Gerade in diesen offenbaren sich die Charakterzüge am schönsten, der übermütige Humor in den Jugendbriefen, das tiefe Gemüt in den Briefen an den sterbenden Vater, an die todgeweihte Schwester, die wundervolle Fähigkeit des Einfühlens in den Briefen an das zehnjährige Söhnchen, das heimwehkranke dreizehnjährige Töchterchen, an frühere Schüler, die nun seine Kollegen geworden waren. Aber auch der schneidend-scharfe Brief an eine befreundete Dame, die ihm kleine Auslagen taktloser Weise zurückerstattet hatte, charakterisiert den Mann. Sie sind alle zugleich Beispiele der ihm natürlichen, unabsichtlich künstlerischen Formung.

Ein besonders hervorstechender Zug ist die echt liberale, tolerante, aber auch ebenso freimütige und tapfere Gesinnung in bezug auf öffentliche Angelegenheiten. Jede Ungerechtigkeit, jede Unterdrückung von Individuen, Völkern, Richtungen ist ihm verhaßt. Die Dreyfus-Affäre in Frankreich, die schon erwähnten ungerechten Kriege Amerikas und Englands erregen und bekümmern ihn aufs tiefste, immer wieder kommt er darauf zurück. Selbst die staatlichen Anordnungen gegen die Mindcurers und die Christian Science veranlassen ihn zu Protesten, obschon er es dadurch mit den medizinischen Kollegen verdirbt. Auch seine Beteiligung an der Psychic Research beruhte außer einer gewissen Vorliebe für das Ungewöhnliche und die geheimnisvollen Untergründe unseres Daseins auf dieser Forderung des Gewährenlassens, des „sportsmanlike fairplay". [222]

Seine Naturliebe ist ein weiterer Zug des Menschen James. Besonders schwärmt er für weite Blicke und die intime Landschaft. Diese Naturschilderungen sind überall genußreich zu lesen. Von den Herrlichkeiten europäischer Landschaften zieht es ihn immer wieder zurück in den »virgin forest« der Heimat, der in Europa nicht seinesgleichen hat.

Trotz warmer Anerkennung der Vorzüge anderer Nationen fühlt sich James doch durchaus als Amerikaner. 1901 schreibt er mir, er wünsche nunmehr zu Hause zu bleiben und durch seine Schriften ein wenig die amerikanischen Ideale zu beeinflussen und vor imperialistischen Verirrungen zu schützen, was man nur aus der Nähe tun könne. Er fürchtet für diese Ideale. „There are splendid things about America, but the old human leaven of national adventure and aggrandizement is threatening to substitute its brute instinctive power for our historic and hereditary principles, and liberal Americans will have a hard fight to keep the country an the Kappier and more beneficent traditional track." Und so tritt auch in den veröffentlichten Briefen seine sorgliche Liebe zum Heimatlande und sein hoher Begriff von den wahren nationalen Aufgaben vielfach zutage.

Für uns Deutsche ist seine Sympathie, ja Liebe zu deutschem Land und Wesen erfreulich und unter den gegenwärtigen Umständen ermutigend. Von Venedig über Wien nach Prag kommend, das ihm damals (1882) den Eindruck einer durchaus deutschen Stadt machte, schreibt er seiner Gattin: „Damn Italy! It is n't a good thing to stay with one's inferiors. With the nourishing breath of the german air, and the sort of smoky and leathery german smell, vigor and good spirits have set in. I have walked well and slept well and eaten well and read well, and in short begin to feel as I expected I should when I decided upon this arduous pilgrimage." In der Weigerung eines Parkwärters, uns kurz nach Torschluß einzulassen, mit den Worten: „Dienst ist Dienst!" findet er „das deutsche Motto allerwärts". 1902 hat er Goethes Gedichte wieder einmal gelesen und schreibt an Miss Frances R. Morse, eine besonders vertraute Korrespondentin: „In general, though I'm a traitor for saying so, it seems to me that the German race has been a more massive organ of expression for the travail of the Allmighty than the Anglo-Saxon, though we did seem to have something more like it in Elisabethian times. Or are clearness and dapperness the absolutely final shape of creation?" Seiner Tochter schreibt er aus Nauheim noch im letzten Lebensjahre: „Die deutsche Zivilisation ist gut! Einem Marsbewohner, der herabkäme und nichts anderes sähe, würde dieser Platz eine falsche Vorstellung von unserer gottverlassenen Erde geben. Kein dunkler Punkt (außer den kranken Herzen der Patienten), keine Armut, keine Laster, nichts als Annehmlichkeit und Einfachheit des Lebens." Einige [223] Tage darauf an Bowditch: „Deutschland ist groß, ohne Zweifel! Aber welcher Gegensatz zwischen dem stattlichen, wohlgepflegten, schneidig dareinschauenden Deutschen von heute und seinem ziemlich plump gekleideten, unklar und unweltläufig blickenden Vater vor 40 Jahren! Aber etwas von der alten *Gemütlichkeit* ist geblieben. Die freundlichen Manieren, die Bereitwilligkeit, mit dir zu sprechen, dich ernst zu nehmen und alles, was da kommt, von der ernsten Seite zu betrachten."

Es tut wohl, in unserem von ungeheurer Übermacht niedergeworfenen, unerhört gedemütigten, geknechteten und dadurch selbst moralisch vielfach zerrütteten Zustande solche Worte zu hören. Daß dasselbe Volk nur vier Jahre später den Weltkrieg frevelhaft entfesselt haben sollte – diese verruchte Lüge hätte sich James sicher nicht aufschwatzen lassen. So sauber wie in Nauheim sah es zwar auch damals nicht an allen Orten Deutschlands aus, und so gutmütig waren nicht alle seine Bewohner; das war auch James nicht unbekannt. Aber in die Seele unseres Volkes hat der große Psychologe doch tiefer geblickt als sein englischer Nachfolger auf dem Lehrstuhl an der Harvard-Universität, der (nach dem Referat im vorigen Bande der Kantstudien, S. 603) noch 1920 in einem Buche mit dem Untertitel „Skizze der Grundsätze der Kollektivpsychologie nebst einer Deutung des nationalen Lebens und Charakters" die Kriegsverleumdungen kritiklos wiederholt hat. Seltsame Kollektivpsychologie, die die Nationen untereinander verhetzt!

Was aber James immer wieder an den Deutschen und besonders an den deutschen Professoren tadelt, das ist erstens die Pedanterie, das Überwiegen der technischen Kleinigkeiten (wenn er z. B. nach der Lektüre von Balfours „Foundations of Belief" schreibt, es sei mehr reale Philosophie darin als in 50 deutschen Büchern, deren Vorzug in gehäuften Subtilitäten und Künstlichkeiten bestehe; oder wenn er nach dreimaliger Lektüre von Avenarius' „Weltbegriff" das Buch, in dem er einen einzigen originalen, aber falschen Gedanken findet, mit seiner ganzen Terminologie auf Nimmerwiedersehen verabschiedet), und zweitens die grimmige gegenseitige Befehdung. Selbst die Stimmen der Deutschen scheinen ihm rauh. Aber von Zeit zu Zeit hört er sie doch gern. An Miller, August 1896: „Ich wollte, ich wäre mit Ihnen in München gewesen [Kongreß] und hätte die lungenkräftigen Deutschen gegeneinander brüllen hören. Es läge mir nichts an den Sachen, von denen sie reden, wenn ich nur die Stimmen hören könnte."

Für die deutsche Sprache hegt er große Vorliebe. „Italienisch und Deutsch sind die Sprachen." Es ist ein durchgehender Zug seines Stils, daß er deutsche

Ausdrücke und ganze deutsche Sätze in seine Briefe einmischt, wo ihm besonders bezeichnende Wendungen einfallen (wie z. B.: „I sail in 2 hours for *die liebe Heimat*"). In vergnügter Laune, nach der glücklichen Ankunft eines Töchterchens, teilt er das Ereignis [224] in einer durchgehends deutschen Postkarte einem englischen Freunde mit. Nur über die zusammengesetzten Wortbildungen, die einen ganzen Satz in die Substantivform pressen, amüsiert er sich schon in Dresden und versucht ergötzliche Nachbildungen im Englischen, wo es übrigens auch nicht ganz daran fehlt.

Versuchen wir schließlich nach Anleitung der Briefe unter vergleichender Heranziehung der Werke einen Einblick in die Entwicklungsgeschichte der philosophischen Anschauungen William James' zu gewinnen. Wir sahen, wie er durch seinen Studiengang von der Medizin zunächst zur Psychologie geführt wurde, aber nach Abschluß seines großen Werkes sich mit ganzer Seele der Metaphysik verschrieb und die Psychologie sogar recht gering dagegen einschätzte. Er billigte es auch nicht, daß D. S. Miller in seinem Buche über ihn soviel Gewicht auf die Psychologie legte. Immerhin wird das Urteil darüber, in welchem Gebiet er sein Bestes geleistet hat, individuell verschieden sein. Ich selbst würde dabei entschieden seine Psychologie in den Vordergrund stellen, da ich seinen im prägnanteren Sinne philosophischen Anschauungen fast in keinem Punkte rückhaltlos zustimmen kann und selbst die Methoden seines Denkens in diesem Gebiete nicht streng genug finde. Vermutlich werden auch die dauerndsten Wirkungen von seiner Psychologie ausgehen, obgleich gerade auf diesem Felde infolge des raschen Fortschrittes vieles schneller veraltet. Kapitel wie die über Automaton-Theory, Mind Stuff-Theory, Stream of Thought werden selbst die, die sich heute am fortgeschrittensten wähnen, noch immer mit reicher Belehrung lesen. Jedenfalls aber bildet dieses Werk einen der Marksteine in der Entwicklungsgeschichte der Psychologie. Im englischen Sprachgebiete ist seit Locke keine auch nur annähernd so tiefdringende und weitschauende Durchforschung des psychischen Lebens in seiner Eigenart vollzogen worden. Das ganze an sich so bewunderungswürdige Gebäude der englischen Assoziationspsychologie war dadurch in seinen Grundfesten erschüttert und ein richtiger gezeichneter Grundriß des Seelenlebens entworfen. Auch nach Vollendung der Principles hat er neben den typenpsychologischen Forschungen an diesen Grundfragen weitergearbeitet, in besonders wertvoller Weise in der Eröffnungsrede zum amerikanischen Psychologenkongreß 1894: „The Knowing of Things together" (wiederabgedruckt in Coll. Ess.). Es handelt sich da um die Frage nach Einheit und Vielheit des Seelenlebens. Er diskutiert sie nach vielen Seiten hin und gibt zuletzt seine eigene frühere Lehre, wonach der Bewußtseins-zustand immer streng einfach wäre, auf, ohne aber zur Assoziationstheorie zurückzukehren. Bewußtseinszustände, heißt es jetzt, sind weder bloße Summen noch strenge Einheiten. Sie sind Komplexe und haben [225] Teile. Aber diese Begriffe der Komplexität und der Teile müssen eben in ihrer ganzen Eigentümlichkeit als Züge des psychischen Lebens erfaßt und anerkannt werden. Unsere „Ganzheits-Psychologen" dürften da (wie freilich auch schon bei Lotze und Brentano) ihre keineswegs neuen Gedanken mit Befriedigung bereits vorgebildet finden. Nicht minder die Vertreter einer teleologischen Struktur des Bewußtseins, welche James ausdrücklich bereits 1870 gegen Herbert Spencer verteidigt hat (Coll. Ess. S. 61, 86. Vgl. oben S. 209 Anm.).

Über die Entstehungsgeschichte der „Principles of Psychology" geben die Briefe keinen näheren Aufschluß. Man wird auch vergeblich versuchen, sie in die Spezialgeschichte irgendeiner Schule einzufügen oder einen einzelnen Psychologen vor James als vorzugsweise einflußreich auf seine Entwicklung nachzuweisen. Er hat viel gelesen, sich aber seine Selbständigkeit bewahrt. Er hat vor allem die Sache selbst auf sich wirken lassen und sich in zehnjährigem Kampfe mit den Problemen unter anhaltender Vertiefung in die Tatsachen des eigenen Bewußtseins zu seinen Anschauungen durchgerungen.

Am wenigsten steht er in irgendeiner Abhängigkeit von Wundt, der sonst die amerikanische Psychologie so stark beeinflußte. Zu der Erkenntnis, daß die Psychologie sich eng an die Physiologie anschließen müsse, und zur Begründung eines psychologischen Laboratoriums hatte ihn sein eigener Bildungsgang geführt. Von Wundts Grundgedanken, ja von seiner ganzen wissenschaftlichen Denk- und Arbeitsmethode fand er sich vielmehr fast überall abgestoßen. Wundts Begriff der Apperzeption und sein „allgemeines Gesetz der Beziehung" erschienen ihm unverständlich, und der Ärger über die vergebliche Mühe, die ihm die Enträtselungsversuche gekostet hatten, macht sich, wo er darauf zu sprechen kommt, im Tone seiner Darstellung Luft. Es ist ja auch anderen (schon Fechner) damit ebenso ergangen. In einem Briefe an mich von 1887, der vom Herausgeber ohne mein Vorwissen ausgewählt worden ist, und in einem späteren an Royce von 1892 anläßlich des „Systems der Philosophie" von Wundt finden sich arge Sarkasmen, die stärksten in einem ungedruckten an mich aus demselben Jahre. Der gemeinsame Kampf gegen die Assoziationspsychologie hätte ihn zwar (wie auch die Brentano-Schule) mit Wundt verbinden müssen, aber methodische Grundsätze bildeten eine unübersteigliche Wand.

Dagegen findet man Lotze und Brentano, die großen Meister der analytischen Psychologie und der Selbstbeobachtung, in den „Principles" immer mit Zustimmung und Bewunderung erwähnt. Dabei scheint J. von Lotze (ich kann es jetzt nicht mehr genauer kontrollieren) nur die „Medizinische Psychologie" gekannt zu haben, nicht den „Mikrokosmus", der sich namentlich im Punkte der Willensfreiheit ganz mit James' eigenen Überzeugungen deckt. Sonst wären seine Sympathien [226] sicher noch gestiegen. Brentanos Kapitel von der Einheit des Bewußtseins zitiert er mit größter Anerkennung, seinem prinzipiellen Einwurf gegen die Ableitung des Fechnerschen Gesetzes stimmt er zu, ebenso seiner scharfen Unterscheidung des Urteilens vom bloßen Vorstellen. Über die ausführliche Besprechung der „Principles" durch Marty, der viel auszusetzen fand (Zschr. f. Psych. Bd. 3), schrieb er mir, sie sei ihm sehr lehrreich gewesen. „Vieles und das meiste von seinen Einwürfen sitzt, einiges beruht auf Mißverständnissen. Aber er verfährt zu mikroskopisch, berücksichtigt zu wenig die allgemeine pädagogische Einstellung eines solchen Buches. Wer außer mir wird denn einen so langen Bericht überhaupt lesen? Aber ich fühle mich geehrt und gerührt dadurch, daß einer das Buch so gründlich studiert hat. Nur Deutsche sind einer solchen Hingabe fähig." Darauf kann man doch auch nur wieder sagen: selbst gegenüber einer rein sachlich orientierten Kritik, wie der Martys, würde nicht jeder sich so geehrt und gerührt gefunden haben. Darin zeigt sich eben wieder der ganze James.

Aus unserer Korrespondenz betreffs einzelner psychologischer Fragen von allgemeinerer Tragweite möchte ich nur hervorheben, daß er in der Frage des einheitlichen oder mehrheitlichen Hörens, über deren Diskussion in meiner „Tonpsychologie" ein Motto aus seinen „Principles" steht, damals keine entschiedene Stellung genommen hat. Er bekennt sich als „musikalischen Barbaren" und fürchtet, daß seine Fähigkeit der Analyse gleichzeitiger Töne immer nur minimal sein würde. Gewiß aus diesem Grunde hat er die Theorie der Tonempfindungen in seinem Buche überhaupt fortgelassen. Er findet meine „Mehrheitslehre", welche die Annahme nicht unterschiedener gleichzeitiger Empfindungen einschließt, unvereinbar mit den Auffassungen seines Buches, glaubt auch, daß sie sich nahe berühre mit der von mir doch abgelehnten Lehre von einer „psychischen Chemie". Die Frage sei wohl nur im Zusammenhange mit einer erkenntnistheoretischen Untersuchung über die Beziehung des Geistes zu seinen Objekten zu lösen, indem man zeige, wie wir dazu kommen, die Erfahrungsdaten einmal als Dinge, ein anderes Mal als mentale Repräsentationen von Dingen zu betrachten. Mit dieser Überschiebung des Problems auf das erkenntnistheoretische Gebiet, welche an die Helmholtz'sche Theorie in ihrer ersten, von Helmholtz selbst aufgegebenen Fassung erinnert, konnte ich allerdings nicht einverstanden sein. 1898 kommt er von dem allgemeineren, oben berührten Standpunkte der psychologischen Einheitslehre darauf zurück und erläutert seine frühere Meinung dahin: „Wir mögen c, e, g, c^1 als Teile des Akkordes bezeichnen, wenn wir wollen, aber sie sind nicht Stücke von ihm, nicht identisch mit den c, e, g, c^1 anderwärts (in isoliertem Zustande); sie sind diesen nur ähnlich und repräsentieren sie" (know this contents or objects representatively, Coll. Ess. S. 398).

Auch in der Frage der einfachen oder unmittelbaren Ähnlichkeit zwischen Sinnesinhalten (Tonpsychologie I 112) sind wir zunächst verschiedener Meinung. Er findet die Folgerung unabweisbar, daß Ähnlichkeit jederzeit in partielle Identität auflösbar sein müsse. 1893 aber diskutiert er die Frage wegen ihrer erkenntnistheoretischen Bedeutung mit Bradley im Mind (seine zwei Artikel sind in Coll. Ess. wiederabgedruckt) und bekennt sich dabei zu meiner These, daß nicht alle Ähnlichkeiten in partielle Gleichheiten aufzulösen seien.

Am meisten interessiert ihn im 1. Bande meines Buches der Kampf gegen die Relativitätslehre, der ihm in seinem Streite mit den Neuhegelianern Waffen zu liefern schien, im 2. Bande das Kapitel über die Klangfarbe wegen der allgemeinen Frage nach der Definition und Entstehung von Komplexeigen-[227]schaften, die mich ja auch selbst nach Jahrzehnten zu einer neuen und ausführlicheren Untersuchung veranlaßt hat.

Meine Abhandlung über Gemütsbewegungen, die ganz speziell gegen seine sensualistische Deutung dieser Zustände gerichtet war, legte er lange zurück, da sie in die Zeit seiner ersten schweren Herzerkrankung fiel, die ihm nur allzu deutliche Bestätigungen seiner Auffassung zu liefern scheinen mochte, und hat sich wohl auch später, da eben die Psychologie seinen Interessen fernergerückt war, nicht mehr eingehender damit beschäftigt. Er betont nur, daß jedenfalls bei den violenten Affekten körperliche Empfindungen die Hauptsache seien, worin mir immerhin eine gewisse Konzession zu liegen scheint. Die veröffentlichten Briefe enthalten einzelnes aus dieser Zeit, das er im Sinne seiner Theorie deutet, so II, 158 aus Nauheim: „Wonach ich mich am meisten sehne, das ist irgendeine wilde amerikanische Landschaft. Es ist ein seltsames Bedürfnis organischer Empfindungen ... Wir vermischen uns mehr mit der Landschaft als die Europäer ..., mit unserem Kampieren und unseren allgemeinen Verwandtschaftsbeziehungen zu den wilden Tieren."

Unter den deutschen Psychologen hat diese Deutung der Gemütsbewegungen sich nicht durchsetzen können; dagegen wird sie von Psychiatern noch jetzt verteidigt.[7]

In bezug auf die Entwicklung seiner im engern Sinne philosophischen Anschauungen, wie sie sich an der Hand der Briefsammlung darstellt, ist vor allem zu beachten, daß eine religiöse Grundstimmung James von Jugend auf erfüllte, und daß die inneren Kämpfe sowohl infolge seiner naturwissenschaftlichen

---

7 Vgl. Niessl v. Mayendorf, Über Wahnentstehung, Zsch. f. d. ges. Neurologie u. Psychiatrie, Bd. 127, 1927.

Studien als auch infolge persönlicher Lebensstimmungen, tiefer Depressionen des Gemütes in seiner Jugendzeit, die alten, ersten und letzten Fragen der Philosophie in ihm lebendig erhielten.

Betreffs der naturwissenschaftlichen Überlegungen ist ein Brief an Th. W. Ward vom März 1869 bezeichnend. „Ich bin in eine empirische Philosophie versunken. Ich fühle, daß wir durch und durch Natur, daß wir gänzlich bedingt sind, daß nicht ein Schwänzeln (wiggle) unseres Willens als Folge der physikalischen Gesetze übrigbleibt; und dennoch sind wir in Fühlung mit der Vernunft. Wie soll man das begreifen? Wer weiß es? Ich bin überzeugt, daß die Verteidigungstaktik der französischen Spiritualisten, die einen standhaften Rückzug vor dem Materialismus ausführen, niemals etwas leisten wird. Es ist nicht so, daß wir ganz Natur wären außer einem Punkte, der Vernunft ist, sondern alles ist Natur und alles ist zugleich Vernunft. Wir werden sehen, Donnerwetter! Wir werden sehen!" In diesem Zeitpunkte sah er also, wie so viele Mediziner und Naturforscher jener Epoche, die Lösung des Problems von Leib und Seele, Natur und Geist in einem ausnahmslosen psychophysischen Parallelismus, der die Willensfreiheit im Sinne des Indeterminismus ausschließt, war sich aber des Provisorischen dieses Standpunktes bewußt.

In der Lebensstimmung aber trat eine Krise um dieselbe Zeit auf, die ihn ganz kurz nach dieser Formulierung davon abdrängte. „Schlechte [228] Gesundheit," sagt der Herausgeber, „Gefühl der Fruchtlosigkeit des eigenen Daseins versetzten ihn in eine krankhafte Depression, deren Tiefe er seinen Angehörigen verbarg." In diesem nervös-angegriffenen Zustand hatte er ein Erlebnis, das er 30 Jahre später in den „Varieties" in dem Kapitel „Sick soul" schilderte, aber einem französischen Korrespondenten zuschrieb. Im Dunkeln befiel ihn plötzlich eine entsetzliche Furcht vor seinem eigenen Dasein, während ihm zugleich das halluzinatorische Bild eines kurz vorher gesehenen blödsinnigen Irrenhauspatienten erschien. Er fühlte: so wirst du sein, wenn die Zeit gekommen ist. Es war, als sei in seiner Brust etwas entzweigegangen und er selbst sei nur noch „eine Masse zitternder Furcht". Die ganze Welt schien ihm fortan verändert. Jeden Morgen wachte er mit argen Schreckensgefühlen auf. Er war später der Meinung, daß er tatsächlich irrsinnig geworden wäre, wenn er sich nicht Worte der Schrift zugerufen hätte, wie: „Der ewige Gott ist meine Zuflucht", „Kommt zu mir alle, die ihr mühselig und beladen seid", „Ich bin die Auferstehung und das Leben".

Dieses Erlebnis fällt wahrscheinlich in den Winter 1869/70. Und nun folgen am 30. April 1870 Tagebuchbemerkungen über die innere Wandlung, die ihn zu seiner neuen Weltanschauung führte. Er hatte Renouviers zweiten „Essai" gelesen und fand in dessen Lehre vom <u>freien Willen</u>, von der Beherrschung des eigenen Gedankenlaufes einen Ausweg. I, 148: „Mein erster Akt des freien Willens soll sein, an den freien Willen zu glauben. Ich will mich bloßer Spekulation und kontemplativer *Grübelei* enthalten und das Gefühl der moralischen Freiheit pflegen ... Nicht in Maximen, nicht in *Anschauungen*, sondern in gehäuften Akten des Denkens liegt die Rettung. In letzter Zeit erschien mir der Selbstmord als männlichste Form des Wagemutes, jetzt will ich einen Schritt weitergehen: ich will glauben an meine individuelle Realität und schöpferische Kraft ... , ich will glauben an die selbstherrliche Widerstandsfähigkeit des Ich gegenüber der Welt. Leben soll aufgebaut werden auf Handeln, Ertragen, Schaffen."

Im Mai desselben Jahres schreibt er dem Bruder (I, 158): „Mir scheint, alles, wovon ein Mensch in der Welt abhängen soll, besteht zuletzt in der rohen Kraft des Widerstandes. Ich kann mich nicht, wie viele, dahin bringen, das Übel nicht zu sehen. Es ist so real wie das Gute. Es muß akzeptiert und gehaßt und bekämpft werden, solange Atem in unserer Brust ist."

Seit dieser Zeit lehrt James mit aller Entschiedenheit Willensfreiheit im absoluten Sinne des Wortes, als <u>ursachlose</u> Entscheidung, als unbedingten Anfang einer neuen Kausalkette, ganz so, wie Lotze sie faßte. In den 10 Jahre später erschienenen „Principles" äußert er sich darüber allerdings zurückhaltender, aber nur darum, weil der entscheidende Grund für ihn eben nicht ein psychologischer, sondern ein ethischer war. [229]

Er wehrte sich gegen jede Umdeutung, die etwa in der Art von Leibniz die Willensfreiheit mit dem Kausalgesetz zu vereinigen sucht. In dieser Richtung sind besonders mehrere Briefe 1885–86 an den englischen Freund Shadworth R. Hodgson von Interesse, dessen frühere Schriften er in den „Principles" oft zustimmend zitiert, der auch von positivem Einfluß auf seine psychologischen Anschauungen gewesen zu sein scheint, der aber eine solche Vermittlung mit dem Determinismus lehrte (I, 243, 256). Es kann kaum eine eindringlichere Verteidigung des Indeterminismus geben. Allen Distinktionen und Kompromissen zum Trotz bleibt er bei der unmittelbaren Aussage seines Bewußtseins. Er schließt mit förmlichen Beschwörungen: „Ah, Hodgson! Hodgson *mio*! from whom hoped so much! Most spirited, most clean, most thoroughbred of philosophers! *Perchè di tanto inganni i figli tuoi?*"[8] „Wenn Sie uns mit dem Determinismus auf rationalem Wege versöhnen wollen, schreiben Sie eine Theodizee, versöhnen Sie uns mit dem Übel, aber reden Sie nicht von der Unterscheidung zwischen Hindernissen von innen und von außen, wenn die inneren und äußeren, von denen Sie sprechen, beide innerhalb des Ganzen liegen, das nach Ihrer Philosophie allein wirksam ist. Es gibt keinen solchen [so törichten] Aberglauben wie die Anbetung des

---

8 [Cf. G. Leopardi, *A Silvia:* „O natura, o natura, / Perchè non rendi poi / Quel che prometti allor? perchè di tanto / Inganni i figli tuoi?" (Anm. des Herausgebers, R.M.)]

Ganzen ... Er macht mich krank im Herzen, dieser Zwiespalt unter den einzigen Menschen, die miteinander übereinstimmen sollten."

Die indeterministische Weltauffassung, zu der sich James nunmehr bekannte, nannte er seit 1897 Pluralismus, weil sie beständig neue Anfänge, neue Schöpfungen in die Weltentwicklung einführt, gegenüber dem Monismus, nach welchem alles bis ins kleinste für alle Zukunft determiniert ist, wie bei Spinoza oder Hegel. Später finden wir auch den Ausdruck „Tychismus", auch gelegentlich „Aktivismus", „Synechismus". Nach der methodischen Seite nennt er sie radikalen Empirizismus, weil sie (vom rein intellektuellen Standpunkte) nur das, aber auch alles das als real anerkennt, was erfahrungsmäßig gegeben ist. Nichts vertuschen, nichts wegräsonnieren, die Dinge nehmen wie sie sind – das ist wohl die allgemeinste Maxime dieser Erkenntnislehre. Eine speziellere, wohl spätere, haben wir o. S. 220 kennengelernt.

Mit außerordentlicher, stets wachsender Schärfe kämpft er jetzt gegen das „Absolute" im Sinne der Hegelianer. Immer kehrt die Losung wieder: „There is no Absolute"; ja, er nennt sich einmal in seiner drastischen Weise „eager for the scalp of the Absolute". Auch dieser Ingrimm, der natürlich nur in den Briefen, nicht in den Schriften zu finden ist, hat seine persönlichen Wurzeln: äußerlich darin, daß ihm der englischamerikanische Neu-Hegelianismus als Hauptgegner vorschwebt (eine hübsche photographische Aufnahme von 1903 zeigt ihn lebhaft mit Royce diskutierend, darunter steht: „Damn the Absolute!"), innerlich aber in der aus seinen Herzenskämpfen erwachsenen Überzeugung, daß das [230] Problem des Übels nun und nimmer auf dem Boden des rationalistischen Pantheismus zu lösen sei, daß dieser zu der Illusion, als sei das Übel selbst eine Illusion, und zu einem quietistischen Vertrauen auf den Weltlauf führe. Darum besonders und in diesem Sinne galt dem Absoluten der Kampf seines ganzen späteren Lebens. Die rationale Theologie erschien ihm definitiv und vollständig abgetan, auch die theistische, sofern sie nicht noch neben Gott irgendein anderes Prinzip anerkennt. Den Begriff eines allmächtigen und allwissenden Gottes nennt er (9. IV. 1907) „a disease of the philosophy-shop". Auch moderne Argumentationen, wie die Lotzes aus der allgemeinen Wechselwirkung, oder die Anwendung von Wahrscheinlichkeitsbetrachtungen auf das Problem der Teleologie läßt er nicht gelten (über die erstere ausführlich in Pluralistic Universe, über die letztere in den Briefen II, 154 und in einem Briefe an mich vom 17. III. 1900).

Bis zu diesem Punkt erscheint James' Philosophie in ihrer Gotteslehre durchaus negativ, mit radikalem Atheismus entweder identisch oder doch verträglich. Der Gott, den er so gefunden, würde nur in der eigenen Brust wohnen. Seine Gotteslehre wäre etwa die Ludwig Feuerbachs.

Aber bald, vielleicht schon von Anfang dieser philosophischen Periode, tritt auch die positive Seite seiner Welt- und Gottesanschauung in die Erscheinung. Wie die negative methodisch durch den radikalen Empirismus, so ist die positive methodisch durch den Pragmatismus gestützt. Beide ergänzen sich, dürfen aber nicht identifiziert werden (II, 267).[9]

Der Kern der vielumstrittenen Pragmatismustheorie, die er beständig vor Mißverständnissen zu stützen bestrebt ist, liegt wohl darin, daß Wahrheit nicht bloß durch den gewöhnlichen Erkenntnisprozeß geschaffen oder gefunden werde, sondern auch durch den Willen. Darum wird sie geradezu definiert durch die Förderung oder Befriedigung, die sie gewährt. An ihren Früchten sollt ihr sie erkennen – das ist der Kanon des Pragmatismus. Oder in Definitionsform: wahr ist, was sich bewährt. Es hat nicht bloß keinen Nutzen, sondern eben darum auch keinen Sinn, über Alternativen zu streiten, die für das Leben im weitesten Sinne, das Gemütsleben inbegriffen, absolut keinen Unterschied machen. Andererseits hat aber auch jede lebensfördernde Vorstellung auf Wahrheit Anspruch. Es lag James vor allem daran, sich so die Befugnis zu erwirken, über das in der Erfahrung Gegebene hinauszugehen, oder – in seinem Sinne vielleicht richtiger gesprochen – den Kreis des Gegebenen selbst zu erweitern. Das religiöse Bedürfnis war die Haupttriebfeder. „Religion ist das große Interesse meines Lebens." Aber auch jener liberale Grundzug seiner Natur, von dem wir sprachen, hängt mit seinem Pragmatismus zusammen: denn auch in Fragen der Weltanschauung soll dem [231] einzelnen je nach seinen Gemütsbedürfnissen und nach seiner ganzen Veranlagung möglichste Freiheit gewahrt bleiben.

In einem sehr wichtigen Briefe an Ch. A. Strong (9. IV. 1907) erklärt James, warum er selbst nicht zum Atheismus übergegangen sei. „Dies würde einen zu entschiedenen Glaubenswillen nach der negativen Seite für mich bedeuten. Es würde ein dogmatisches Nichtglauben an die Existenz irgendeines über dem normalen Menschengeist stehenden Bewußtseins bedeuten, und dies angesichts des höchst lebendigen seelischen Verkehrs von Menschen mit einem Ideal, das sich dem Gefühl aufdrängt, als ob es gleichfalls wirklich wäre (ich habe keinen solchen Verkehr – ich wollte, ich hätte ihn –, aber ich kann meine Augen nicht vor seiner Lebhaftigkeit bei anderen verschließen), und angesichts solcher Analogien, wie sie Fechner heranzieht, um die Existenz anderer Bewußtseine als der menschlichen zu beweisen. Wenn aber andere existieren, warum nicht höhere und mächtigere? Warum sollen wir nicht im Universum

---

9 Näher handelt über dieses Verhältnis der Herausgeber der „Essays in Radical Empiricism" im Vorwort S. VIff.

leben wie unsere Hunde und Katzen in unserem Wohn- und Arbeitszimmer? Es ist ein Glaubenswille auf beiden Seiten: ich bin ganz einverstanden, wenn andere nicht glauben, warum sollen Sie sich nicht toleranterweise für das Schauspiel meines Glaubens interessieren?"

Daß er selbst keine religiösen Erfahrungen habe, schrieb er schon 1904 an Leuba; es steht ebenso in seinen Antworten auf Pratts Fragebogen aus demselben Jahre. Aber andere haben solche Erlebnisse, und eben darum hat er sie in den Varieties gesammelt und beschrieben. Auf diese mystischen Erlebnisse legt er solches Gewicht, daß ihm sogar die Hypothesen des Unterbewußten und des Pluralismus unwesentlich erscheinen gegenüber dem „mystischen Keim" und seinem Einfluß auf das Denken (o. S. 215).

Man könnte fragen, warum James nicht die obenerwähnte tiefe religiöse Erschütterung anläßlich einer Halluzination, von der er in den Varieties unter anderem Namen berichtet, als eine eigene Erfahrung in dieser Richtung bewertet habe. Aber er ist darin sich selbst gegenüber sehr kritisch: er bezeichnet sie in einem Brief an den französischen Übersetzer des Werkes mit medizinischer Nüchternheit als „acute Neurasthenia with Phobia" (s. Flournoy, La philosophie de Will. James, 1910, S. 149). Ein halbes Jahr vor seinem Tode hat er aber angegeben (Coll. Ess. 500ff.), daß er in den letzten fünf Jahren viermal auch an sich selbst mystische Erlebnisse beobachtet habe, dreimal in Form einer plötzlichen, unbestimmten Erweiterung seines Selbst, einmal in Form einer Verflechtung dreier Träume, die ihm den Eindruck machte, als hätten sich die Träume anderer in seine eigenen eingemischt. Dennoch ist er auch hier von blindem Vertrauen auf den unmittelbaren Eindruck weit entfernt und verfehlt nicht, allerlei Fragezeichen zu machen.

Ehe wir die Ausbildung seiner Gottes- und Weltanschauung weiter verfolgen, seien Bemerkungen über die Entstehungsgeschichte und [232] den Sinn des Pragmatismus eingeschaltet, die sich aus den Briefen im Zusammenhange mit den Schriften ergeben. James selbst nennt einmal zwei Denker die „Großväter" dieser Theorie: Ch.S. Peirce und S.H. Hodgson, diesen wegen seiner Art, die Probleme anzupacken. Der Brief ist an den letzteren selbst gerichtet und klagt, daß er sein eigenes Enkelkind nicht anerkennen wolle, sondern als eine Art Wechselbalg betrachte (II, 328). Man darf daher vermuten, daß James hier mehr ad hominem argumentiere. In der Tat hat er anderwärts nur Peirce als den eigentlichen Urheber der Lehre wie auch des Ausdruckes Pragmatismus angegeben und gerühmt (Philosophical Conceptions and Practical Results, 1898, abgedruckt in den Coll. Ess., ebenso Pragmatism 1907 S. 47). Von Peirce habe er beides schon in den ersten siebziger Jahren in Cambridge (Harvard-Univ.) vernommen. Peirce, der als mathematisierender Logiker bekannt ist, hat demnach die erste äußere Anregung gegeben. In den Briefen wird er sonst nur ganz gelegentlich, einmal als ein wunderliches Wesen (queer being) genannt. Die Hauptquelle der Lehre lag doch sicher in James' eigener Entwicklung und Persönlichkeit. Das Wesentliche trägt er zuerst 1878 in einem Aufsatz über die „méthode subjective" für Renouviers Zeitschrift unter dessen Beifall vor (abgedruckt in den Coll. Ess.). Auch in den Principles (1890) kann man in der Urteilslehre die Grundgedanken finden. 1896 sind sie der Kern des für James' spätere Geistesrichtung sehr bedeutungsvollen und von ihm selbst oft zitierten Artikels „The Will to Believe", dessen Titel später auf eine ganze Sammlung damit zusammenhängender Abhandlungen übergegangen ist. Zu Beginn unseres Jahrhunderts haben dann Schiller in Oxford (Humanism 1903) und seine Genossen, sowie Dewey in Chicago (Studies in Logical Theory 1904) und seine Schule ähnliche Lehren vertreten. Diese beiden begrüßte James sofort lebhaft als Mitkämpfer. Er selbst wurde durch sein Buch „Pragmatism" 1907 der Führer dieser ganzen Bewegung, die in Deutschland allerdings wenig Anklang gefunden hat, wenn auch Mach und die Positivisten ebenso wie Eucken ihr nahestanden. Mit dem Namen Pragmatismus war James nicht einverstanden, setzte 1898 und 1904 dafür öfters „Practicalism", wollte ihn aber nicht aufgeben, da er ihm taktisch wertvoll erschien (II, 298, 300). Auch die Formel „Will to Believe" möchte er später einmal in den Briefen durch „Right to Believe" ersetzen.

Für die vielumstrittene Definition des Pragmatismus[10] ist es wichtig, daß James nicht bloß die Befriedigung der Gemütsbedürfnisse, sondern auch die der Verstandesbedürfnisse (wenn man sich so ausdrücken kann) als Wahrheitskriterium ansieht. An den alten Freund François Pillon, den Herausgeber der Critique philosophique, dem schon die „Principles of Psych." gewidmet waren, schreibt er noch in seinen letzten Monaten: „Zu meinem Bedauern haben selbst Sie noch nicht den wahren Kern meines Wahrheitsbegriffes erfaßt. Sie sprechen, als ob ich keine *valeur de connaissance proprement dite* zugäbe, was eine gänzlich falsche Beschuldigung ist. Wenn eine Vorstellung erfolgreich wirkt unter allen anderen Vorstellungen, die sich auf den durch sie im Bewußtsein repräsentierten Gegenstand beziehen, indem sie sich harmonisch mit ihnen verbindet und angleicht, so bleiben die Wirkungen völlig innerhalb der intellektuellen Sphäre, und der Wert der Vorstellung ist rein intellektuell, wenigstens bei dieser Gelegenheit. Das ist meine und Schillers Lehre, aber sie scheint sehr schwer so ausdrückbar zu sein, daß sie Verständnis findet!" Ob der Wahrheitsbegriff und das Wahrheitskriterium des Pragmatismus damit, für solche Fälle wenigstens, ganz aus dem emotionalen Gebiet herausgenommen werden,

---

10 In einem der Aufsätze, die in dem Buche „The Meaning of Truth" 1909 vereinigt sind, widerlegt James der Reihe nach nicht weniger als <u>acht</u> Mißverständnisse.

könnte man immerhin fragen, und wahrscheinlich würde James selbst, wenn einer diese Konsequenz gezogen hätte, darauf erwidert haben, daß überall, wo von Befriedigung und Harmonie die Rede ist, doch schon irgend etwas Emotionelles im Spiele sei, und daß eben hierdurch seine Wahrheitslehre sich von der bisherigen unterscheide. In [233] diesem Sinne heißt es denn auch in einem Briefe an Dickinson S. Miller 1907 (wo er sich gegen die Annahme verteidigt, als leugne er die Außenwelt)[11]: „Alles, was Schiller und ich behaupten, ist, daß es keine Wahrheit gibt ohne irgendein Interesse und daß nicht-intellektuelle Interessen ebensogut eine Rolle spielen wie intellektuelle." Interesse ist aber eben auch schon etwas Emotionelles.

Soviel nur zur Erläuterung seiner Wahrheitsdefinition aus den Briefen. Über ihre Richtigkeit oder Brauchbarkeit haben wir hier nicht zu befinden. Doch möchte ich nicht verschweigen, daß ich bei aller Anerkennung des Verdienstes, das sich der Pragmatismus durch die Bekämpfung von Fragestellungen, die keinerlei Aussicht auf Beantwortung haben oder bloße Wortangelegenheiten sind, erworben hat, seine Definition des Wahrheitsbegriffes selbst nicht unterschreiben kann. In einem öffentlichen Briefwechsel v. J. 1907 zwischen James und John E. Russel (abgedruckt in Coll. Ess.) vergleicht dieser sie mit der Definition eines guten Messers als eines solchen, das gut schneidet. Man kann vielleicht keinen treffenderen, die pragmatistische Absicht besser ausdrückenden Vergleich finden. Aber Russel fügt m. E. mit Recht hinzu: daß es gut schneidet, muß doch in einer bestimmten Beschaffenheit gründen, und diese Beschaffenheit kann angegeben werden. Die entsprechende Beschaffenheit der Urteile unzweideutig und unmißverständlich anzugeben, ist freilich nicht so ganz einfach, muß aber möglich sein. Im übrigen dürften doch auch die subjektivistischen, ja individualistischen Konsequenzen des Pragmatismus einen schweren Einwand bilden. Wenn z. B. jemand fände, daß der Monismus, und zwar just der Hegelsche, ein stärkeres Gefühl der Befriedigung in ihm auslöse als der Pluralismus – wie will man ihm beikommen? Erweist sich nicht damit der Pragmatismus gerade auch für die Interessen, um deren willen er eingeführt und verteidigt wurde, als untaugliches Werkzeug? Wir kämen eben auf Protagoras zurück. Vielleicht ist dies wirklich im Sinne mancher Pragmatisten, schwerlich aber in James' Sinne.

Die Welt- und Gottesanschauung, zu der James auf diesem Wege gelangt, hat eine große, auch von James selbst hervorgehobene Verwandtschaft mit der

---

[11] Man muß wohl zugeben, daß James' Ausführungen namentlich in den älteren Aufsätzen gelegentlich stark an die Berkeleys oder Machs streifen (Coll. Ess. 373 ff.). 1904 aber verteidigte er den Realismus (Essays in Radical Empiricism S. 76 ff.).

Fechners, ausgenommen allerdings den Punkt des Pluralismus. Es gibt zahllose Bewußtseine, die durch ein gemeinsames Unterbewußtsein mehr oder weniger zusammenhängen. Aus diesem gehen an vielen Stellen Einflüsse in das empirische Einzelbewußtsein hinüber, und darin liegt das Wesen der religiösen Erlebnisse. Aber dieses überindividuelle Bewußtsein, so weit umfassend es auch gedacht werden mag, muß nach James noch etwas außer sich haben und infolgedessen endlicher Art sein, wenn anders das Übel und das Böse begreiflich sein sollen. Der monistische Pantheismus, ebenso aber auch der strenge Monotheismus bleiben ihm unannehmbar. So kommt James zu einem endlichen Gott, der aber an unseren Leiden und unseren Kämpfen mit den Mächten der Finsternis teilnimmt.

Von großem Interesse sind die in der Briefsammlung mitgeteilten Antworten James' auf einen 1904 von J.B. Pratt versandten Fragebogen über die Stellung der Gefragten zur Religion. Die 10 Fragen sind in obi-[234]gem Sinne, aber höchst knapp und prägnant beantwortet. Am Schlusse lehnt er den Bibelglauben der englisch-amerikanischen Positiven mit bemerkenswerter Schärfe ab, indem er auf die Frage nach dem göttlichen Ursprung der Bibel antwortet: „No. No. No. It is so human a book that I don't see how belief in its divine authorship can survive the reading of it." Dennoch wissen wir, wie tief manches biblische Wort in seinem Gemüte haftete und wirkte. Zum Christentum als Gesinnung hat er sich immer bekannt.

In Hinsicht des Verhältnisses zwischen dem empirischen Einzelbewußtsein und jenem Unter- oder überbewußtsein (Subliminal = Transmarginal, Coll. Ess. 502) könnte zunächst eine pantheistische Auffassung als die angemessenste, ja einzig mögliche erscheinen, wie denn eine solche auch Fechners Anschauung entspricht. Aber gegen die Unklarheiten und Widersprüche des gewöhnlichen Bewußtseinspantheismus, die Fechner nach seiner, in diesen Dingen mehr poetischen Denkweise kein Kopfzerbrechen verursachten, hat James gerade in seinem letzten Werk äußerst scharfe Angriffe gerichtet. Unmöglich können wir, die wir uns selbst als bewußte Wesen erfassen, nur Bewußtseinsinhalte oder Teile eines höheren göttlichen Bewußtseins sein. Über diesen Widerspruch, der ihn viele Jahre lang quälte, hat ihm nun aber <u>Bergson</u> hinweggeholfen, dem das Reale innerlichst als alogisch gilt. Darum hat er mit solcher Begeisterung Bergsons anti-intellektualistische Lehre ergriffen, in der ihm überdies die Zentralbegriffe des „élan vital" und der schöpferischen Entwicklung aufs höchste sympathisch sein mußten.

Auch das „infernale Problem" des Verhältnisses von <u>Leib und Seele</u> hat ihn in der letzten Zeit und gerade im Zusammenhange mit seinen Bergson-Studien noch stark beschäftigt. Ist es doch auch aufs engste mit den metaphysischen Problemen verwachsen. Er ventiliert den Gedanken, daß das Gehirn nicht als wirkende Ursache, sondern nur als eine Art von Filter für das Bewußtsein diene, und weist Bergson auf sein Büchlein über die Unsterblichkeit v. J. 1898 hin, das ähnliche Gedanken enthalte. (Er erklärte es dort für eine mögliche Hypothese, daß das Gehirn nicht eine produktive, sondern eine „transmissive" Funktion bezüglich des Seelenlebens habe, ähnlich wie ein farbiges Glas nur bestimmte Strahlen des Sonnenlichtes durchlasse. Auf eine verwandte Vorstellung ist bald darauf auch Schiller gekommen.)

Es ist hier nicht unsere Absicht, allen Wendungen zu folgen, die James' Denken im Laufe der Jahre durchgemacht hat, noch weniger, die Diskrepanzen im einzelnen aufzuzeigen, die sich auch in seiner letzten Gestalt noch finden. Sollten Philosophiehistoriker oder Verfasser von Dissertationen dieses Ziel verfolgen, so wird es unumgänglich nötig sein, die Briefsammlung mit zu Rate zu ziehen. Sie bildet eine wesentliche Ergänzung zu James' veröffentlichten Schriften. Er selbst war gerne [235] bereit, Ungenauigkeiten und Unstimmigkeiten zuzugeben, aber er hielt nicht viel auf philologisch-minutiöse Studien und wünschte, daß die Kritik sich mehr an die Grundgedanken halte.

Freilich eben diese Grundgedanken möchte man vollkommen klar und widerspruchslos ausgedrückt wünschen; und in dieser Beziehung können wir einige Bemerkungen nicht unterdrücken. Die Mystik in allen Ehren – vielleicht führt jedes tiefere Denken über die letzten Dinge auf mystische Bahnen, auf gefühlsmäßige Ahnungen dessen, was sich nicht mehr in Begriffe fassen läßt –, aber so lange wir Wissenschaft treiben, also mit Begriffen operieren, müssen diese beiden Forderungen, Klarheit und Widerspruchslosigkeit, ausnahmslos festgehalten werden. Ich kann nicht glauben, daß ein so energischer und aufrichtiger Denker wie James sich weiterhin dauernd mit der Zuflucht zu einer mit inneren Widersprüchen behafteten Weltanschauung hätte beruhigen können. Wenn er in den Briefen wiederholt die Absicht äußert, nach den mehr populär-exoterischen Schriften zur Metaphysik zuletzt noch eine ganz exakte, trockene Darstellung zu verfassen, ein System der Philosophie im üblichen Sinne des Wortes, um auch die Anhänger der reinen Verstandesphilosophie, selbst die deutschen Pedanten zu gewinnen und zu überzeugen, so liegt doch wohl das Gefühl zugrunde, daß logische Schwierigkeiten überall nur durch Logik, durch die gewöhnlichen Hilfsmittel des nüchternen Intellekts zu lösen sind.

Vor allem käme es darauf an, den genauen Sinn seines Pluralismus zu erfassen. Eine Art Pluralismus ist auch der gemeine Materialismus, da er die letzten Bestandteile der Welt als ebenso viele letzte, von keinem gemeinsamen Prinzip abhängige Realitäten faßt. An einen solchen denkt James natürlich nicht. Eine andere Art von Pluralismus lehren die großen griechischen Denker, die dem göttlichen νοῦς eine ὕλη zur Seite stellen, in der die Beschränktheit und die Übel der Welt wurzeln. Diesem undefinierbaren Etwas kommt das „Andere", das James verlangt, schon näher. Und wenn Schelling in der Schrift über die Freiheit, die den Anfang seiner theosophischen Periode bildet, das Übel auf einen dunklen „Ungrund" in Gott, der doch nicht Gott selbst sei, zurückführt, so ist es dasselbe in pantheistischem Gewande. Wie sehr auch Schelling sich gegen den Titel eines Pluralisten gesträubt hätte: ein gewisser Dualismus ist da eben doch in Gott hineingetragen. Aber James denkt nicht nur an ein derartiges dunkles Prinzip neben oder in Gott, sondern an eine gleich ursprüngliche Mehrheit psychischer Wesen oder Kräfte. Der Sternnebel des „Anderen" wird aufgelöst in eine Vielheit selbständiger Fixsterne, und diese sind geistiger Art.

James betont, daß sein Pluralismus dem gewöhnlichen Menschenverstande näher stehe als der strenge Monotheismus. Betrachtet man den Volksglauben und uralte religiöse Vorstellungen als Ausdruck des [236] natürlichen Menschenverstandes, so läßt sich dies gewiß nicht leugnen. Denn die guten und bösen Dämonen der Primitiven, auch der Chinesen und Tibetaner, ebenso Ormuzd und Ahriman im Parsismus, Gott und Teufel in theologisch unbeeinflußten Christengemütern fallen unter dieselbe Form des Pluralismus. Hätte James, wie Fechner, einen neuen „Zendavesta" geschrieben, so wäre er darin dem alten noch erheblich näher gekommen als Fechner. Er hat auch damit recht, daß es in der Philosophie zuweilen nützlich ist, sich an den gesunden Menschenverstand zu erinnern. Ein beweisendes Argument freilich liegt in solcher Übereinstimmung nicht; hat sich doch die Wissenschaft selbst in Gebieten, wo der Augenschein eine fast zwingende Gewalt auf das Denken ausübt, weit davon entfernen müssen; man vergleiche die moderne Physik. Im übrigen ist nicht zu vergessen, daß James' Pluralismus nicht bloß eine erklärende Hypothese für die Realität des Übels, sondern zugleich und sogar in erster Linie praktisch motiviert ist. Denn gegen diese finsteren außer-göttlichen Mächte gilt es zu streiten, und es gibt nur eine Möglichkeit, sich ihrer Umklammerung zu entziehen: den freien Willensakt. Pluralismus und Indeterminismus sind für James unlöslich verbunden.

Gibt denn aber nicht gerade die Lehre von der Willensfreiheit für den, der sie anerkennt, ein Mittel in die Hand, die Tatsachen des Übels mit dem strengen Monotheismus zu vereinigen? Bekanntlich hat die alte Kirchenlehre die guten und bösen Dämonen des Orients in sich aufgenommen und ihnen trotzdem einen einheitlichen, unendlich vollkommenen Schöpfer übergeordnet. Sie tat es mit Hilfe der Lehre von der Willensfreiheit. Alle Engel sind gut geschaffen, ein Teil aber mißbraucht seine Willensfreiheit, empört sich gegen Gott und wird zu Teufeln. Der Fürst der Finsternis verführt dann die ersten Menschen, aus deren Sündenfall das physische Übel, Krankheit und Tod, als Strafe des allgerechten Gottes entsprungen ist. Also das physische Übel aus dem moralischen, dieses aus der

Willensfreiheit, die Willensfreiheit aber ein hohes Gut. Somit, wie schon Plato sagte: „αἰτία ἑλομένου · θεὸς ἀναίτιος". Gottes unendliche Güte erscheint gerettet. Man darf nicht verkennen, daß trotz der kindlich-naiven Form viel Überlegung, viel ernstes Nachdenken dem alten Mythus zugrunde liegt.

Warum hat nun James nicht einfach diesen Weg, vielleicht in modernisierter, abstrakterer Form beschritten? Nun, er mochte sich die ungeheuren Diskussionen vergegenwärtigen, die sich seit den Kirchenvätern daran geknüpft haben. Warum, fragte man sich, hat der Allwissende, der auch den Mißbrauch der Freiheit voraussehen mußte, nicht diejenigen Geschöpfe, bei denen er ihn voraussah, ungeschaffen gelassen? Muß daher nicht doch die tiefste Wurzel des Übels wieder im Allheiligen gesucht werden? Solche Fragen mögen es gewesen sein, die James zur radikalen Lösung durch seinen Pluralismus führten. Man könnte fast [237] sagen, seine Lehre sei die alte Kirchenlehre, nur enthauptet, d. h. ohne die Herleitung der Engel und Teufel aus dem gemeinsamen Urgrund der göttlichen Einheit. Eine ähnliche Lehre liegt schon in dem „Personalismus" Renouviers vor, dem James sein letztes (postum erschienenes) Buch mit der Motivierung widmete, daß er ohne ihn sich niemals von dem monistischen Aberglauben frei gemacht hätte. Desgleichen ist Schillers Pluralismus von derselben Art.[12] An die Stelle der rationalen Theologie muß dann eben eine rationale Dämonologie treten, wie sie schon die Stoiker entwickelten, – wenn anders diese besser als jene möglich ist. An einer Stelle, in einem Artikel aus der letzten Zeit über Miss Piper (Coll. Ess., S. 486 ff.), geht James tatsächlich schon ziemlich weit in Vermutungen über „pneumatologische Möglichkeiten". Soviel glaubt er aber schon nach den religiösen Erfahrungen sagen zu können, daß unter den guten Geistern einer ist, mit dem wir durch das Unterbewußtsein zusammenhängen und der uns im Kampfe hilft: das ist der Gott des religiösen Bewußtseins. So ist auch Schiller bemüht, den theistischen Gottesbegriff mit allen seinen Merkmalen, nur Unendlichkeit, Zeitlosigkeit und Weltschöpfung ausgenommen, zu retten.

Am Schlusse seines Buches über das pluralistische Universum findet James sogar den Begriff des Absoluten doch nicht mehr so unmöglich wie früher. Wenigstens als Hypothese läßt er es zu, daß alle endlichen Geister von einem übermenschlichen Bewußtsein umfaßt seien, das nur eben „irgend etwas Fremdes"

---

12 Riddles of the Sphinx 1891, zuerst anonym „by a Troglodyte" (nicht A. Troglodyte, wie in einer Philosphiegeschichte steht). Bei uns scheint Schopenhauer in seiner Entwicklungszeit vorübergehend einem ähnlichen Pluralismus gehuldigt zu haben. Herr Dr. Hochstetter macht mich auf Stellen des handschriftlichen, von ihm veröffentlichten Nachlasses aufmerksam, wo von „den Willen" in der Mehrzahl, deren Erscheinungen die Einzeldinge seien, die Rede ist (Sämtl. Werke, Bd. XI, S. 179, 182, 208).

außer sich habe und folglich endlicher Natur sei. Die vielen übermenschlichen Bewußtseine scheinen hier als entbehrlich aus der Hypothese herausgefallen zu sein. Im wesentlichen wäre dies wieder der antike Dualismus, Gott und Natur oder Materie.

In Deutschland ist aus ähnlichen Bedürfnissen wie bei James und Schiller 1871 eine solche Weltanschauung in einer anonymen, aber von Lotze durch ein Vorwort eingeführten Schrift: „Das Evangelium der armen Seele" vertreten worden. Der Verfasser hat sich damals auch mir anvertraut, ich war es aber nicht selbst. Diese Schrift wäre noch mehr nach James' als nach Lotzes Sinne gewesen. In einer warm-persönlichen, an die Schriften der mittelalterlichen Mystiker erinnernden Sprache, einem Zwiegespräch der Seele mit Gott, wird die Anschauung von Gott als einem endlichen, aber unserer Seele näherstehenden Wesen entwickelt. Er hat nichts mit der Natur zu tun, aber er ist unser Heil und unsere Rettung in den inneren Nöten. Die [238] Natur ist jenes „Andere", Außergöttliche. So wird auf die einfachste Weise zwischen Religion und Naturwissenschaft Frieden gestiftet. Lotze fühlte sich von der Beichte der armen Seele gerührt: „Mir aber hatte sie es angetan. Wie eine alte halbverklungene Sage kam mir die Erinnerung an die jugendlichen Tage wieder, in denen wir alle noch unsere Gedanken über die höchsten Dinge nur aus dem lebendigen Drange des begeisterten Herzens schöpften." Aber er schied seinen Weg alsbald von den Weisungen dieses Evangeliums. „Mir wird es nicht gelingen, in Gott anstatt des Schöpfers Himmels und der Erden nur den freundlichen Genius zu verehren, der über die Leiden einer Welt tröstet, in der er so fremd ist wie wir selbst." Der Anonymus ist in späteren Schriften selbst zu anderen Anschauungen gekommen. Aber das Büchlein verdient als Ausdruck eines Dualismus, zu dem die deutsche Philosophie sonst nicht hinneigt, in religionsphilosophischen Kreisen wohl mehr Beachtung als ihm trotz Lotzes Empfehlung zuteil geworden ist. James kannte es sicher nicht.

Nur auf das Verständnis, nicht auf eine Kritik des Pluralismus bei James war es hier abgesehen. Die Philosophie wird sich auch weiterhin bemühen, die Realität und furchtbare Größe des Übels mit dem Begriff eines einheitlichen letzten Weltgrundes zu vereinigen und diesen Begriff eben so zu formulieren, daß er weder den Tatsachen noch sich selbst widerspricht. Irgendwie aber muß er sicherlich gegenüber dem eines Willkür-Herrschers im alten Sinne umgebildet, muß die immanente Notwendigkeit der Naturgesetze in Gottes Wesen aufgenommen werden. Dies war auch ein Grundgedanke der spekulativ-idealistischen Systeme. Nur gerade so war er nicht durchzuführen. Wer immer diese Probleme in sich herumwälzt, der wird, wenn er auch James' radikale Lösung sich nicht zu eigen machen kann, doch die Schärfe besser verstehen, mit der er gegen das Absolute des

Pantheismus angeht, in dem mittels kunstvoller Dialektik, aber nichts weniger als zwingender Logik alle Rätsel der Welt ihre Lösung finden sollten.

---

37 Jahre sind seit dem Erscheinen der „Principles of Psychology", 17 Jahre seit James' Tode verflossen. Wie hat die Psychologie, wie haben Erkenntnistheorie und Metaphysik sich seitdem weiterentwickelt? In der Psychologie haben wir anscheinend den Zustand wieder, dem Brentano abhelfen wollte, als er im Vorwort seines Werkes die Hoffnung aussprach, daß an die Stelle der Psychologien eine Psychologie treten werde. Es ist von einer ganzen Anzahl neuer Psychologien die Rede, deren Schöpfer geneigt sind, die gesamte bisherige Arbeit als belanglos einzuschätzen. Tatsächlich besteht aber die Entwicklung nur darin (und erweist sich gerade dadurch als wahrer Fortschritt), daß genau so, wie es in allen Erfahrungswissenschaften fortwährend geschieht, relativ [239] zu wenig beachtete Gebiete oder Erklärungsprinzipien einem reichen Bestande hinzugefügt werden, der dadurch nur vermehrt, auch wohl verbessert, aber nicht gänzlich entwertet und umgestoßen werden kann. Weder die experimentelle Psychologie, noch selbst die alte, während dreier Jahrhunderte entwickelte Assoziationspsychologie sind so mausetot wie viele glauben. Gewiß, das psychische Leben kann nicht in bloße „Und-Verbindungen" aufgelöst werden und die Assoziationsgesetze bedürfen selbst der Revision; aber eine Fülle des Lehrreichen und gut Beobachteten liegt ihnen zugrunde und bleibt bestehen. Auch die experimentelle Psychologie ist mitnichten abgewirtschaftet, hat vielmehr in der Untersuchung der Anschauungsbilder und der Komplexe, Gestalten, Bewegungen, aber auch in den weiten Gebieten der Kinder- und der Tierpsychologie eine Fülle neuer, dankbarer Aufgaben gefunden. Daß ihr relativ, d. h. im Verhältnis zur Breite des psychischen Lebens, recht enge Grenzen gezogen sind, daß in allen höheren Gebieten des Seelenlebens die bloße Beobachtung und Analyse weitaus überwiegen und der Fortschritt hier nur in ihrer Vertiefung gesucht werden muß, ebenda wo ihn auch James mit Lotze und Brentano gesucht hat, verstand sich für Einsichtige allezeit von selbst.[13]

---

13 Vergl. die bedeutsamen Ausführungen Bühlers im letzten Bande dieser Zeitschrift über die Krise in der Psychologie, insbesondere den Behaviorismus in James' Heimatlande und die „verstehende Psychologie" bei uns in Deutschland. Wenn ich im obigen die Rolle des Experimentes in der Denk- und Willenspsychologie für sehr gering ansehe, so dürfte auch hierin kein ernstlicher Unterschied gegenüber Bühlers Anschauungen liegen. Denn seine eigene Erstlingsschrift, mit der er diese Richtung eröffnete, verdankt ihre wesentlichsten Ergebnisse doch den aus seiner Selbstbeobachtung geschöpften Deutungen, und schließlich fließen auch die Aussagen der Versuchspersonen aus keiner anderen Quelle als ihrer Selbstbeobachtung.

Der Okkultismus und die jetzt so genannte Parapsychologie, die James fruchtbarer erschienen als die damalige Experimentalpsychologie, haben seitdem unstreitig in Deutschland mehr Freunde gewonnen, darunter einige bedeutende Naturforscher, deren einer sich sogar zu der Überzeugung bekennt, daß wir von Geistern umgeben seien, also auf dem besten Wege zum Pluralismus und zur Dämonologie ist. Daß hierbei nicht so sehr psychologische als metaphysische Interessen im Spiele sind, würde an sich ihren Wert nur erhöhen. Aber, aber – der Fragezeichen, mit denen bereits James nicht sparte, sind es inzwischen kaum weniger geworden.

Die Metaphysik selbst, die einschließlich der Erkenntnistheorie James in seinen letzten Dezennien fast ganz in Anspruch nahm, hat seitdem in der Gunst der philosophischen Welt die Psychologie unstreitig noch überflügelt. Aber ihre Lage entspricht wohl kaum James' Hoffnungen und Wünschen. Ihre Weiterentwicklung in Amerika ist mir allerdings nicht genügend bekannt; unsere philosophischen Amerika-[240]fahrer können mehr davon erzählen. In Deutschland aber ist weder der Pluralismus und Pragmatismus noch der Bergsonianismus durchgedrungen. Unter den heimischen Gewächsen steht manches Achtungswerte neben vielem Unkraut; aber von einer durchgreifenden Erneuerung, einem imposanten Aufschwung der Philosophie ist noch nichts zu spüren. Das Gesamtbild ist, wenn mich nicht der Pessimismus des Alters trügt, mehr das jenes gärenden Durcheinander von Altem und Neuem, das für Übergangszeiten charakteristisch ist. Wir leiden nicht so sehr an einem Mangel kräftiger Talente als an einem Überfluß von Parteibildungen, ganz wie in unserem politischen Leben. Unnötige Wortschöpfungen und Systemtitulaturen gehen damit einher. Es sind Fehler, die James immer an uns rügte.

Das Trockene, Pedantische der Form ist nicht immer vermeidbar, solange Gründlichkeit der Untersuchung als Hauptsache gilt; und das muß sie bleiben. Immerhin dürfte sich auch das Gründlichste, Tiefste der Wissenschaft in einer, wenn nicht geradezu allgemeinverständlichen, doch wenigstens den Fachmännern der konkreten Wissenschaften verständlichen Form sagen lassen. Bereits Kant hat vielfach wertvolle Gedanken durch eine mit ungenügend definierten technischen Ausdrücken überladene Darstellung mehr verhüllt als klargelegt und dadurch freilich auch der Kritik ihre Arbeit erschwert. Man kann es James, der ihn hochachtete, seit der Jugend eifrig studierte und in der reifsten Zeit Seminarübungen zugrunde legte, nicht verdenken, wenn er sich als Meister des lebendigen Stiles davon zurückgestoßen fühlte. Selbst einen Ausruf wie: „Es lebe der angelsächsische Amateur, Schüler von Locke und Hume, und *pereat* der deutsche Fachmann!" dürfen wir in einem Brief an den geistesverwandten Schiller, dem er sein Herz ausschüttet, nicht zu tragisch nehmen.

Ob die Philosophie sachlich recht getan hätte, auf Hume weiterzubauen und seine Untersuchungsweise nur konsequenter als er selbst durchzuführen (Coll. Ess. 434 ff. u.ö.), bleibe hier dahingestellt. Es ist anders gekommen und hat nicht anders kommen können, als es gekommen ist. Aber in die Verachtung der angelsächsischen Geistesrichtung, wie sie im Kreise der spekulativen Denker üblich war, dürfen wir nicht wieder zurückfallen, müssen uns vielmehr ihre eigentümlichen Vorzüge anzueignen suchen, ohne die unsrigen aufzugeben. In keinem Falle kann die Rückkehr zu den Ruinen der spekulativen Systeme das Losungswort sein. Wir mögen sie um ihres hohen Schwunges willen lieben, um ihrer Gedankenbaukunst willen bewundern, aber zu bewohnen sind sie nicht mehr und auch nicht zu reparieren. Den immer dringender werdenden Mahnungen dazu möchte man – nur zur Verrechnung und ohne Gewähr gegen Mißbrauch – mit Goethes Versen erwidern:

> Amerika, du hast es besser
> Als unser Kontinent, das alte,
> Hast keine verfallne Schlösser
> Und keine Basalte.
>
> Dich stört nicht im Innern
> Zu lebendiger Zeit
> Unnützes Erinnern
> Und vergeblicher Streit.[14]

---

14 Diese Verse hatte ich eben abgeschrieben, als mir v. Asters Übersetzung des Unsterblichkeitsbüchleins von James (1926) zu Gesichte kam. Da stellt der Übersetzer gleichfalls James' frische Denk- und Schreibweise dem „verzopften und geschichtlich belasteten Europa" als Muster hin. Ob er an dieselben Zöpfe vorzugsweise gedacht hat, weiß ich allerdings nicht.

Zu S. 210 vorliegender Abhandlung möchte ich noch mitteilen, daß nach einer Zuschrift Prof. Österreichs (Tübingen) eine Sammlung der „parapsychologischen" Aufsätze W. James' unter dem Titel „Études et Reflexions d'un Psychiste" 1914 bei Payot in Paris erschienen ist.

Abbreviations

Autobiography	Stumpf, Carl (1924): "Carl Stumpf" [Selbstdarstellung]. In: Raymund Schmidt (Ed.): *Die Philosophie der Gegenwart in Selbstdarstellung*. Vol. 5. Leipzig: Meiner, pp. 1–57. Quoted form the Eng. trans. "Autobiography". In Carl Murchison (Ed.). *A History of Psychology in Autobiography*. Vol. 1. Worcester: Clark University Press, pp. 389–441 (1930).
Corr.	James, William (1992–2004): *The Correspondence of William James*. Ignas K. Skrupskelis/Elisabeth M. Berkeley (Eds.). 12 vols. Charlottesville-London: University of Virginia Press.
Essays on Stumpf	Denis Fisette/Riccardo Martinelli (Eds.) (2015). *Philosophy from an Empirical Standpoint. Essays on Carl Stumpf*. Amsterdam-Leiden-Boston: Brill-Rodopi.
Principles of Psychology	James, William (1890): *The Principles of Psychology*. 2 vols. New York: Holt.
Raumvorstellung	Stumpf, Carl (1873): *Über den psychologischen Ursprung der Raumvorstellung*. Leipzig: Hirzel.
Reden und Vorträge	Stumpf, Carl (1910): *Philosophische Reden und Vorträge*. Leipzig: Barth.
Stumpf Collection	Takasuna, Miko (2003): "Reconstruction of Stumpf Collection and Barth Collection: Using Bibliographical Cards as Resource in the Main Library at Kyushu University". In: *History of Psychology and Psychological Studies* 5, pp. 37–68.
Thought and Character	Perry, Ralph Barton (1935): *The Thought and Character of William James, as revealed in unpublished correspondence and notes, together with his published writings*. 2 vols. London: Humphrey Milford (Oxford: Oxford University Press).
Tone Psychology 1	Stumpf, Carl (2020): *Tone Psychology: Volume 1. The Sensation of Successive Single Tones*. Robin Rollinger (Ed.). London and New York: Routledge [English translation of *Tonpsychologie* 1].
Tonpsychologie 1	Stumpf, Carl (1883): *Tonpsychologie*. Vol. 1. Leipzig: Hirzel.
Tonpsychologie 2	Stumpf, Carl (1890): *Tonpsychologie*. Vol. 2. Leipzig: Hirzel.
Varieties	James, William (1902): *The Varieties of Religious Experience: A Study in Human Nature*. New York-London: Longmans, Green & Co. [*Works* 15].
Will to Believe	James, William (1897): *The Will to Believe and Other Essays in Popular Philosophy*. New York-London: Longmans, Green & Co. [*Works* 6].
William James	Stumpf, Carl (1927): "William James nach seinen Briefen. Leben. Character. Lehre". In: *Kant-Studien* 32, pp. 205–241.
Works	James, William (1975–1988): *The Works of William James*. Frederick H. Burkhardt/Fredson Bowers/Ignas K. Skrupskelis (Eds.). 17 vols. Cambridge-London: Harvard University Press.

References

Allesch, Christian (2015): "Ästhetik als praktische Philosophie: Zur impliziten Ästhetik von Carl Stumpf". In: *Essays on Stumpf*, pp. 293–313.
Araujo de Freitas, Saulo (2016): *Wundt and the Philosophical Foundations of Psychology. A Reappraisal*. Cham-Heidelberg-New York-Dordrecht-London: Springer.
Aristotle (1957): *On the Soul. Parva Naturalia. On Breath*. Walter Stanley Hett (Ed.). Loeb Classical Library 288. Cambridge-London: Harvard University Press.
Ash, Graham Mitchell (1995): *Gestalt Psychology in German Culture, 1890–1967. Holism and the Quest for Objectivity*. Cambridge: Cambridge University Press.
Avenarius, Richard (1888–90): *Kritik der reinen Erfahrung*. 2 vols. Leipzig: Reisland.
Baldwin, James Mark (1896): "The Third Congress of Psychology". In: *The Nation. A Weekly Journal Devoted to Politics, Literature, Science and Art* 63, No. 1628, pp. 192–193.
Banks, Erik (2003): *Ernst Mach's World Elements. A Study in Natural Philosophy*. Dordrecht: Springer.
Banks, Erik (2014): *The Realistic Empiricism of Mach, James, and Russell. Neutral Monism Reconceived*. Cambridge: Cambridge University Press.
Barzun, Jacques (1983): *A Stroll with William James*. Chicago-London: The University of Chicago Press.
Baumgartner, Wilhelm (2015): "The Young Carl Stumpf. His Spiritual, Intellectual, and Professional Development". In: *Essays on Stumpf*, pp. 61–74.
Berlioz, Hector (1878): *Mémoires de H. Berlioz, comprenant ses voyages en Italie, en Allemagne, en Russie et en Angleterre (1803–1865)*. Paris: Calmann-Lévy.
Bjork, Daniel W. (1983): *The Compromised Scientist: William James in the Development of American Psychology*. New York: Columbia University Press.
Blackmore, John T./Hentschel, Klaus (Eds.) (1985): *Ernst Mach als Aussenseiter. Machs Briefwechsel über Philosophie und Relativitätstheorie mit Persönlichkeiten seiner Zeit*. Wien: Braumüller.
Bonacchi, Silvia/Boudewijnse, Geert-Jan (Eds.) (2011): *Carl Stumpf. From Philosophical Reflection to Interdisciplinary Scientific Investigation*. Wien: Krammer.
Bradley, Francis Herbert (1893a): "Professor James on Simple Resemblance". In: *Mind* n.s. 2, pp. 366–369.
Bradley, Francis Herbert (1893b): "On Professor James's Doctrine of Simple Resemblance". In: *Mind* n.s. 2, pp. 83–88.
Bradley, Francis Herbert (1904): "On Truth and Practice". In: *Mind* n.s. 13, pp. 309–335.
Brentano, Franz (1874): *Psychology from an Empirical Standpoint*. Linda McAlister (Ed.). London-New York: Routledge, 2009.
Brentano, Franz (1896): "Über Individuation, multiple Qualität und Intensität sinnlicher Erscheinungen". In: *Untersuchungen zur Sinnespsychologie*. Hamburg: Meiner (1979), pp. 66–89.
Brentano, Franz (1989): *Briefe an Carl Stumpf 1867–1917*. Gerhard Oberkofler (Ed.). Graz: Akademische Druck- und Verlagsanstalt.
Calkins, Mary Whiton (1901): *An Introduction to Psychology*. New York-London: Macmillan.
Carlson, Thomas (1997): "James and the Kantian Tradition". In: *The Cambridge Companion to William James*. Ruth Anna Putnam (Ed.). Cambridge: Cambridge University Press, pp. 363–383.

Carrette, Jeremy (2014): "Growing up Zig-Zag: Reassessing the Transatlantic Legacy of William James". In: Martin Halliwell/Joel D.S. Rasmussen (Eds.). *William James and the Transatlantic Conversation. Pragmatism, Pluralism, and Philosophy of Religion*. Oxford: Oxford University Press, pp. 199–217.

Centi, Beatrice (2011): "Stumpf and Lotze on Space, Reality, Relation". In: Silvia Bonacchi/Geert-Jan Boudewijnse (Eds.). *Carl Stumpf. From Philosophical Reflection to Interdisciplinary Scientific Investigation*. Wien: Krammer, pp. 69–81.

Cesalli, Laurent (2015): "Stumpf's (Early) Insights and Marty's Way to His (Later) Sprachphilosophie". In: *Essays on Stumpf*, pp. 359–384.

Christensen, Dieter (2000): "Erich M. von Hornbostel, Carl Stumpf, and the Institutionalization of Comparative Musicology" In: Arthur Simon (Ed.). *Das Berliner Phonogramm-Archiv 1900–2000. Sammlungen der traditionellen Musik der Welt*. Berlin: Verlag für Wissenschaft und Bildung, pp. 141–150.

Clendenning, John (1999): *The Life and Thought of Josiah Royce*. Nashville: Vanderbilt University Press.

Cooper, Wesley (2002): *The Unity of William James's Thought*. Nashville: Vanderbilt University Press.

Cranch, Christopher Pearse (1844): *Poems*. Philadelphia: Carey & Hart.

Dazzi, Nino (1999): "James and Stumpf. Similarities and Differences". In: *Psychologie und Geschichte* 6, pp. 244–257.

Dewey, John (1903): *Studies in Logical Theory*. Chicago: The University of Chicago Press.

Dilthey, Wilhelm (2010): "Ideas for a Descriptive and Analytic Psychology". In: *Selected Works*, vol. 2: *Understanding the Human World*. Rudolph A. Makkreel/Fritjohf Rodi (Eds.). Princeton-Oxford: Princeton University Press.

Dunham, Jeremy (2015): "Idealism, Pragmatism and the Will to Believe: Charles Renouvier and William James". In: *British Journal for the History of Philosophy* 23, pp. 756–778.

Edie, James M. (1987): *William James and Phenomenology*. Bloomington: Indiana University Press.

Ellis, Alexander J. (1922): "Über die Tonleitern verschiedener Völker". In: *Sammelbände für vergleichende Musikwissenschaft* 1, pp. 1–76.

Emerson, Ralph Waldo (1884): "Friendship". In: *Essays*. Boston: Houghton Mifflin.

Fisette, Denis/Martinelli, Riccardo (Eds.) (2015): *Philosophy from an Empirical Standpoint. Essays on Carl Stumpf*. Amsterdam, Leiden, Boston: Brill-Rodopi.

Fisette, Denis (2019): "Carl Stumpf". In: *The Stanford Encyclopedia of Philosophy*. Edward N. Zalta (Ed.). https://plato.stanford.edu/archives/spr2019/entries/stumpf/, visited on 10 July 2019.

Fisette, Denis (2013): "Mixed Feelings. Carl Stumpf's Criticism of James and Brentano on Emotions". In: *Themes from Brentano*. Denis Fisette/Guillaume Fréchette (Eds.). Amsterdam-New York: Rodopi, pp. 281–305.

Fisette, Denis (2015): "Bibliography of the Publications of Carl Stumpf. Bibliographie der Schriften von Carl Stumpf". In: *Essays on Stumpf*, pp. 529–541.

Flourens, Pierre (1858): *De la vie et de l'intelligence*. Paris: Garnier.

Flournoy, Théodore (1911): *La Philosophie de William James*. Saint-Blaise: Foyer Solidariste. Eng. trans. *The Philosophy of William James*. New York: Holt & Co. (1917).

Flournoy, Théodore/James, William (1966): *The Letters of William James and Théodore Flournoy*. Robert Le Clair (Ed.). Madison-Milwaukee-London: The University of Wisconsin Press.

Ford, Marcus (1998): "William James's Psychical Research and Its Philosophical Implications". In: *Transactions of the Charles S. Peirce Society* 34, pp. 605–626.
Fréchette, Guillaume/Taieb, Hamid (Eds.) (2017): *Mind and Language. On the Philosophy of Anton Marty*. Berlin: De Gruyter.
Fullerton, George Stuart (1887): *The Conception of the Infinite, and the Solution of the Mathematical Axioms: A Study in Psychological Analysis*. Philadelphia: Lippincott.
Funke, Otto (1880): "Der Tastsinn und die Gemeingefühle". In: Ludimar Hermann (Ed.). *Handbuch der Physiologie*. Vol. 3, t. 2: *Handbuch der Physiologie der Sinnesorgane*. Leipzig: Vogel, pp. 289–413.
Gerhart, Volker/Mehring, Reinhard/Rindert, Jana (1999): *Berliner Geist. Eine Geschichte der Berliner Universitätsphilosophie bis 1946*. Berlin: Akademie-Verlag.
Gioia, Lia (2013): *William James e Carl Stumpf. Un rapporto scientifico e personale attraverso le lettere*. PhD Thesis, University of Trieste. http://hdl.handle.net/10077/10147, last visit 10 July 2019.
Goethe, Johann Wolfgang (1827): "Den vereinigten Staaten" (from *Zahme Xenien*). In: *Sämtliche Werke, Briefe, Tagebücher und Gespräche*. Sect. 1, vol. 2: *Gedichte 1800–1832*, Frankfurt a.M.: Suhrkamp (1988).
Graefe, Karl Alfred/Saemisch, Theodor (Eds.) (1874–1922): *Handbuch der gesamten Augenheilkunde*. Leipzig: Engelmann.
Gundlach, Horst (2018): "William James and the Heidelberg Fiasco". In: *History of Psychology* 21, pp. 47–72.
Gurney, Edmund (1889): *The Power of Sound*. London: Smith, Elder & Co.
Gurney, Edmund/Myers, Frederic W.H./Podmore, Frank (1886): *Phantasms of the Living*. 2 vols. London: Trübner.
Halliwell, Martin/Rasmussen, Joel D.S. (Eds.). (2014): *William James and the Transatlantic Conversation. Pragmatism, Pluralism, and Philosophy of Religion*. Oxford: Oxford University Press.
Hauptmann, Carl (1893): *Die Metaphysik in der modernen Physiologie. Eine kritische Untersuchung*. Dresden: Ehlermann.
Helmholtz, Hermann von (1856–67): *Handbuch der physiologischen Optik*. 3 vols. Leipzig: Voss.
Helmholtz, Hermann von (1863): *Die Lehre von den Tonempfindungen, als physiologische Grundlage für die Theorie der Musik*. Braunschweig: Vieweg.
Hering, Ewald (1879): "Raumsinn des Auges. Augenbewegung". In: Ludimar Hermann (Ed.). *Handbuch der Physiologie*. Vol. 3, t. 1: *Handbuch der Physiologie der Sinnesorgane*, Leipzig: Vögel, pp. 343–600.
Hermann, Ludimar (Ed.) (1879–83): *Handbuch der Physiologie*. 6 vols. Leipzig: Vogel.
Herzog, Max (1995): "William James and the Development of Phenomenological Psychology in Europe". In: *Journal of the Human Sciences* 8, pp. 29–46.
Hugo, Victor (1862): *Les Misérables*. Bruxelles: Lacroix.
James, Henry (1881): *The Portrait of a Lady*. Boston: Houghton Mifflin & Co.
James, Henry (1877): *The American*. Boston: Osgood & Co.
James, Henry 1st. (1884): *The Literary Remains of the Late Henry James*. Edited with an Introduction by William James. Boston-New York: Houghton Mifflin.
James, Henry 3rd (Ed.) (1920): *The Letters of William James*. Boston: Little & Brown.
James, William (1875): "Review of Wundt, Grundzüge der physiologischen Psychologie (1875)" [unsigned]. In: *North American Review* 121, pp. 195–201 [*Works* 17: 296–303].

James, William (1876): "The Teaching of Philosophy in our Colleges" [unsigned]. In: *Nation* 23, pp. 178–179 [*Works* 5: 3–6].
James, William (1878a): "Brute and Human Intellect". In: *Journal of Speculative Philosophy* 12, pp. 236–276 [*Works* 13: 1–37].
James, William (1878b): "Remarks on Spencer's Definition of Mind as Correspondence". In: *Journal of Speculative Philosophy* 12, pp. 1–18 [*Works* 5: 7–22].
James, William (1879a): "The Sentiment of Rationality". In: *Mind* 4, pp. 317–346 [*Works* 5: 32–64]. Combined with "Rationality, Activity and Faith" of 1882 and reprinted under the title "The Sentiment of Rationality" in *Will to Believe* [*Works* 6: 57–89]).
James, William (1879b): "The Spatial Quale". In: *Journal of Speculative Philosophy* 13, pp. 64–87 [*Works* 13: 62–82].
James William (1879c): "Review of Herbert Spencer's Data of Ethics" [unsigned]. In: *Nation* 29, pp. 178–179 [*Works* 17: 347–353].
James, William (1880a): *The Feeling of Effort*, Anniversary Memoirs of the Boston Society of Natural History. Boston [*Works* 13: 83–124].
James, William (1880b): "Great Men, Great Thoughts and their Environment". In: *Atlantic Monthly* 46, pp. 441–459. Reprinted as "Great Men and their Environment" in *Will to Believe* [*Works* 6: 163–189].
James, William (1881): "Reflex Action and Theism". In: *Unitarian Review* 16, pp. 389–416. Reprinted in *Will to Believe* [*Works* 6: 90–113].
James, William (1882): "Rationality, Activity and Faith". In: *Princeton Review* 2, pp. 58–86. Combined with selections from "The Sentiment of Rationality" and reprinted under the title "The Sentiment of Rationality" in *Will to Believe* [*Works* 6: 57–89].
James, William (1884a): "On Some Omissions of Introspective Psychology". In: *Mind* 9, pp. 1–26 [*Works* 13: 142–167].
James, William (1884b): "What is an Emotion?". In: *Mind* 9, pp. 188–205 [*Works* 13: 168–187].
James, William (1884c): "Introduction" to *The Literary Remains of the Late Henry James*. Boston-New York: Houghton Mifflin [*Works* 11: 3–63].
James, William (1884d): "Review of Th. Lipps's Psychologische Studien" [unsigned]. In: *Science* 6, 1885, pp. 308–310 [*Works* 17: 391–394].
James, William (1885): "Review of J. Royce's *The Religious Aspect of Philosophy*" [unsigned]. In: *Atlantic Monthly* 55, pp. 840–843 [*Works* 17: 383–388].
James, William (1886a): "The Perception of Time". In: *Journal of Speculative Philosophy* 20, pp. 374–407. Reprinted almost *verbatim* in *Principles of Psychology*, ch. 15 (Perception of Time) [*Works* 8: 570–604].
James, William (1886b): "Report on the Committee on Hypnotism" [with M. Carnochan]. In: *Proceedings of the American Society for Psychical Research* 1, pp. 95–102 [*Works* 13: 190–197].
James, William (1886c): "Report on the Committee on Mediumistic Phenomena". In: *Proceedings of the American Society for Psychical Research* 1, July, pp. 102–106 [*Works* 16: 14–18].
James, William (1887a): Review of "E. Gurney's, F.W.H. Myers's, and F. Podmore's Phantasms of the Living". In: *Science* 9, pp. 18–20 [*Works* 16: 24–28].
James, William (1887b): "The Perception of Space". In: *Mind* 12, pp. 1–30, 183–211, 321–353, 516–548. Reprinted with considerable revision in *Principles of Psychology*, ch. 20 (Perception of Space) [*Works* 9: 776–912].

James, William (1887c): "Correction to 'The Perception of Space' (1887)" [untitled]. In: *Mind* 12, p. 318 [*Works* 17: 126–127].
James, William (1889): "Report on the Congress of Physiological Psychology at Paris". In: *Mind* 14, pp. 614–615 [*Works* 13: 243–246].
James, William (1890a): *The Principles of Psychology*. New York: Holt [*Works* 8–10].
James, William (1890b): "The Hidden Self". In: *Scribner's Magazine* 7, pp. 361–373 [*Works* 13: 247–268].
James, William (1891a): "The Proposed Shortening of the College Course". In: *Harvard Monthly* 11, pp. 127–137 [Works 17: 32–41].
James, William (1891b): "The Moral Philosopher and the Moral Life". In: *International Journal of Ethics* 1, pp. 330–354. Reprinted in James, *Will to Believe* [*Works* 6: 161–142].
James, William (1892a): *Psychology. Briefer Course*. New York, Holt [*Works* 14].
James, William (1892b): "Review of H. Schmidkunz's Psychologie der Suggestion". In: *Philosophical Review* 1, pp. 306–309 [*Works* 17: 419–423].
James, William (1893a): "The Galileo Festival at Padua". In: *Nation* 56, pp. 8–9 [*Works* 17: 41–46].
James, William (1893b): "Mr. Bradley on Immediate Resemblance". In: *Mind* n.s. 2, pp. 208–210 [*Works* 5: 65–68].
James, William (1893c): "Immediate Resemblance". In: *Mind* n.s. 2, pp. 509–510 [with a note by Francis Herbert Bradley, p. 510] [*Works* 5: 69–70].
James, William (1894a): "Review of G.T. Ladd's Psychology: Descriptive and Explanatory". In: *Psychological Review* 1, pp. 286–293 [*Works* 17: 478–485].
James, William (1894b): "Professor Wundt and Feelings of Innervation". In: *The Psychological Review* 1, pp. 70–73 [*Works* 13: 295–299].
James, William (1895a): "The Knowing of Things Together". In: *Psychological Review* 2, pp. 105–124 [*Works* 5: 71–89].
James, William (1895b): "Preface to Paulsen's *Introduction to Philosophy*". New York: Holt [*Works* 5: 90–93].
James, William (1897a): *The Will to Believe and Other Essays in Popular Philosophy*. New York-London: Longmans, Green & Co. [*Works* 6].
James, William (1897b): "Final American Report: Letter to Henry Sidgwick". In: *Dritter International Congress für Psychologie in München vom 4–7 August 1896*. München: Lehmann [*Works* 16: 73–74].
James, William (1898): *Human Immortality: Two Supposed Objections to the Doctrine*. Boston-New York: Houghton Mifflin [*Works* 11: 75–101].
James, William (1899a): *Talks to Teachers on Psychology: and to Students on Some of Life's Ideals*. New York: Holt [*Works*: 12].
James, William (1899b): *Der Wille zum Glauben und andere popularphilosophische Essays*, m. e. Geleitwort von Friedrich Paulsen (pp. iii–xviii). Stuttgart: Frommann.
James, William (1902): *The Varieties of Religious Experience. A Study in Human Nature*, being the Gifford Lectures on Natural Religion delivered at Edinburgh in 1901–1902. New York-London: Longmans, Green & Co. [*Works* 15].
James, William (1904a): "Does Consciousness Exist?" In: *Journal of Philosophical Psychology, and Scientific Methods* 1, pp. 477–491 [*Works* 3: 3–19].
James, William (1904b): "Reviewed Work[s]: *Personal Idealism: Philosophical Essays by Eight Members of the University of Oxford*, by Henry Sturt". In: *Mind* n.s. 12, pp. 93–97 [*Works* 17: 540–545].

James, William (1904c): "Humanism and Truth". In: *Mind* n.s. 13, pp. 457–475. Reprinted with revision and integration from another essay in *The Meaning of Truth* [*Works* 2: 37–60].
James, William (1907): *Pragmatism: A New Name for Some Old Ways of Thinking*. New York-London: Longmans, Green & Co. [*Works*: 1].
James, William (1909a): *The Meaning of Truth. A Sequel to 'Pragmatism'*. New York-London: Longmans, Green & Co. [*Works* 2].
James, William (1909b): *A Pluralistic Universe. Hibbert Lectures at Manchester College on the Present Situation in Philosophy*. New York-London: Longmans, Green & Co. [*Works*: 4].
James, William (1909c): "On the Function of Cognition". In: *The Meaning of Truth. A Sequel to 'Pragmatism'*. London: Longmans, Green & Co. [*Works* 2: 13–32]. Reprinted from: *Mind* 10, pp. 27–44 (1885).
James, William (1911a): *Some Problems of Philosophy. A Beginning of an Introduction to Philosophy*. New York-London: Longmans, Green & Co. [*Works*: 7].
James, William (1911b): *Memories and Studies*. Henry James Jr. (Ed.). New York-London: Longmans, Green & Co.
James, William (1912): *Essays in Radical Empiricism*. Ralph Barton Perry (Ed.). New York-London: Longmans, Green & Co. [*Works* 3].
James, William (1926): *Unsterblichkeit*. Ernst von Aster (Ed.). Berlin: Philo-Verlag.
James, William (1975–1988): *The Works of William James*. Frederick H. Burkhardt/Fredson Bowers/Ignas K. Skrupskelis (Eds.). 17 vols. Cambridge-London: Harvard University Press.
James, William (1992–2004): *The Correspondence of William James*. Ignas K. Skrupskelis/Elisabeth M. Berkeley (Eds.). 12 vols. Charlottesville-London: University Press of Virginia.
Janet, Pierre (1889): *L'automatisme psychologique. Essai de psychologie expérimentale sur les formes inférieures de l'activité humaine*. Paris: Alcan.
Janet, Pierre (1892–94): *État mental des hystériques*, 2 vols.: *Les stigmates mentaux*; *Les accidents mentaux*. Paris: Rueff et Cie.
Janet, Pierre (Ed.) (1901): *Quatrième Congrès International de Psychologie*. Tenu à Paris, du 20 au 26 Août 1900 [...]. *Compte rendu des séances et texte des mémoires publiés par les soins de P. Janet*. Paris: Alcan.
Kant, Immanuel (1998): *Critique of Pure Reason*. Paul Guyer and Allen Wood (Eds.). The Cambridge Edition of the Works of Immanuel Kant. Vol. 2. Cambridge: Cambridge University Press.
Kaiser-el-Safti, Margret (1994): "Carl Stumpfs Lehre vom Ganzen und den Teilen". In: *Axiomathes* n.s. 5, pp. 87–122.
Köhler, Wolfgang (1913): "Über unbemerkte Empfindungen und Urteilstäuschungen". In: *Zeitschrift für Psychologie* 66, pp. 51–80. Eng. trans. "On Unnoticed Sensations and Errors of Judgment". In: *The Selected Papers of Wolfgang Köhler*. Mary Henle (Ed.). New York: Liveright, pp. 13–39 (1971).
Kraushaar, Otto (1936): "Lotze's Influence on the Psychology of William James". In: *The Psychological Review* 43, pp. 235–257.
Kraushaar, Otto (1938): "What James's Philosophical Orientation Owed to Lotze". In: *The Psychological Review* 47, pp. 517–526.
Kraushaar, Otto (1939): "Lotze as a Factor in the Development of James's Radical Empiricism and Pluralism". In: *The Psychological Review* 48, pp. 455–471.
Kraushaar, Otto (1940): "Lotze's Influence on the Pragmatism and Practical Philosophy of William James". In: *Journal of the History of Ideas* 1, pp. 439–458.

Kucklick, Bruce (1977): *The Rise of American Philosophy. Cambridge, Massachusetts, 1860–1930.* New Haven-London: Yale University Press.
Ladd, Geroge Trumbull (1894): *Psychology: Descriptive and Explanatory. A Treatise of the Phenomena, Laws and Development of Human Mental Life.* New York: Scribner.
Lamberth, David (1999): *William James and the Metaphysics of Experience.* Cambridge: Cambridge University Press.
Langfeld, Herbert Sidney (1937): "Carl Stumpf: 1848–1936". In: *The American Journal of Psychology* 50, pp. 316–320.
Langfeld, Herbert Sidney (1909): *Über die heterochrome Helligkeitsvergleichung.* Inaugural-Dissertation zur Erlangung der Doktorwürde, Universität zu Berlin. Leipzig: Barth.
Langfeld, Herbert Sidney (1937): "Stumpf's 'Introduction to Psychology'". In: *The American Journal of Psychology* 50, pp. 33–56.
Lewin, Kurt (1937): "Carl Stumpf". In: *The Psychological Review* 44, pp. 189–194.
Lindsay, Thomas M. (1873): "On the Psychological Origin of the Idea of Space" [Review of C. Stumpf, *Über den psychologischen Ursprung der* Raumvorstellung]. In: *The Academy* 6, No 71, pp. 172–173.
Lipps, Theodor (1883): *Grundtatsachen des Seelenlebens.* Bonn: Cohen.
Lipps, Theodor (1885): *Psychologische Studien. Der Raum der Gesichtswahrnehmung. Das Wesen der musikalischen Harmonie und Disharmonie.* Leipzig: Dürr.
Livingstone, Alexander (2016): *Damn Great Empires! William James and the Politics of Pragmatism.* Oxford: Oxford University Press.
Lorenz, Carl (1890): "Untersuchungen über die Auffassung von Tondistanzen". In: *Philosophische Studien* 6, pp. 26–103.
Lukens, Hermann Tyson (1898): "Notes Abroad". In: *The Pedagogical Seminary* 6, No 1, pp. 114–125.
Mach, Ernst (1883): *Die Mechanik in ihrer Entwickelung historisch-kritisch dargestellt.* Leipzig: Brockhaus.
Mach, Ernst (1886): *Beiträge zur Analyse der Empfindungen.* Jena: Fischer. Eng. trans. *Contributions to the Analysis of the Sensations.* Chicago: Open Court (1897).
Mach, Ernst (1887): "Zur Analyse der Tonempfindungen". In: *Sitzungsberichte der Kaiserlichen Akademie der Wissenschaften. Mathematisch-naturwissenschaftliche Klasse* 92.
Mach, Ernst (1910): "Sinnliche Elemente und naturwissenschaftliche Begriffe". In: *Pflügers Archiv für die gesamte Physiologie des Menschen und der Tiere* 136, pp. 263–274. Eng. trans. "Sensory Elements and Scientific Concepts". In: *Ernst Mach. A Deeper Look. Documents and New Perspectives.* John T. Blackmore (Ed.). Dordrecht: Kluwer, pp. 118–126.
Madelrieux, Stéphane (Ed.) (2011a): *Bergson et James, cent ans après.* Paris: Presses Universitaires de France.
Madelrieux, Stéphane (2011b): "De l'âme à l'inconscient. Métaphysique et psychologie chez James et Bergson". In: *Bergson et James, cent ans après.* Paris: Presses Universitaires de France, pp. 99–121.
Martinelli, Riccardo (2011): "Intentionality and God's Mind. Stumpf on Spinoza". In: *Carl Stumpf: From Philosophical Reflection to Interdisciplinary Scientific Investigation.* Silvia Bonacchi/Geert-Jan Boudewijnse (Eds.). Vienna: Krammer, pp. 51–67.
Martinelli, Riccardo (2014): "Melting Musics, Fusing Sounds. Stumpf, Hornbostel, and Comparative Musicology in Berlin". In: Rens Bod/Jaap Maat/Thijs Weststeijn (Eds.).

The Making of the Humanities. Vol. 3: *The Modern Humanities*. Amsterdam: Amsterdam University Press, pp. 391–401.
Martinelli, Riccardo (2015a): "Stumpf on Categories". In: *Essays on Stumpf*, pp. 203–227.
Martinelli, Riccardo (2015b): "A Philosopher in the Lab. Carl Stumpf on Philosophy and Experimental Sciences". *Philosophia Scientiae* 19, pp. 23–43.
Marty, Anton (1884–96): "Über subjectlose Sätze und das Verhältniss der Grammatik zur Logik und Psychologie". In: *Vierteljahrsschrift für wissenschaftliche Philosophie* (parts 1–2–3, 8, pp. 56–94, 161–192, 292–340; parts 4–5, 16, pp. 320–356, 421–471; parts 6–7, 19, pp. 19–87, 263–334).
Marty, Anton (1886–92): "Über Sprachreflex, Nativismus und absichtliche Sprachbildung". In: *Vierteljahrsschrift für wissenschaftliche Philosophie* 8, 1884, pp. 456–478; 10, 1886, pp. 69–105, 346–364; 13, 1889, pp. 195–220, 304–344; 14, 1890, pp. 442–484; 15, 1891, 445–467; 16, 1892, pp. 104–122.
Marty, Anton (1892): "Anzeige von William James' Werk 'Principles of Psychology'". In: *Zeitschrift für Psychologie und Physiologie der Sinnesorgane* 3, pp. 297–333.
Milkov, Nikolay (2015): "Carl Stumpf's Debt to Hermann Lotze". In: *Essays on Stumpf*, pp. 101–122.
Müller, Georg Elias (1891): *Theorie der Muskelcontraktion*, 1er Teil. Leipzig: Veit.
Müller, Johannes (1835): *Handbuch der Physiologie: für Vorlesungen*. Coblenz: Hölscher.
Müller, Karl Alexander von (1957): "Cossmann, Paul". In: *Neue Deutsche Biographie* vol. 3, pp. 374–375.
Münsterberg, Hugo (1889–92): *Beiträge zur experimentellen Psychologie*, 4 parts. Freiburg i.Br.: Mohr.
Münsterberg, Hugo (1900): *Grundzüge der Psychologie*, Leipzig: Barth.
Münsterberg, Hugo (1901): *American Traits from the Point of View of a German*. Boston-New York: Houghton Mifflin (Cambridge: The Riverside Press).
Münsterberg, Hugo (1904): *Die Amerikaner*. Berlin: Mittler & Sohn.
Myers, Gerald E. (1986): *William James. His Life and Thought*. New Haven-London: Yale University Press.
Newcomb, Simon (1886): "Address of the President". In: *Proceedings of the American Society for Psychical Research* 1, No 2, pp. 63–86.
Oppenheim, Janet (1985): *The Other World: Spiritualism and Psychical Research in England, 1850–1914*. Cambridge: Cambridge University Press.
Paul, Hermann (2018): "German Thoroughness in Baltimore: Epistemic Virtues and National Stereotypes". In: *History of Humanities* 3, pp. 327–350.
Paulsen, Friedrich (1892): *Einleitung in die Philosophie*. Berlin: Hertz.
Paulsen, Friedrich (1895): *Introduction to Philosophy*, New York: Holt.
Pawelsky, James (2007): *The Dynamic Individualism of William James*. Albany: SUNY Press.
Perry, Ralph Barton (1920): *Annotated Bibliography of the Writings of William James*. New York: Longmans, Green & Co.
Perry, Ralph Barton (1935): *The Thought and Character of William James, as revealed in unpublished correspondence and notes, together with his published writings*. 2 vols. London: Humphrey Milford (Oxford: Oxford University Press).
Pfungst, Oskar (1907): *Das Pferd des Herrn von Osten. Der Kluge Hans*. Leipzig: Barth.
Piéron, Henri (1954): "Histoire succincte des Congrès internationaux de Psychologie". In: *L'année psychologique* 54, pp. 397–405.

Putnam, Ruth Anna (Ed.). (1997): *The Cambridge Companion to William James*. Cambridge: Cambridge University Press.
Ratcliffe, Matthew (2005): "William James on Emotion and Intentionality" In: *International Journal of Philosophical Studies* 13, pp. 179–202.
Reed, Edward (1995): "The Psychologist's Fallacy as a Persistent Framework in William James's Psychological Theorizing". In: *History of the Human Sciences* 8, pp. 61–72.
Reisenzein, Rainer/Schönpflug, Wolfgang (1992): "Stumpf's Cognitive-Evaluative Theory of Emotion". In: *American Psychologist* 47, pp. 34–45.
Richardson, Robert (2006): *William James: in the Maelstrom of American Modernism. A Biography*. Boston: Houghton Mifflin.
Rollinger, Robin (1999): *Husserl's Position in the School of Brentano*. Dordrecht: Kluwer.
Rollinger, Robin (2008a): *Austrian Phenomenology: Brentano, Husserl, and Meinong on Mind and Object*. Frankfurt a.M.: Ontos.
Rollinger, Robin (2008b): "Stumpf on Phenomena and Phenomenology". In: *Austrian Phenomenology: Brentano, Husserl, and Meinong on Mind and Object*. Frankfurt a.M.: Ontos, pp. 139–156.
Rollinger, Robin (2008c): "The Concept of Causality in Stumpf's Epistemology". In: *Austrian Phenomenology, pp. Brentano, Husserl, and Meinong on Mind and Object*. Frankfurt a.M.: Ontos, pp. 263–300.
Royce, Josiah (1885): *The Religious Aspect of Philosophy. A Critique of the Bases of Conduct and of Faith*. Boston-New York: Houghton Mifflin.
Ruetenik, Tadd (2018): *The Demons of William James. Religious Pragmatism Explores Unusual Mental States*. London: Palgrave Macmillan.
Salter, William Mackintire (1885): *Die Religion der Moral*. Georg von Giżycki (Ed.). Leipzig: Friedrich.
Salter, William Mackintire (1889): *Ethical Religion*. Boston: Roberts.
Savourin, Michel/Cooper, Saths (2014): "The first International Congress of Physiological Psychology (Paris, August 1889): The Birth of the International Union of Psychological Science". In: *International Journal of Psychology* 49, pp. 222–232.
Schiller, Friedrich (1980): "Der Antritt des neuen Jahrhunderts". In: *Sämtliche Werke*. Jochen Golz (Ed.). Vol. 1: *Gedichte*. Aufbau-Verlag: Berlin, pp. 497–498.
Schmidkunz, Hans (1891a): "Der Hypnotismus in der neuesten 'Psychologie'". In: *Vierteljahrsschrift für wissenschaftliche Philosophie* 15 (2), pp. 210–215.
Schmidkunz, Hans (1891b): "Berichtigung". In: *Vierteljahrsschrift für wissenschaftliche Philosophie* 15 (3), pp. 348–350.
Schuhmann, Karl (1996): "Carl Stumpf (1848–1936)". In: Liliana Albertazzi et al. (Eds.). *The School of Franz Brentano*. Dordrecht: Kluwer, pp. 109–129.
Schumann, Friedrich (Ed.) (1912): *Bericht über den fünften Kongreß für experimentelle Psychologie in Berlin vom 16. bis 20. April 1912*. Leipzig: Barth.
Siegfried, Charlene Haddock (1990): *William James's Radical Reconstruction of Philosophy*. Albany: SUNY Press.
Simon, Arthur (Ed.) (2000): *Das Berliner Phonogramm-Archiv 1900–2000. Sammlungen der traditionellen Musik der Welt*. Berlin: Verlag für Wissenschaft und Bildung.
Simon, Linda (1998): *Genuine Reality. A Life of William James*. New York: Harcourt Brace & Co.
Slater, Michael R. (2009): *William James on Ethics and Faith*. Cambridge: Cambridge University Press.
Spencer, Herbert (1879): *The Data of Ethics*. London: Williams & Norgate.

Spiegelberg, Herbert (1960): *The Phenomenological Movement. A Historical Introduction.* Den Haag: Nijhoff, pp. 112–113.
Sprigge, Timothy L.S. (1993): *James and Bradley. American Truth and British Reality.* Chicago-La Salle: Open Court.
Sprung, Helga (2006): *Carl Stumpf. Eine Biographie. Von der Philosophie zur experimentellen Psychologie.* Von Helga Sprung unter Mitarbeit von Lothar Sprung. München-Wien: Profil.
Sprung, Lothar (2006): "Brüder im Geiste. Franz Brentano und William James". In: *Carl Stumpf. Eine Biographie. Von der Philosophie zur experimentellen Psychologie.* Von Helga Sprung unter Mitarbeit von Lothar Sprung. München-Wien: Profil, pp. 184–202.
Stricker, Salomon (1880): *Studien über die Sprachvorstellungen.* Wien: Braumüller.
Stricker, Salomon (1885): *Du langage et de la musique.* Paris: Alcan.
Stumpf, Carl (1873): *Über den psychologischen Ursprung der Raumvorstellung.* Leipzig: Hirzel.
Stumpf, Carl (1874): "Die empirische Psychologie der Gegenwart". In: *Im neuen Reich* 4, No 2, pp. 201–226.
Stumpf, Carl (1878): "Aus der vierten Dimension". In: *Philosophische Monatshefte* 14, pp. 13–30.
Stumpf, Carl (1883): *Tonpsychologie,* vol. 1. Leipzig: Hirzel.
Stumpf, Carl (1885a): "Musikpsychologie in England". In: *Vierteljahrsschrift für Musikwissenschaft* 1, pp. 261–349.
Stumpf, Carl (1885b): "Review of Lipps, Psychologische Studien I". In: *Deutsche Literaturzeitung* 45, No 7. cols. 1580–1581.
Stumpf, Carl (1885c): "Sur la représentation des mélodies". In: *Revue philosophique de la France et de l'étranger* 20, pp. 617–618;
Stumpf, Carl (1886a): "Über die Vorstellung von Melodien". In: *Zeitschrift für Philosophie und philosophische Kritik* n.s. 89, pp. 45–47.
Stumpf, Carl (1886b): "Lieder der Bellakula-Indianer". In: *Vierteljahrsschrift für Musikwissenschaft* 2, pp. 405–426.
Stumpf, Carl (1886c): "Rev. of Alexander J. Ellis, 'On the Musical Scale of various Nations' [In: *Journal of The Society of Arts* 33, No. 1688 (1885)]". In: *Vierteljahrsschrift für Musikwissenschaft* 2, pp. 511–524.
Stumpf, Carl (1886d): "Review of E. Mach, Beiträge zur Analyse der Empfindungen". In: *Deutsche Litteraturzeitung* 27, No 3, cols. 947–948.
Stumpf, Carl (1886e): "Review of H. Spencer, System der synthetischen Philosophie, 5er Bd.: Die Principien der Psychologie". In: *Deutsche Litteraturzeitung* 7, No 34, cols. 1194–1196.
Stumpf, Carl (1890a): *Tonpsychologie,* vol. 2, Leipzig: Hirzel.
Stumpf, Carl (1890b): "Über Vergleichung von Tondistanzen". In: *Zeitschrift für Psychologie und Physiologie der Sinnesorgane* 1, pp. 419–462.
Stumpf, Carl (1891a): "Wundts Antikritik". In: *Zeitschrift für Psychologie und Physiologie der Sinnesorgane* 2, pp. 266–293.
Stumpf, Carl (1891b): "Bemerkung zu S. 290 des vorigen Heftes". In: *Zeitschrift für Psychologie und Physiologie der Sinnesorgane* 2, p. 426.
Stumpf, Carl (1891c): "Mein Schlusswort gegen Wundt". In: *Zeitschrift für Psychologie und Physiologie der Sinnesorgane* 2, pp. 438–443.
Stumpf, Carl (1892): "H. Münsterberg: Vergleichung von Tondistanzen. Münsterbergs *Beiträge zur experimentellen Psychologie,* Heft 4, S. 147–177". In: *Zeitschrift für Psychologie und Physiologie der Sinnesorgane* 5, 1893, pp. 114–117.

Stumpf, Carl (1895): "Hermann von Helmholtz and the New Psychology". In: *Psychological Review* 2, pp. 1–12. Germ. trans. "Hermann von Helmholtz und die neuere Psychologie". In: *Archiv für Geschichte der Philosophie* n.s. 8, No 3, pp. 303–314.
Stumpf, Carl (1897): "Eröffnungsrede des Präsidenten, Prof. Dr Carl Stumpf". In: *Dritter International Congress für Psychologie in München vom 4–7 August 1896*. München: Lehmann, pp. 3–16. Reprinted (with modifications) as "Leib und Seele" in *Reden und Vorträge*, pp. 65–93.
Stumpf, Carl (1898): "Konsonanz und Dissonanz". In: *Beiträge zur Akustik und Musikwissenschaft* 1, pp. 1–108.
Stumpf, Carl (1899a): "Über den Begriff der Gemüthsbewegung". In: *Zeitschrift für Psychologie und Physiologie der Sinnesorgane* 21, pp. 47–99.
Stumpf, Carl (1899b): *Der Entwicklungsgedanke in der gegenwärtigen Philosophie*. Berlin: Lange. Reprinted in *Reden und Vorträge*, pp. 194–224.
Stumpf, Carl (1900): "Review of E. Mach, Die Analyse der Empfindungen und das Verhältnis des Physischen zum Psychischen". In: *Deutsche Litteraturzeitung* 51/52, No 15, cols. 3291–3294.
Stumpf, Carl (1903): *Leib und Seele. Der Entwicklungsgedanke in der gegenwärtigen Philosophie. Zwei Reden.* Leipzig: Barth.
Stumpf, Carl (1906a): "Erscheinungen und psychische Funktionen". In: *Abhandlungen der Königlich-Preußischen Akademie der Wissenschaften, Philosophisch-historische Classe* 6, pp. 3–40.
Stumpf, Carl (1906b): "Zur Einteilung der Wissenschaften". In: *Abhandlungen der Königlich-Preußischen Akademie der Wissenschaften, Philosophisch-historische Classe* 5, pp. 1–94.
Stumpf, Carl (1907a): *Die Wiedergeburt der Philosophie. Rede zum Eintritt des Rektorates der königlichen Friedrich-Wilhelms-Universität Berlin*, 15 Oktober 1907. Berlin: Francke. Reprinted in *Reden und Vorträge*, pp. 161–196.
Stumpf, Carl (1907b): "Über Gefühlsempfindungen". In: *Zeitschrift für Psychologie und Physiologie der Sinnesorgane* 44, pp. 1–49; also in Friedrich Schumann (Ed.), *Bericht über den II. Kongreß für xwexperimentelle Psychologie in Würzburg vom 18–21 April 1906*. Leipzig: Barth, pp. 209–213 (1906).
Stumpf, Carl (1910a): *Philosophische Reden und Vorträge*. Leipzig: Barth.
Stumpf, Carl (1910b): "Konsonanz und Konkordanz. Nebst Bemerkungen über Wohlklang und Wohlgefälligkeit musikalischer Zusammenklänge". In: *Zeitschrift für Psychologie und Physiologie der Sinnesorgane* 58, pp. 321–355; also in *Beiträge zur Akustik und Musikwissenschaft* 6, 1910, pp. 151–165.
Stumpf, Carl (1919a): "Spinozastudien". In: *Abhandlungen der Königlich-Preußischen Akademie der Wissenschaften*, Berlin: Verlag der Königlich Akademie der Wissenschaften, pp. 1–57.
Stumpf, Carl (1919b): "Erinnerungen an Franz Brentano". In: Oskar Kraus (Ed.). *Franz Brentano. Zur Kenntnis seines Lebens und seiner Lehre*. Munich: Beck.
Stumpf, Carl (1924): "Carl Stumpf" [Selbstdarstellung]. In: Raymund Schmidt (Ed.): *Die Philosophie der Gegenwart in Selbstdarstellung*. Vol. 5. Leipzig: Meiner, pp. 1–57. Eng. trans. "Autobiography". In Carl Murchison (Ed.). *A History of Psychology in Autobiography*. Vol. 1. Worcester: Clark University Press, pp. 389–441.
Stumpf, Carl (1927): "William James nach seinen Briefen. Leben. Character. Lehre". In: *Kant-Studien* 32, pp. 205–241.
Stumpf, Carl (1928): *William James nach seinen Briefen*. Berlin: Pan Verlag.

Stumpf, Carl (1939–40): *Erkenntnislehre*. 2 vols. Felix Stumpf (Ed.). Leipzig: Barth.
Stumpf, Carl (2012): *The Origins of Music*. David Trippett (Ed.). Oxford: Oxford University Press.
Stumpf, Carl (2020): *Tone Psychology: Volume 1. The Sensation of Successive Single Tones*. Robin Rollinger (Ed.). London-New York: Routledge [English Translation of Carl Stumpf, *Tonpsychologie*, vol. 1, 1883].
Sturt, Henry (Ed.) (1902): *Personal Idealism: Philosophical Essays by Eight Members of the University of Oxford*. London: Macmillan.
Sully, James (1880): *Sensation and Intuition. Studies in Psychology and Aesthetics*. London: Kegan Paul.
Sully, James (1884): "Review of C. Stumpf, Tonpsychologie (1)". In: *Mind* 9, pp. 593–602.
Sully, James (1886): "Review of Stumpf, Musikpsychologie in England". In: *Mind* 11, pp. 580–585.
Sully, James (1891): "Review of C. Stumpf, Tonpsychologie (2)". In: *Mind* 16, pp. 274–280.
Takasuna, Miko (2003): "Reconstruction of Stumpf Collection and Barth Collection: Using Bibliographical Cards as Resource in the Main Library at Kyushu University". In: *History of Psychology and Psychological Studies* 5, pp. 37–68.
Takasuna, Miko (2006): "Die Stumpf-Sammlung in Japan". In: H. Sprung, *Carl Stumpf. Eine Biographie. Von der Philosophie zur experimentellen Psychologie*, München-Wien: Profil, pp. 450–454.
Tuchman, Arleen (1993): "Helmholtz and the German Medical Community". In: David Cahan (Ed.). *Hermann von Helmholtz and the Foundations of Nineteenth-Century Science*. Berkeley: University of California Press, pp. 50–108.
Valentine, Elisabeth (2001): "Carl Stumpf and English Music Psychology". In: *Brentano-Studien* 9, pp. 251–266.
Weinfeld, David (2018): "*Les Intellectuels* in America: William James, the Dreyfus Affair, and the Development of the Pragmatist Intellectual". In: *The Journal of American History* 6, pp. 19–44.
Wilshire, Bruce (1979): *William James and Phenomenology: A Study of "The Principles of Psychology"*. New York: AMS Press.
Wundt, Wilhelm (1874): *Grundzüge der physiologischen Psychologie*. Leipzig: Englemann.
Wundt, Wilhelm (1884): "Stumpf, Dr. Carl, Prof., Tonpsychologie, 1. Bd. Leipzig, 1883. Hirzel. (XIV, 424, S.S.)" [unsigned]. In: *Literarisches Centralblatt* 16, 12 Apr. 1884, col. 547.
Wundt, Wilhelm (1885): *Essays*. Leipzig: Engelmann.
Wundt, Wilhelm (1886): *Ethik. Eine Untersuchung der Tatsachen und Gesetze des sittlichen Lebens*. Stuttgart: Enke.
Wundt, Wilhelm (1890): "Über Vergleichungen von Tondistanzen". In: *Philosophische Studien*, 6, pp. 605–640.
Wundt, Wilhelm (1891a): "Eine Replik C. Stumpf's". In: *Philosophische Studien* 7, pp. 298–327.
Wundt, Wilhelm (1891b): "Auch ein Schlusswort". In: *Philosophische Studien* 7, pp. 633–636.
Wundt, Wilhelm (1893): *Grundzüge der physiologischen Psychologie*, 4te umgearbeitete Auflage. Leipzig: Engelmann.
Wundt, Wilhelm (1899): *System der Philosophie*. Leipzig: Engelmann.
Zarncke, Friedrich Karl Theodor (1850): [Untitled]. In: *Literarisches Centralblatt für Deutschland* 1 Oct., cols. 1–2.

Index of Names

Adams, Henry 264
Agassiz, Louis 252
Albertazzi, Liliana 5
Allesch, Christian 101
Aquinas, Thomas 19, 171
Araujo de Freitas, Saulo 14
Aristotle 19, 103
Ash, Graham Mitchell 8, 13, 37, 38, 63
Aster, Ernst von 11, 287
Auwers, Arthur Julius von 154, 155, 157, 158, 236
Avenarius, Richard 37, 79, 122

Bain, Alexander 23, 61, 64
Baldwin, James Mark 20, 125, 127, 134, 135, 136, 137, 139, 228
Balfour, Arthur 71
Banks, Erik 17
Barzun, Jacques 6
Baumgartner, Wilhelm 5
Beneke, Friedrich Eduard 265
Bergson, Henri 168, 180, 243, 261, 263, 280, 281
Berkeley, Elisabeth 45
Berlioz, Hector 176
Bernard, Claude 252
Bernheim, Hippolyte 92
Binet, Alfred 92, 125
Bjork, Daniel 12
Blackmore, John 16
Bod, Rens 77
Bonacchi, Silvia 18
Bonaparte, Napoléon 14, 85, 122
Boudewijnse, Geert-Jan 18, 35
Bowditch, Henry Pickering 268
Bowers, Fredson 47
Bradley, Francis Herbert 30, 123, 176, 272
Brentano, Franz 4, 5, 13, 14, 17, 18, 19, 58, 145, 209, 232, 265, 270, 285
Brown, Thomas 23
Buchner, Edward Franklin 135, 228
Burkhardt, Frederick 47

Cahan, David 129
Caird, Edward 254
Calkins, Mary Whiton 12, 167
Carlson, Thomas 42
Carlyle, Thomas 251
Carrette, Jeremy 5
Carrière, Louis 145, 232
Centi, Beatrice 18, 23
Cesalli, Laurent 4
Christensen, Dieter 77
Clendenning, John 85
Coggeshall, Frederic 96
Comte, Auguste 253
Cooper, Saths 20
Cooper, Wesley 9, 23
Cossmann, Paul Nikolaus 97, 99, 107, 221, 223
Cranch, Christopher Pearse 121

Darwin, Charles 68, 212
Dazzi, Nino 23, 29
Delboeuf, Joseph 51, 54, 92, 208
Descartes, René 19
Dewey, John 176, 278
Dilthey, Wilhelm 13, 63, 118, 127, 140, 152, 156, 159, 162, 235, 236, 237, 238, 252
Donaldson, Henry Herbert 125
Driesch, Hans 264
Du Bois-Reymond, Emil 252
du Prel, Carl Freiherr 94, 220
Dunham, Jeremy 6

Edie, James 19
Ellis, Alexander J. 76, 186, 214
Emerson, Ralph Waldo 5, 121
Esterhazy, Ferdinand Walsin 148, 149
Eucken, Rudolf Christoph 278
Exner, Sigmund 254

Fechner, Gustav Theodor 28, 35, 78, 215, 276, 279, 282
Ferrier, David 53

Feuerbach, Ludwig 275
Fichte, Johann Gottlieb 34
Fischer, Kuno 156, 236, 252
Fisette, Denis 3, 7, 18, 19
Flourens, Pierre 85
Flournoy, Théodore 138, 193, 249, 256, 261, 263, 264, 265
Ford, Marcus 40
Forel, Auguste 92
Fourier, Charles 5
Fréchette, Guillaume 4, 19
Freud, Sigmund 264
Fullerton, George Stuart 71, 77, 83
Funke, Otto 58, 209

Galilei, Galileo 115
Gerhart, Volker 13
Gioia, Lia X, 44
Giżycki, Georg von 71, 97, 99, 221
Gley, Eugène 92
Goethe, Johann Wolfgang 11, 12, 263, 287
Goldmark, Pauline 258
Golz, Jochen 89
Graefe, Karl Alfred 77, 214
Grimm, Gisela 252
Grimm, Herman 252
Gundlach, Horst 14
Gurney, Edmund 40, 57, 68, 69, 71, 83, 89, 209, 212
Guyer, Paul 11

Hagen, Hermann August 129
Halliwell, Martin 5
Hauptmann, Carl 122
Hegel, Georg Wilhelm Friedrich 34, 35, 76, 82, 137, 214, 217, 251, 252, 275
Heinze, Max 152, 156, 157, 235, 236
Helmholtz, Hermann von 25, 31, 51, 54, 57, 72, 83, 88, 125, 129, 208, 252, 253, 254, 257, 271
Hentschel, Klaus 17
Herakleitos 28
Hering, Ewald 3, 58, 64, 88, 183, 209, 254
Hermann, Ludimar 58
Herzog, Max 19

Hochstetter, Erich 283
Hodgson, Shadworth 274, 277
Höffding, Harald 156, 236
Hornbostel, Erich M. von 76, 77
Hugo, Victor 12, 85, 122
Hume, David 286
Husserl, Edmund 19

James, Alexander Robertson (William's son) 22
James, Alice (William's sister) 22
James, Alice Howe Gibbens (William's wife) 3, 10, 14, 22, 44, 56, 183, 188, 245
James, Garth Wilkinson (William's brother) 56
James, Henry (William's brother) 22, 58, 101, 185, 187, 191, 192, 194, 250
James, Henry 1st (William's father) 38, 56
James, Henry 3rd (William's son) 34, 43, 109, 189, 194, 246
James, Herman (William's son) 58, 71
James, Margaret Mary (William's daughter) 22
James, William 2nd (William's son) 22, 250
Jastrow, Joseph (1863–1944) 125
Joachim, Joseph 7, 170
Jung, Carl Gustav 264

Kaiser-el-Safti, Margret 23, 25
Kant, Immanuel 4, 10, 11, 23, 25, 52, 137
Koffka, Kurt 63
Köhler, Wolfgang 31, 63, 151, 234
Kraus, Oskar 5
Kraushaar, Otto 27
Kucklick, Bruce 6, 87

Labori, Fernand 145, 232
Ladd, Geroge Trumbull 125, 128
Lamberth, David 32, 34, 163
Langfeld, Herbert Sidney 26, 82, 104, 127, 132, 140, 181, 182, 244
Le Clair, Robert 138, 193
LeConte, Joseph 88
Leuba, James Henry 277

Lewin, Kurt 15
Liegeois, Jules 92
Lindsay, Thomas 24
Lipps, Theodor 24, 70, 71, 168, 192, 248
Livingstone, Alexander 22, 161
Locke, John 62, 269, 286
Lorenz, Carl 15
Lotze, Rudolf Hermann 5, 18, 23, 270, 274, 275, 284, 285
Ludwig, Carl 252, 275
Lukens, Hermann Tyson 140, 230

Maat, Jaap 77
Mach, Ernst 3, 14, 16, 17, 30, 35, 37, 51, 56, 64, 72, 76, 177, 183, 242, 254, 278
Makkreel, Rudolph A. 63, 156
Marillier, Léon 92
Martinelli, Riccardo 3, 8, 35, 74
Marty, Anton 3, 52, 54, 56, 58, 64, 66, 79, 110, 113, 184, 208, 209, 211, 216, 225, 271
Maudsley, Henry 18, 58
McAlister, Linda 58
McKeen Cattell, James 125
Mehring, Reinhard 13
Miklosich, Franz 58
Milkov, Nikolay 5, 18, 24
Mill, John Stuart 23
Miller, Dickinson Sergeant 139, 268, 269, 279
Molière [Poquelin, Jean-Baptiste] 69
Morse, Frances R. 267
Müller, Georg Elias 12, 115, 256
Müller, Johannes 26
Müller, Karl Alexander von 97
Münsterberg, Hugo 12, 92, 110, 112, 114, 125, 126, 127, 132, 135, 136, 138, 143, 148, 164, 165, 168, 170, 175, 224, 229, 239, 256
Munthe, Axel 42
Myers, Frederic William Henry 40, 154

Newcomb, Simon 71, 82, 83
Niecks, Friedrich Maternus 164

Oberkofler, Gerhard 13, 145
Oppenheim, Janet 39, 40, 83
Ostwald, Wilhelm 168

Palladino, Eusapia 255
Panizzardi, Alessandro 145, 232
Papini, Giovanni 261
Paul, Hermann 11
Paulsen, Friedrich 116, 117, 118, 122, 123, 140, 159, 226, 237
Pawelsky, James 9
Peirce, Charles Sanders 277
Perry, Ralph Barton 46, 266
Pettenkofer, Max von 112, 224
Pfungst, Oskar 178
Pierce, Arthur Henry 130
Piéron, Henri 20
Pierre, Janet 92
Pillon, François 278
Piper, Leonora 255, 283
Podmore, Frank 40, 89
Pole, William 68, 212
Pratt, James Bissett 280
Putnam, Ruth Anna 42

Rankin, Henry W. 260
Rasmussen, Joel D.S. 5
Ratcliffe, Matthew 18
Reed, Edward 31
Reisenzein, Rainer 19
Renouvier, Charles Bernard 5, 6, 160, 162, 238, 253, 273, 278, 283
Ribot, Théodule 145
Richardson, Robert 3, 5, 6, 39, 42, 114, 142
Richet, Charles 92, 154
Riehl, Alois 110
Rindert, Jana 13
Robertson, George Croom 87
Rodi, Fritjohf 63, 156
Rollinger, Robin 8
Royce, Josiah 72, 86, 254, 259, 270, 275
Ruetenik, Tadd 39
Russel, John E. 279

Saemisch, Theodor 77
Saint Teresa 173
Salter, William Mackintire 71, 107, 223
Savourin, Michel 20
Schaarschmidt, Carl 53, 208
Schegg, Peter Johann 171
Schiller, Friedrich 89
Schleiermacher, Friedrich Daniel 252
Schmidkunz, Hans 94, 99, 220, 221
Schoen, Wilhelm 88
Schönpflug, Wolfgang 19
Schrenck-Notzing, Albert Freiherr von 92, 94, 137, 192, 220, 248
Schuhmann, Karl 5, 18
Schumann, Friedrich 132
Schwartzkoppen Maximilian von 145, 232
Scripture, Edward Wheeler 125
Sidgwick, Henry 137
Siegfried, Charlene Haddock 37
Sigwart, Christoph von 162, 238
Simon, Arthur 77
Simon, Linda 3, 5, 56, 89, 107, 142
Skrupskelis, Ignas 45, 47
Slater, Michael 38
Spencer, Herbert 68, 76, 81, 86, 123, 152, 212, 214, 217, 235, 270
Spiegelberg, Herbert 20
Spinoza, Baruch 35, 36, 275
Sprigge, Timothy Lauro Squire 30, 123
Sprung, Helga 3
Sprung, Lothar 17
Stéphane, Madelrieux 40, 168
Stratton, George Malcolm 131
Stricker, Salomon 72, 254
Strong, Charles Augustus 135, 139, 276
Stumpf, Elisabeth (Carl's daughter) 22, 169
Stumpf, Felix (Carl's son) 7, 22, 66, 173, 177, 213, 241, 242
Stumpf, Hermine Biedermann (Carl's wife) 22, 44, 52, 56, 64, 70, 73, 89, 96, 104, 150, 185, 187, 196, 227
Stumpf, Rudolf (Carl's son) 22, 52, 64, 129, 133, 139, 146, 173, 177, 179, 185, 232, 241, 242

Sturt, Henry 176
Sully, James 64, 67, 68, 79, 83, 89, 100, 106, 164, 212, 216, 218, 221, 222
Swedenborg, Emanuel 5, 251

Taieb, Hamid 4
Takasuna, Miko 45
Thomsen, Anton 17
Tracz, R. Brian X, 44, 49
Trippett, David 77
Troeltsch, Ernst 259
Tuchman, Arleen 129
Tweedy, Edmund 10

Ueberweg, Friedrich 18, 58

Vahlen, Johannes 162, 238
Valentine, Elisabeth 68
van der Wijck, Bernard Hendrik K. 156
Virchow, Rudolf 252
Volkmann, Alfred Wilhelm 88

Wadsworth, Oliver Fairfield 135
Ward, Thomas W. 273
Weinfeld, David 22
Weststeijn, Thijs 77
Wilshire, Bruce 19
Windelband, Wilhelm 168
Wobbermin, Georg 260
Wolff, Christian 10, 14, 86
Wood, Allen 11
Wundt, Wilhelm 11, 13, 14, 15, 26, 35, 51, 67, 79, 80, 81, 85, 86, 94, 105, 106, 107, 115, 118, 122, 152, 157, 211, 216, 217, 220, 222, 223, 226, 227, 235, 252, 253, 270
Wyman, Jeffries 252

Zalta, Edward 3
Zarncke, Friedrich Karl Theodor 79
Zeller, Eduard 127
Ziegler, Theobald 156, 236
Zöllner, Johann Karl Friedrich 52

Index of Subjects

Absolute 11, 34, 96, 219, 254, 275
Academy of Sciences 152, 153, 162, 238
America 9, 11, 39, 94, 116, 127, 134, 158, 165, 169, 182, 267
Americanism 9, 132, 135, 138, 258
anti-imperialism 22, 164
appearances 31, 33, 35, 106
articulation-feelings 26, 73
associationism 24
Athanasian Creed 173

consciousness 25, 28, 36, 41, 42, 63, 77, 120, 123, 171, 175

depression 3, 5, 21, 128, 273
Dreyfus affair 22, 143, 145, 148, 232
dualism 35, 117, 282, 284

education 5, 7, 11, 36, 55, 56, 58, 61, 71, 72, 75, 83, 86, 109, 116, 128, 137, 142, 144, 148, 153, 155, 167, 168, 173, 177, 178, 182, 209
emotions 18, 19, 27–34, 145, 146, 147, 154, 232, 260, 272
empiricism 38
experimentation 7, 13, 51, 72, 79, 110, 115, 127, 128, 130, 132, 137, 138, 143, 148, 286

faith 38, 42, 59, 70, 173, 175
feelings 11, 27–34, 41, 53, 55, 62, 70, 71, 78, 81, 107, 118, 121, 142, 147, 148, 161, 171, 173, 185, 208, 254
fourth dimension 53
friendship 3–8, 17, 106, 118, 121, 144, 145, 147, 158, 159

German character 9, 130
Gifford lectures 36, 42, 142, 143, 144, 148, 153, 154, 155, 157, 160, 163, 164, 165, 258, 259

hypnosis 72, 78, 92, 94, 99, 215, 220, 221

idealism 33, 34, 35, 77, 87, 214
immortality 39, 40, 41, 42, 140, 172, 175
indeterminism 36, 273, 274, 282
individual psychology 172
infallibility of the Pope 5
innervation-feelings 14, 26, 53, 58, 59, 67, 73, 77, 119, 208, 209
intentionality 18, 35, 141

judgments 27, 28, 63, 71, 118, 134, 141

logicalism 26, 61

mental functions 35
metaphysics 6, 7, 23, 29, 34–37, 42, 86, 96, 102, 137, 143, 148, 168, 178
monism 23, 37, 254, 255, 261, 275, 279
morality 5, 7, 38, 67, 148
multiplicity, doctrine of 7, 14, 31, 103, 271

nativism 3, 23, 25

ophthalmoscope 129
over-belief 41, 172, 240
overtones 28, 63, 119

parallelism 16, 35, 139, 273
partial contents 23
partial identity 29, 32, 34, 103
perception 3, 18, 23, 27, 62, 88
phenomenology 19, 20
philosophical seminar 58
pluralism 23, 35, 36, 37, 155, 166, 173, 241, 253, 258, 261, 263, 275, 277, 279, 281, 282, 283, 284, 286
positivism 35
pragmatism 23, 37, 177, 178, 181, 242, 244, 258, 262, 263, 276, 277, 278, 279, 286
psychical resesarch 38–42, 71, 82, 255
Psychological Review 20, 125, 128, 266
psychologist's fallacy 33
psychology X, 6, 7, 13, 14, 16, 18, 20, 23, 28, 31, 33, 34, 35, 39, 44, 58, 62, 64, 68, 71, 72, 76, 79, 80, 82, 89, 92, 94, 96, 98,

https://doi.org/10.1515/9783110525533-010

99, 102, 107, 110, 113, 115, 125, 128, 130, 131, 132, 135, 137, 140, 143, 148, 163, 164, 167, 182, 214, 270
psycho-mythology 26, 61
psychophysical parallelism 35

radical empiricism 17, 23, 27, 32, 34, 37, 104, 166, 265, 276, 279
relations 5, 8, 10, 12, 19, 23–27, 32, 33, 37, 61, 62, 68, 75, 77, 99, 102, 104, 131, 138, 145, 170
relativity of sensations 14, 26, 82
religion 5, 23, 37, 38–42, 67, 69, 87, 142, 163, 166, 168, 171, 175, 191, 192, 211, 212, 239, 240, 251, 255, 257, 258, 259, 261, 263, 276, 280, 284
resemblance 29, 30, 32, 33, 102, 103, 107, 123

seminary 5, 127, 170
sensationalism 20, 25, 26, 27, 61
space 3, 4, 18, 23–24, 25, 27, 33, 45, 52, 62, 70, 79, 88, 90, 99, 100, 103, 107, 129, 140
spiritism 78, 94, 220
St. Louis Exhibition 168, 175

telepathy 94, 118
tonal fusion 29, 57, 102
tone psychology 25, 26, 27, 28, 29, 30, 53, 61, 62, 63, 67, 72, 88, 103, 104, 119
translations 46, 97, 99, 107, 126, 133, 135, 139

unity-hypothesis 32
unnoticed sensations 28, 29, 32, 62

www.ingramcontent.com/pod-product-compliance
Lightning Source LLC
Chambersburg PA
CBHW031757220426
43662CB00007B/442